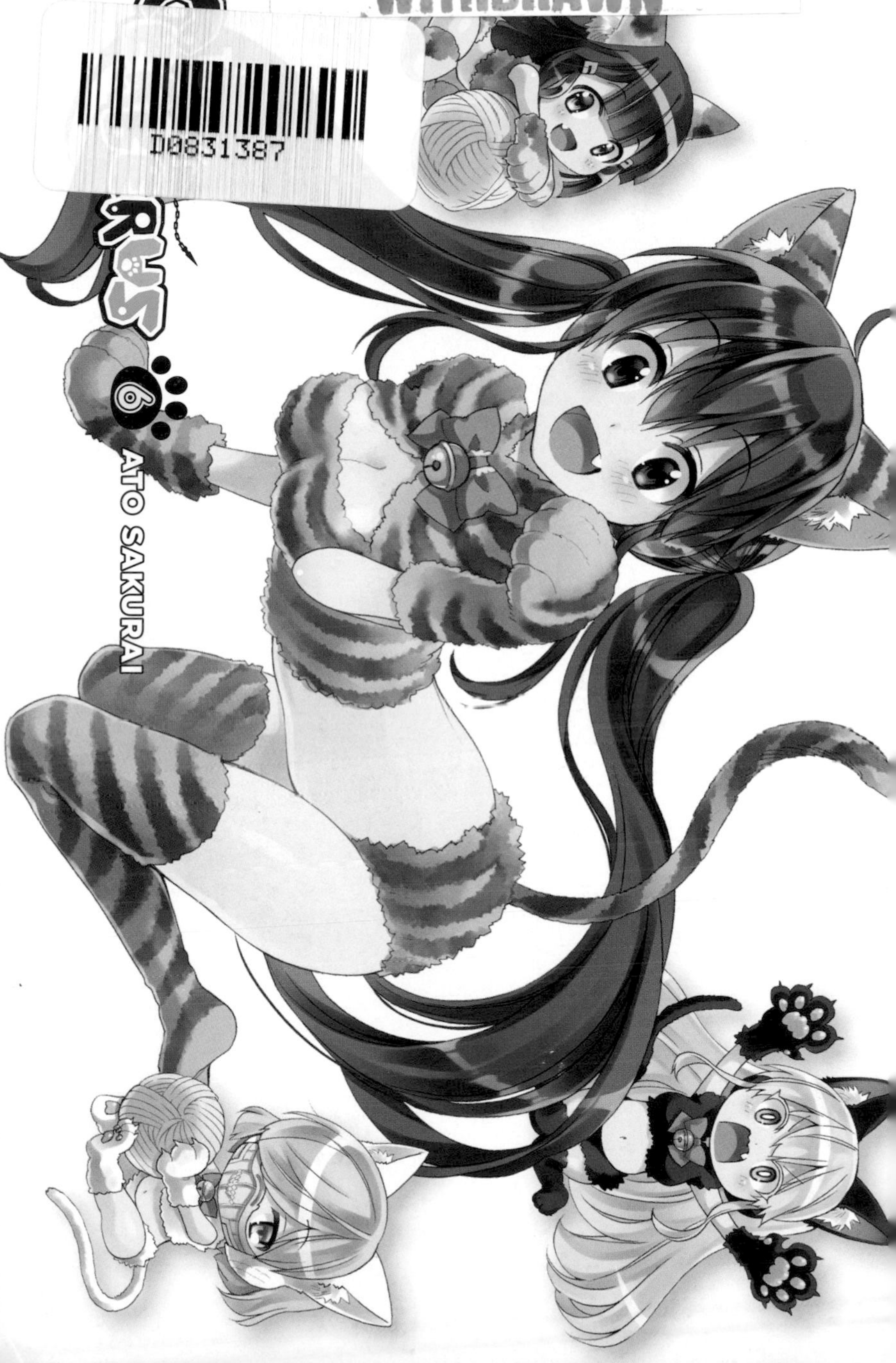
6
ATO SAKURAI

CONTENTS

Chapter 25
The Second
003

Chapter 26
Let's Greet People
043

Chapter 27
Clumsy Dog
075

Chapter 28
Alone
109

Chapter 29
What You Like
141

Extra
Today's Cerberus-san
185

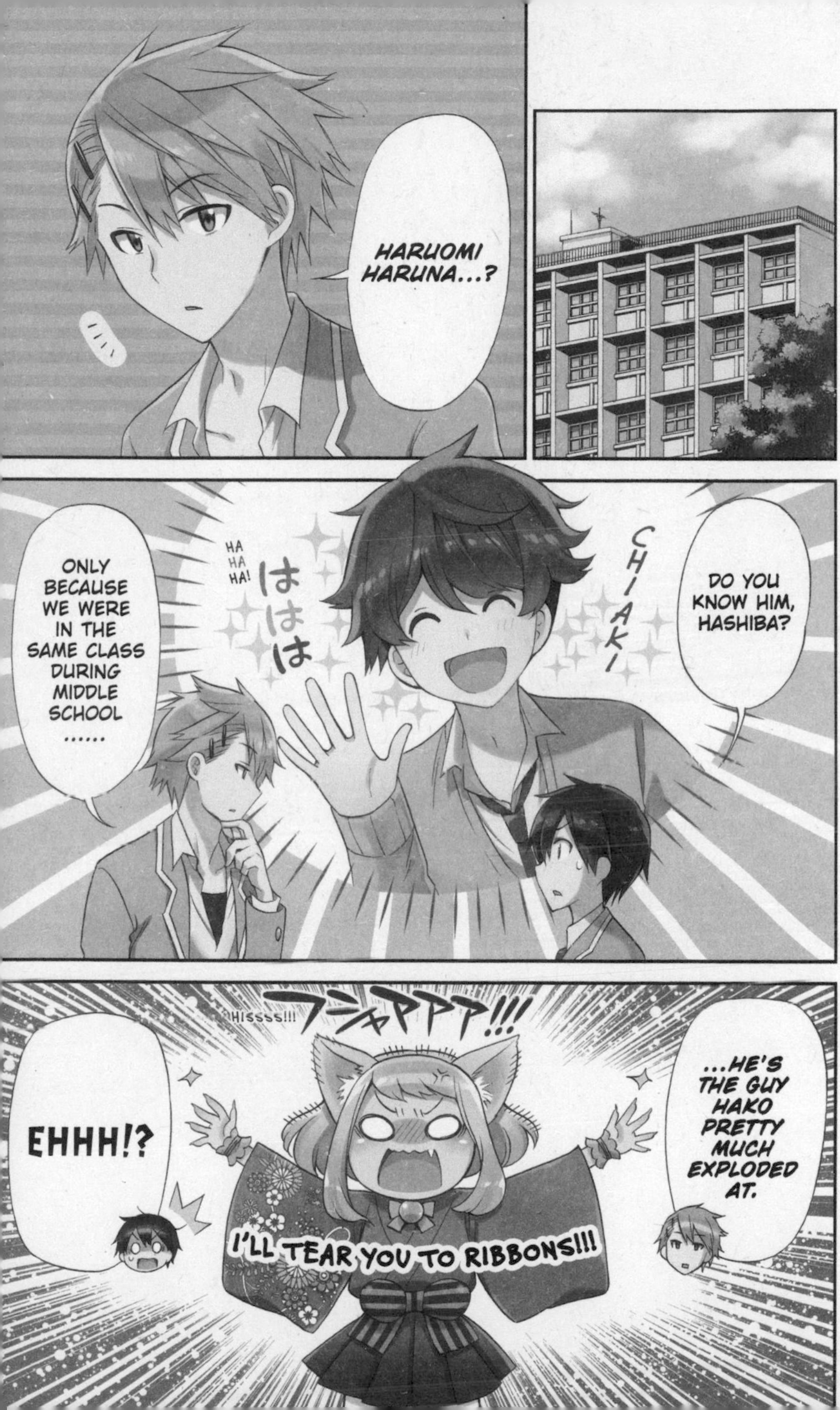
HARUOMI HARUNA...?
DO YOU KNOW HIM, HASHIBA?
CHIAKI
ははは
HA HA HA!
ONLY BECAUSE WE WERE IN THE SAME CLASS DURING MIDDLE SCHOOL ......
...HE'S THE GUY HAKO PRETTY MUCH EXPLODED AT.
フシャアア!!!
HISSSS!!!
I'LL TEAR YOU TO RIBBONS!!!
EHHH!?

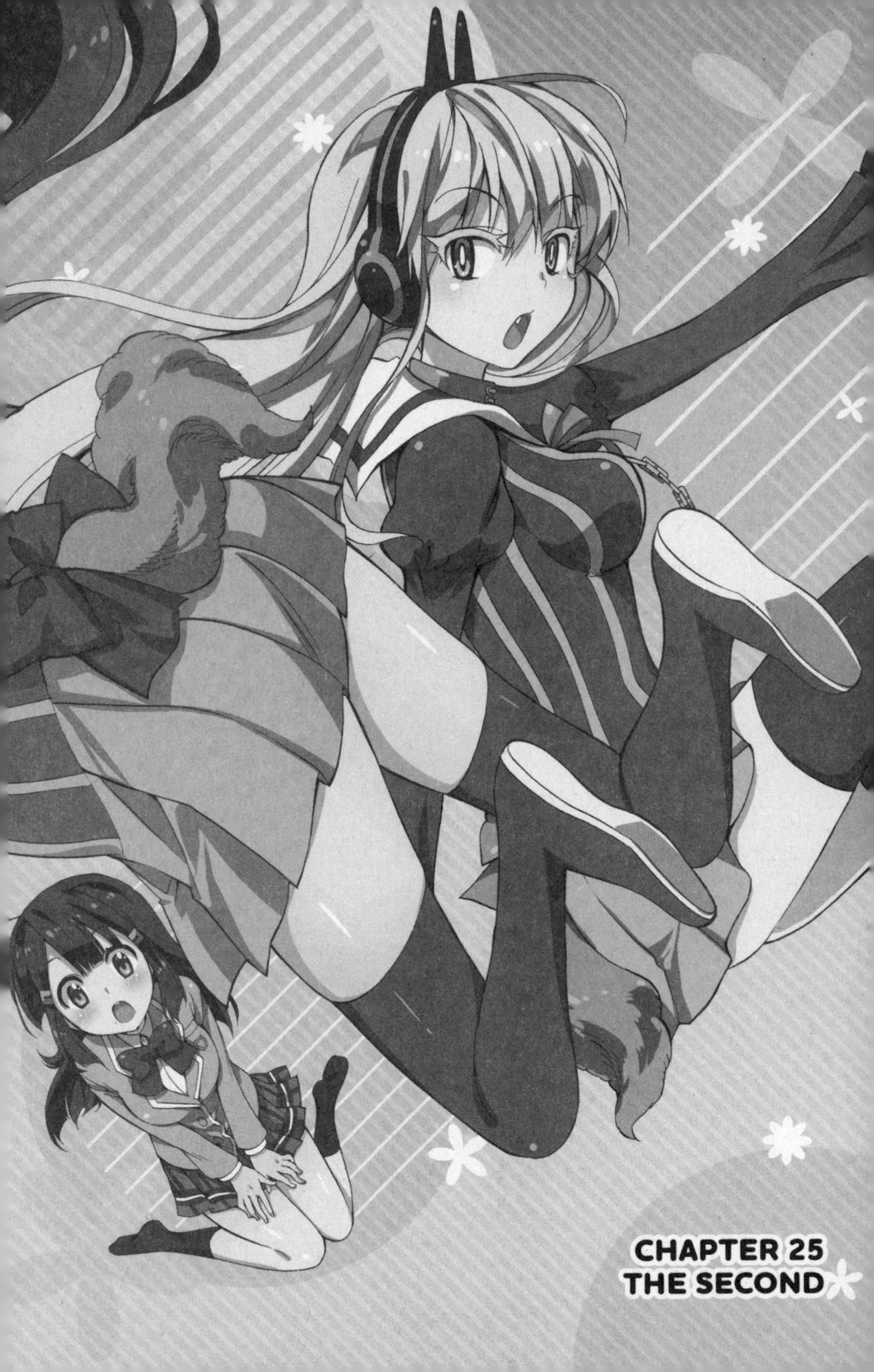

CHAPTER 25
THE SECOND

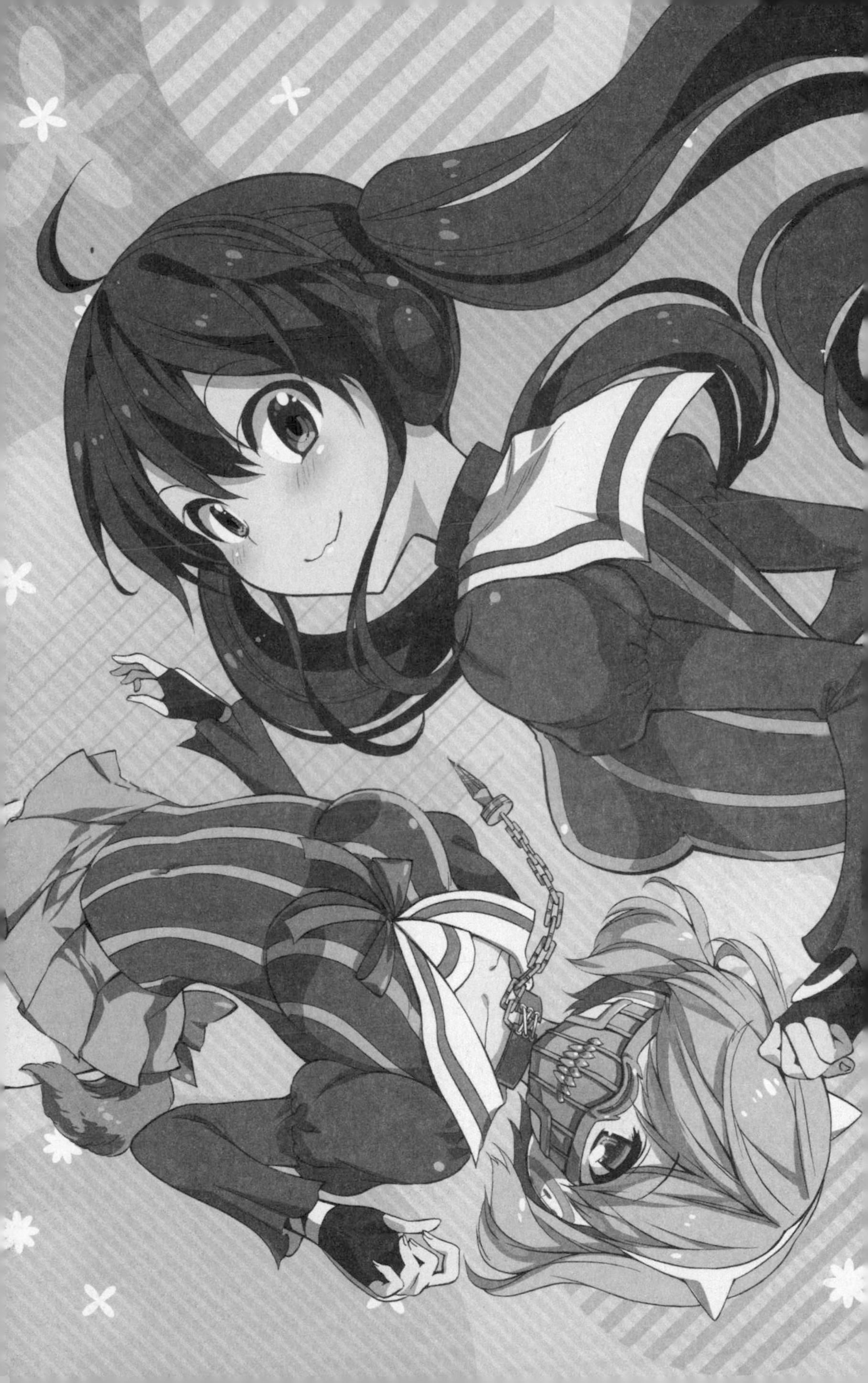

TODAY'S CERBERUS

MEOWWW!!

BOOM

NOT QUITE
LIKE THAT.

EXPLODED
AT...!?

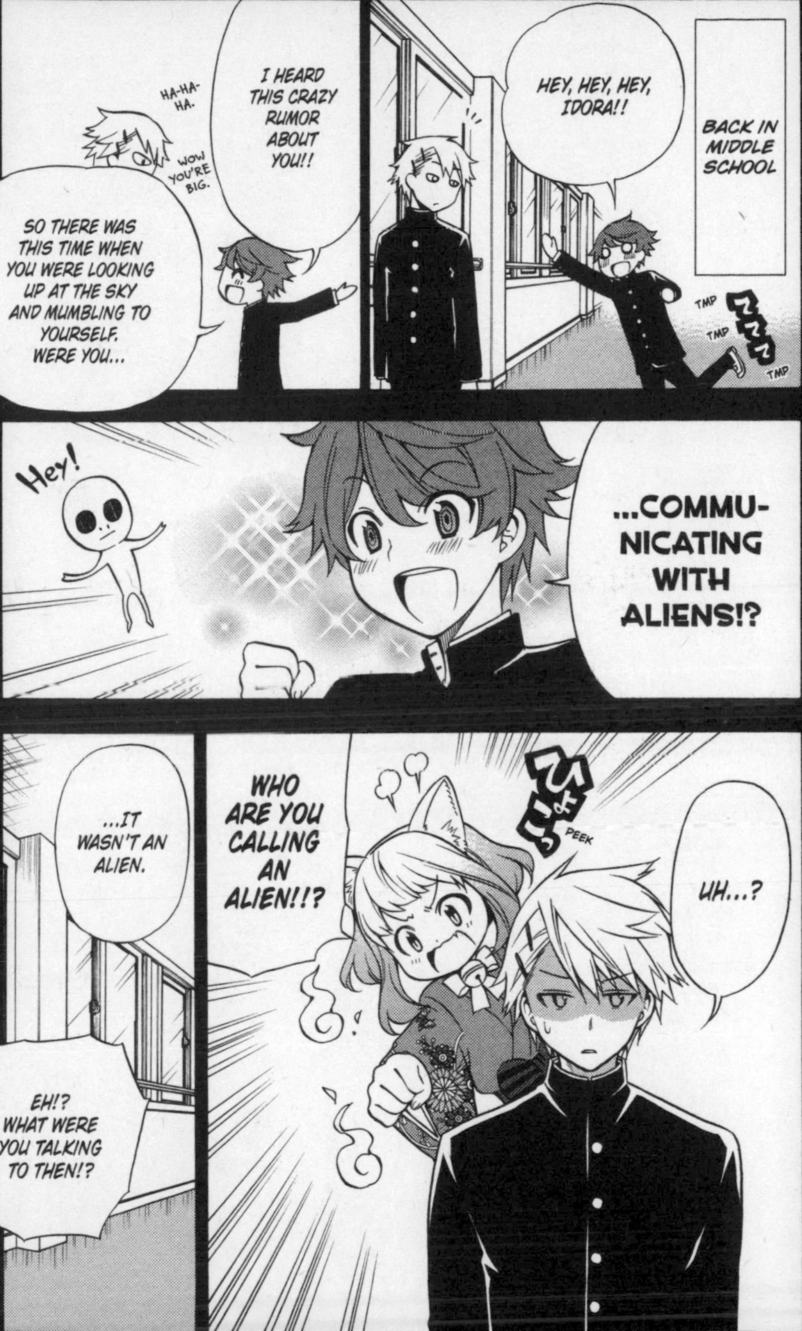
BACK IN MIDDLE SCHOOL
HEY, HEY, HEY, IDORA!!
TMP
TMP
TMP
I HEARD THIS CRAZY RUMOR ABOUT YOU!!
HA-HA-HA.
WOW YOU'RE BIG.
SO THERE WAS THIS TIME WHEN YOU WERE LOOKING UP AT THE SKY AND MUMBLING TO YOURSELF. WERE YOU...
...COMMUNICATING WITH ALIENS!?
Hey!
UH...?
PEEK
WHO ARE YOU CALLING AN ALIEN!!?
...IT WASN'T AN ALIEN.
EH!? WHAT WERE YOU TALKING TO THEN!?

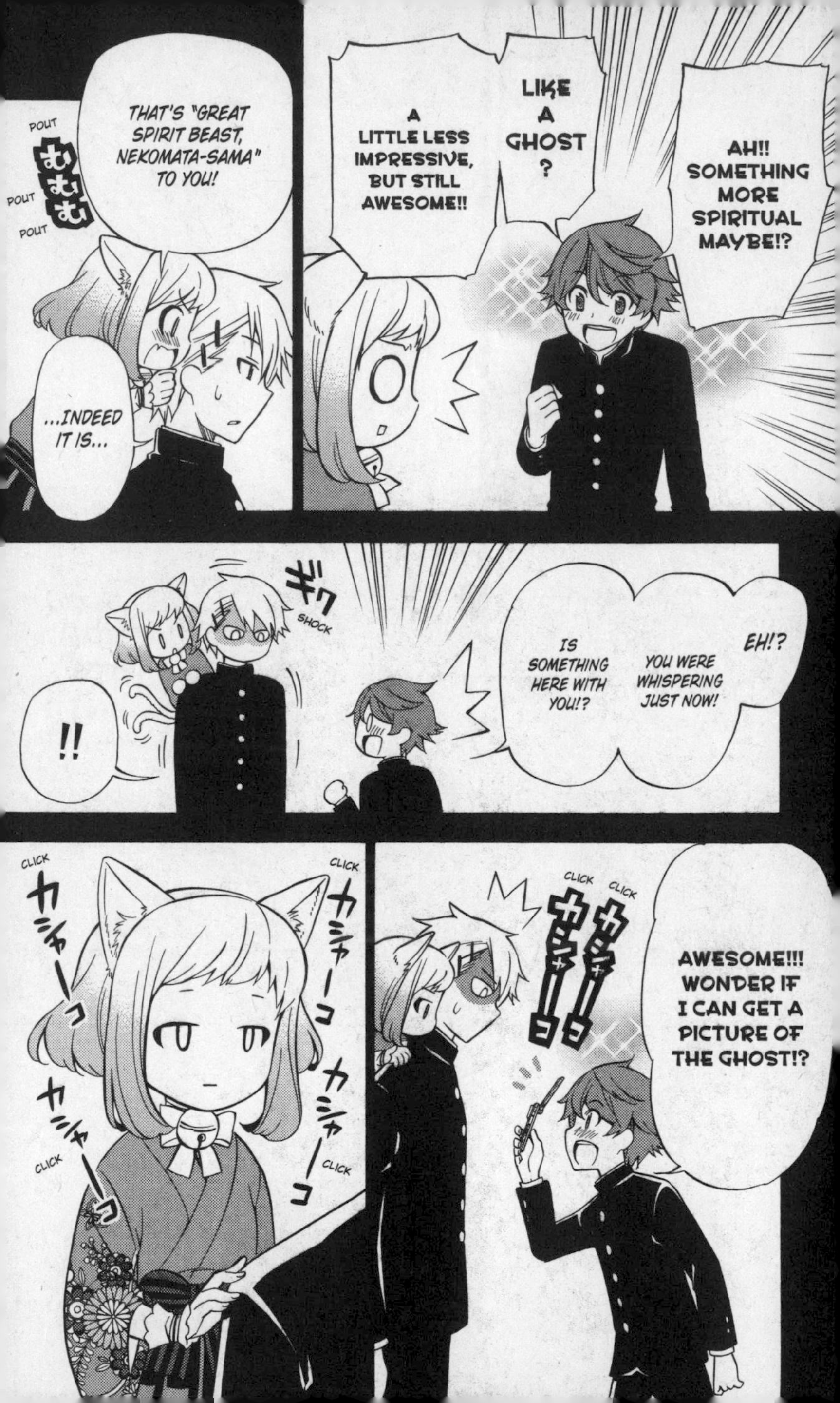
AH!! SOMETHING MORE SPIRITUAL MAYBE!?
LIKE A GHOST?
A LITTLE LESS IMPRESSIVE, BUT STILL AWESOME!!
THAT'S "GREAT SPIRIT BEAST, NEKOMATA-SAMA" TO YOU!
むむむ
POUT POUT POUT
...INDEED IT IS...
EH!? YOU WERE WHISPERING JUST NOW!
IS SOMETHING HERE WITH YOU!?
ギク
SHOCK
!!
AWESOME!!! WONDER IF I CAN GET A PICTURE OF THE GHOST!?
カシャーッ カシャーッ
CLICK CLICK
カシャーッ カシャーッ カシャーッ カシャーッ
CLICK CLICK CLICK CLICK

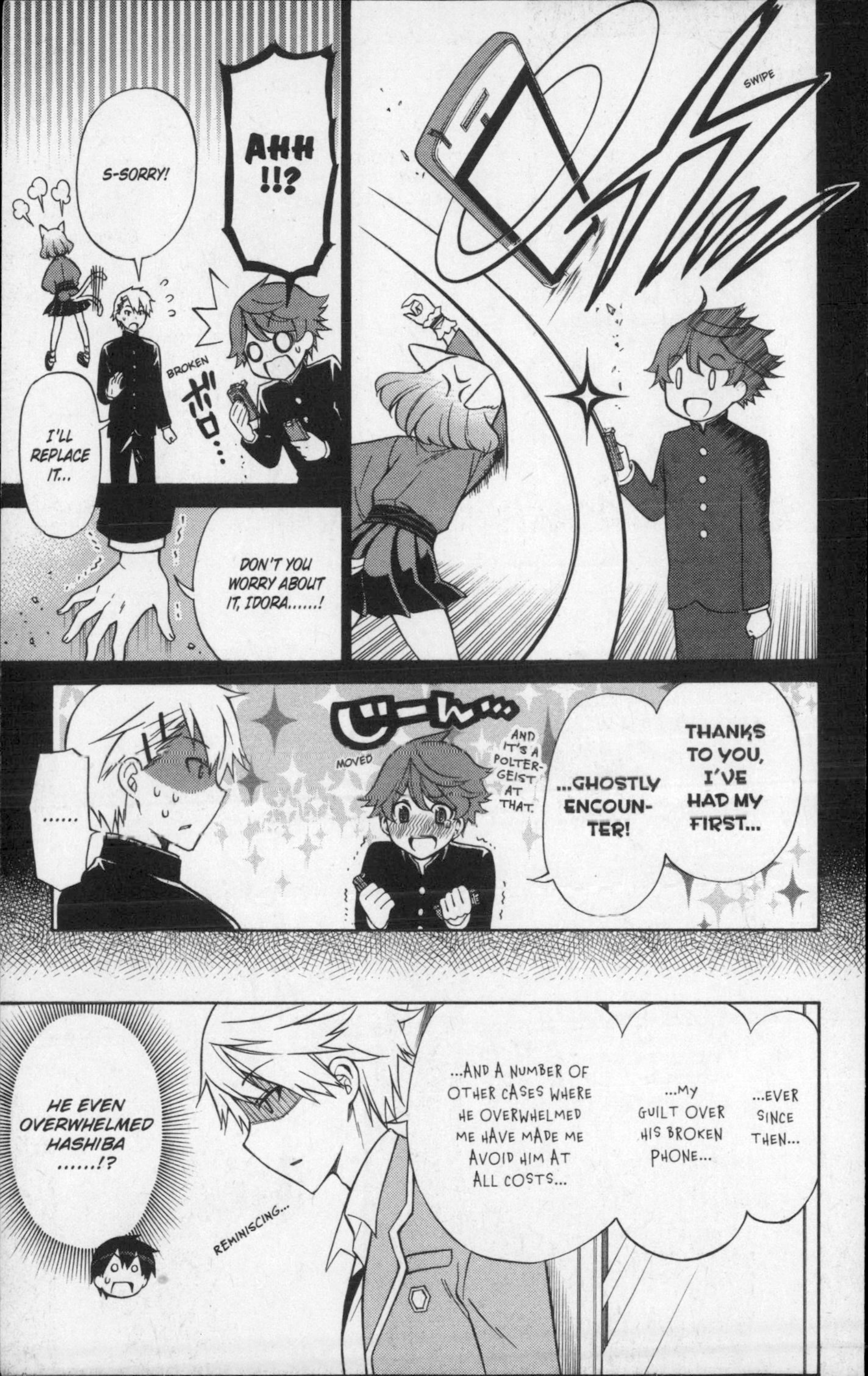
SWIPE
AHH!!?
S-SORRY!
BROKEN
ボロ…
I'LL REPLACE IT...
DON'T YOU WORRY ABOUT IT, IDORA......!
THANKS TO YOU, I'VE HAD MY FIRST...
...GHOSTLY ENCOUNTER!
AND IT'S A POLTERGEIST AT THAT.
MOVED
じーん…
......
...EVER SINCE THEN...
...MY GUILT OVER HIS BROKEN PHONE...
...AND A NUMBER OF OTHER CASES WHERE HE OVERWHELMED ME HAVE MADE ME AVOID HIM AT ALL COSTS...
HE EVEN OVERWHELMED HASHIBA......!?
REMINISCING...

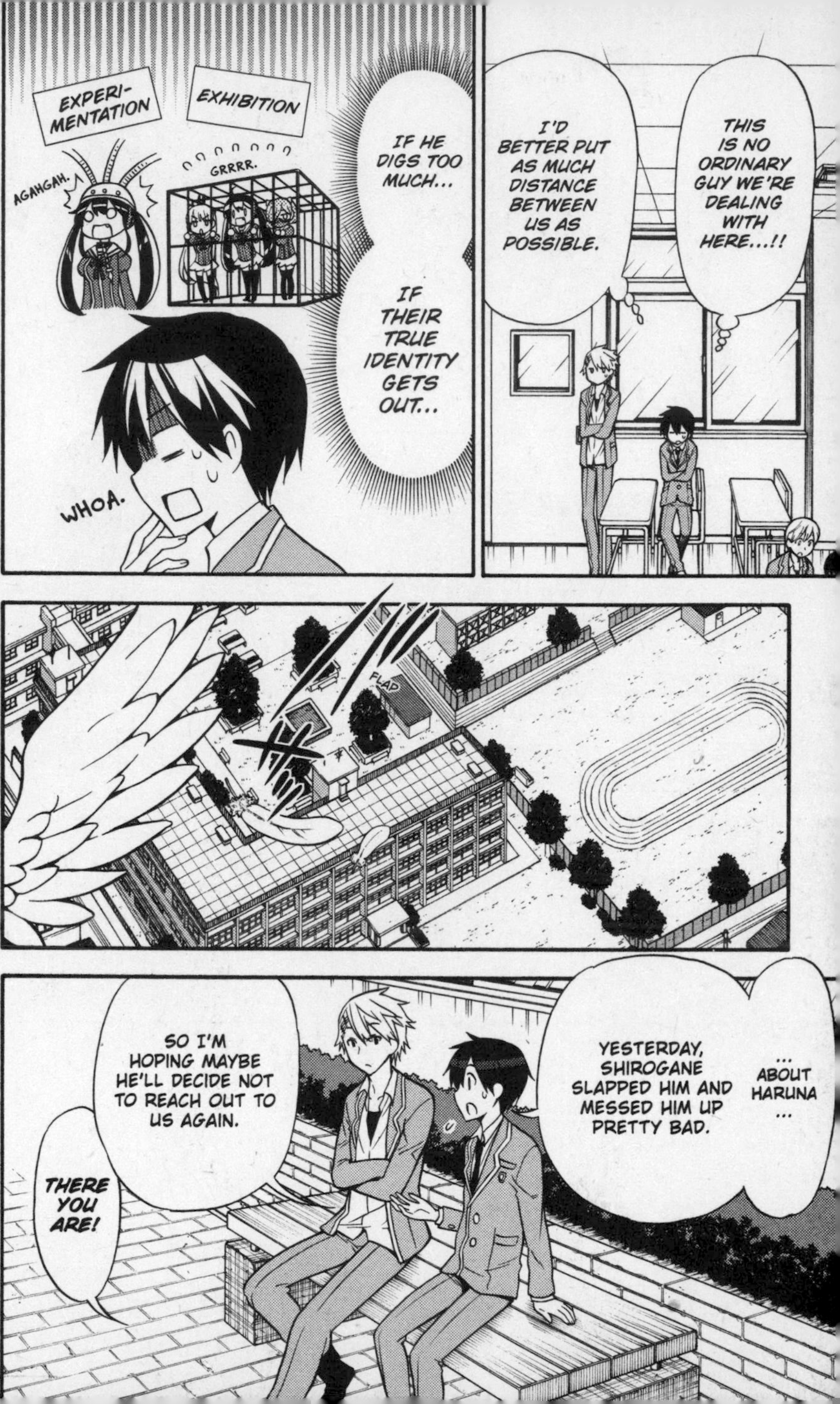
THIS IS NO ORDINARY GUY WE'RE DEALING WITH HERE...!!
I'D BETTER PUT AS MUCH DISTANCE BETWEEN US AS POSSIBLE.
IF HE DIGS TOO MUCH...
IF THEIR TRUE IDENTITY GETS OUT...
EXHIBITION
EXPERI-MENTATION
GRRRR.
AGAHGAH.
WHOA.
FLAP
...ABOUT HARUNA...
YESTERDAY, SHIROGANE SLAPPED HIM AND MESSED HIM UP PRETTY BAD.
SO I'M HOPING MAYBE HE'LL DECIDE NOT TO REACH OUT TO US AGAIN.
THERE YOU ARE!

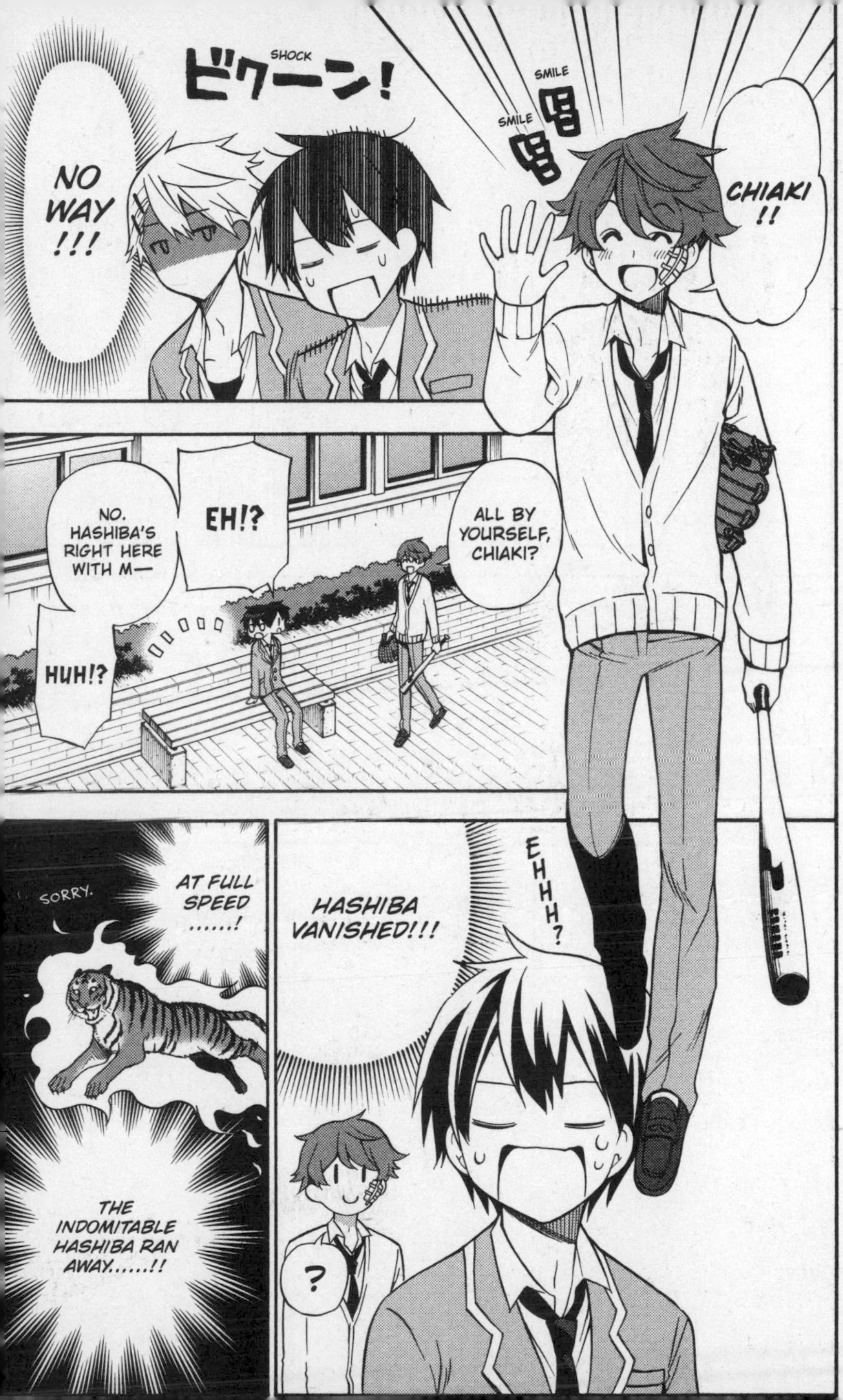
CHIAKI !!
SMILE
SMILE
ビクーン!
SHOCK
NO WAY !!!
ALL BY YOURSELF, CHIAKI?
EH!?
NO. HASHIBA'S RIGHT HERE WITH M—
HUH!?
EHHH?
HASHIBA VANISHED!!!
?
AT FULL SPEED ......!
SORRY.
THE INDOMITABLE HASHIBA RAN AWAY......!!

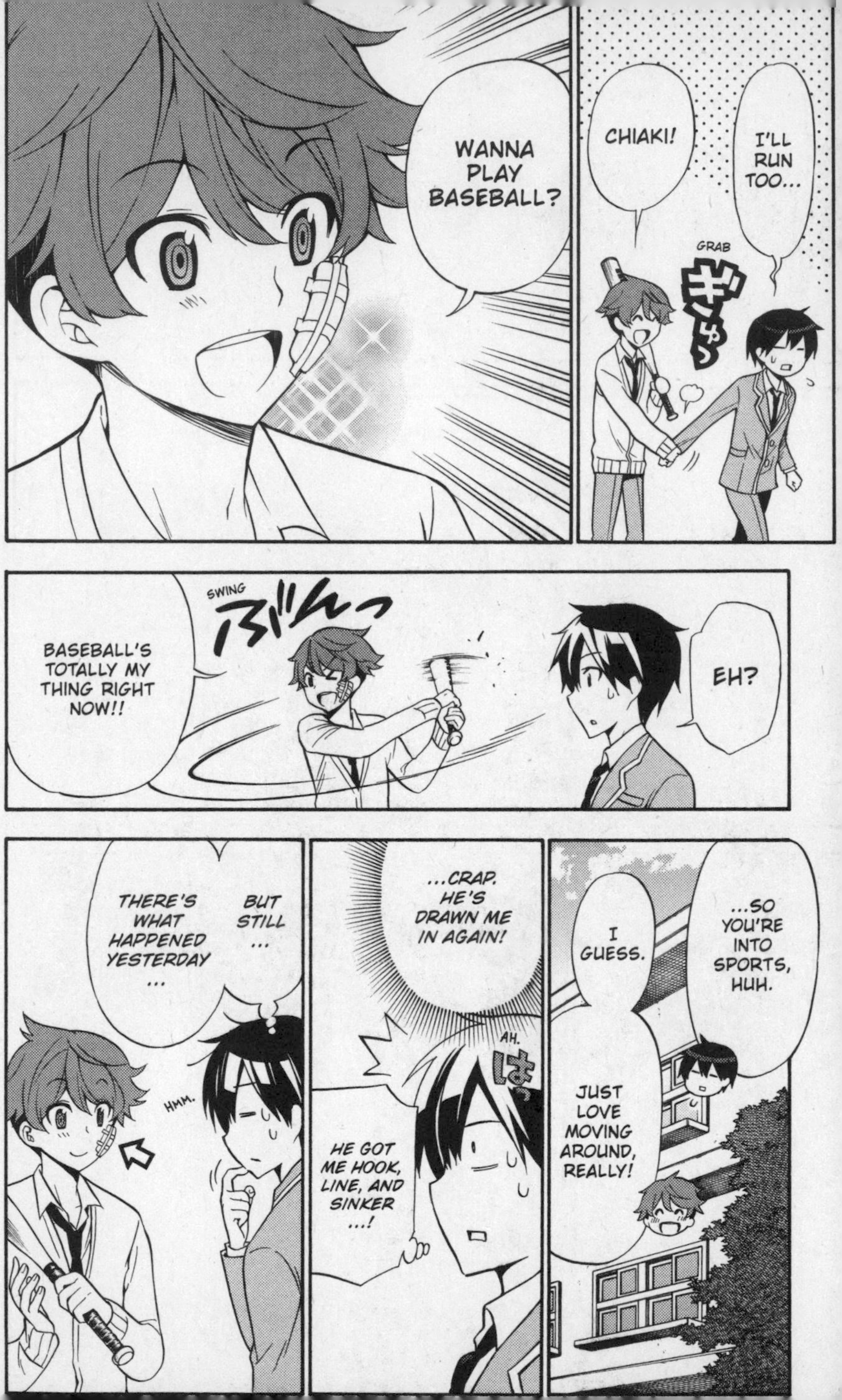
I'LL RUN TOO...
CHIAKI!
GRAB
ぎゅっ
WANNA PLAY BASEBALL?
EH?
SWING
ぶんっ
BASEBALL'S TOTALLY MY THING RIGHT NOW!!
...SO YOU'RE INTO SPORTS, HUH.
I GUESS.
JUST LOVE MOVING AROUND, REALLY!
...CRAP. HE'S DRAWN ME IN AGAIN!
AH.
はっ
HE GOT ME HOOK, LINE, AND SINKER...!
BUT STILL...
THERE'S WHAT HAPPENED YESTERDAY...
HMM.

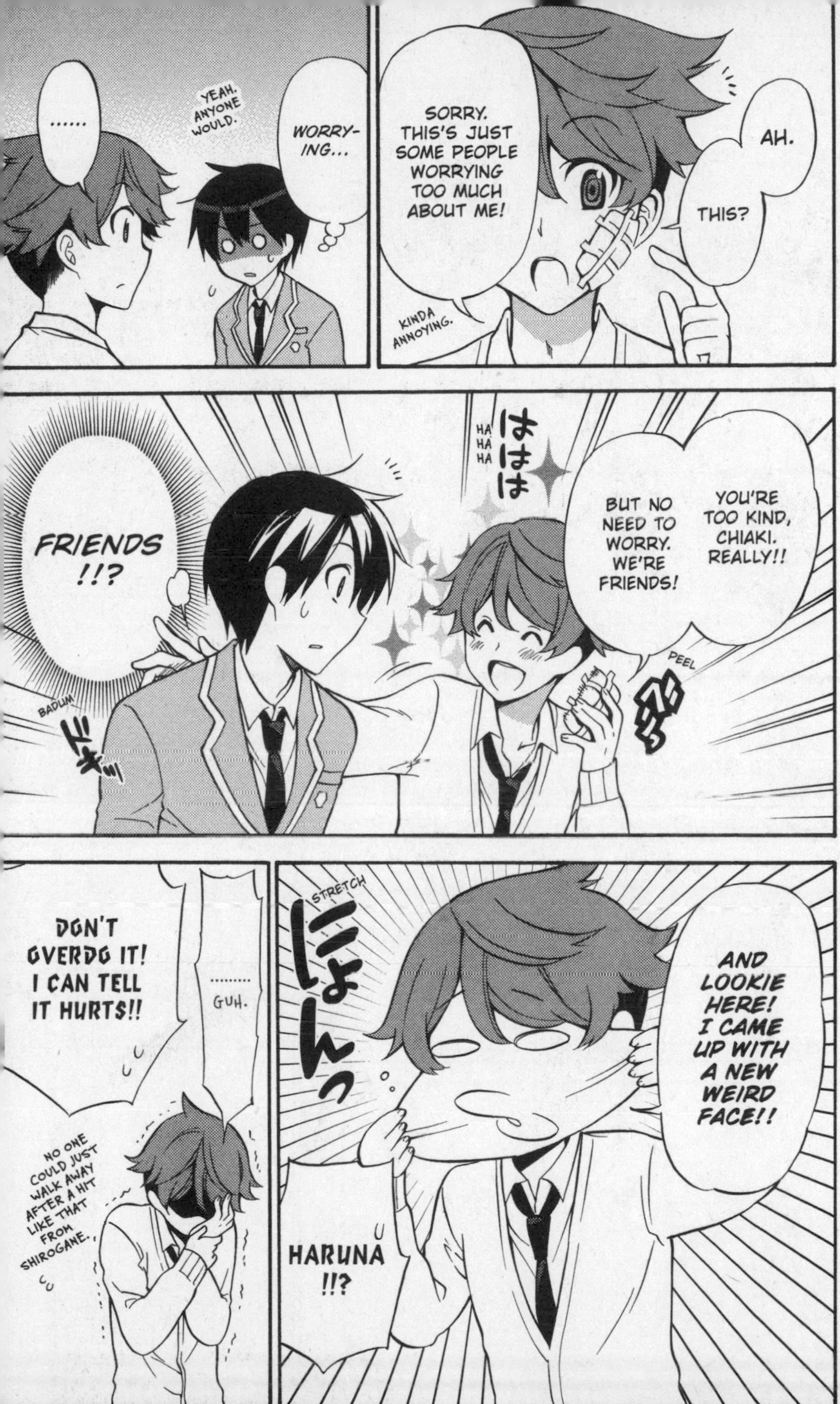
AH.
THIS?
SORRY. THIS'S JUST SOME PEOPLE WORRYING TOO MUCH ABOUT ME!
KINDA ANNOYING.
WORRY-ING...
YEAH, ANYONE WOULD.
......
YOU'RE TOO KIND, CHIAKI. REALLY!!
BUT NO NEED TO WORRY. WE'RE FRIENDS!
HA HA HA
ははは
PEEL
FRIENDS!!?
BADUM
AND LOOKIE HERE! I CAME UP WITH A NEW WEIRD FACE!!
STRETCH
にょんっ
HARUNA!!?
DON'T OVERDO IT! I CAN TELL IT HURTS!!
....
GUH.
NO ONE COULD JUST WALK AWAY AFTER A HIT LIKE THAT FROM SHIROGANE.

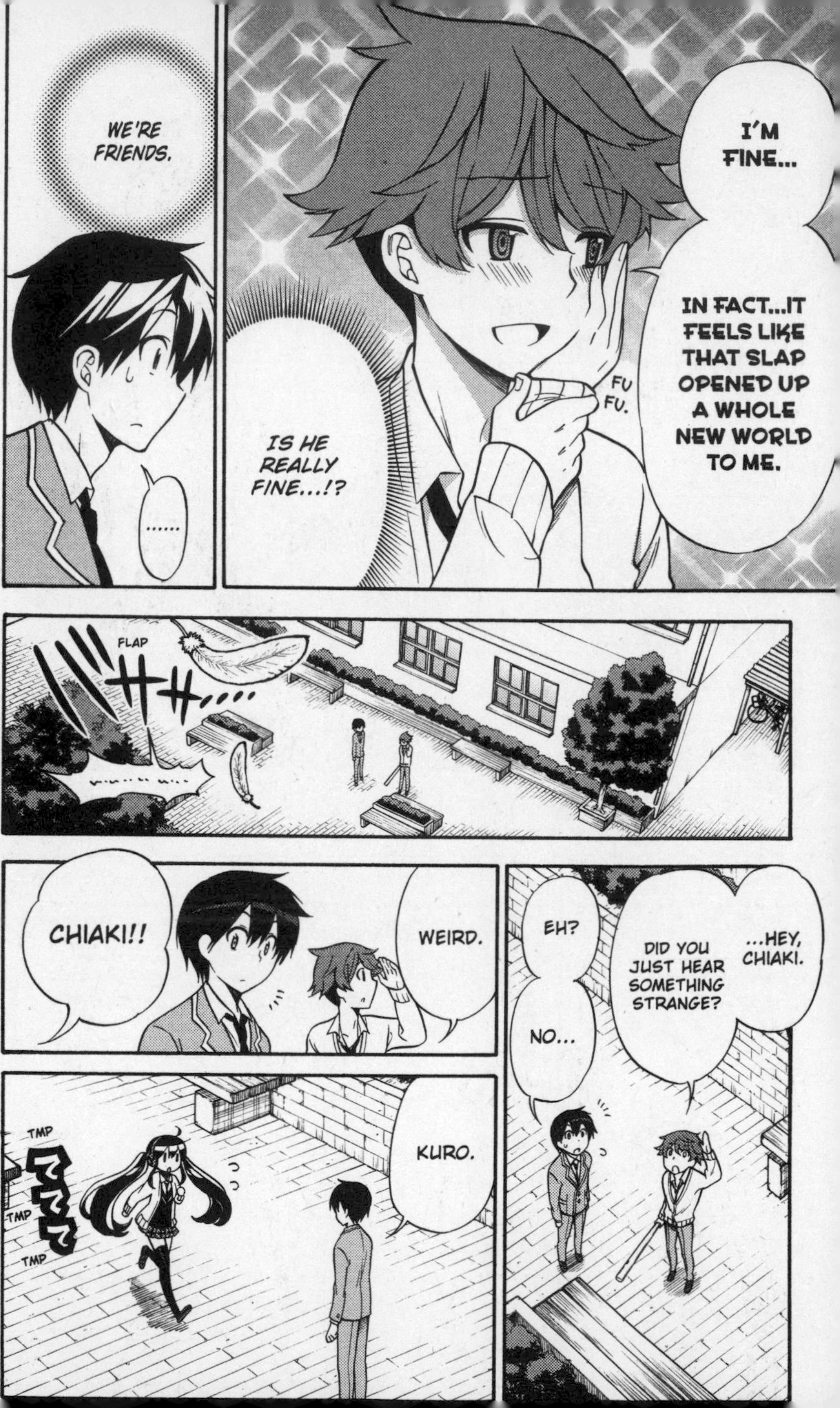
I'M FINE...
IN FACT...IT FEELS LIKE THAT SLAP OPENED UP A WHOLE NEW WORLD TO ME.
FU FU.
IS HE REALLY FINE...!?
WE'RE FRIENDS.
......
FLAP
...HEY, CHIAKI.
DID YOU JUST HEAR SOMETHING STRANGE?
EH?
NO...
WEIRD.
CHIAKI!!
KURO.
TMP
TMP
TMP

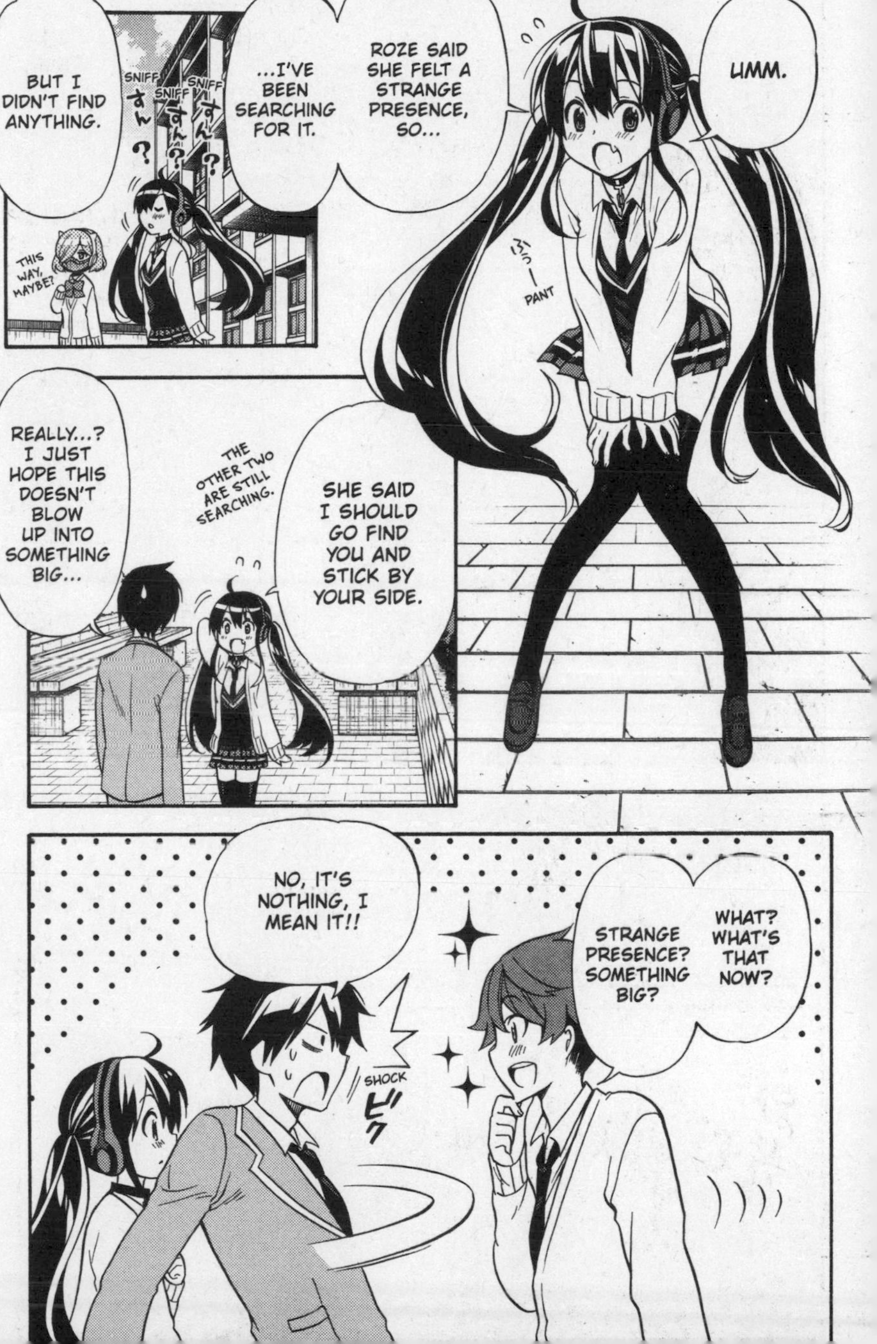
UMM.
ROZE SAID SHE FELT A STRANGE PRESENCE, SO...
...I'VE BEEN SEARCHING FOR IT.
PANT
SNIFF すん
SNIFF すん
SNIFF すん
BUT I DIDN'T FIND ANYTHING.
THIS WAY, MAYBE?
SHE SAID I SHOULD GO FIND YOU AND STICK BY YOUR SIDE.
THE OTHER TWO ARE STILL SEARCHING.
REALLY...? I JUST HOPE THIS DOESN'T BLOW UP INTO SOMETHING BIG...
WHAT? WHAT'S THAT NOW?
STRANGE PRESENCE? SOMETHING BIG?
SHOCK ビク
NO, IT'S NOTHING, I MEAN IT!!

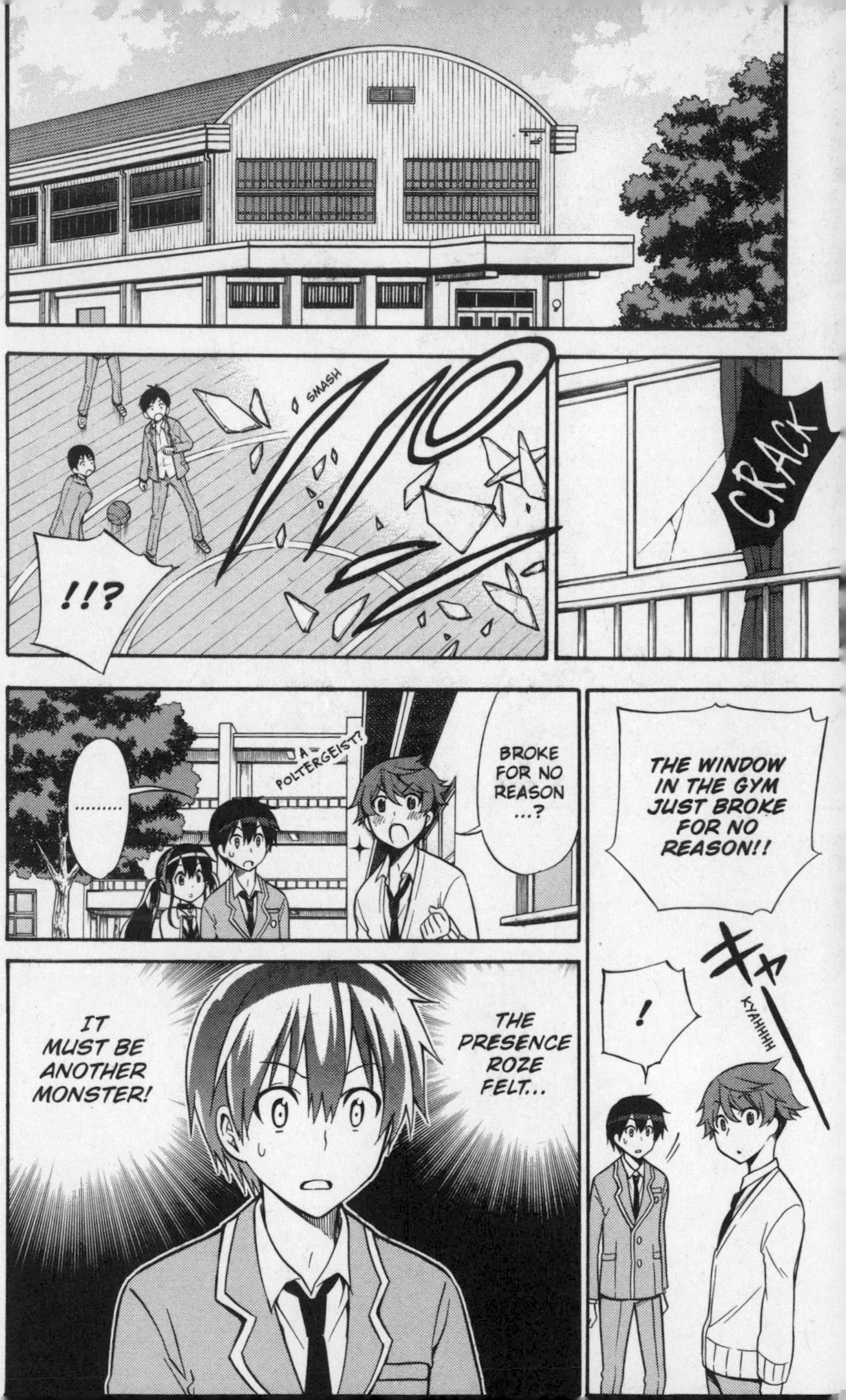
CRACK
SMASH
!!?
THE WINDOW IN THE GYM JUST BROKE FOR NO REASON!!
BROKE FOR NO REASON ...?
A POLTERGEIST?
....
KYAHHHH
!
THE PRESENCE ROZE FELT...
IT MUST BE ANOTHER MONSTER!

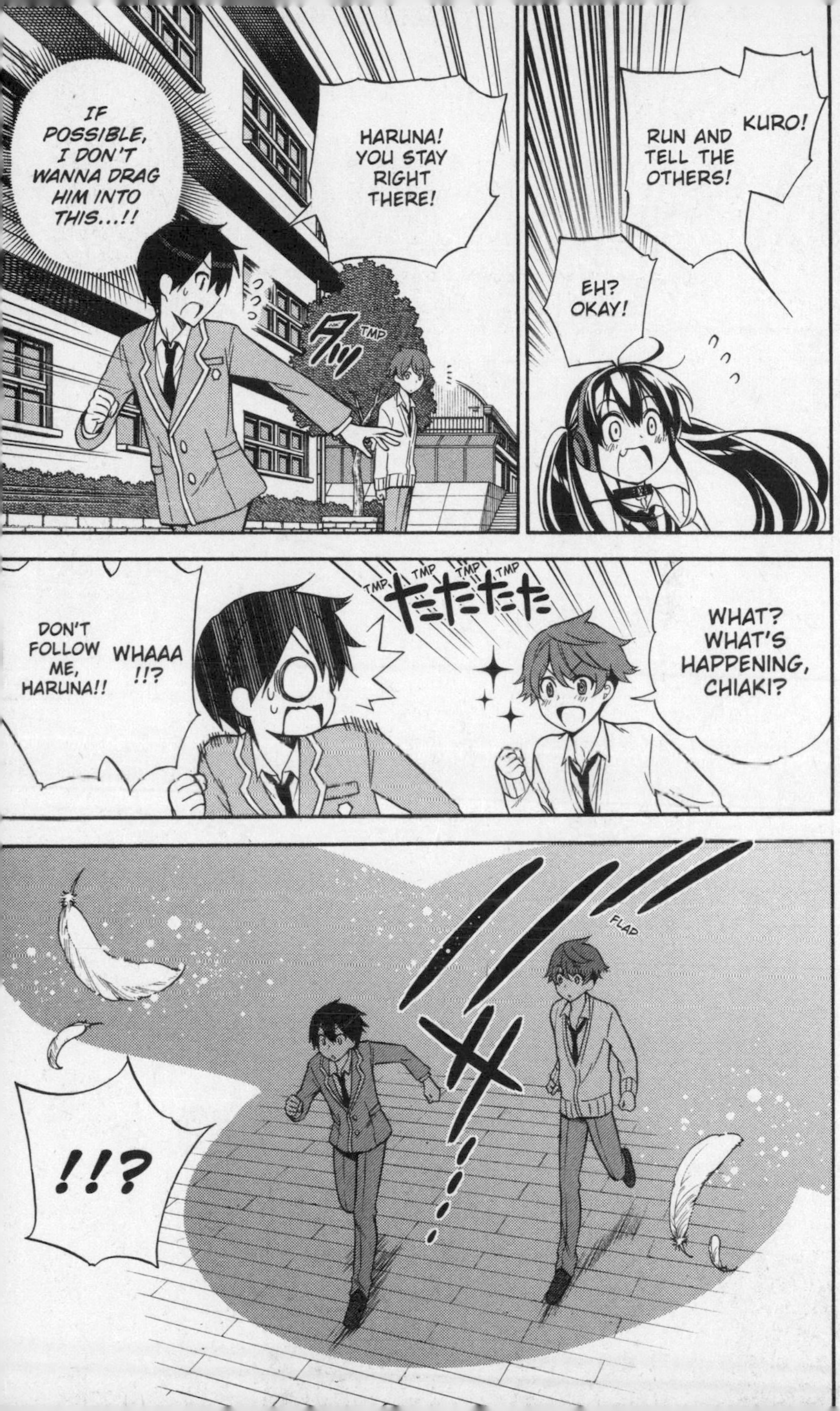
KURO!
RUN AND TELL THE OTHERS!
EH? OKAY!
HARUNA! YOU STAY RIGHT THERE!
IF POSSIBLE, I DON'T WANNA DRAG HIM INTO THIS...!!
TMP
WHAT? WHAT'S HAPPENING, CHIAKI?
TMP TMP TMP TMP
WHAAA!!?
DON'T FOLLOW ME, HARUNA!!
FLAP
!!?

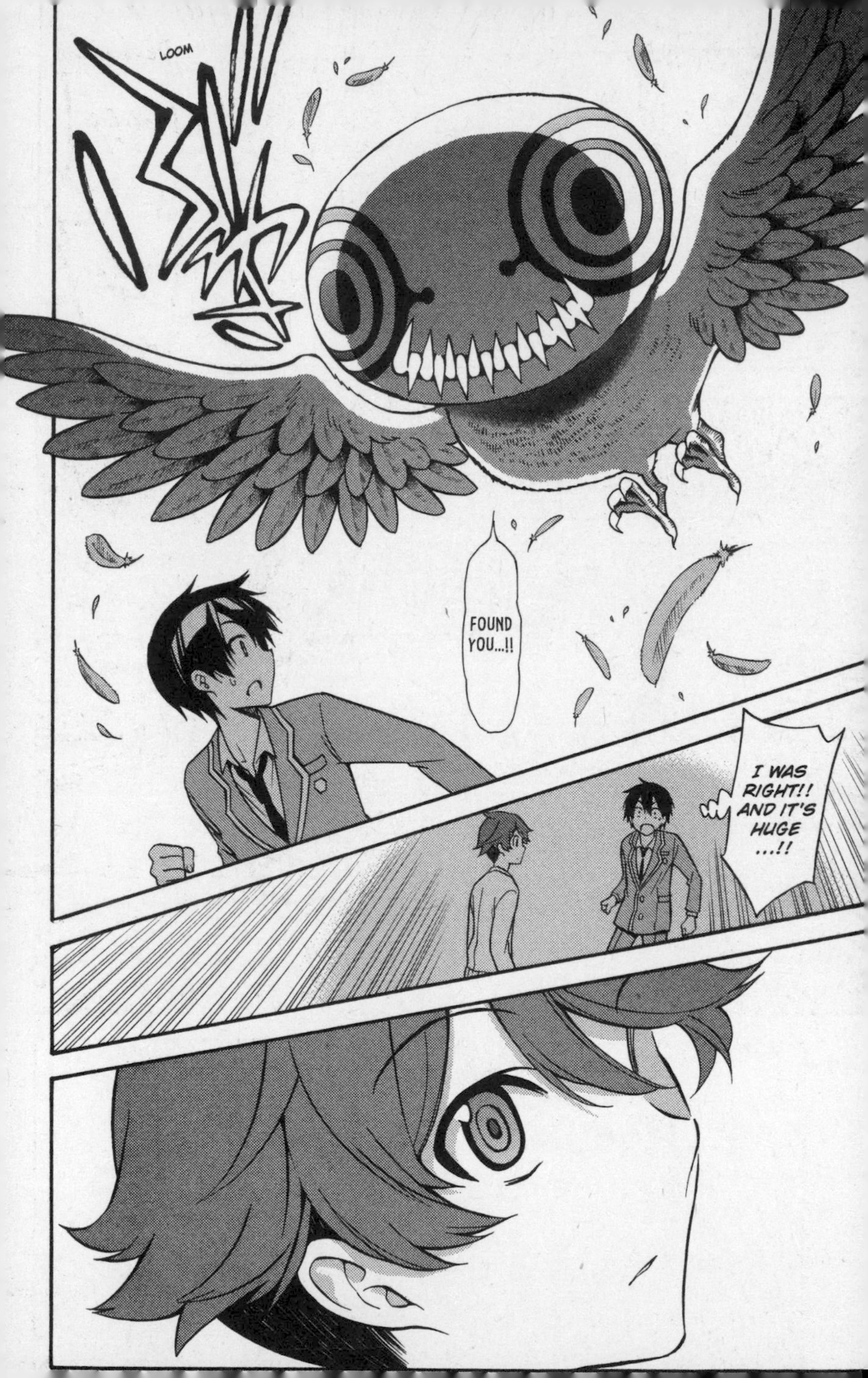
LOOM
FOUND YOU...!!
I WAS RIGHT!! AND IT'S HUGE ...!!

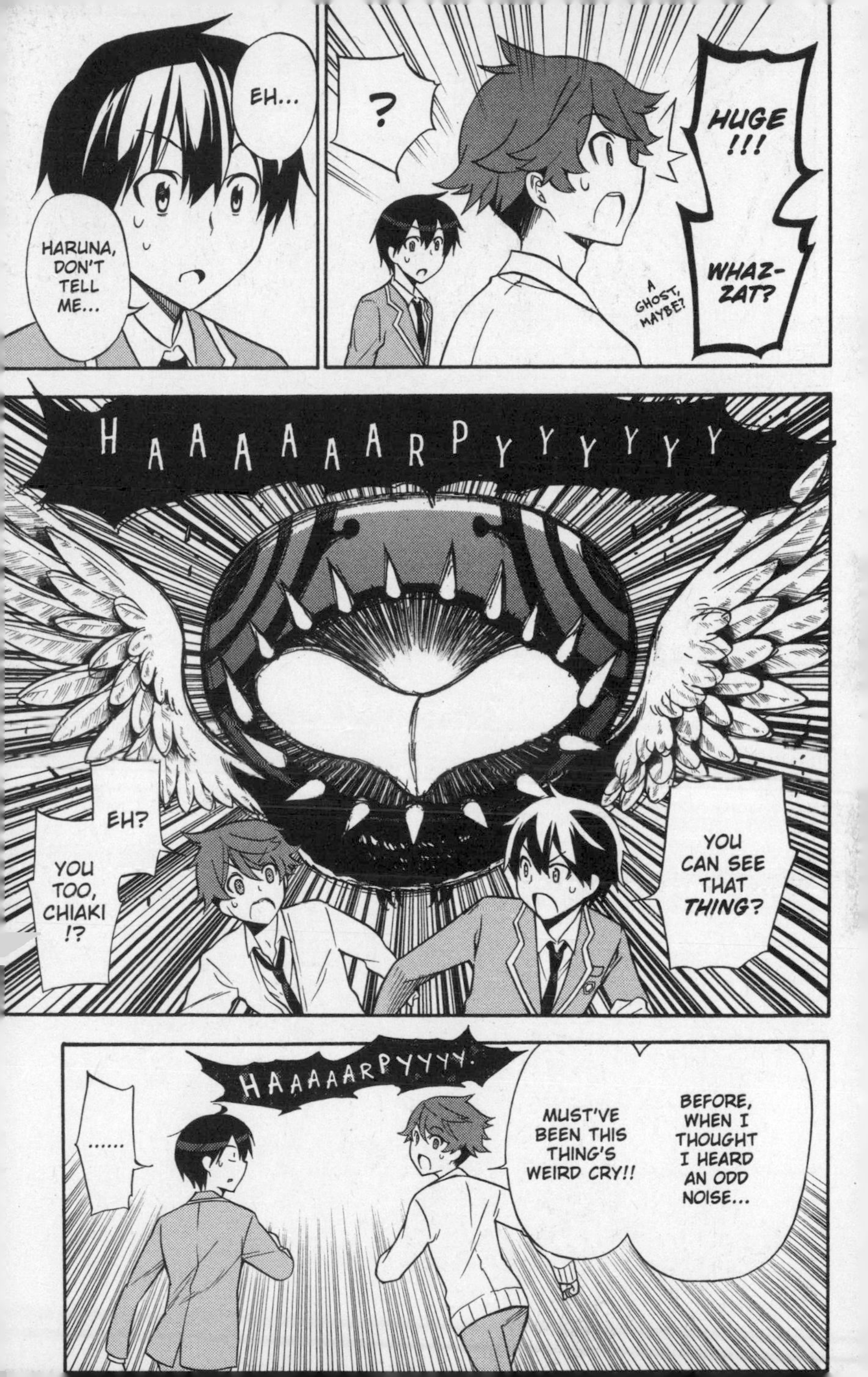
HUGE!!!
WHAZ-ZAT?
?
A GHOST, MAYBE?
EH...
HARUNA, DON'T TELL ME...
HAAAAARPYYYYYY
YOU CAN SEE THAT THING?
EH?
YOU TOO, CHIAKI!?
BEFORE, WHEN I THOUGHT I HEARD AN ODD NOISE...
MUST'VE BEEN THIS THING'S WEIRD CRY!!
HAAAAARPYYYY.
......

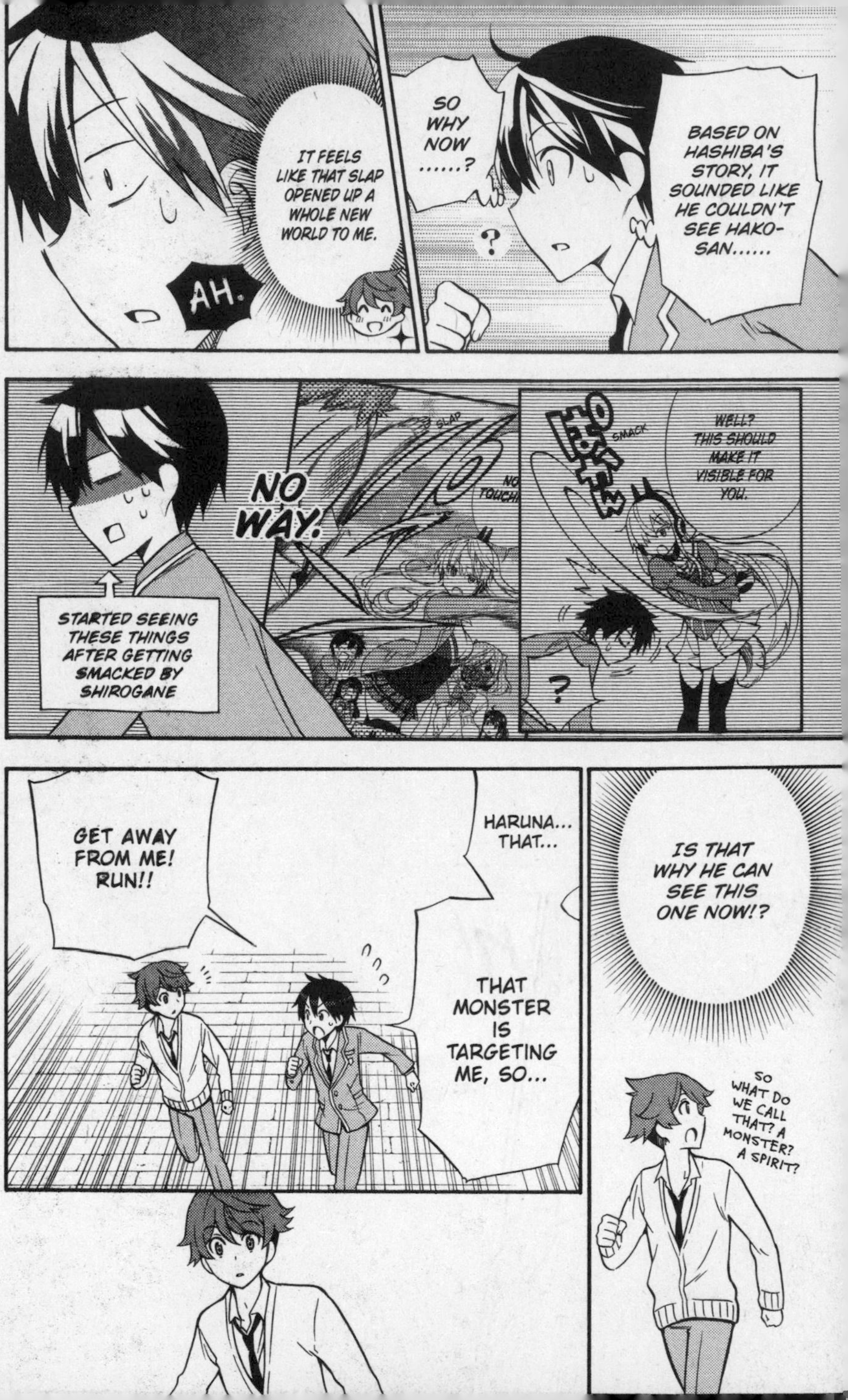
BASED ON HASHIBA'S STORY, IT SOUNDED LIKE HE COULDN'T SEE HAKO-SAN......
SO WHY NOW ......?
?
IT FEELS LIKE THAT SLAP OPENED UP A WHOLE NEW WORLD TO ME.
AH.
WELL? THIS SHOULD MAKE IT VISIBLE FOR YOU.
SMACK
?
SLAP
NO WAY.
STARTED SEEING THESE THINGS AFTER GETTING SMACKED BY SHIROGANE
IS THAT WHY HE CAN SEE THIS ONE NOW!?
SO WHAT DO WE CALL THAT? A MONSTER? A SPIRIT?
HARUNA... THAT...
THAT MONSTER IS TARGETING ME, SO...
GET AWAY FROM ME! RUN!!

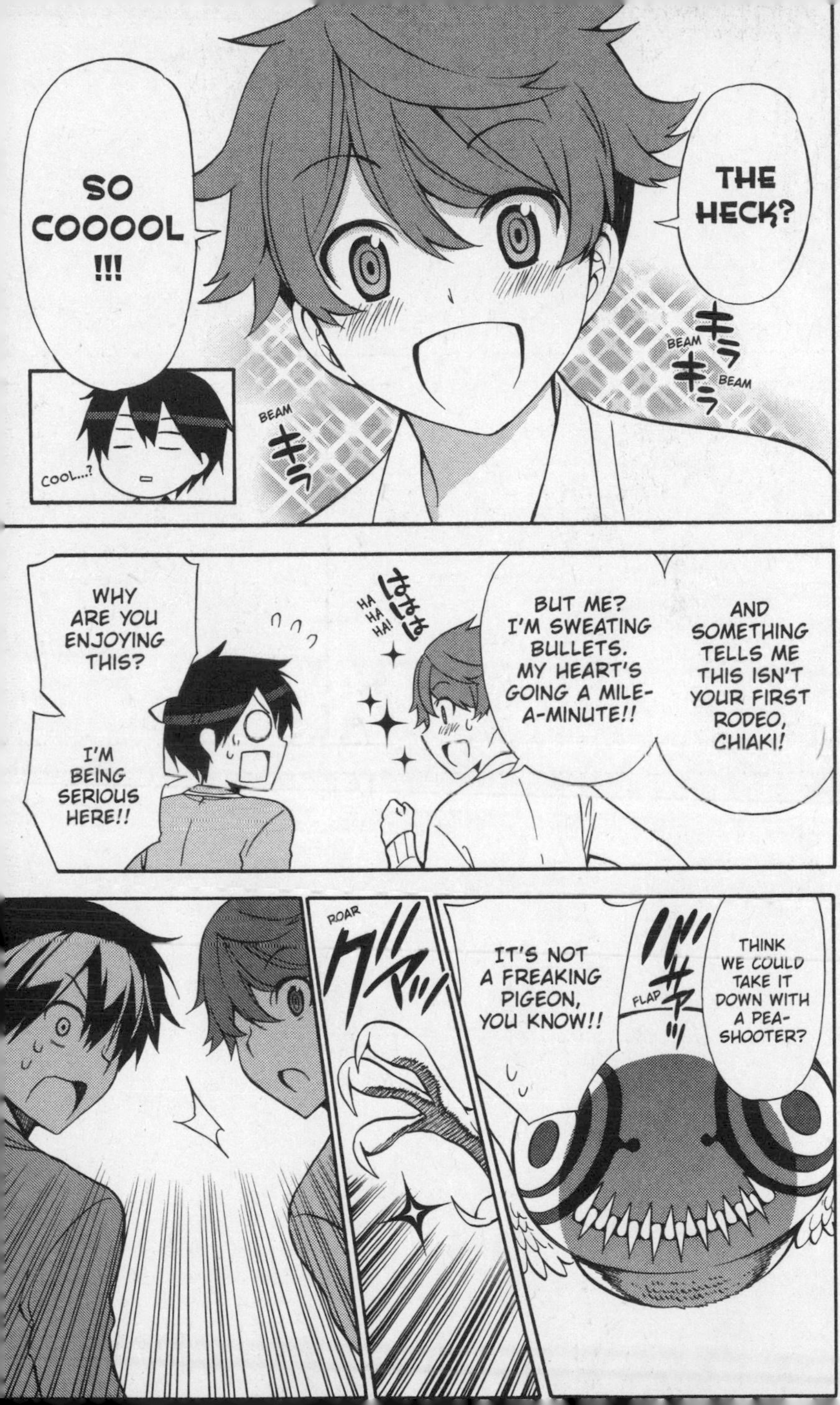
THE HECK?
BEAM キラ
BEAM キラ
BEAM キラ
SO COOOOL !!!
COOL...?
AND SOMETHING TELLS ME THIS ISN'T YOUR FIRST RODEO, CHIAKI!
BUT ME? I'M SWEATING BULLETS. MY HEART'S GOING A MILE-A-MINUTE!!
HA HA HA ははは
WHY ARE YOU ENJOYING THIS?
I'M BEING SERIOUS HERE!!
THINK WE COULD TAKE IT DOWN WITH A PEA-SHOOTER?
FLAP バサッ
IT'S NOT A FREAKING PIGEON, YOU KNOW!!
ROAR グワッ

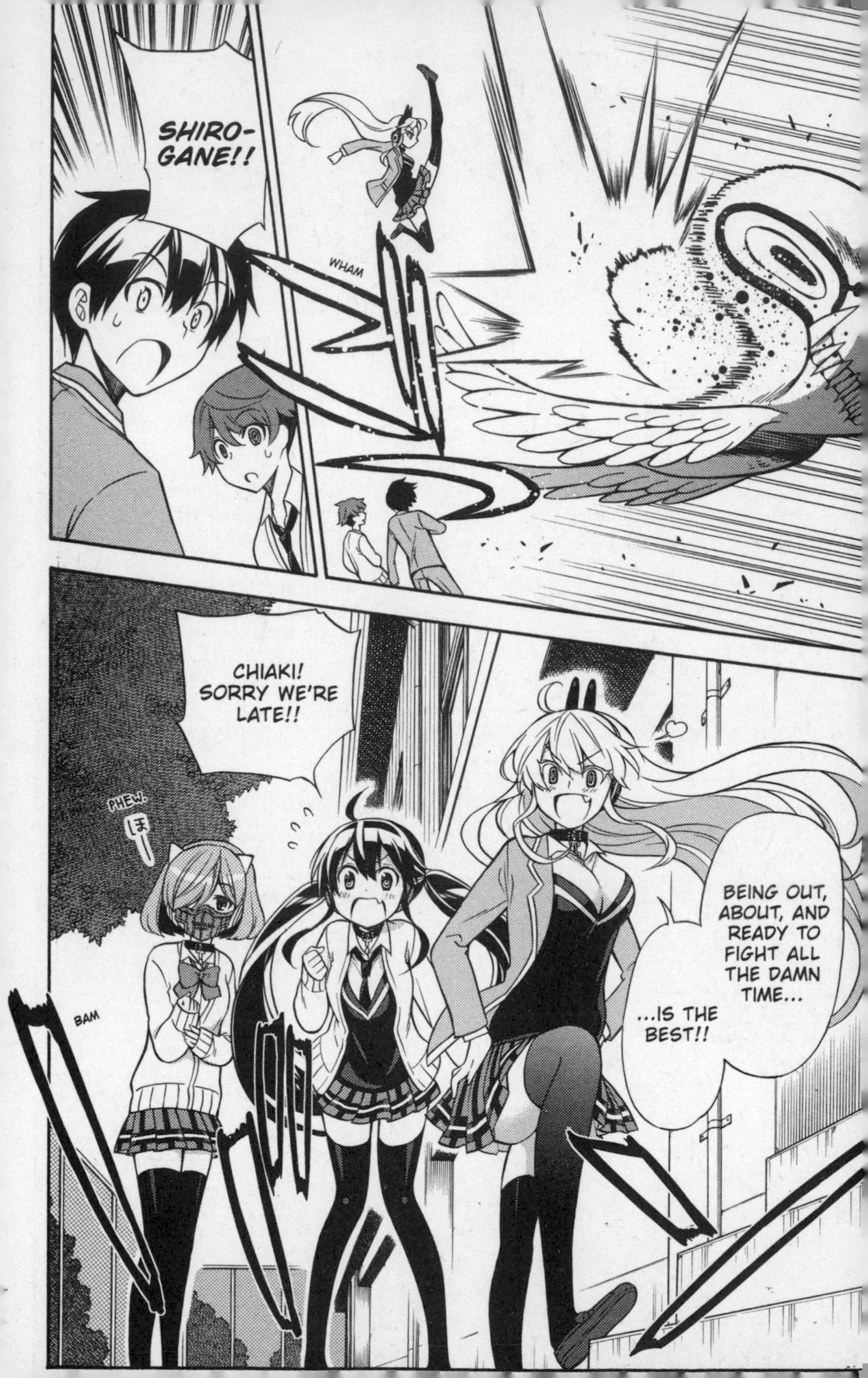
WHAM
SHIRO-GANE!!
BEING OUT, ABOUT, AND READY TO FIGHT ALL THE DAMN TIME...
...IS THE BEST!!
CHIAKI! SORRY WE'RE LATE!!
PHEW.
ほー
BAM

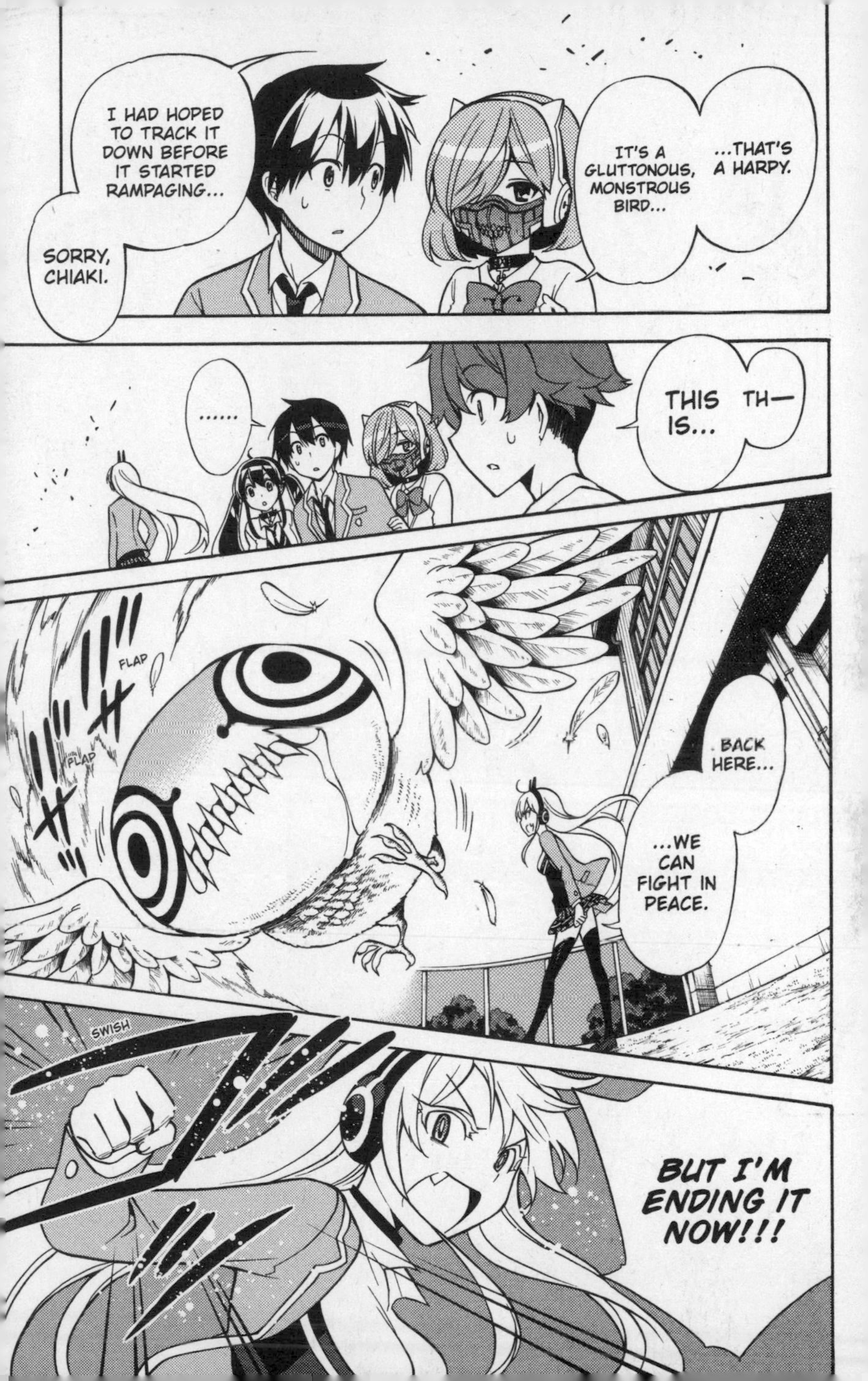
...THAT'S A HARPY.
IT'S A GLUTTONOUS, MONSTROUS BIRD...
I HAD HOPED TO TRACK IT DOWN BEFORE IT STARTED RAMPAGING...
SORRY, CHIAKI.
TH— THIS IS...
......
FLAP
FLAP
. BACK HERE...
...WE CAN FIGHT IN PEACE.
SWISH
BUT I'M ENDING IT NOW!!!

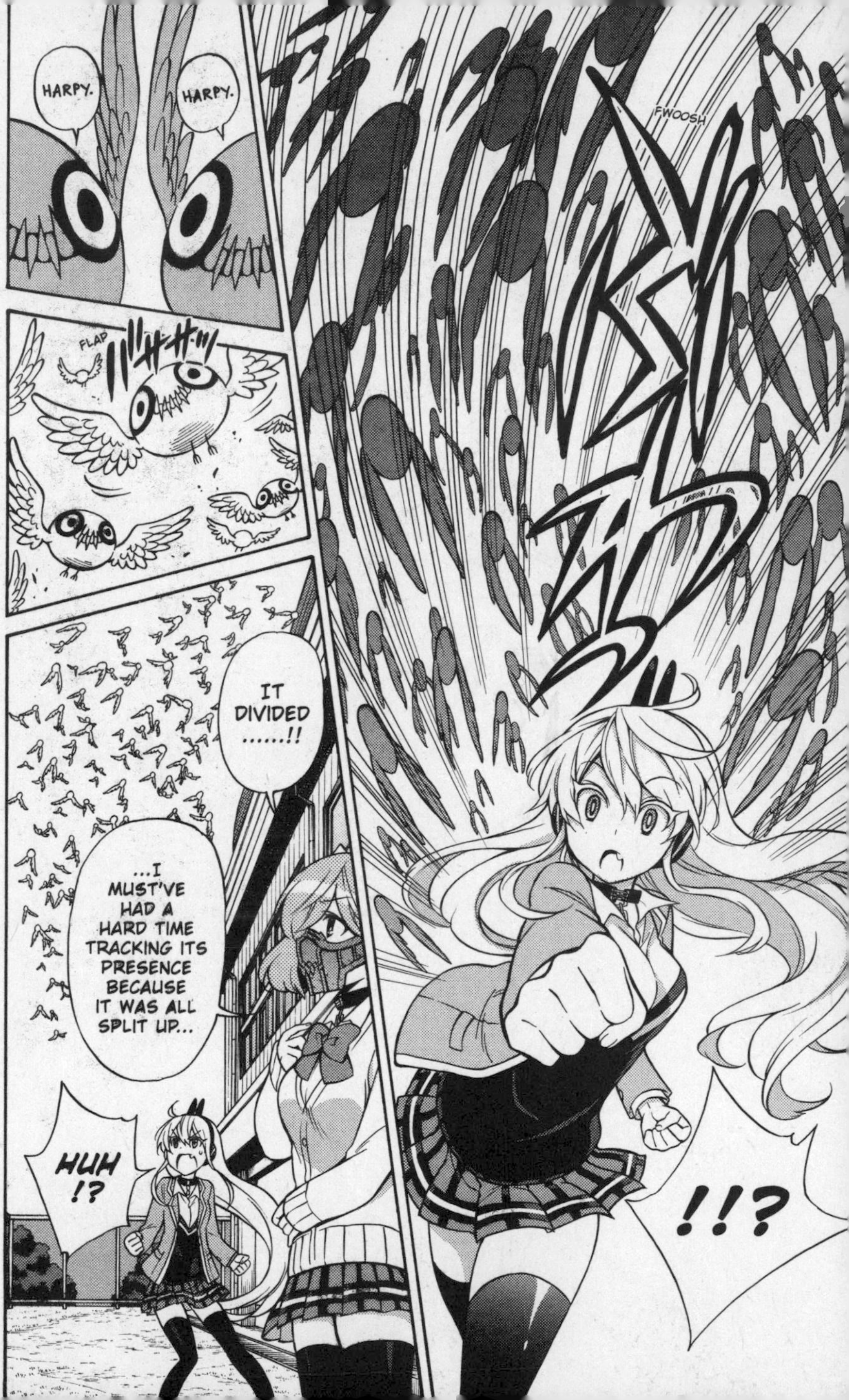
FWOOSH
!!?
HARPY.
HARPY.
FLAP
IT DIVIDED ......!!
...I MUST'VE HAD A HARD TIME TRACKING ITS PRESENCE BECAUSE IT WAS ALL SPLIT UP...
HUH !?

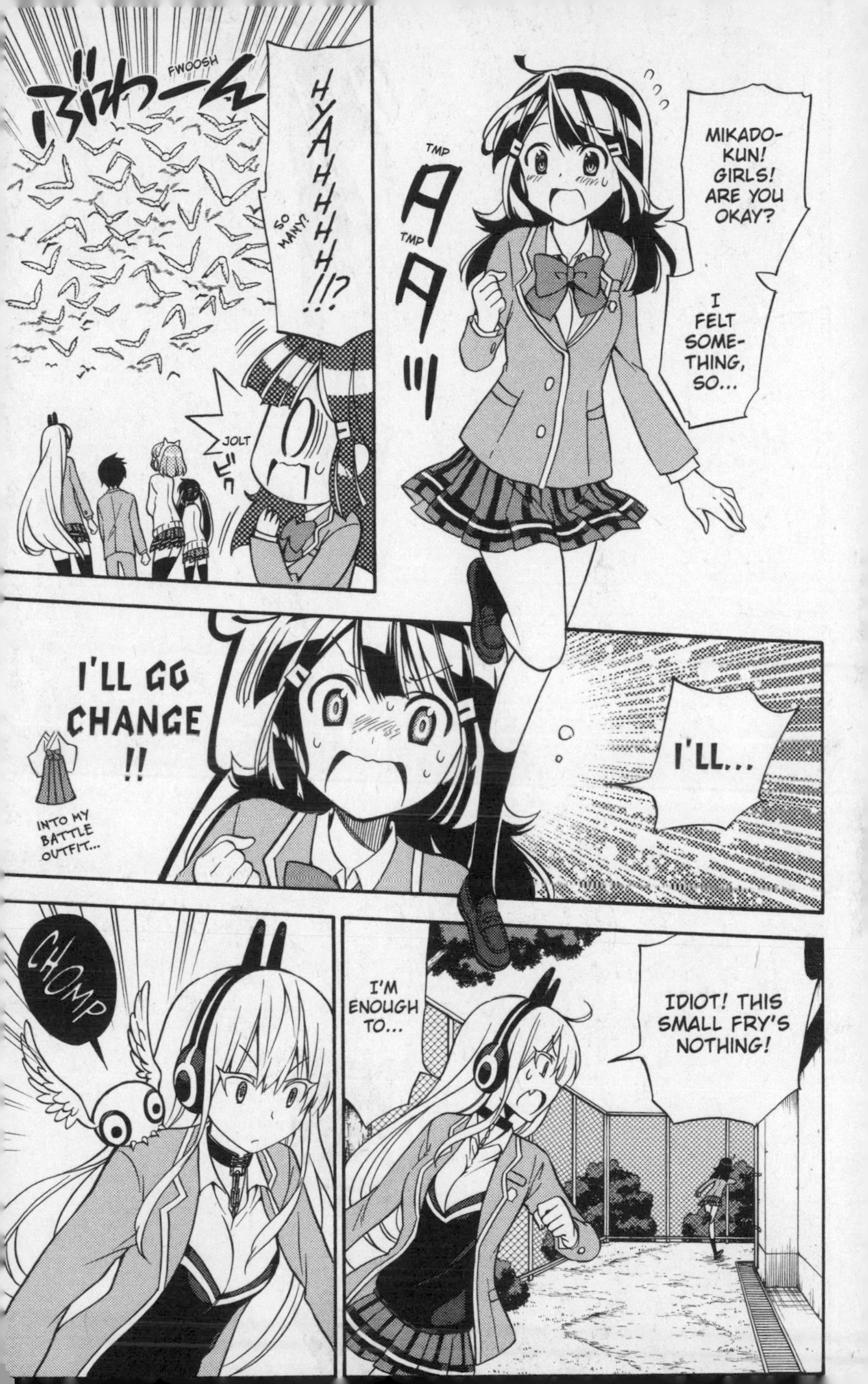
MIKADO-KUN! GIRLS! ARE YOU OKAY?
I FELT SOMETHING, SO...
TMP
TMP
HYAHHHHH!!?
FWOOSH
SO MANY?
JOLT
I'LL...
I'LL GO CHANGE!!
INTO MY BATTLE OUTFIT...
IDIOT! THIS SMALL FRY'S NOTHING!
I'M ENOUGH TO...
CHOMP

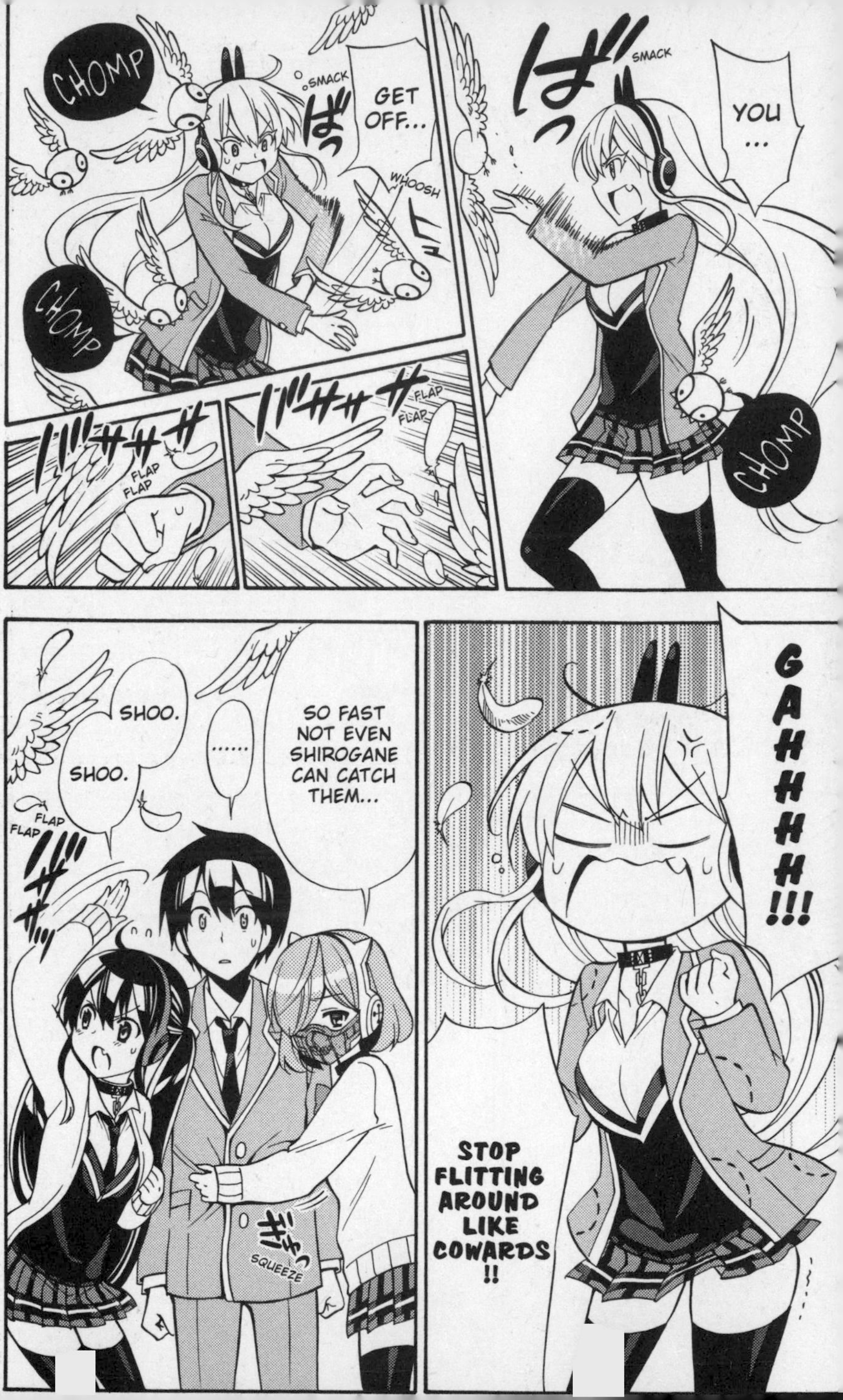
SMACK
YOU ...
CHOMP
GET OFF...
SMACK
WHOOSH
CHOMP
CHOMP
FLAP FLAP
FLAP FLAP
GAHHHHHH!!!
STOP FLITTING AROUND LIKE COWARDS !!
SO FAST NOT EVEN SHIROGANE CAN CATCH THEM...
......
SHOO.
SHOO.
FLAP FLAP
SQUEEZE

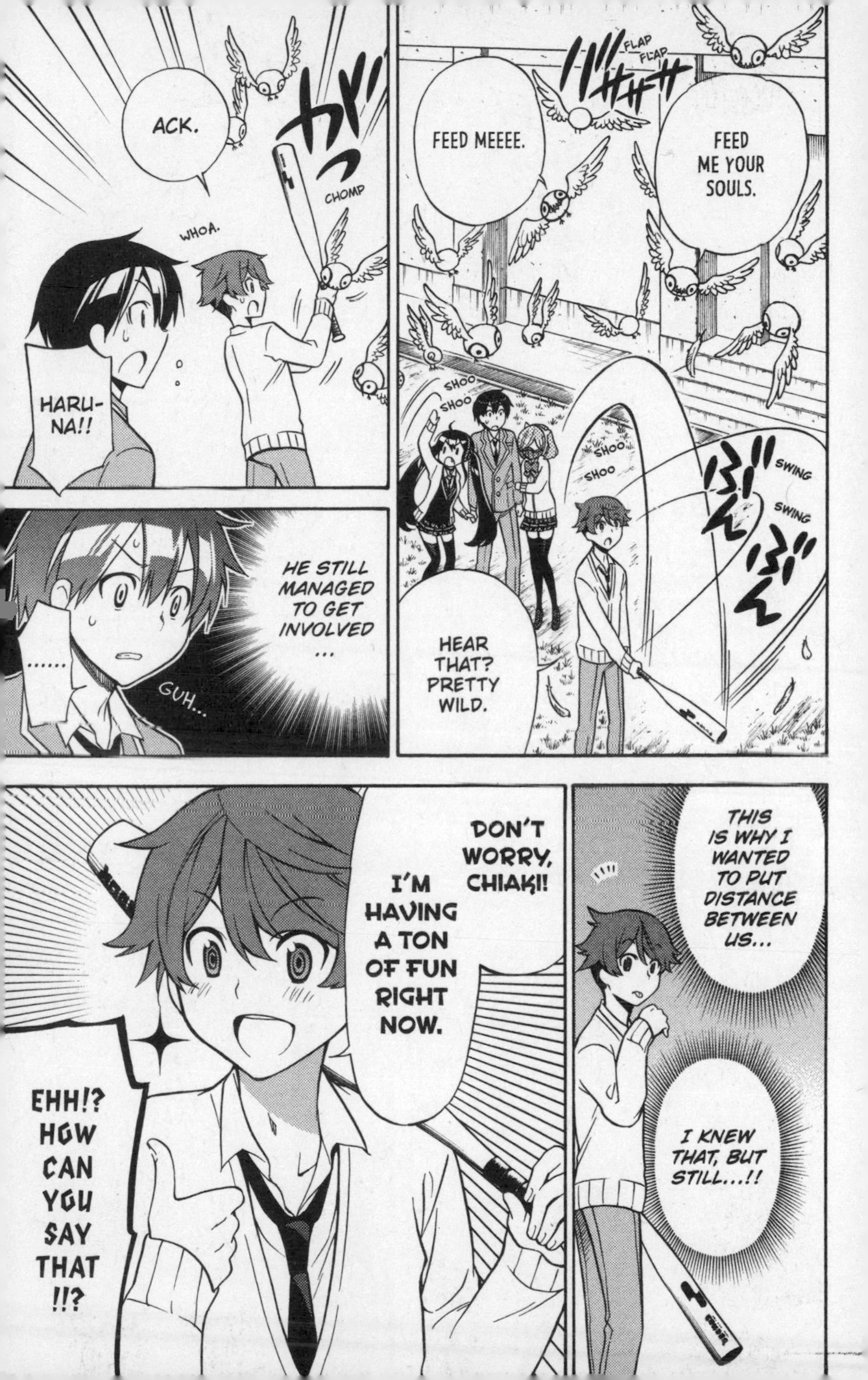
FLAP
FLAP
FEED ME YOUR SOULS.
FEED MEEEE.
SHOO
SHOO
SHOO
SHOO
SWING
SWING
HEAR THAT? PRETTY WILD.
CHOMP
ACK.
WHOA.
HARU-NA!!
HE STILL MANAGED TO GET INVOLVED ...
......
GUH...
THIS IS WHY I WANTED TO PUT DISTANCE BETWEEN US...
!!!
I KNEW THAT, BUT STILL...!!
DON'T WORRY, CHIAKI!!
I'M HAVING A TON OF FUN RIGHT NOW.
EHH!? HOW CAN YOU SAY THAT!!?

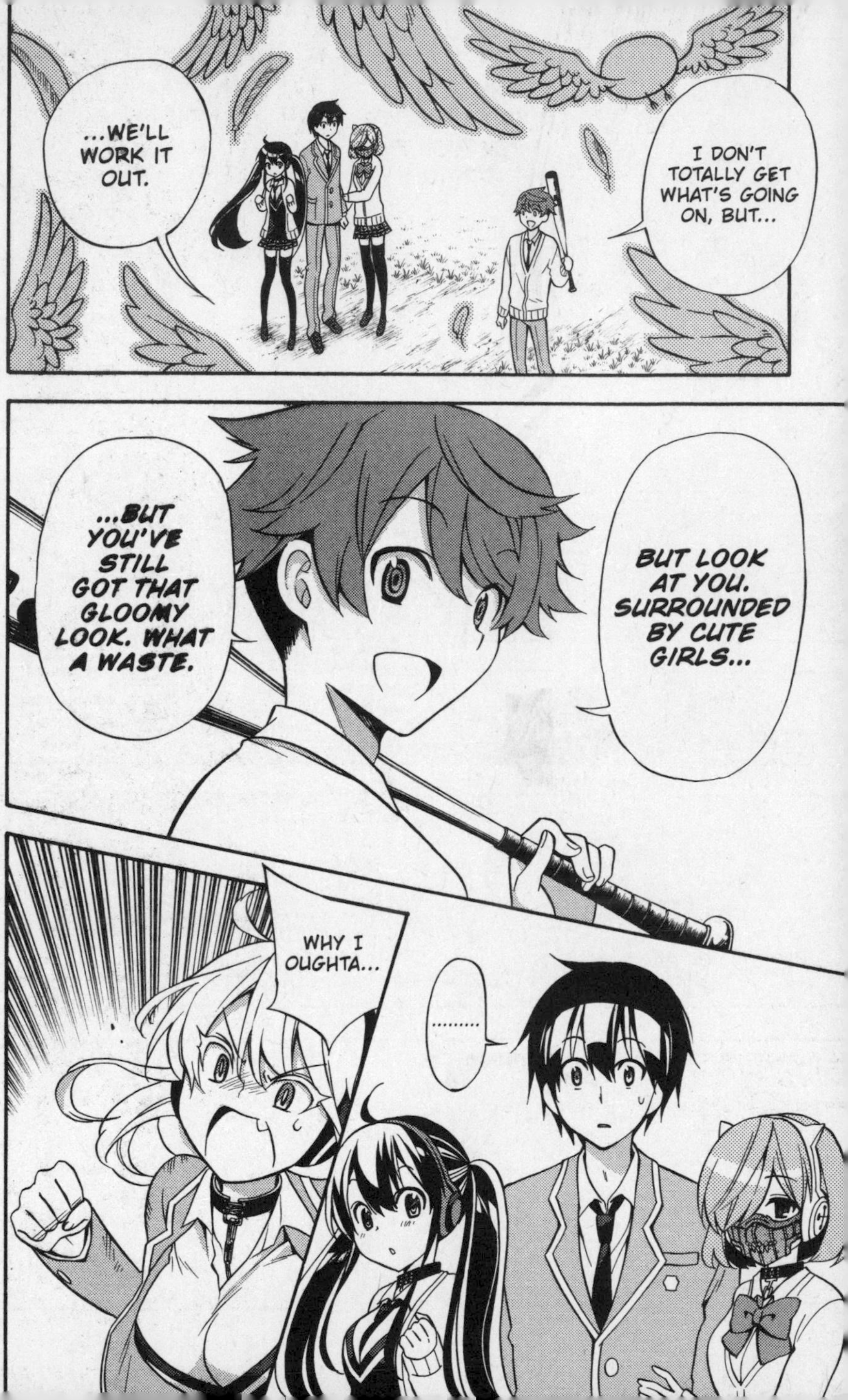
I DON'T TOTALLY GET WHAT'S GOING ON, BUT...
...WE'LL WORK IT OUT.
BUT LOOK AT YOU. SURROUNDED BY CUTE GIRLS...
...BUT YOU'VE STILL GOT THAT GLOOMY LOOK. WHAT A WASTE.
....
WHY I OUGHTA...

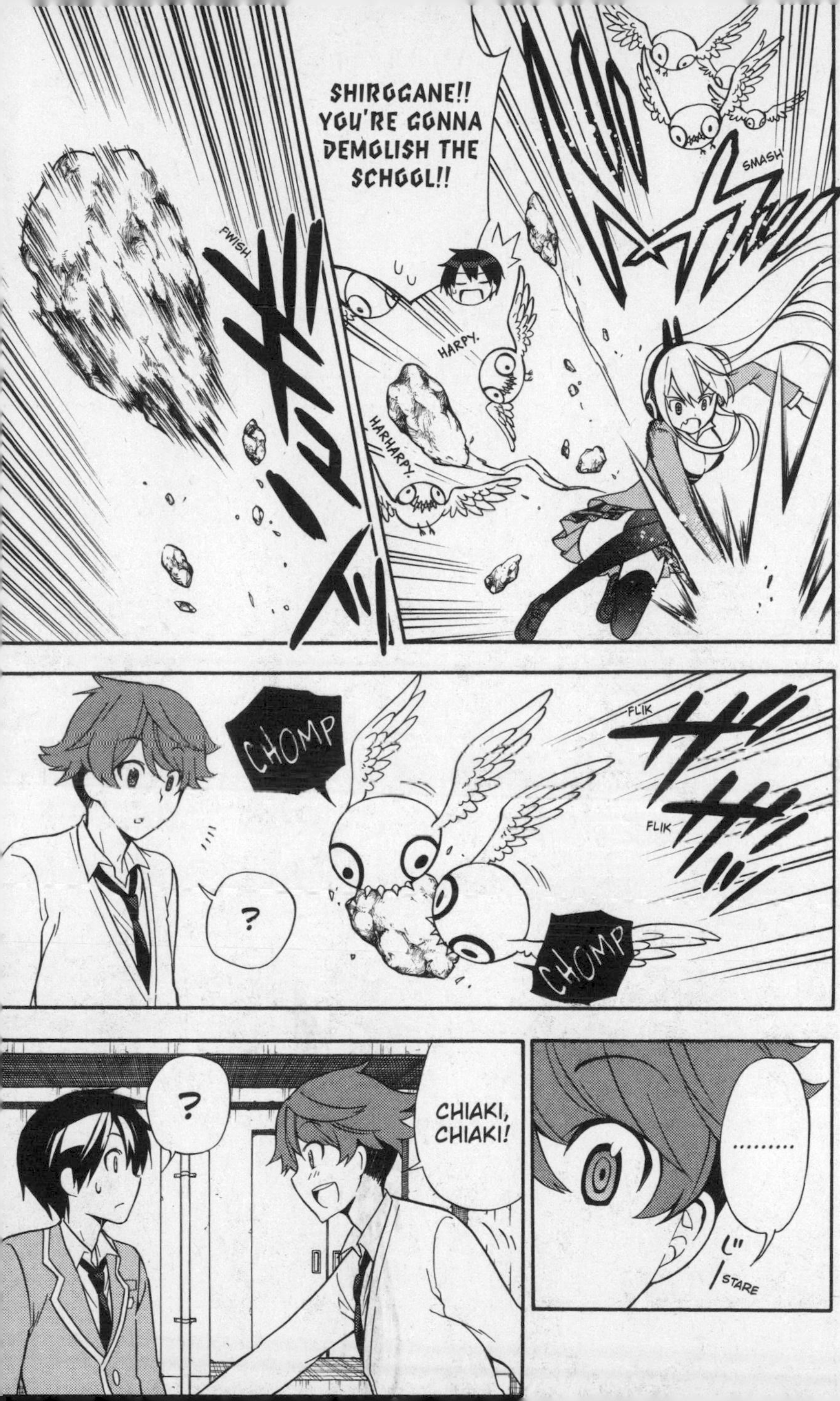

SMASH
SHIROGANE!! YOU'RE GONNA DEMOLISH THE SCHOOL!!
HARPY.
HARHARPY.
PWISH
FLIK
FLIK
CHOMP
CHOMP
?
....
STARE
CHIAKI, CHIAKI!
?

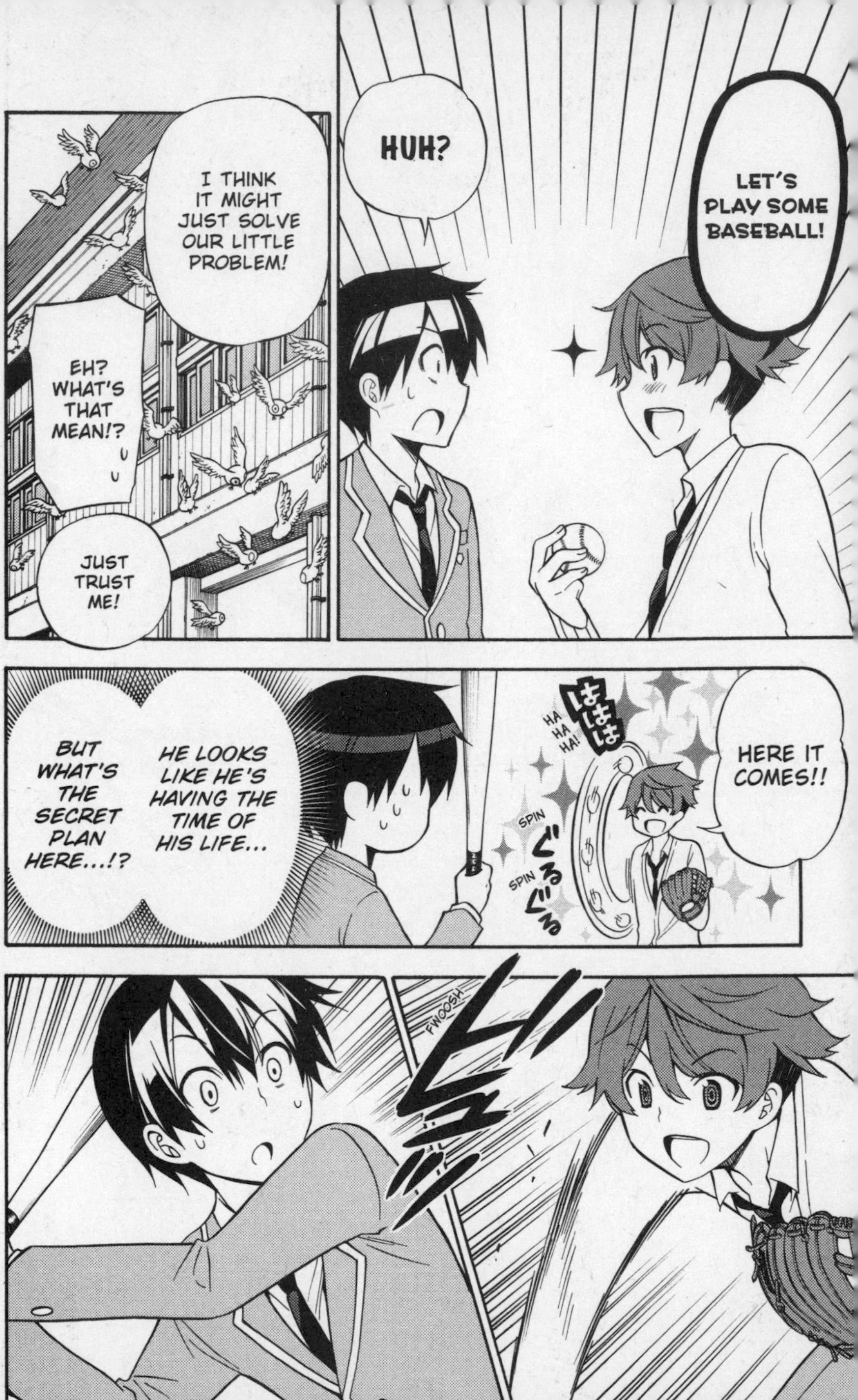
LET'S PLAY SOME BASEBALL!
HUH?
I THINK IT MIGHT JUST SOLVE OUR LITTLE PROBLEM!
EH? WHAT'S THAT MEAN!?
JUST TRUST ME!
HERE IT COMES!!
ははは
HA HA HA!
ぐるぐる
SPIN SPIN
HE LOOKS LIKE HE'S HAVING THE TIME OF HIS LIFE...
BUT WHAT'S THE SECRET PLAN HERE...!?
FWOOSH

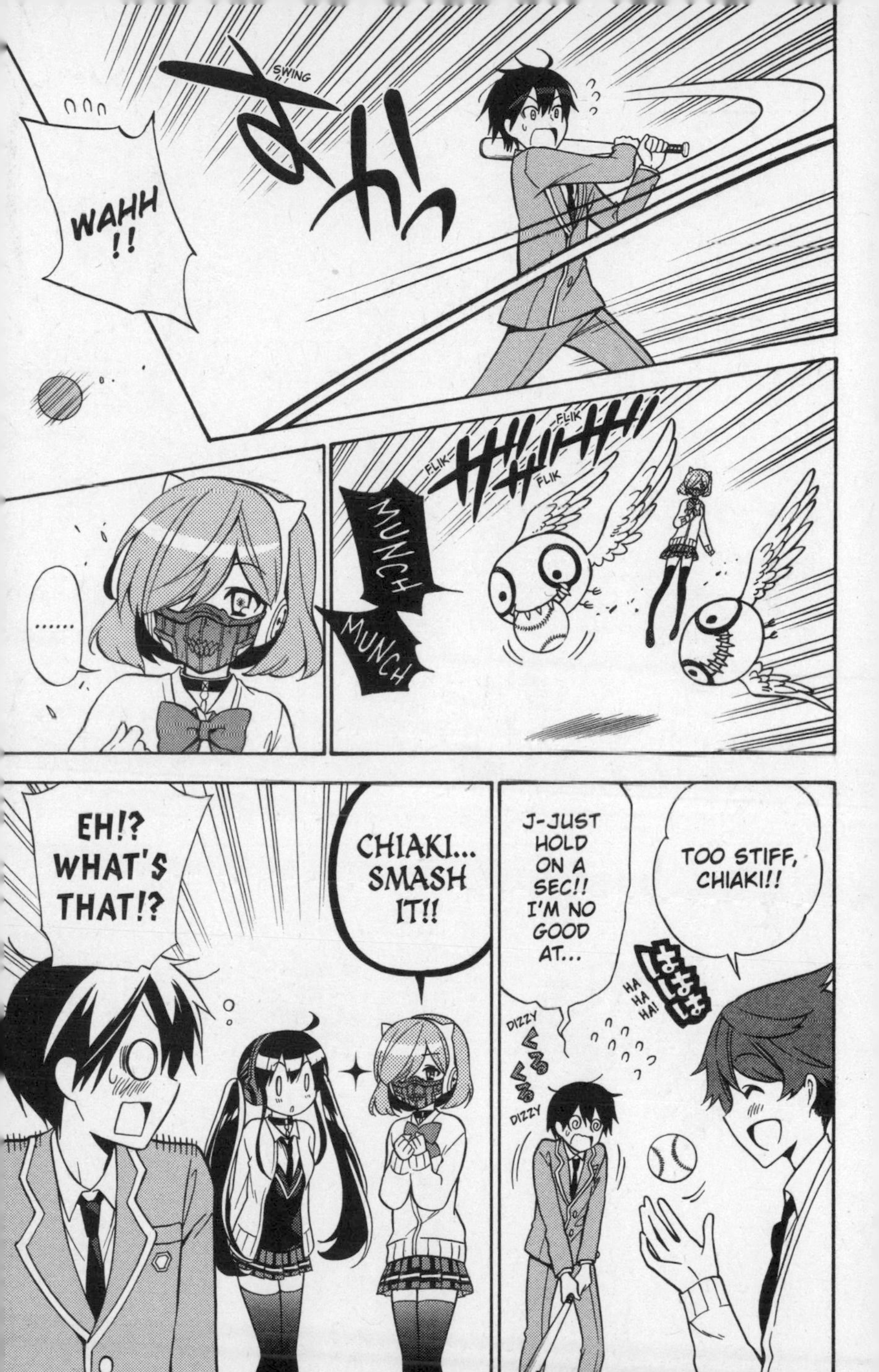
SWING
WAHH !!
FLIK
FLIK
FLIK
MUNCH
MUNCH
......
TOO STIFF, CHIAKI!!
HA HA HA!
J-JUST HOLD ON A SEC!! I'M NO GOOD AT...
DIZZY
DIZZY
CHIAKI... SMASH IT!!
EH!? WHAT'S THAT!?

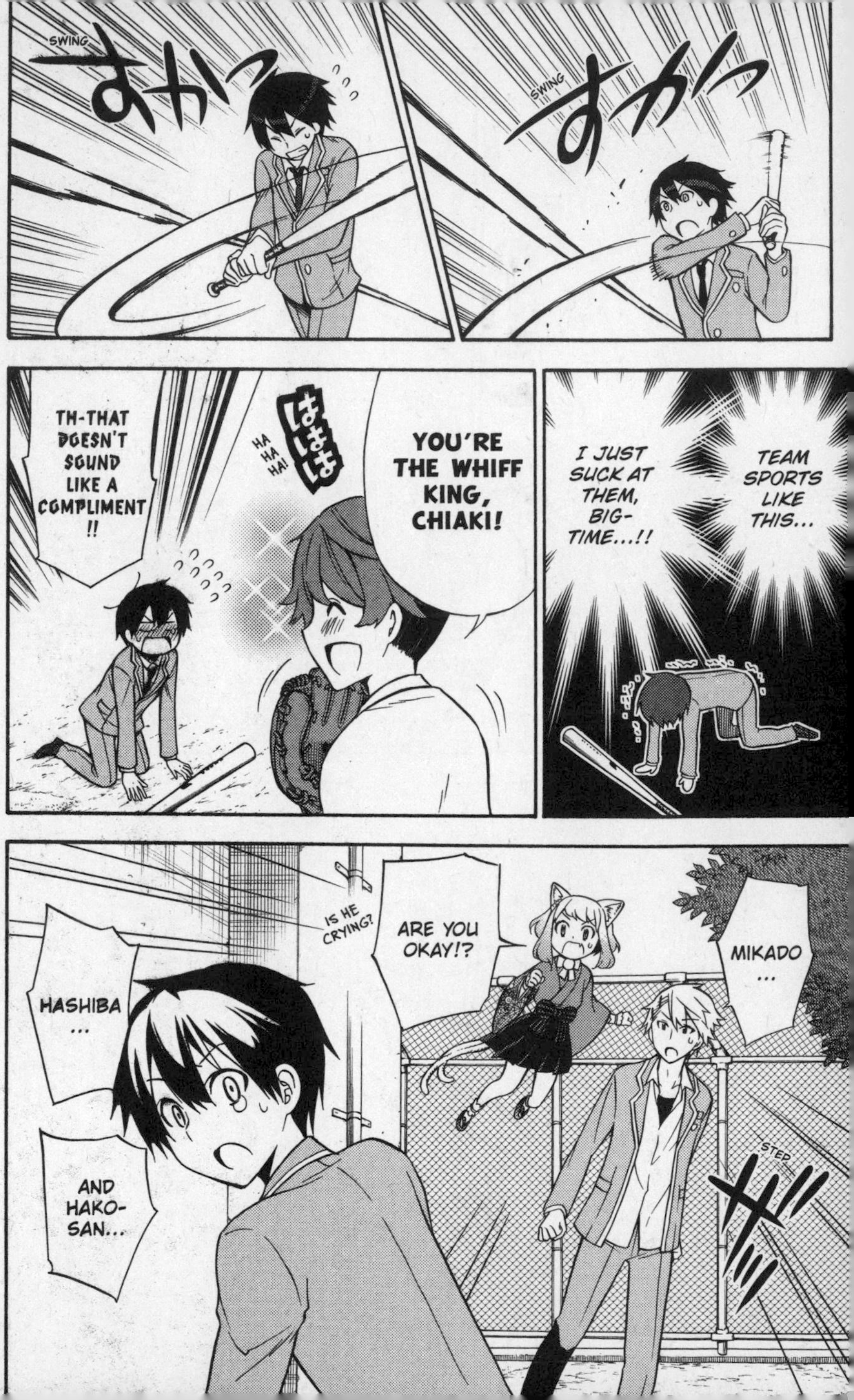
SWING
すかっ
SWING
すかっ
TEAM SPORTS LIKE THIS...
I JUST SUCK AT THEM, BIG-TIME...!!
YOU'RE THE WHIFF KING, CHIAKI!
HA HA HA!
ははは
TH-THAT DOESN'T SOUND LIKE A COMPLIMENT!!
MIKADO...
STEP
ARE YOU OKAY!?
IS HE CRYING?
HASHIBA...
AND HAKO-SAN...

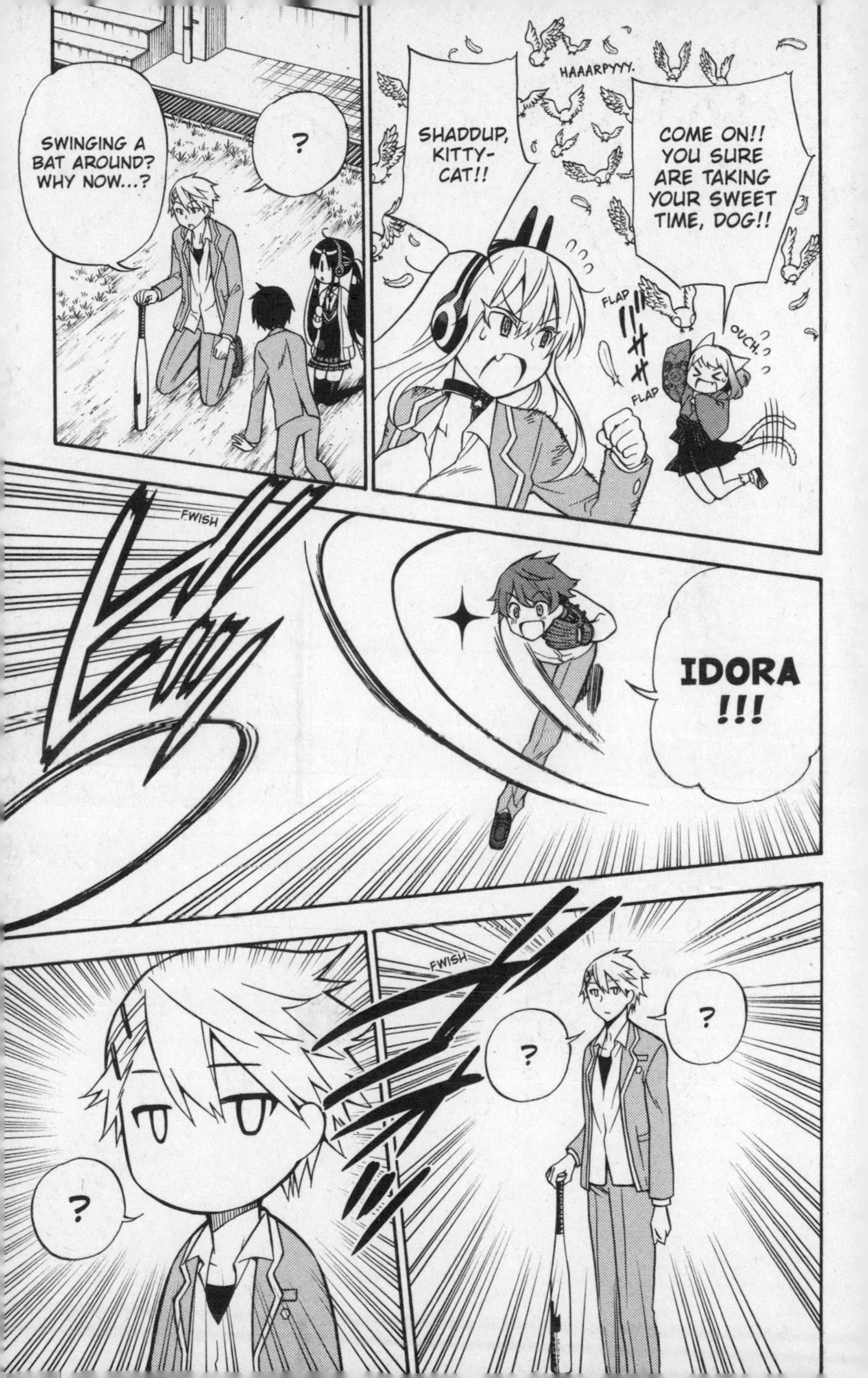
COME ON!! YOU SURE ARE TAKING YOUR SWEET TIME, DOG!!
HAAARPYYY.
SHADDUP, KITTY-CAT!!
OUCH.
FLAP
FLAP
?
SWINGING A BAT AROUND? WHY NOW...?
IDORA!!!
FWISH
?
?
FWISH
?

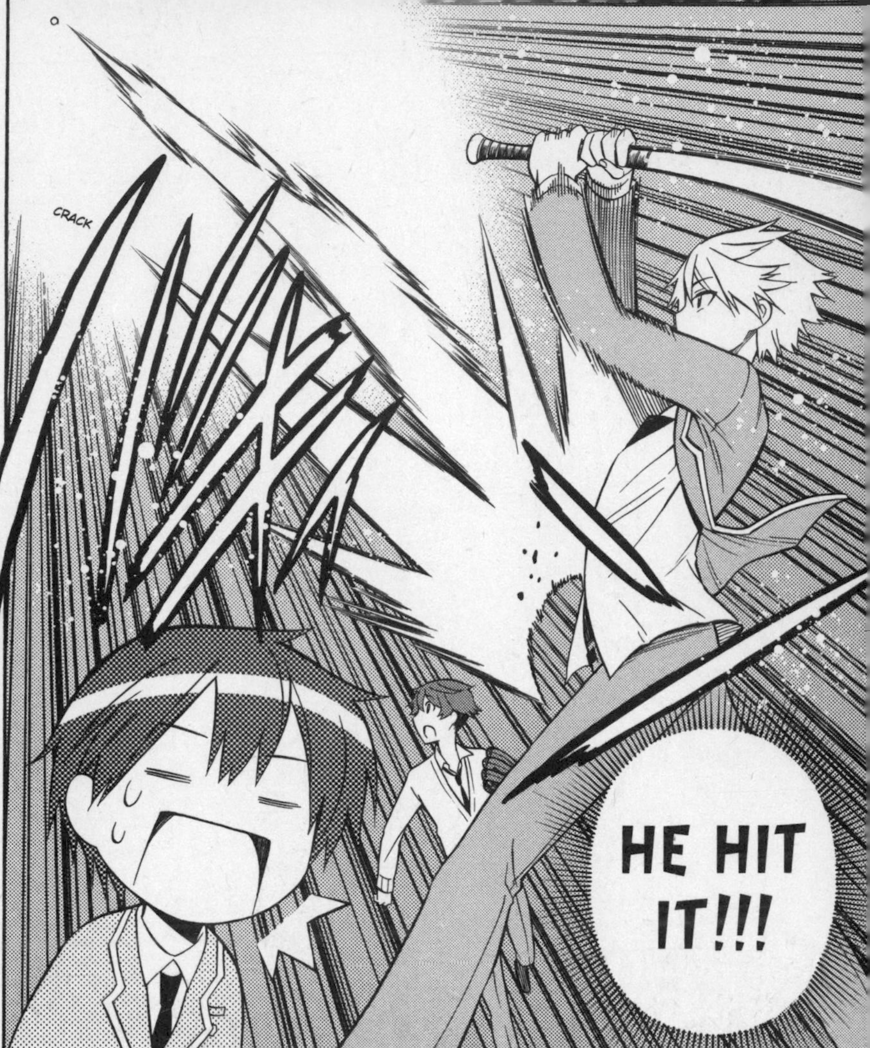
CRACK
HE HIT IT!!!
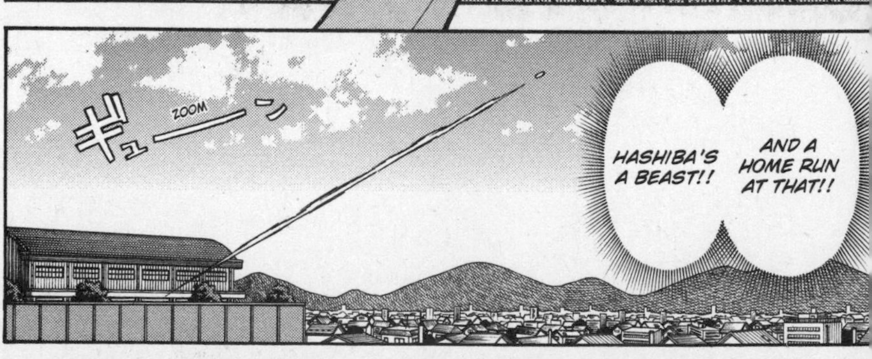
AND A HOME RUN AT THAT!!
HASHIBA'S A BEAST!!
ZOOM

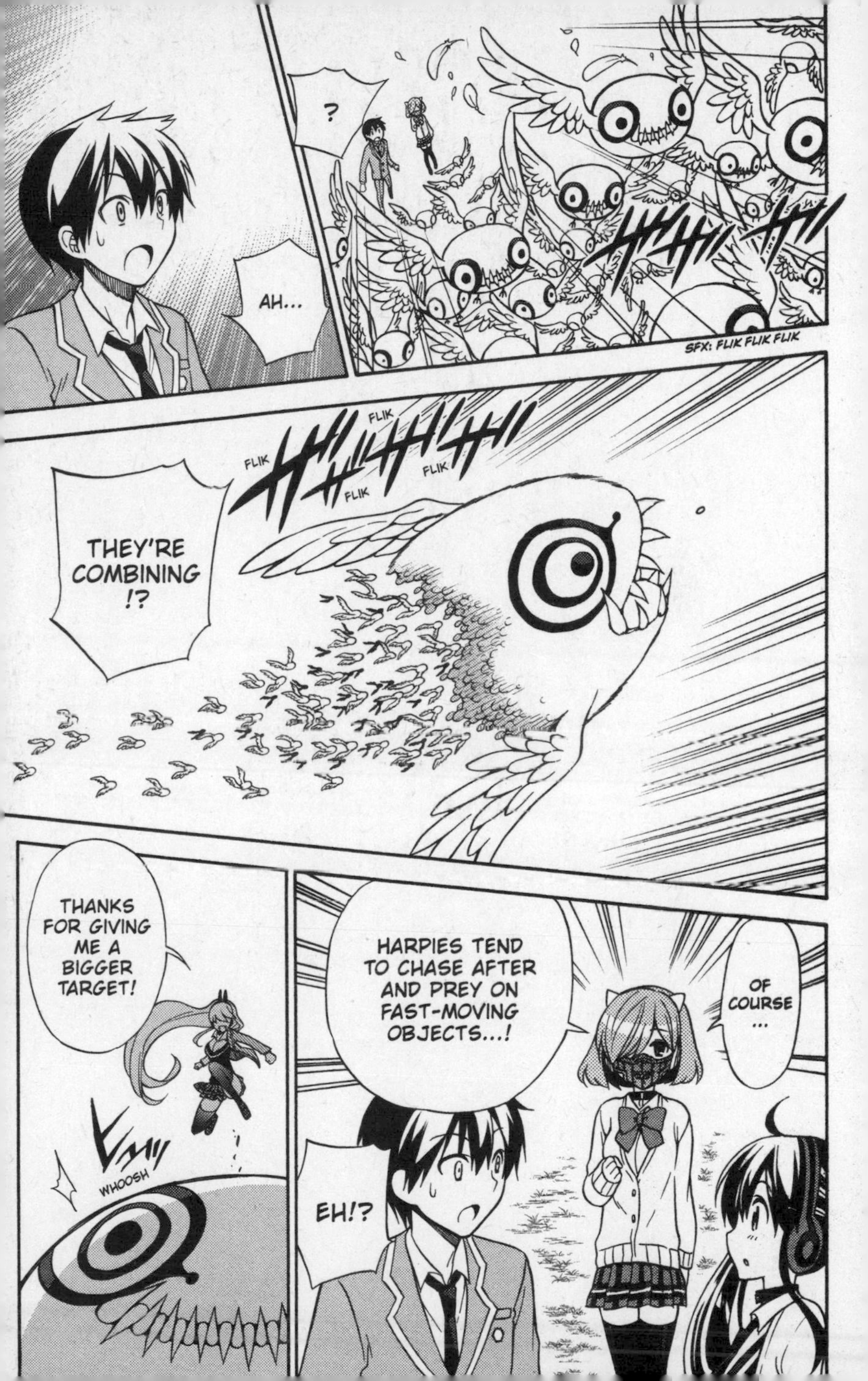
?
SFX: FLIK FLIK FLIK
AH...
FLIK FLIK FLIK FLIK
THEY'RE COMBINING !?
OF COURSE ...
HARPIES TEND TO CHASE AFTER AND PREY ON FAST-MOVING OBJECTS...!
EH!?
THANKS FOR GIVING ME A BIGGER TARGET!
WHOOSH

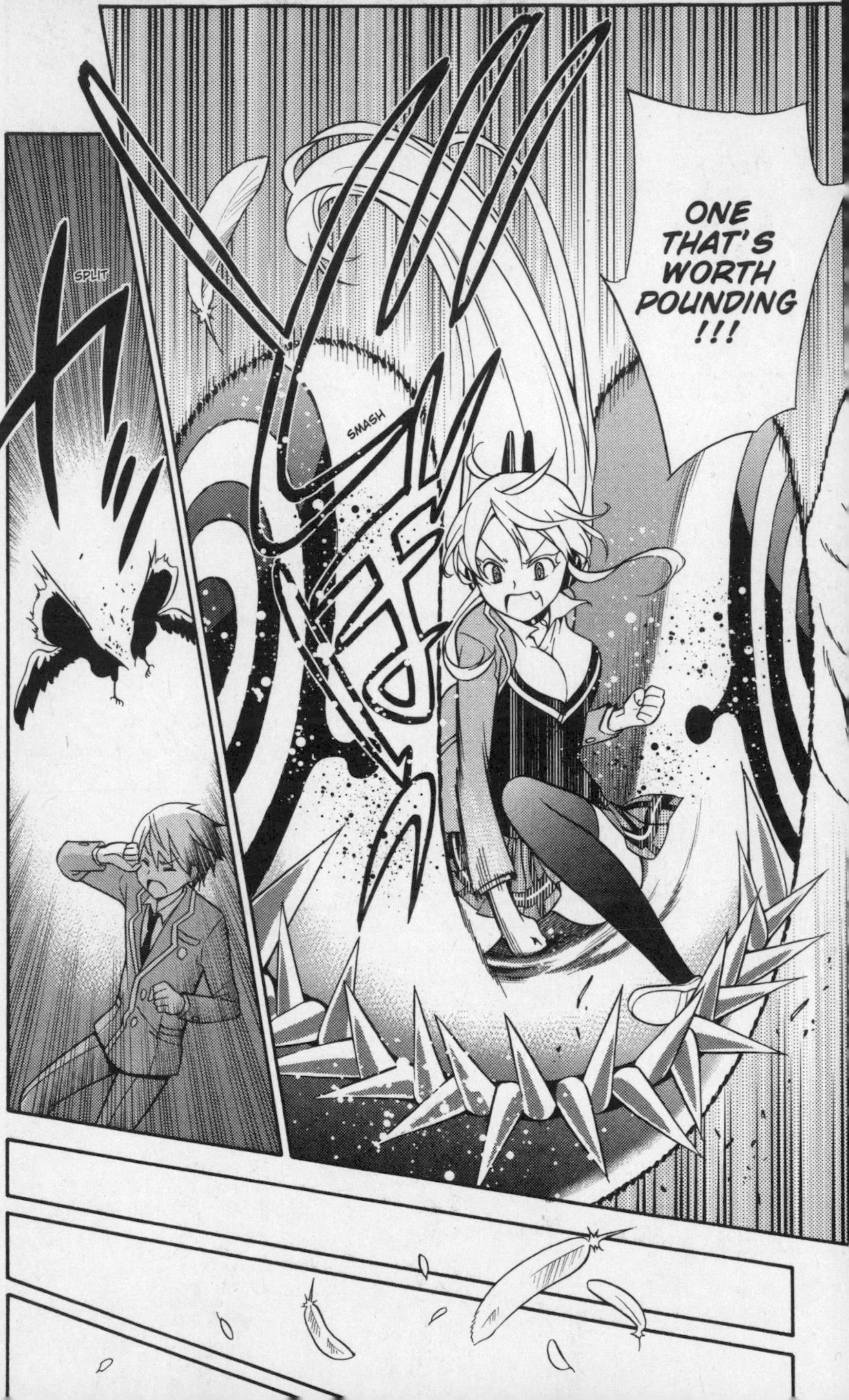
ONE THAT'S WORTH POUNDING !!!
SMASH
SPLIT

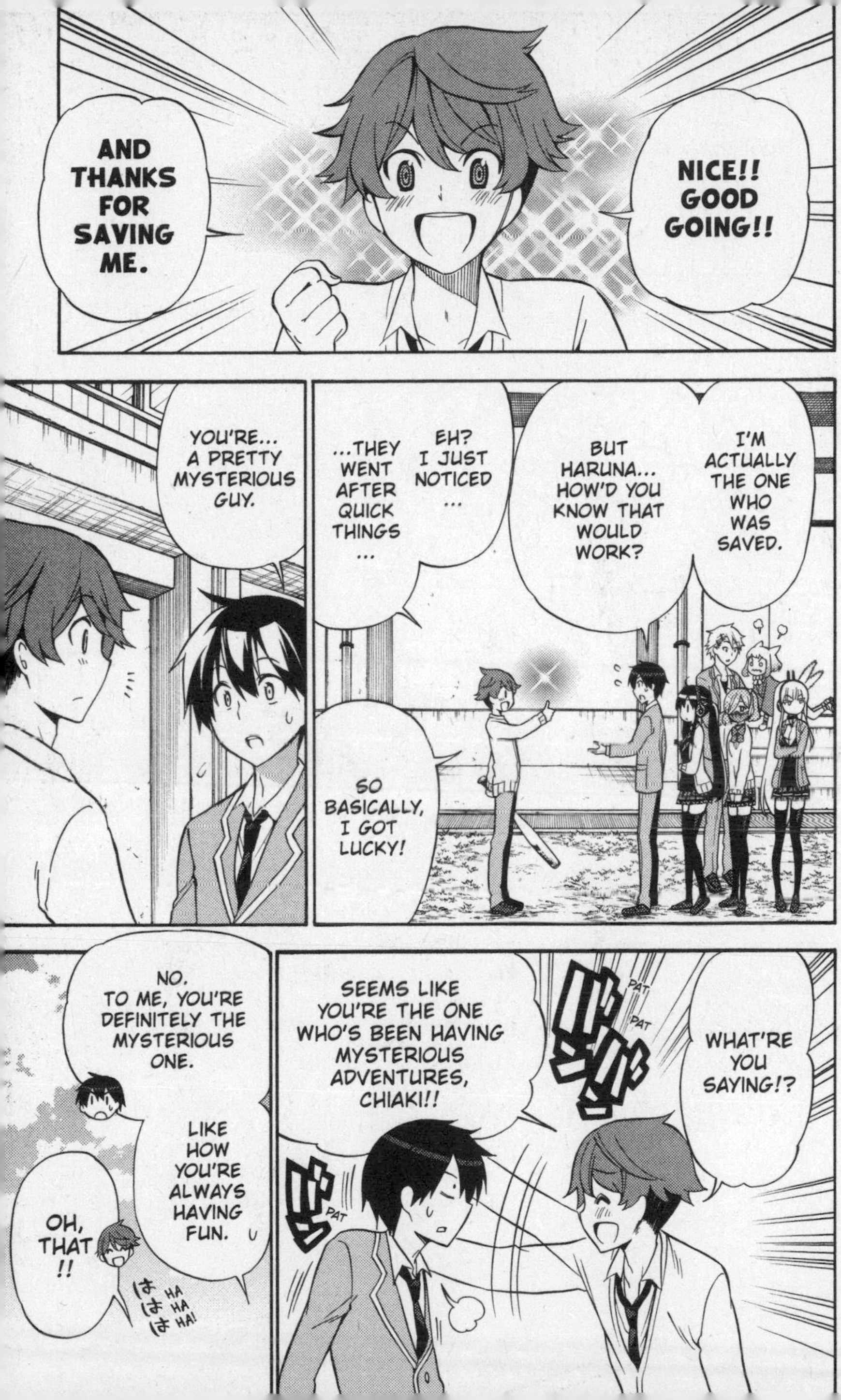
NICE!! GOOD GOING!!
AND THANKS FOR SAVING ME.
I'M ACTUALLY THE ONE WHO WAS SAVED.
BUT HARUNA... HOW'D YOU KNOW THAT WOULD WORK?
EH? I JUST NOTICED ...
...THEY WENT AFTER QUICK THINGS ...
SO BASICALLY, I GOT LUCKY!
YOU'RE... A PRETTY MYSTERIOUS GUY.
WHAT'RE YOU SAYING!?
PAT PAT
SEEMS LIKE YOU'RE THE ONE WHO'S BEEN HAVING MYSTERIOUS ADVENTURES, CHIAKI!!
PAT
NO. TO ME, YOU'RE DEFINITELY THE MYSTERIOUS ONE.
LIKE HOW YOU'RE ALWAYS HAVING FUN.
OH, THAT!!
ははは HA HA HA!

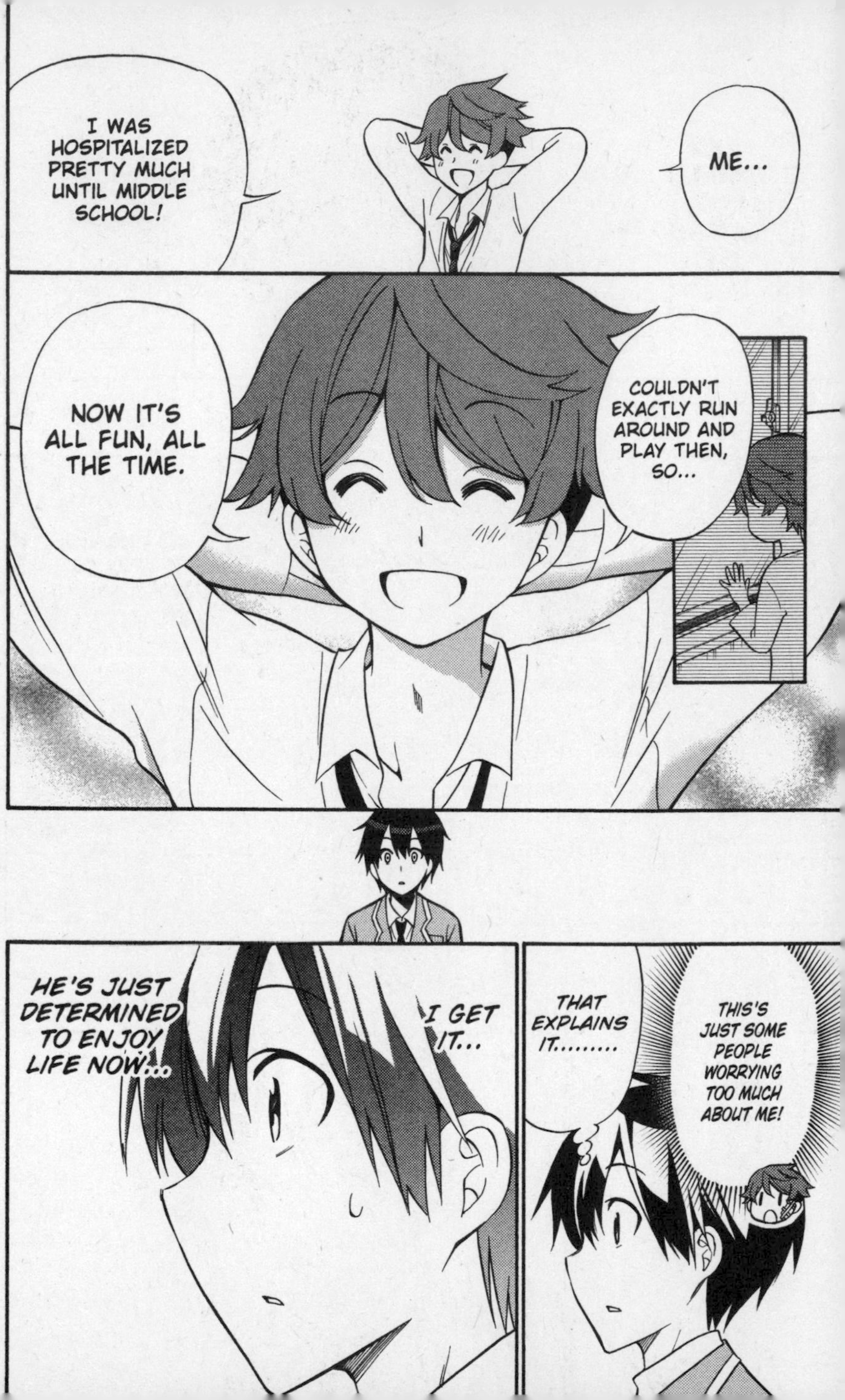
ME...
I WAS HOSPITALIZED PRETTY MUCH UNTIL MIDDLE SCHOOL!
COULDN'T EXACTLY RUN AROUND AND PLAY THEN, SO...
NOW IT'S ALL FUN, ALL THE TIME.
THIS'S JUST SOME PEOPLE WORRYING TOO MUCH ABOUT ME!
THAT EXPLAINS IT.........
I GET IT...
HE'S JUST DETERMINED TO ENJOY LIFE NOW...

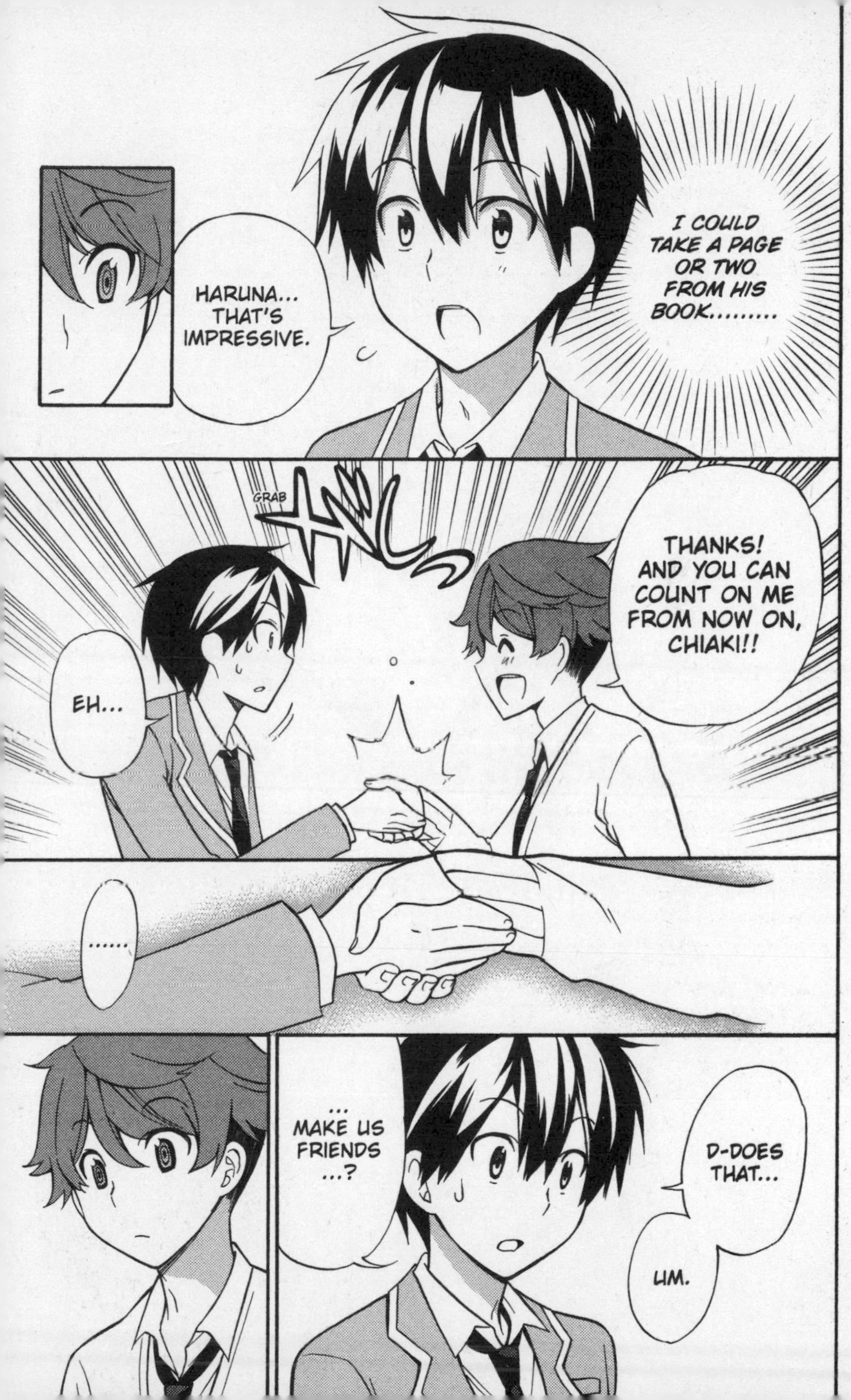
I COULD TAKE A PAGE OR TWO FROM HIS BOOK.........
HARUNA... THAT'S IMPRESSIVE.
THANKS! AND YOU CAN COUNT ON ME FROM NOW ON, CHIAKI!!
GRAB
EH...
......
D-DOES THAT...
...MAKE US FRIENDS ...?
UM.

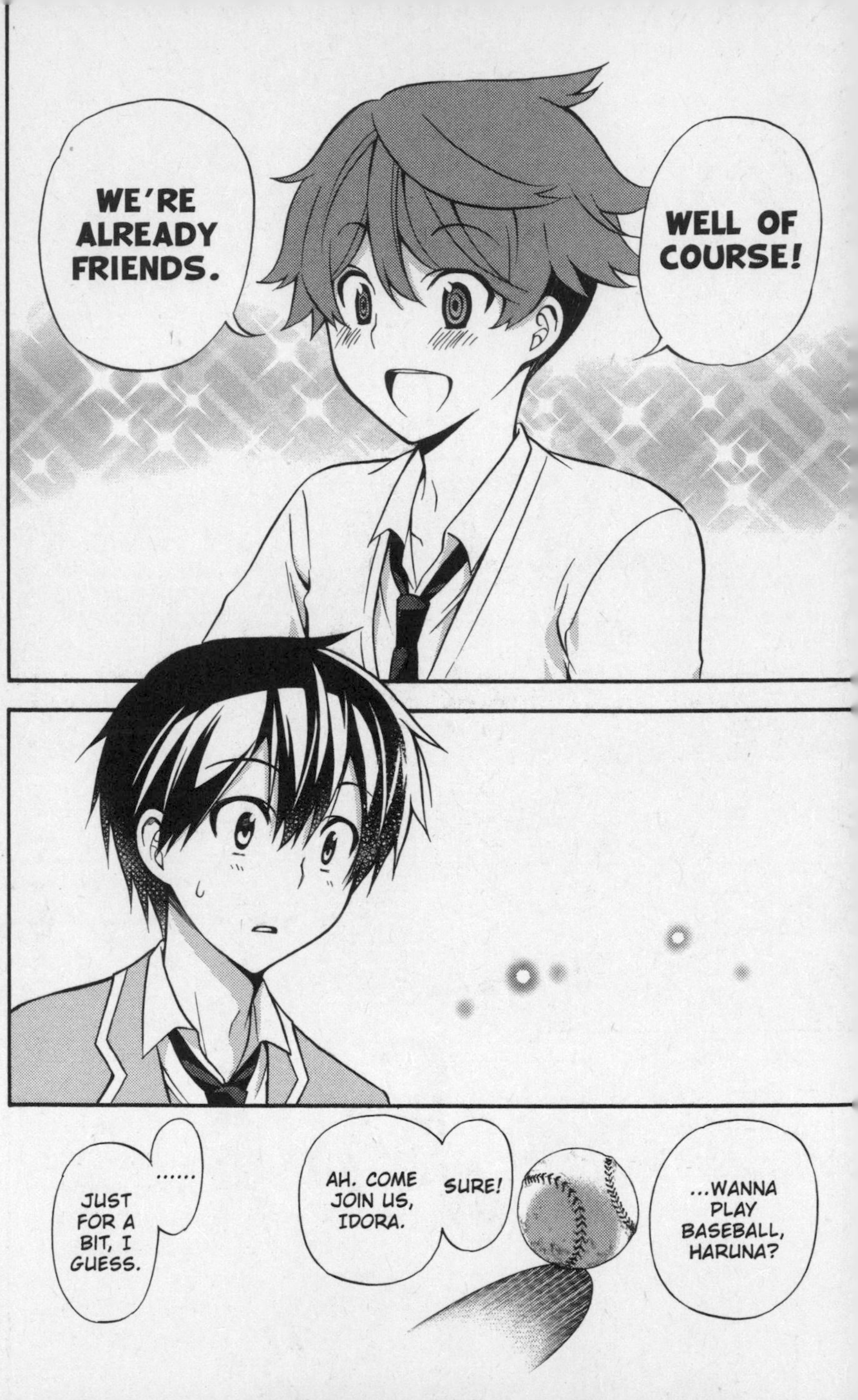
WELL OF COURSE!
WE'RE ALREADY FRIENDS.
...WANNA PLAY BASEBALL, HARUNA?
SURE!
AH. COME JOIN US, IDORA.
......
JUST FOR A BIT, I GUESS.

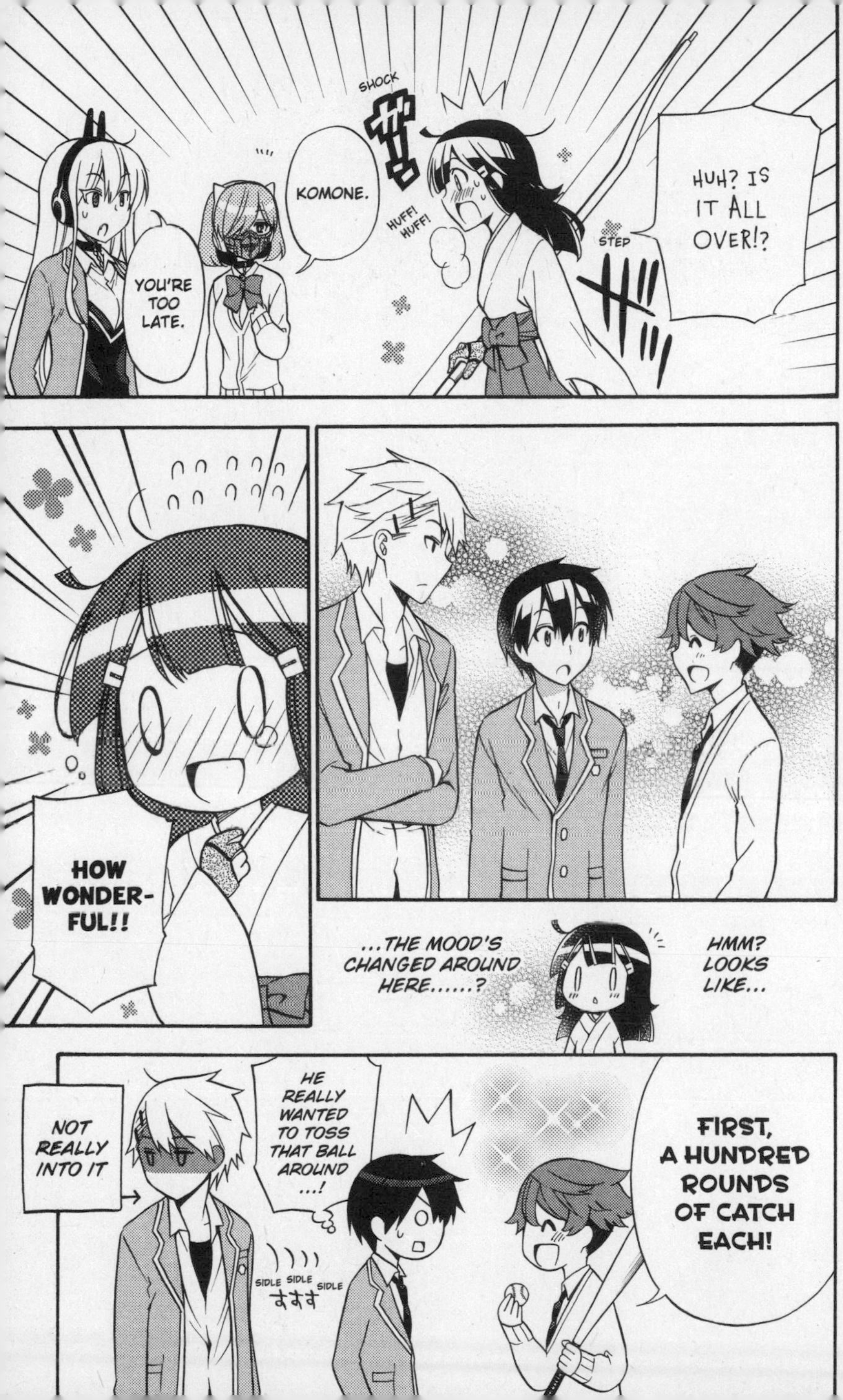
HUH? IS IT ALL OVER!?
STEP
SHOCK
HUFF! HUFF!
KOMONE.
YOU'RE TOO LATE.
HMM? LOOKS LIKE...
...THE MOOD'S CHANGED AROUND HERE......?
HOW WONDER-FUL!!
FIRST, A HUNDRED ROUNDS OF CATCH EACH!
HE REALLY WANTED TO TOSS THAT BALL AROUND ...!
SIDLE SIDLE SIDLE
すすす
NOT REALLY INTO IT

TODAY'S CERBERUS

I'D BETTER PRACTICE CHANGING OUTFITS FASTER.

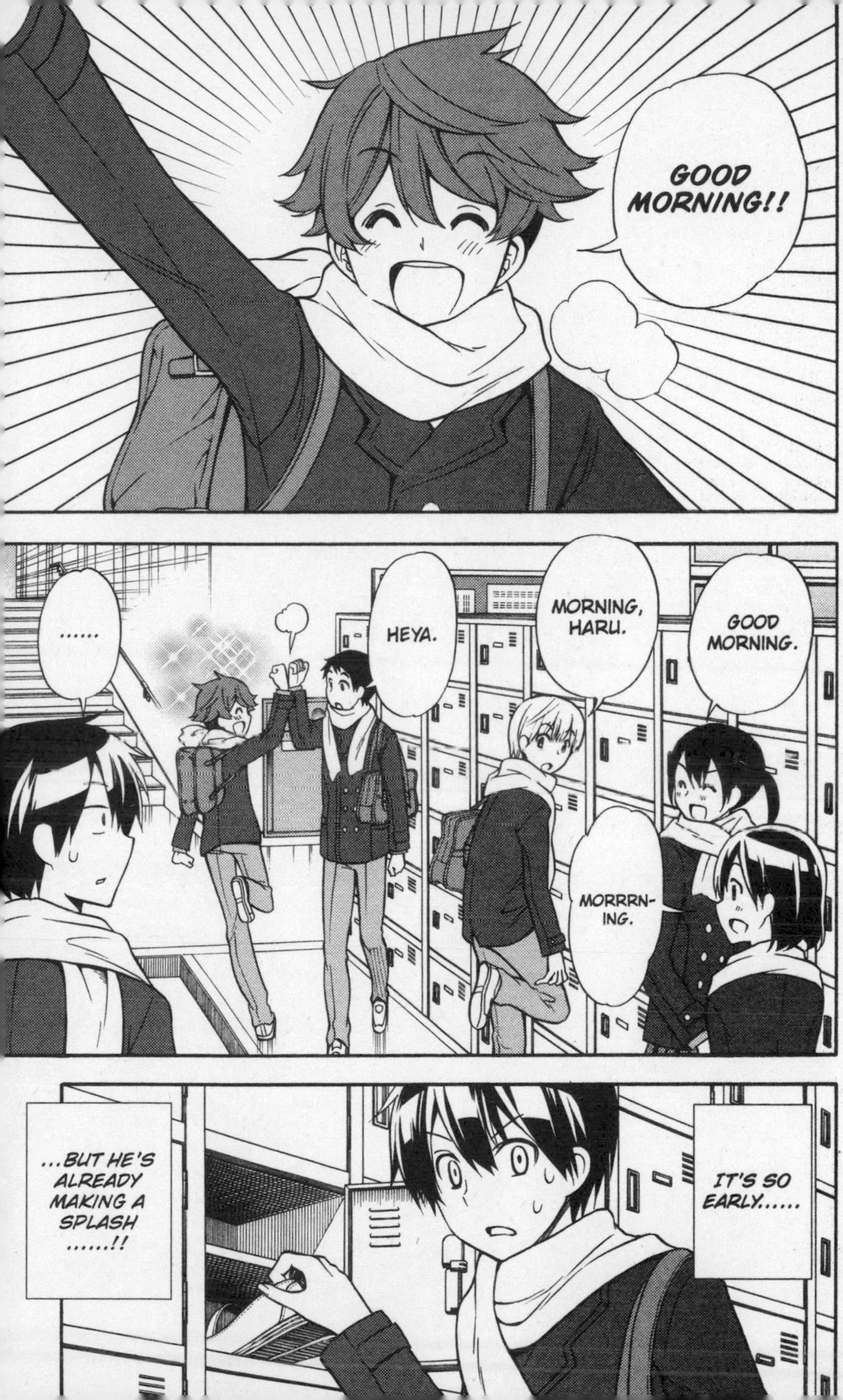
GOOD MORNING!!
GOOD MORNING.
MORNING, HARU.
MORRRN-ING.
HEYA.
......
IT'S SO EARLY......
...BUT HE'S ALREADY MAKING A SPLASH ......!!

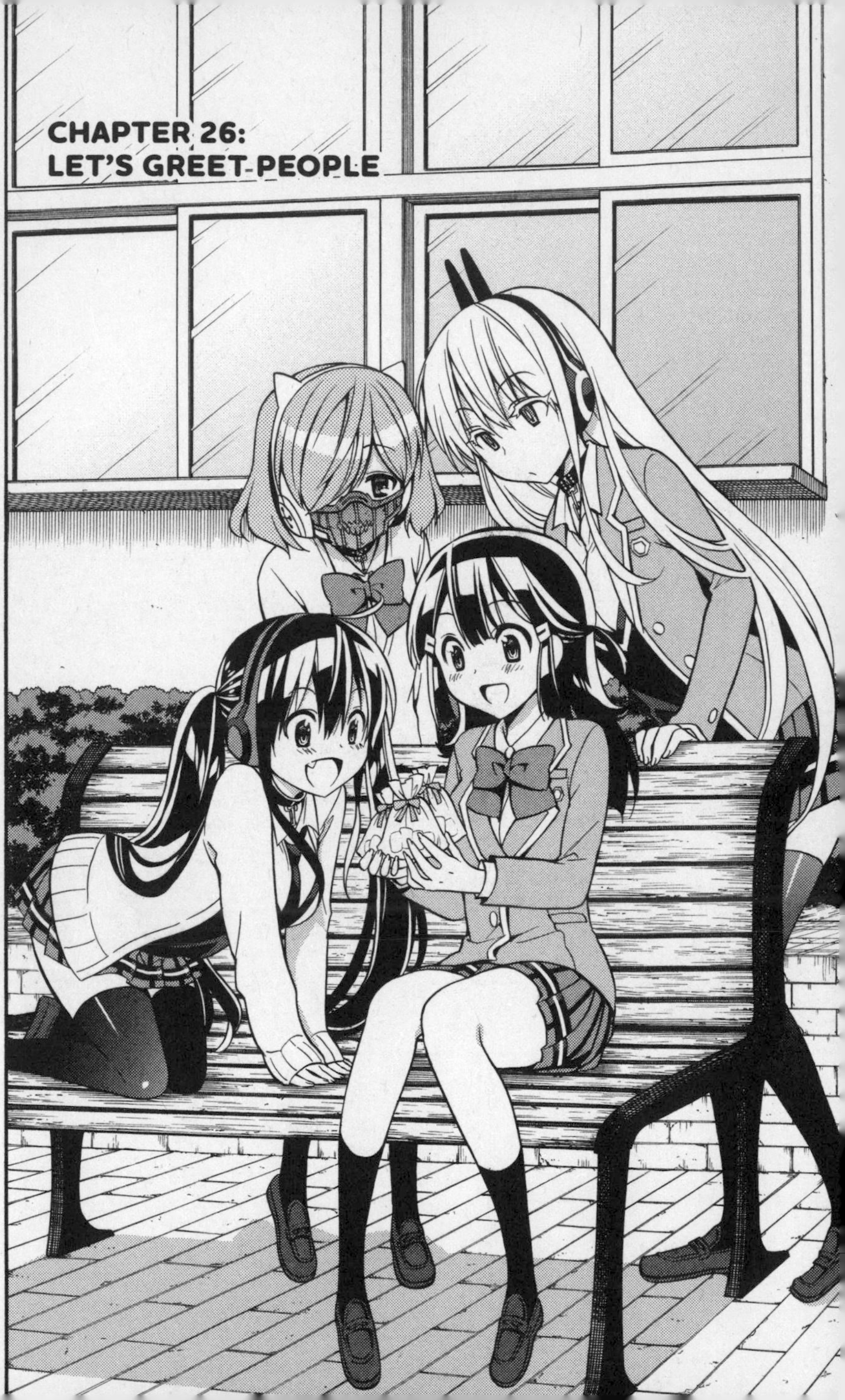
CHAPTER 26:
LET'S GREET PEOPLE

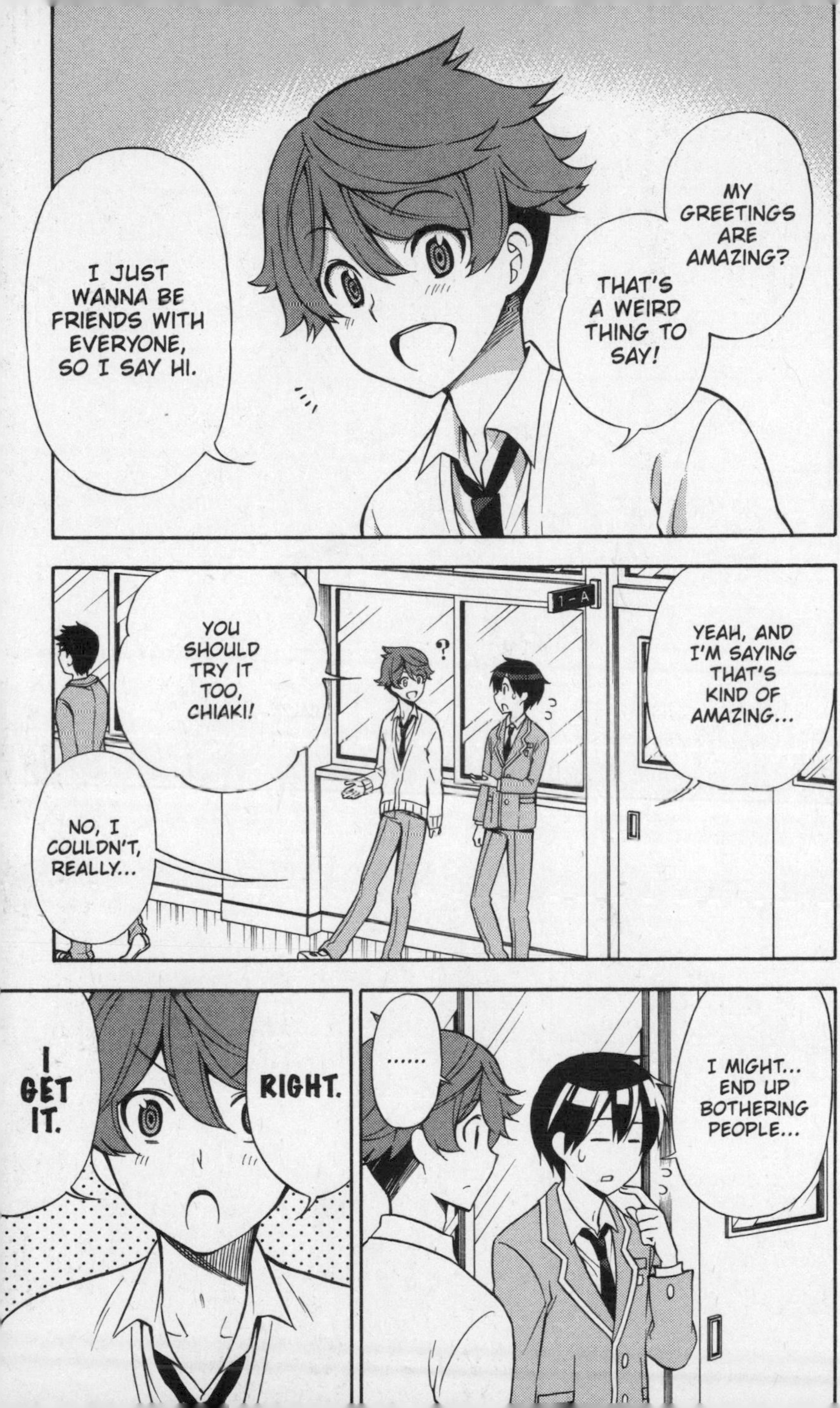
MY GREETINGS ARE AMAZING?
THAT'S A WEIRD THING TO SAY!
I JUST WANNA BE FRIENDS WITH EVERYONE, SO I SAY HI.
YEAH, AND I'M SAYING THAT'S KIND OF AMAZING...
1-A
YOU SHOULD TRY IT TOO, CHIAKI!
NO, I COULDN'T, REALLY...
I MIGHT... END UP BOTHERING PEOPLE...
......
RIGHT.
I GET IT.

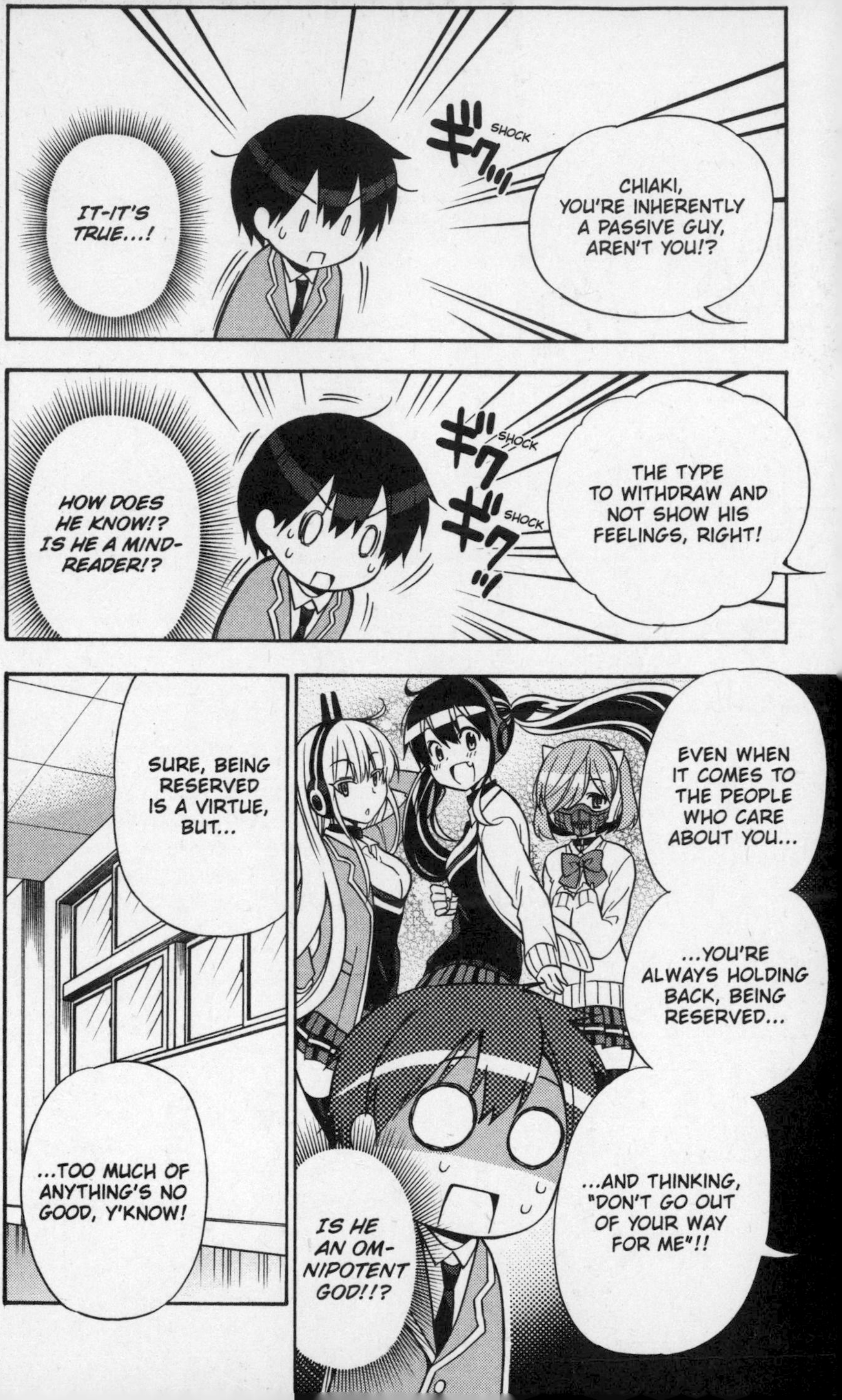
SHOCK
CHIAKI, YOU'RE INHERENTLY A PASSIVE GUY, AREN'T YOU!?
IT-IT'S TRUE...!
SHOCK
SHOCK
THE TYPE TO WITHDRAW AND NOT SHOW HIS FEELINGS, RIGHT!
HOW DOES HE KNOW!? IS HE A MIND-READER!?
EVEN WHEN IT COMES TO THE PEOPLE WHO CARE ABOUT YOU...
...YOU'RE ALWAYS HOLDING BACK, BEING RESERVED...
...AND THINKING, "DON'T GO OUT OF YOUR WAY FOR ME"!!
IS HE AN OM-NIPOTENT GOD!!?
SURE, BEING RESERVED IS A VIRTUE, BUT...
...TOO MUCH OF ANYTHING'S NO GOOD, Y'KNOW!

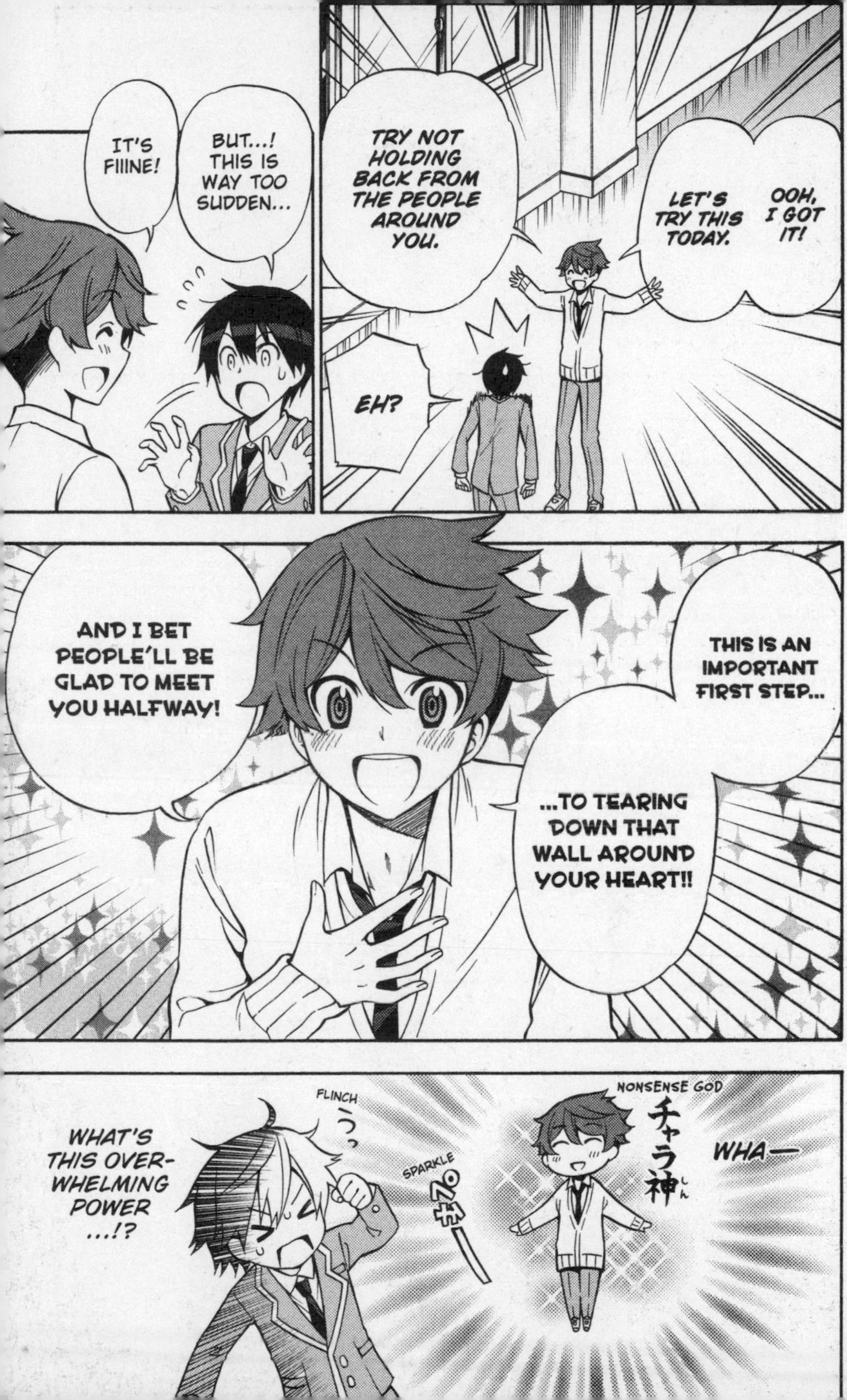
OOH, I GOT IT!
LET'S TRY THIS TODAY.
TRY NOT HOLDING BACK FROM THE PEOPLE AROUND YOU.
EH?
BUT...! THIS IS WAY TOO SUDDEN...
IT'S FIIINE!
THIS IS AN IMPORTANT FIRST STEP...
...TO TEARING DOWN THAT WALL AROUND YOUR HEART!!
AND I BET PEOPLE'LL BE GLAD TO MEET YOU HALFWAY!
WHA—
NONSENSE GOD
チャラ神
SPARKLE
ペカー
FLINCH
うっ
WHAT'S THIS OVER-WHELMING POWER ...!?

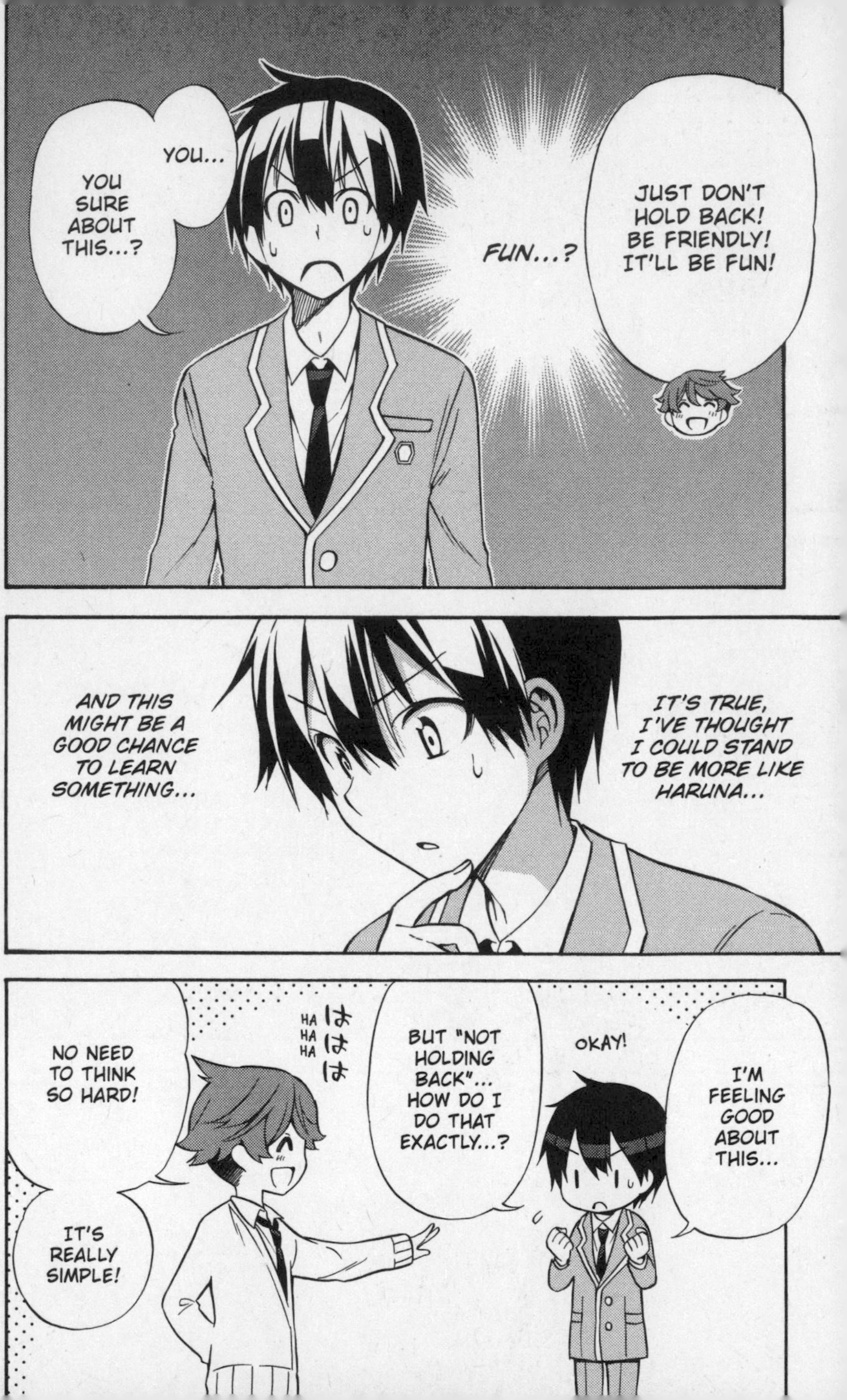
JUST DON'T HOLD BACK! BE FRIENDLY! IT'LL BE FUN!
FUN...?
YOU...
YOU SURE ABOUT THIS...?
IT'S TRUE, I'VE THOUGHT I COULD STAND TO BE MORE LIKE HARUNA...
AND THIS MIGHT BE A GOOD CHANCE TO LEARN SOMETHING...
I'M FEELING GOOD ABOUT THIS...
OKAY!
BUT "NOT HOLDING BACK"... HOW DO I DO THAT EXACTLY...?
ははは
HA HA HA
NO NEED TO THINK SO HARD!
IT'S REALLY SIMPLE!

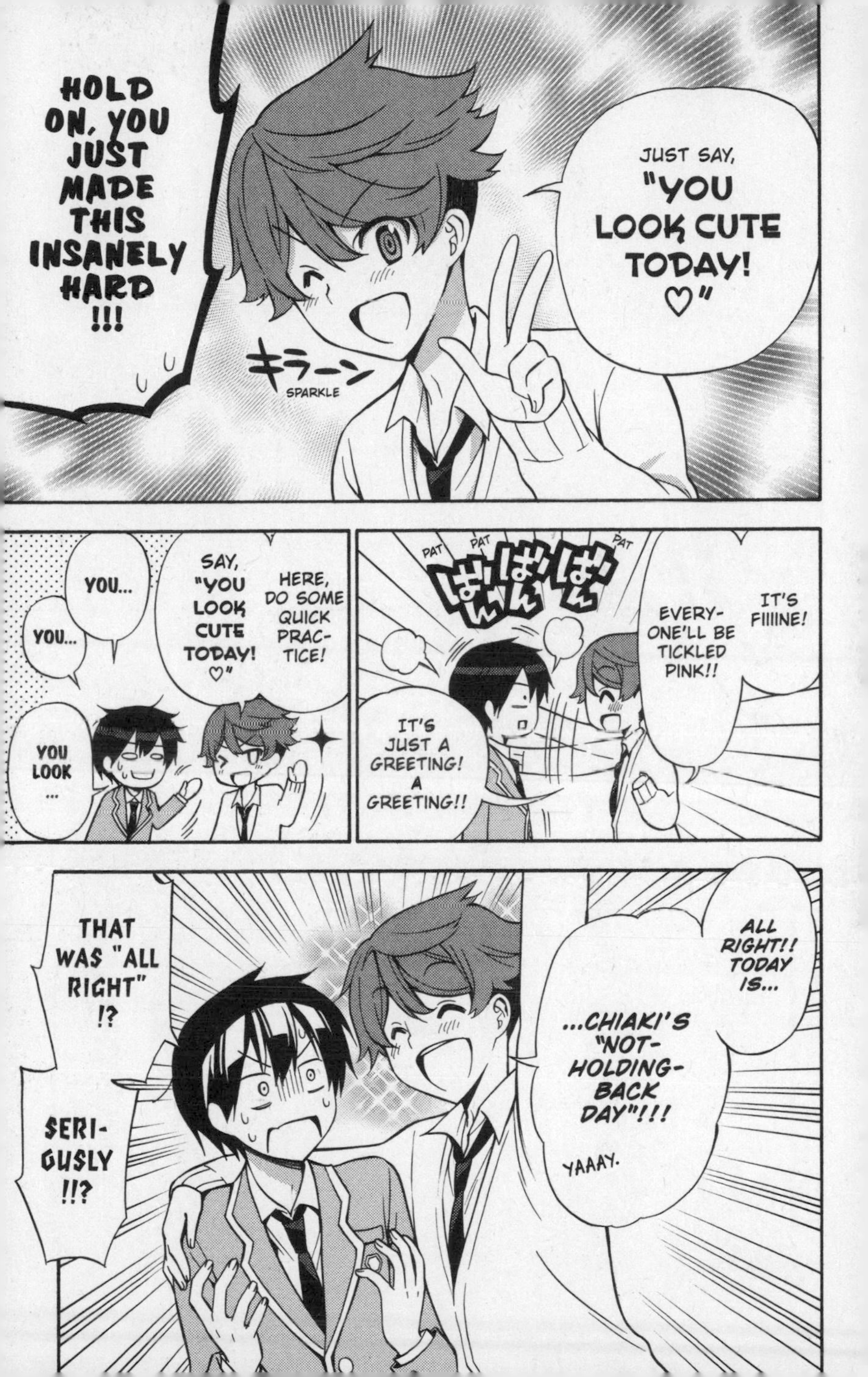
JUST SAY, "YOU LOOK CUTE TODAY! ♡"
キラーン
SPARKLE
HOLD ON, YOU JUST MADE THIS INSANELY HARD!!!
IT'S FIIIINE!
EVERYONE'LL BE TICKLED PINK!!
ぱんぱんぱん
PAT PAT PAT
IT'S JUST A GREETING! A GREETING!!
HERE, DO SOME QUICK PRACTICE!
SAY, "YOU LOOK CUTE TODAY! ♡"
YOU...
YOU...
YOU LOOK ...
ALL RIGHT!! TODAY IS...
...CHIAKI'S "NOT-HOLDING-BACK DAY"!!!
YAAAY.
THAT WAS "ALL RIGHT"!?
SERI-GUSLY!!?

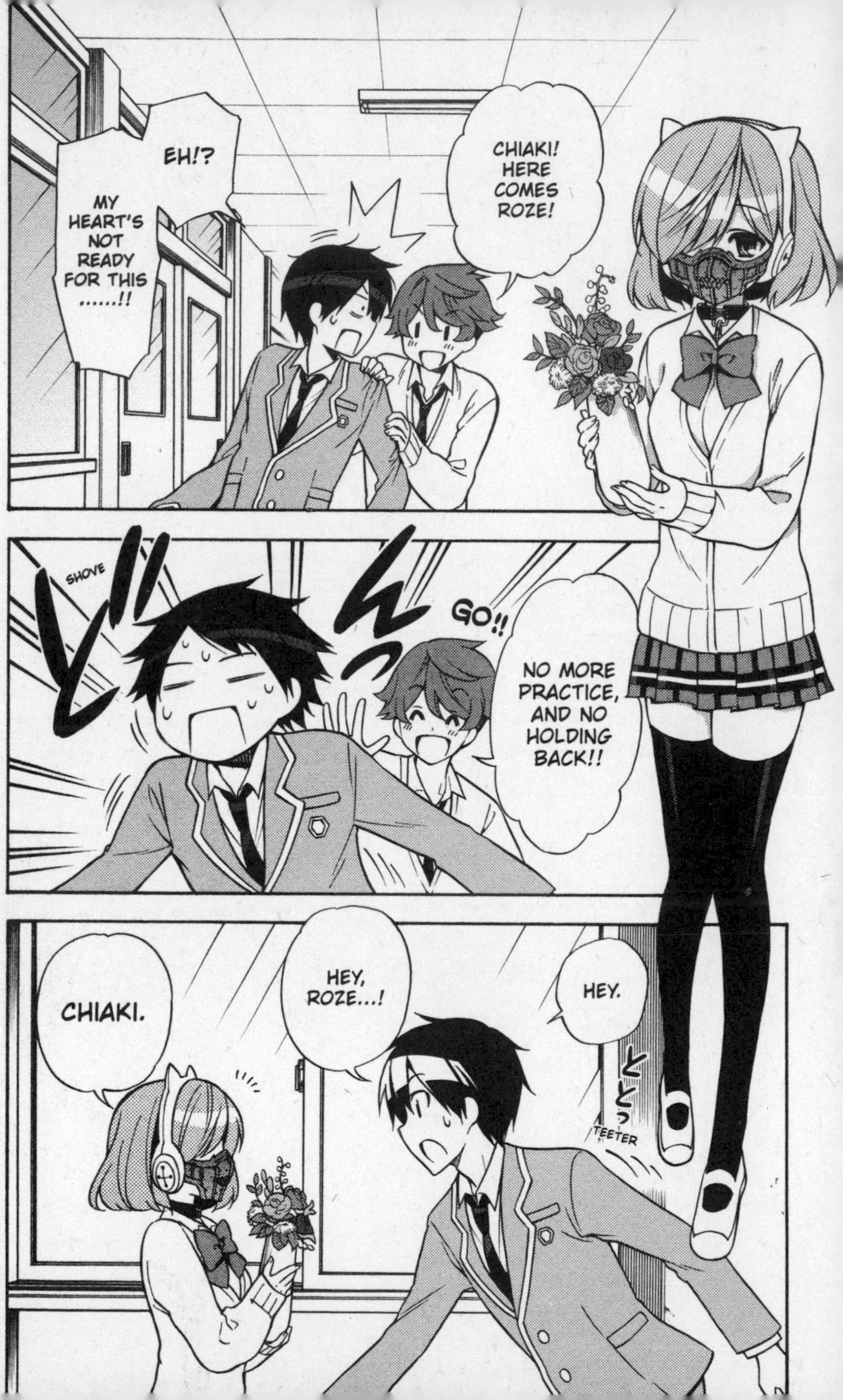
CHIAKI! HERE COMES ROZE!
EH!?
MY HEART'S NOT READY FOR THIS ......!!
NO MORE PRACTICE, AND NO HOLDING BACK!!
GO!!
SHOVE
TEETER
HEY.
HEY, ROZE...!
CHIAKI.

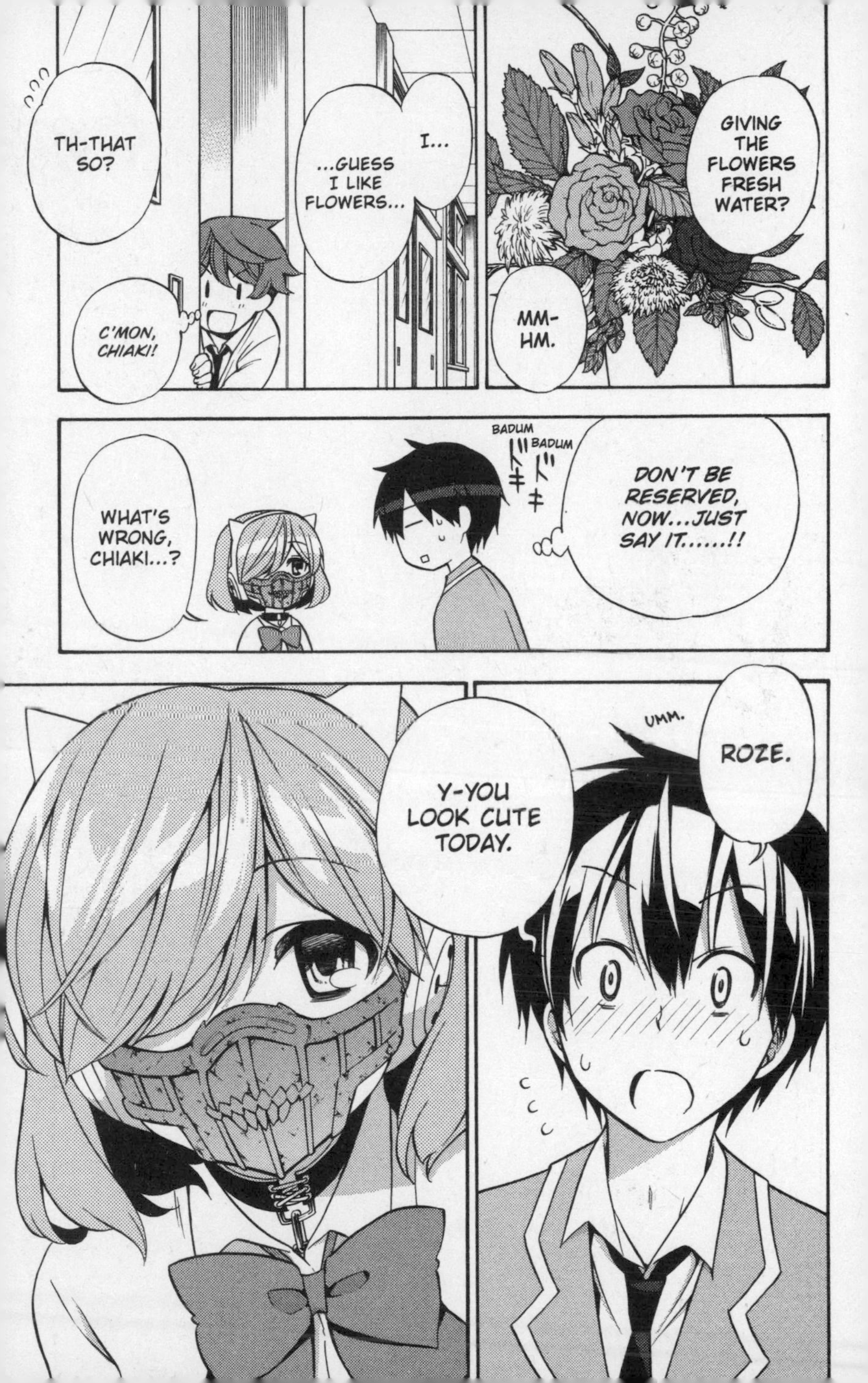
GIVING THE FLOWERS FRESH WATER?
MM-HM.
I... ...GUESS I LIKE FLOWERS...
TH-THAT SO?
C'MON, CHIAKI!
BADUM BADUM
DON'T BE RESERVED, NOW...JUST SAY IT......!!
WHAT'S WRONG, CHIAKI...?
UMM.
ROZE.
Y-YOU LOOK CUTE TODAY.

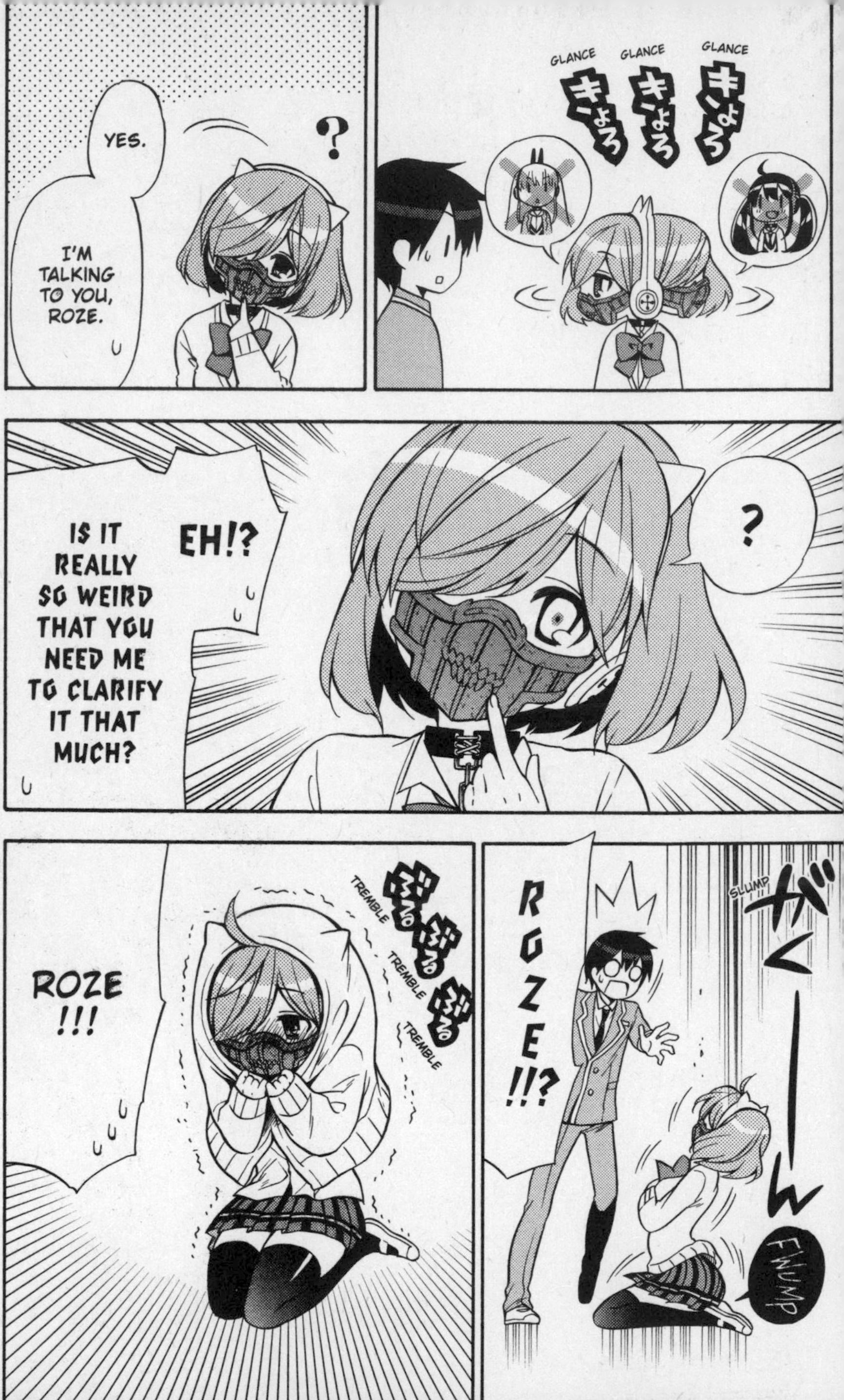

きょろ
GLANCE
きょろ
GLANCE
きょろ
GLANCE
?
YES.
I'M TALKING TO YOU, ROZE.
?
EH!?
IS IT REALLY SO WEIRD THAT YOU NEED ME TO CLARIFY IT THAT MUCH?
がくーん
SLUMP
ROZE!!?
FWUMP
ぶる
TREMBLE
ぶる
TREMBLE
ぶる
TREMBLE
ROZE!!!

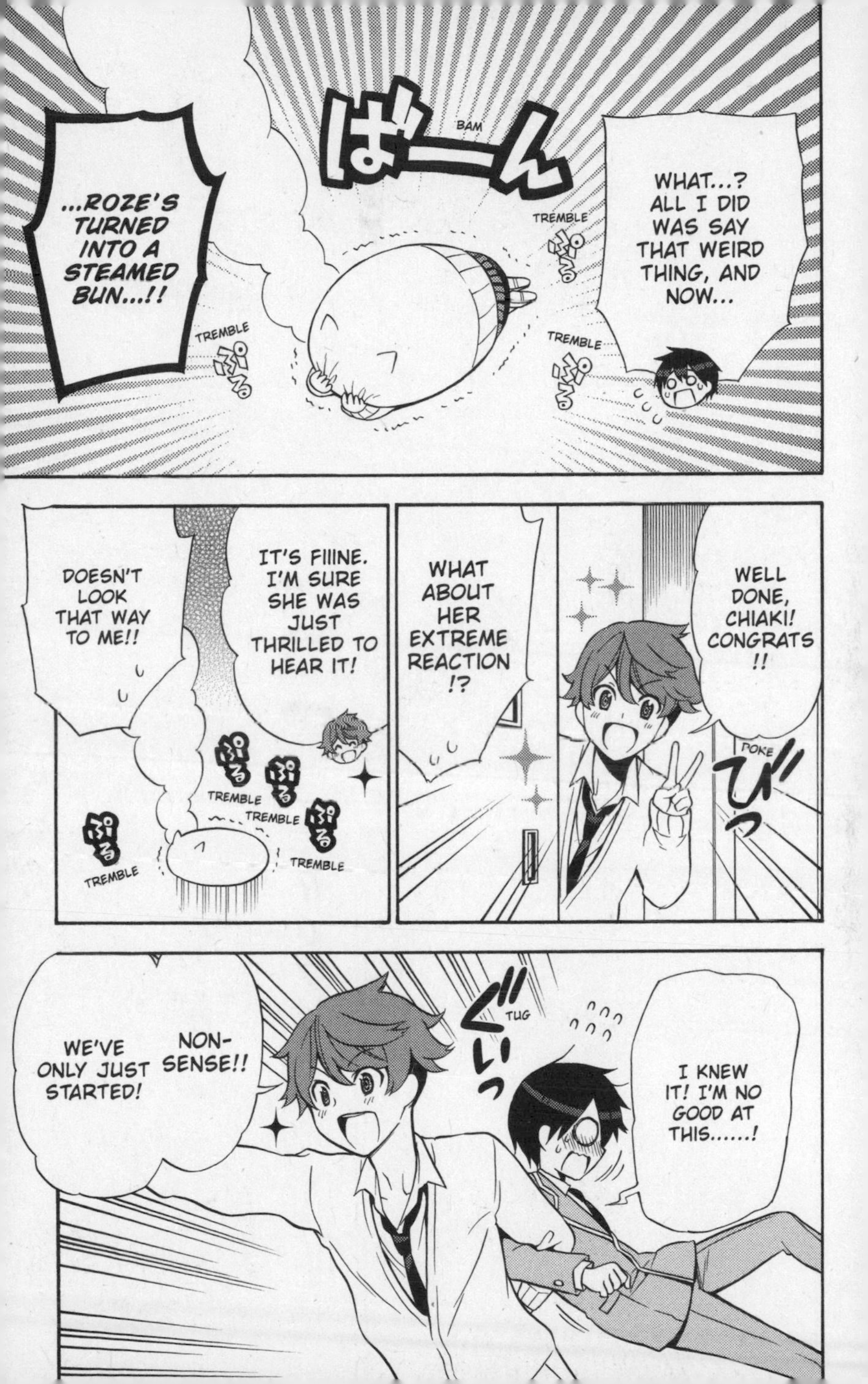
WHAT...? ALL I DID WAS SAY THAT WEIRD THING, AND NOW...
ばーん
BAM
ぷる
TREMBLE
ぷる
TREMBLE
ぷる
TREMBLE
...ROZE'S TURNED INTO A STEAMED BUN...!!
WELL DONE, CHIAKI! CONGRATS!!
ぴっ
POKE
WHAT ABOUT HER EXTREME REACTION!?
IT'S FIIINE. I'M SURE SHE WAS JUST THRILLED TO HEAR IT!
DOESN'T LOOK THAT WAY TO ME!!
ぷる
TREMBLE
ぷる
TREMBLE
ぷる
TREMBLE
ぷる
TREMBLE
I KNEW IT! I'M NO GOOD AT THIS......!
ぐいっ
TUG
NON-SENSE!!
WE'VE ONLY JUST STARTED!

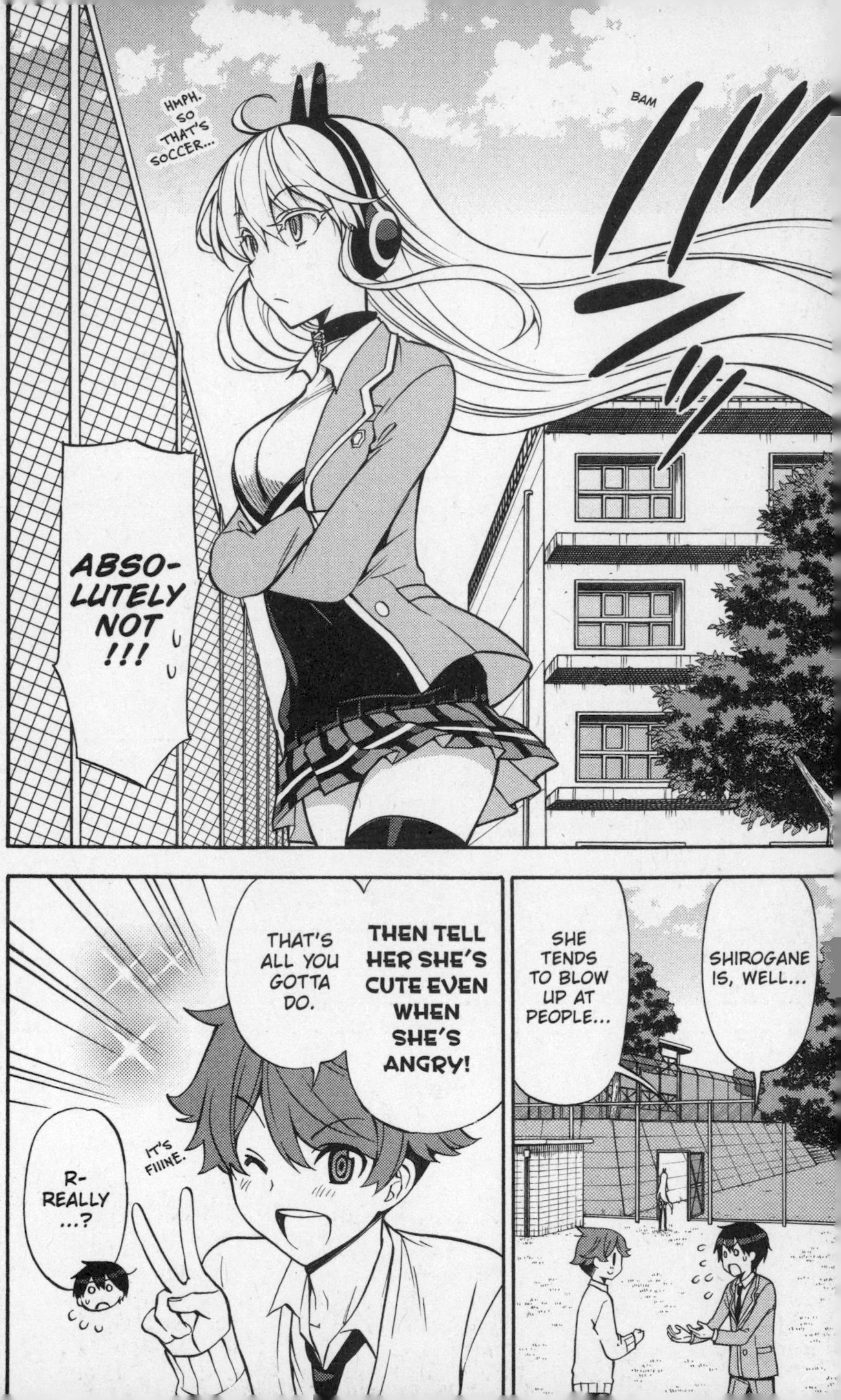
BAM
HMPH. SO THAT'S SOCCER...
ABSO-LUTELY NOT!!!
SHIROGANE IS, WELL...
SHE TENDS TO BLOW UP AT PEOPLE...
THEN TELL HER SHE'S CUTE EVEN WHEN SHE'S ANGRY!
THAT'S ALL YOU GOTTA DO.
IT'S FIIINE.
R-REALLY...?

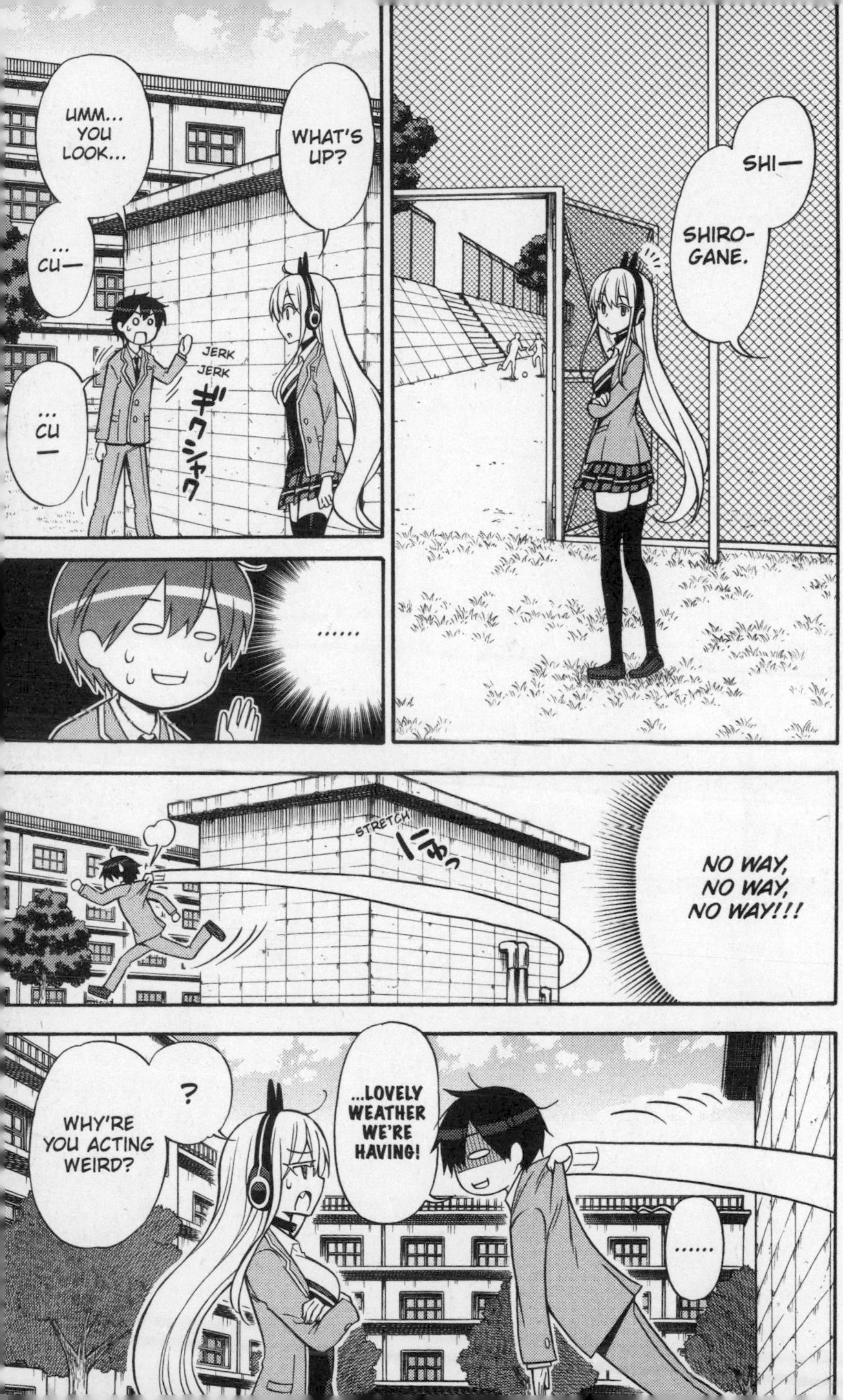
SHI—
SHIRO-GANE.
WHAT'S UP?
UMM... YOU LOOK...
... CU—
... CU —
JERK JERK
ギクシャク
......
STRETCH
NO WAY, NO WAY, NO WAY!!!
......
...LOVELY WEATHER WE'RE HAVING!
?
WHY'RE YOU ACTING WEIRD?

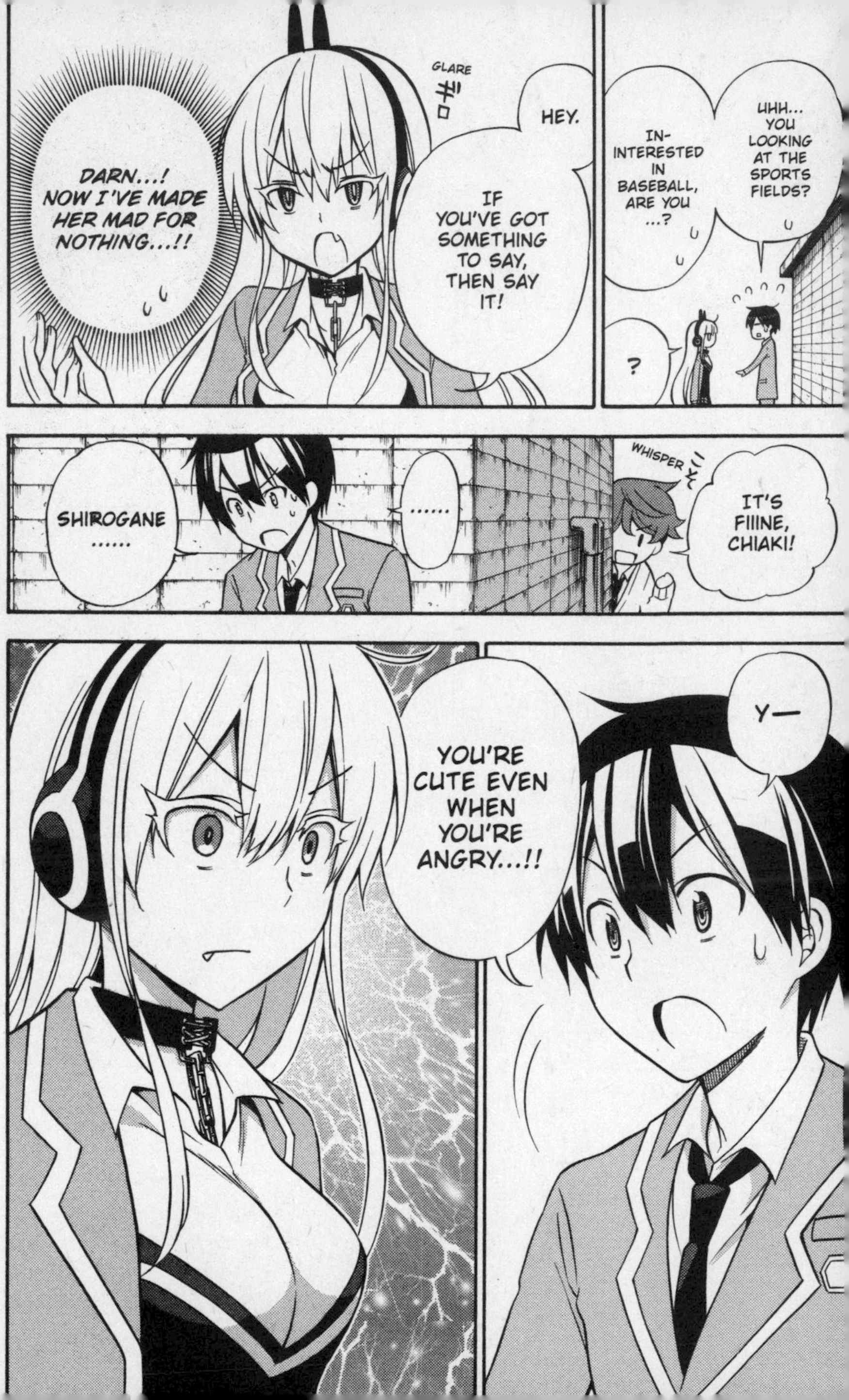
UHH... YOU LOOKING AT THE SPORTS FIELDS?
IN- INTERESTED IN BASEBALL, ARE YOU ...?
?
GLARE
HEY.
IF YOU'VE GOT SOMETHING TO SAY, THEN SAY IT!
DARN...! NOW I'VE MADE HER MAD FOR NOTHING...!!
WHISPER
IT'S FIIINE, CHIAKI!
......
SHIROGANE ......
Y—
YOU'RE CUTE EVEN WHEN YOU'RE ANGRY...!!

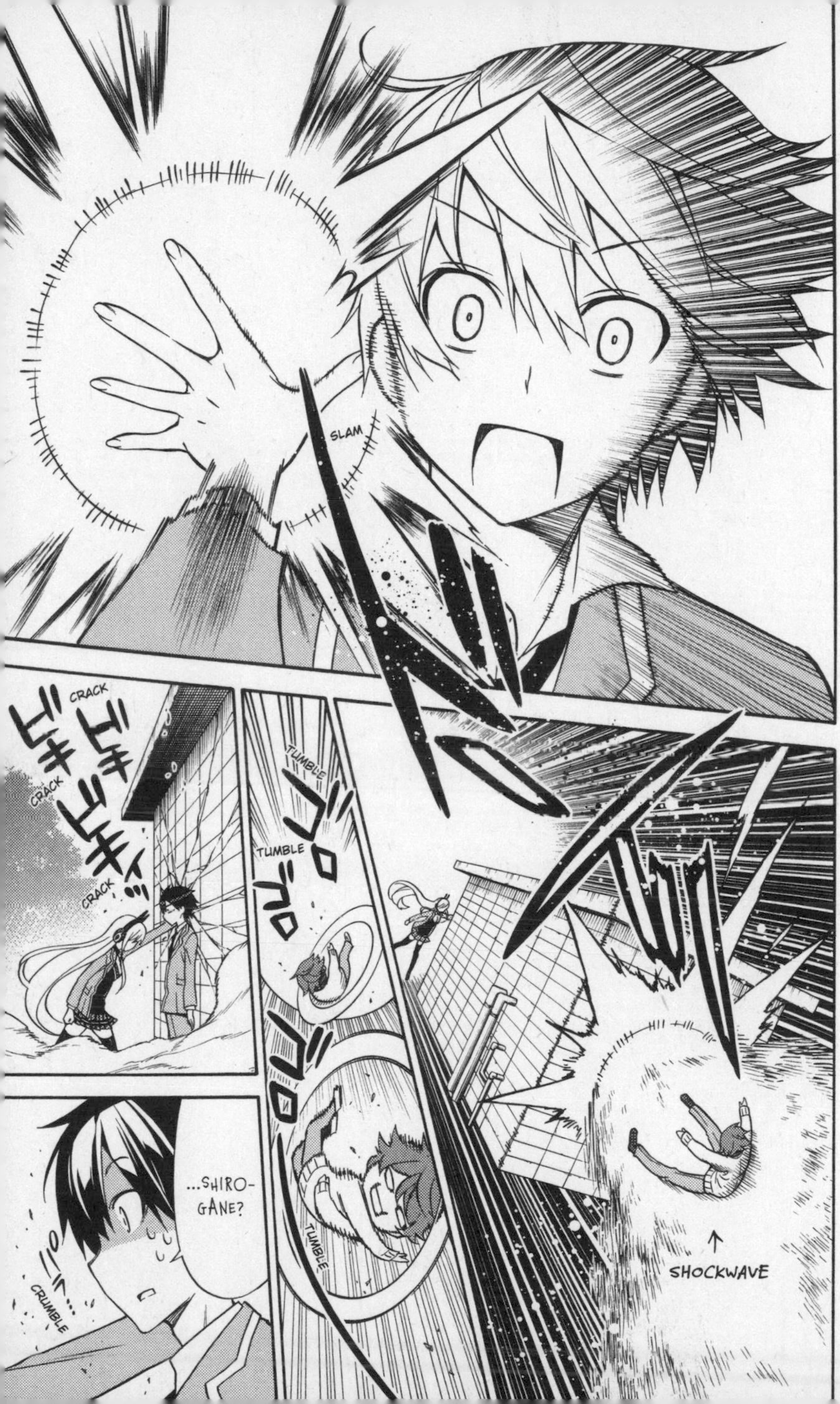
SLAM
SHOCKWAVE
TUMBLE
TUMBLE
TUMBLE
CRACK
CRACK
CRACK
...SHIRO-GANE?
CRUMBLE

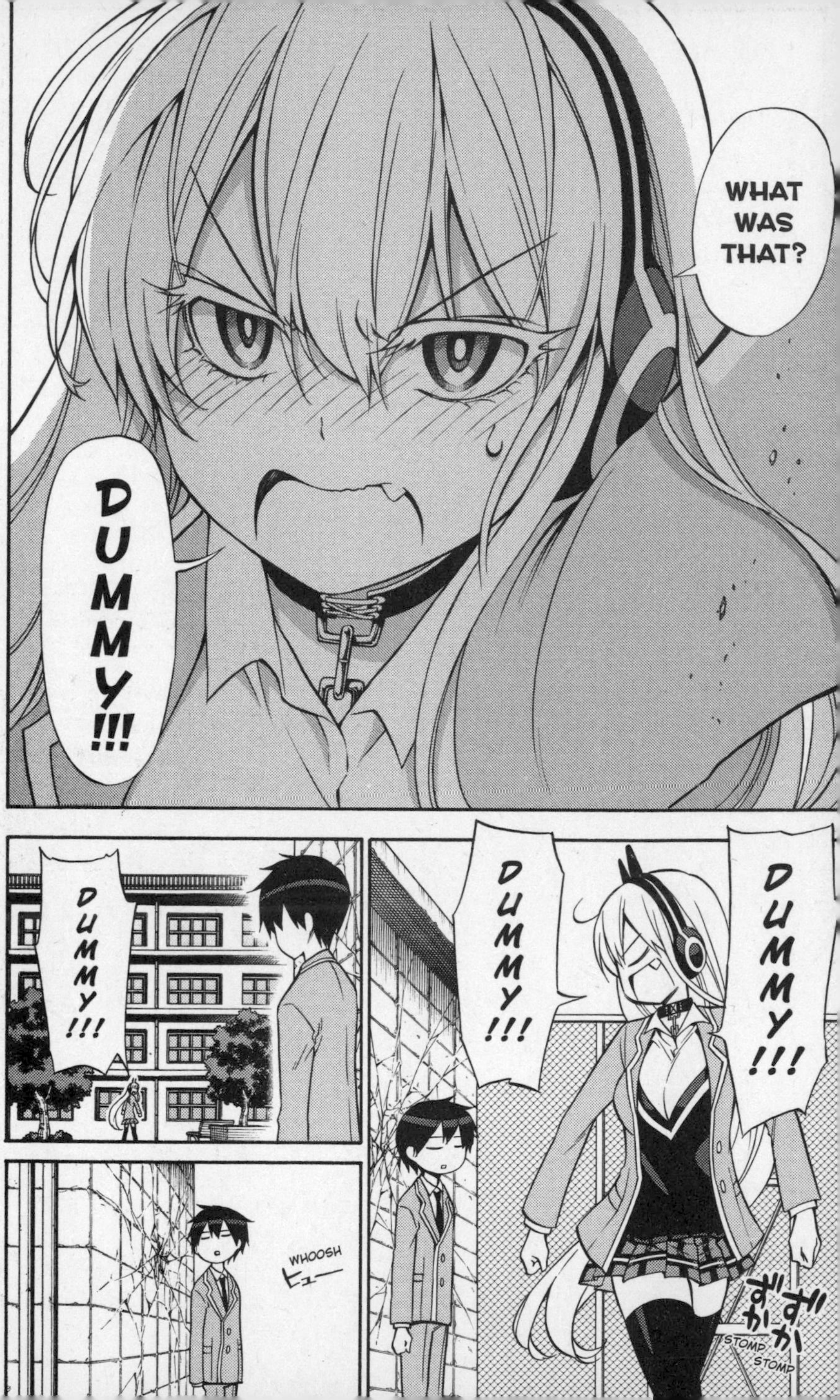
WHAT WAS THAT?
DUMMY!!!
DUMMY!!!
DUMMY!!!
ずかずか
STOMP STOMP
DUMMY!!!
WHOOSH
ヒュー

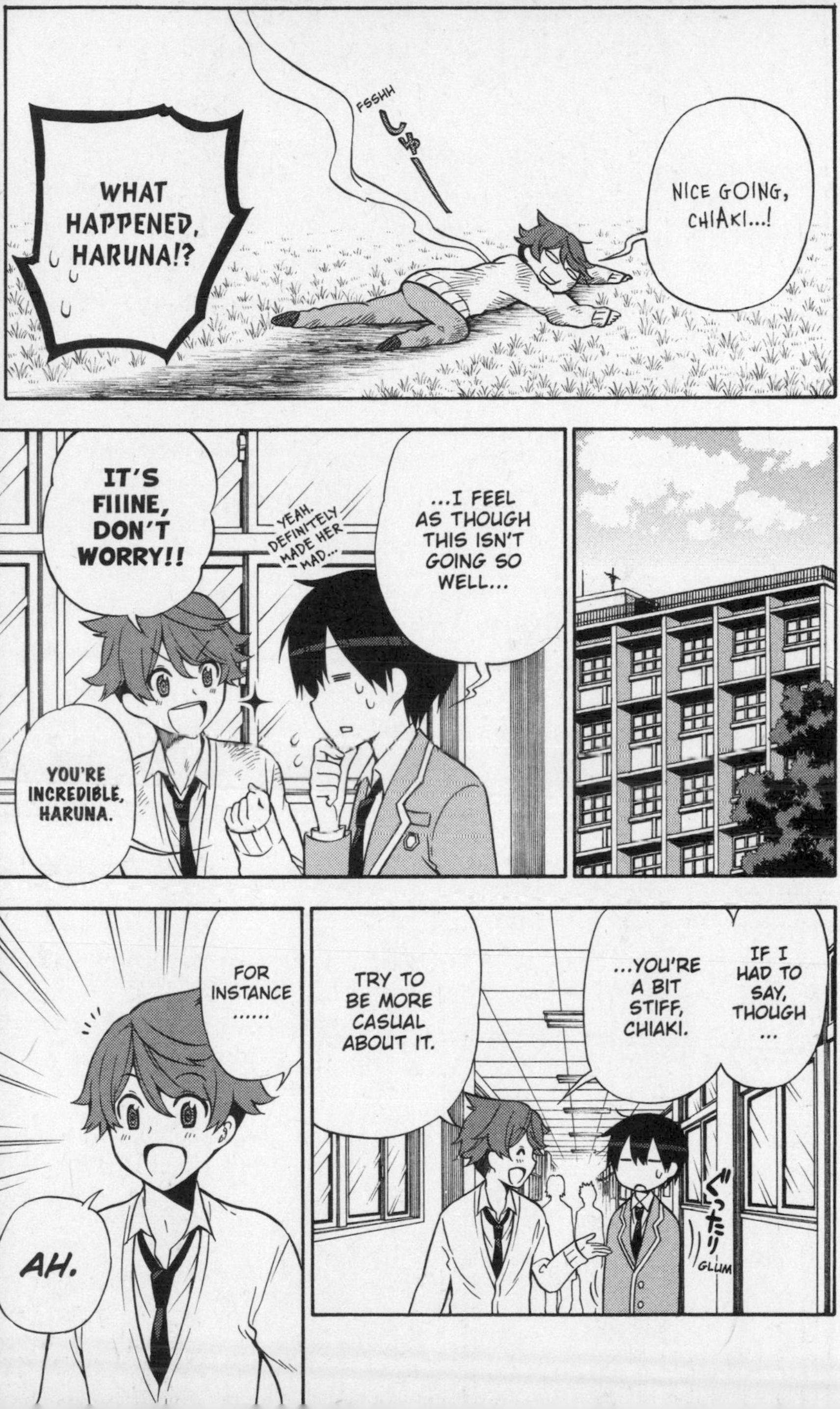
NICE GOING, CHIAKI...!
FSSHH
WHAT HAPPENED, HARUNA!?
...I FEEL AS THOUGH THIS ISN'T GOING SO WELL...
YEAH. DEFINITELY MADE HER MAD...
IT'S FIIINE, DON'T WORRY!!
YOU'RE INCREDIBLE, HARUNA.
IF I HAD TO SAY, THOUGH ...
...YOU'RE A BIT STIFF, CHIAKI.
TRY TO BE MORE CASUAL ABOUT IT.
GLUM
FOR INSTANCE ......
AH.

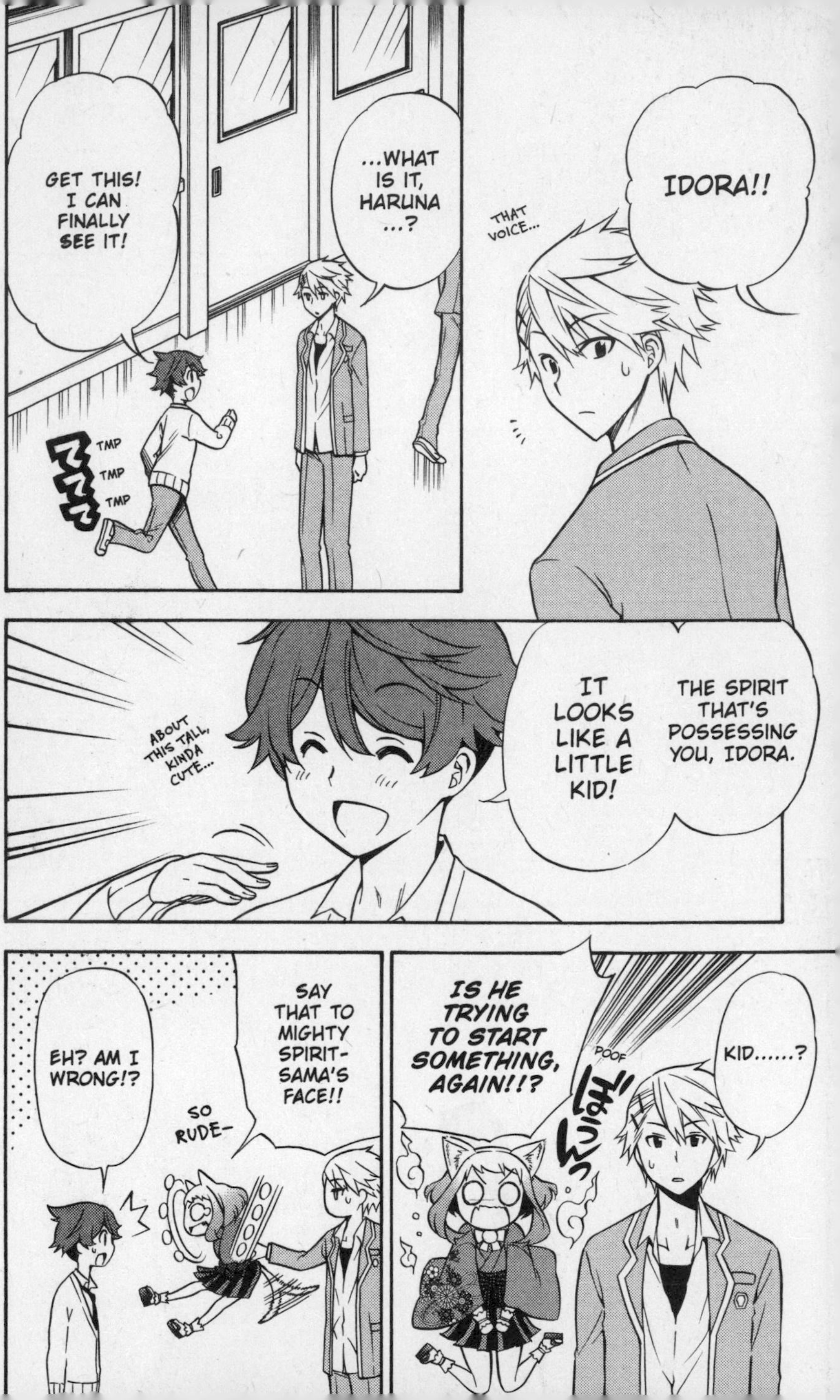
IDORA!!
THAT VOICE...
...WHAT IS IT, HARUNA ...?
GET THIS! I CAN FINALLY SEE IT!
TMP
TMP
TMP
THE SPIRIT THAT'S POSSESSING YOU, IDORA.
IT LOOKS LIKE A LITTLE KID!
ABOUT THIS TALL, KINDA CUTE...
KID......?
POOF
IS HE TRYING TO START SOMETHING, AGAIN!!?
SAY THAT TO MIGHTY SPIRIT-SAMA'S FACE!!
SO RUDE-
EH? AM I WRONG!?

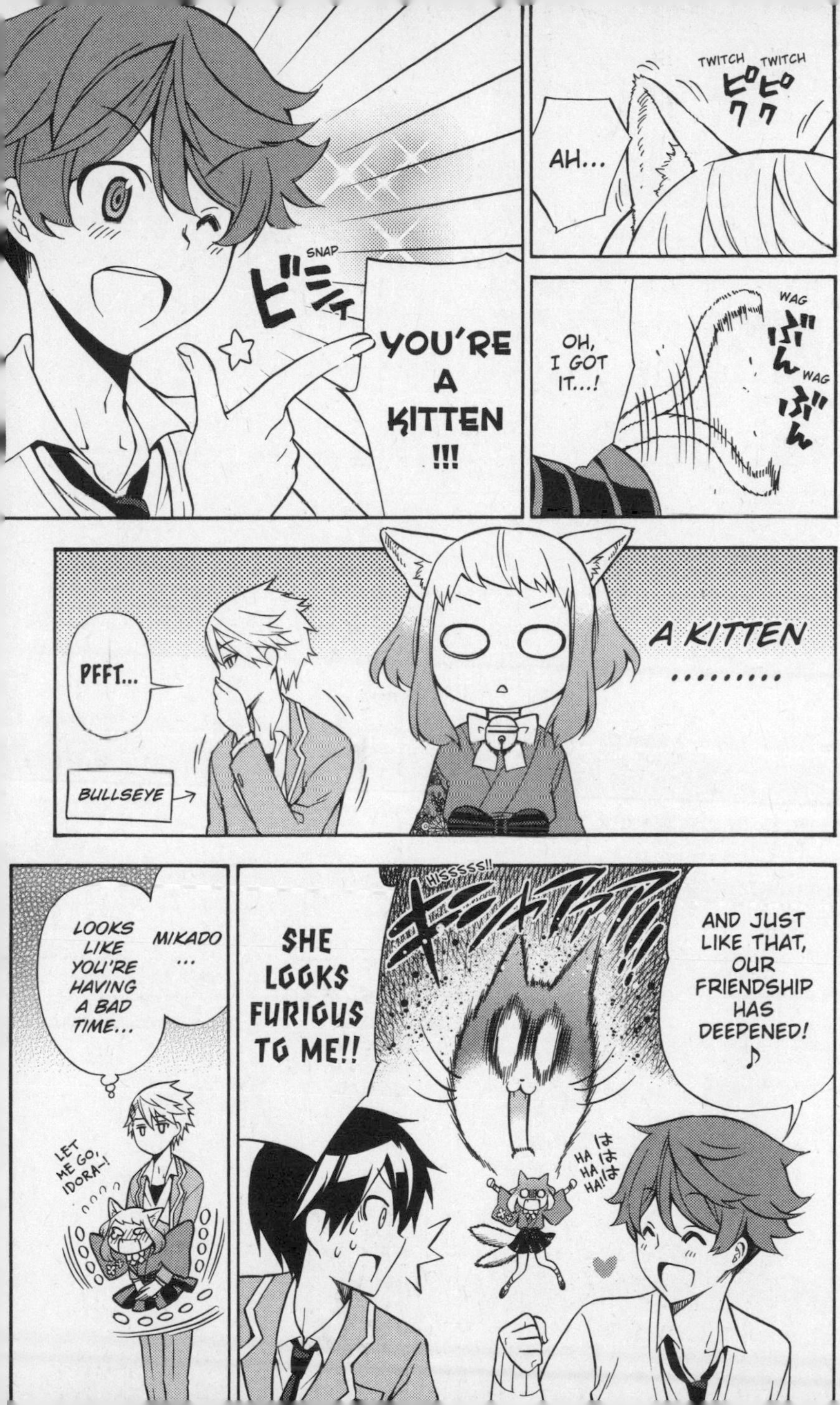
TWITCH TWITCH
ピクピク
AH...
OH, I GOT IT...!
WAG
ぶん
WAG
ぶん
SNAP
ビシィ
YOU'RE A KITTEN!!!
A KITTEN ....
PFFT...
BULLSEYE
HISSSSS!!
AND JUST LIKE THAT, OUR FRIENDSHIP HAS DEEPENED! ♪
SHE LOOKS FURIOUS TO ME!!
HA HA HA
ははは
MIKADO...
LOOKS LIKE YOU'RE HAVING A BAD TIME...
LET ME GO, IDORA--!

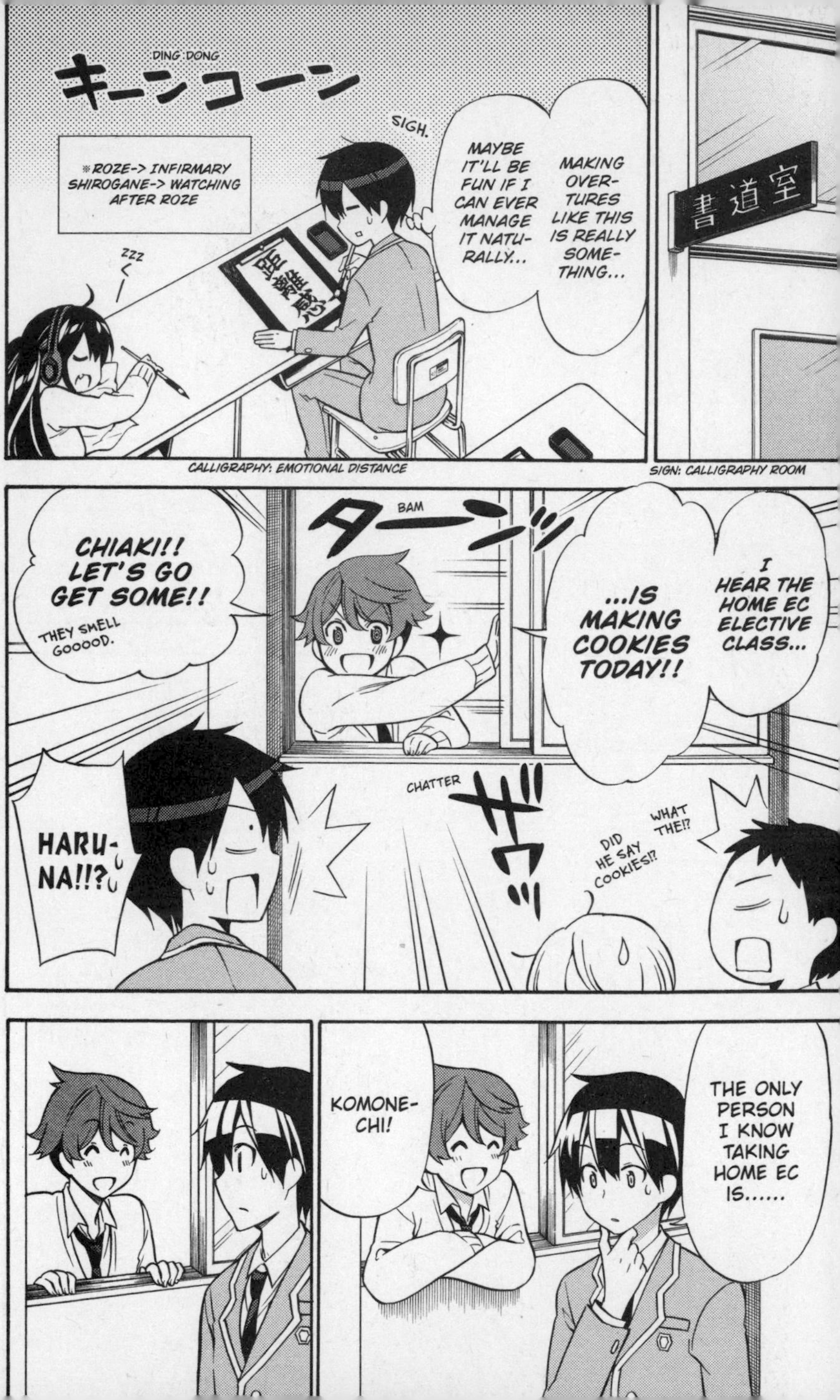
書道室
SIGN: CALLIGRAPHY ROOM
MAKING OVERTURES LIKE THIS IS REALLY SOMETHING...
MAYBE IT'LL BE FUN IF I CAN EVER MANAGE IT NATURALLY...
SIGH.
キーンコーン
DING DONG
※ROZE-> INFIRMARY SHIROGANE-> WATCHING AFTER ROZE
ZZZ
距離感
CALLIGRAPHY: EMOTIONAL DISTANCE
I HEAR THE HOME EC ELECTIVE CLASS...
...IS MAKING COOKIES TODAY!!
ターンッ
BAM
CHIAKI!! LET'S GO GET SOME!!
THEY SMELL GOOOOD.
WHAT THE!?
DID HE SAY COOKIES!?
ザワッ
CHATTER
HARU-NA!!?
THE ONLY PERSON I KNOW TAKING HOME EC IS......
KOMONE-CHI!

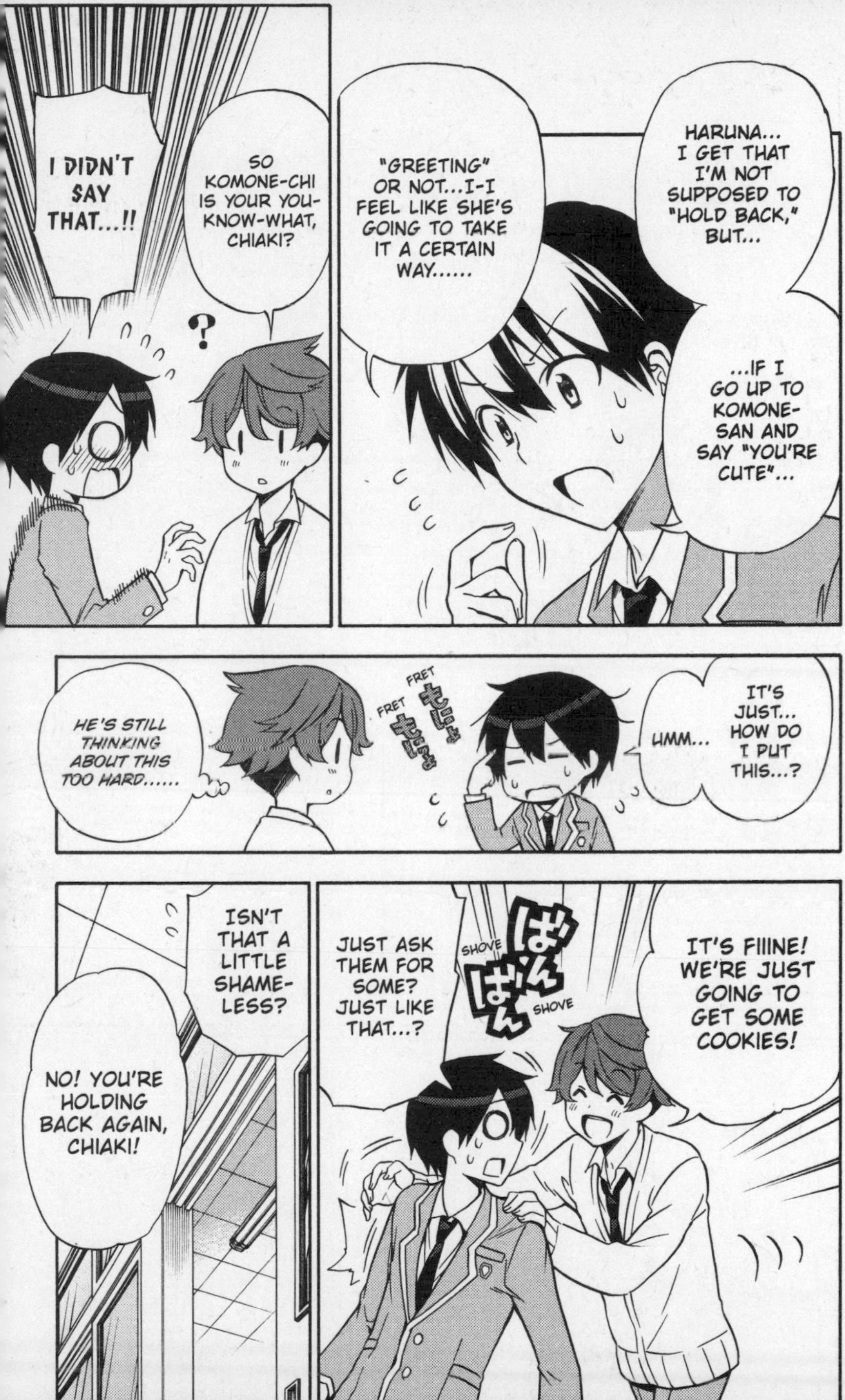
HARUNA... I GET THAT I'M NOT SUPPOSED TO "HOLD BACK," BUT...
...IF I GO UP TO KOMONE-SAN AND SAY "YOU'RE CUTE"...
"GREETING" OR NOT...I-I FEEL LIKE SHE'S GOING TO TAKE IT A CERTAIN WAY......
SO KOMONE-CHI IS YOUR YOU-KNOW-WHAT, CHIAKI?
I DIDN'T SAY THAT...!!
IT'S JUST... HOW DO I PUT THIS...?
UMM...
FRET
FRET
HE'S STILL THINKING ABOUT THIS TOO HARD......
IT'S FIIINE! WE'RE JUST GOING TO GET SOME COOKIES!
SHOVE
SHOVE
JUST ASK THEM FOR SOME? JUST LIKE THAT...?
ISN'T THAT A LITTLE SHAME-LESS?
NO! YOU'RE HOLDING BACK AGAIN, CHIAKI!

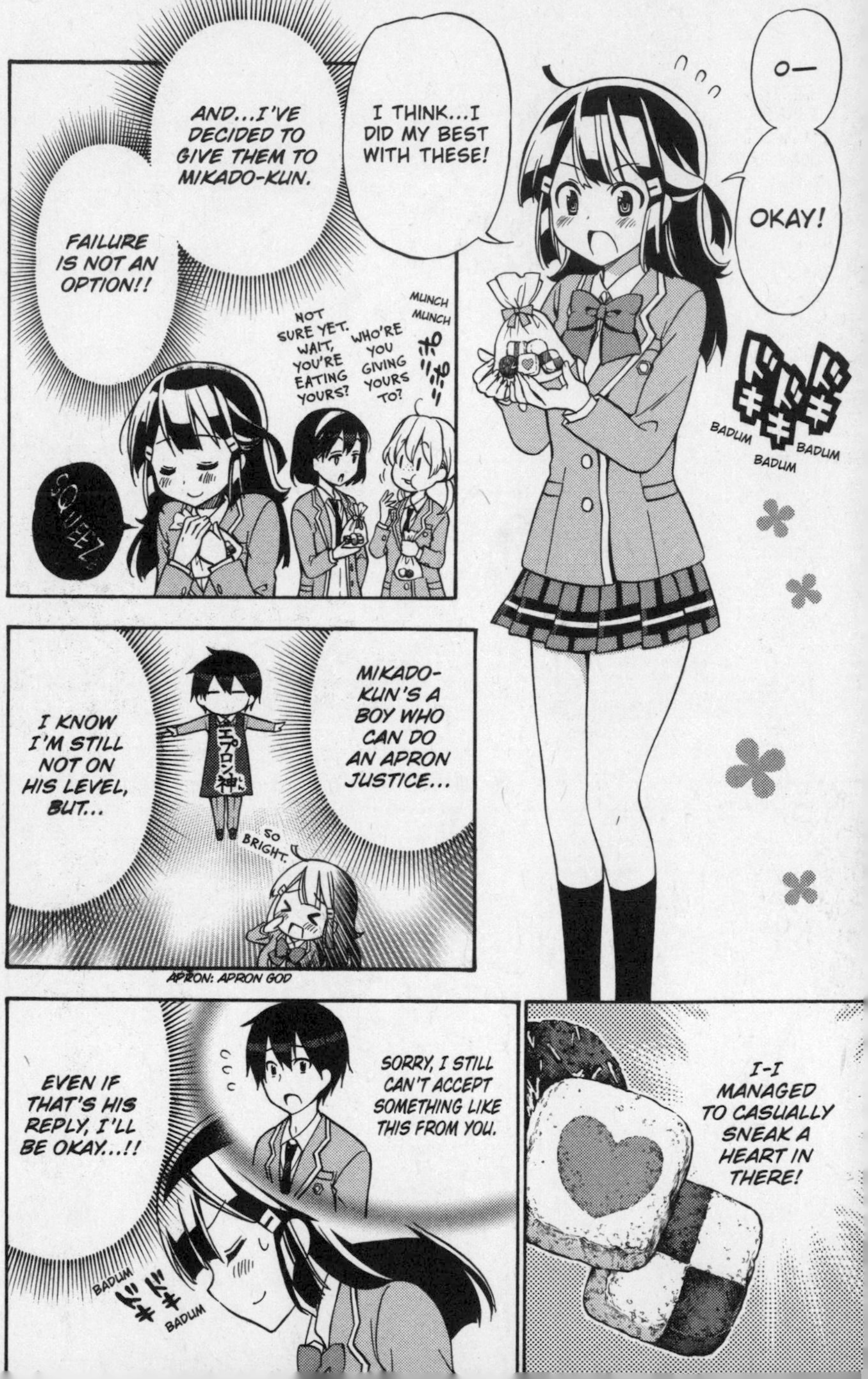
O— OKAY!
BADUM BADUM BADUM
I THINK...I DID MY BEST WITH THESE!
AND...I'VE DECIDED TO GIVE THEM TO MIKADO-KUN.
FAILURE IS NOT AN OPTION!!
MUNCH MUNCH
WHO'RE YOU GIVING YOURS TO?
NOT SURE YET. WAIT, YOU'RE EATING YOURS?
SQUEEZE
MIKADO-KUN'S A BOY WHO CAN DO AN APRON JUSTICE...
I KNOW I'M STILL NOT ON HIS LEVEL, BUT...
エプロン神
SO BRIGHT.
APRON: APRON GOD
I-I MANAGED TO CASUALLY SNEAK A HEART IN THERE!
SORRY, I STILL CAN'T ACCEPT SOMETHING LIKE THIS FROM YOU.
EVEN IF THAT'S HIS REPLY, I'LL BE OKAY...!!
BADUM BADUM

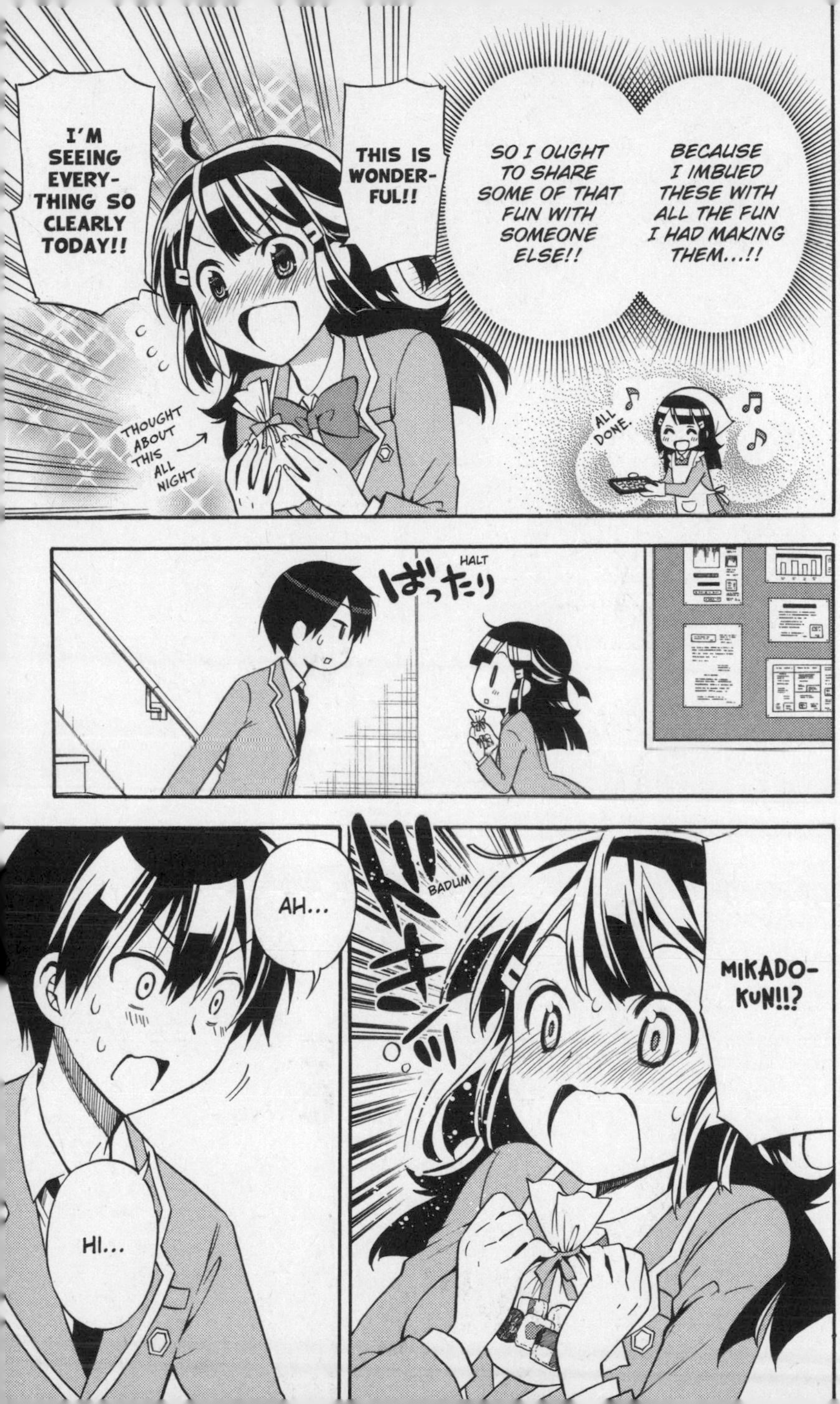
BECAUSE I IMBUED THESE WITH ALL THE FUN I HAD MAKING THEM...!!
SO I OUGHT TO SHARE SOME OF THAT FUN WITH SOMEONE ELSE!!
ALL DONE.
THIS IS WONDERFUL!!
I'M SEEING EVERYTHING SO CLEARLY TODAY!!
THOUGHT ABOUT THIS ALL NIGHT
ばったり
HALT
ドキッ
BADUM
MIKADO-KUN!!?
AH...
HI...

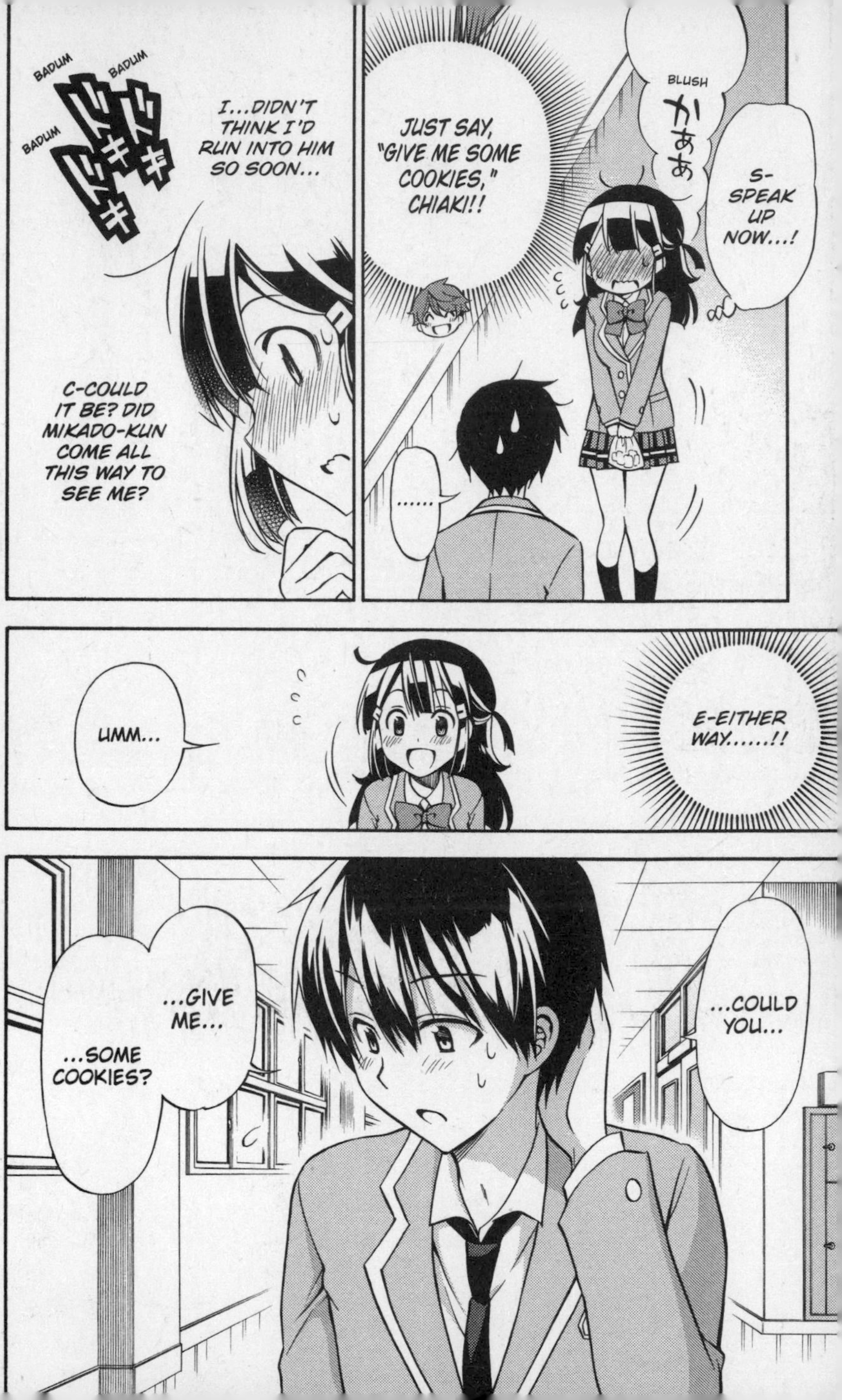

BLUSH
かぁぁ
S-SPEAK UP NOW...!
JUST SAY, "GIVE ME SOME COOKIES," CHIAKI!!
......
BADUM BADUM BADUM
ドキドキドキ
I...DIDN'T THINK I'D RUN INTO HIM SO SOON...
C-COULD IT BE? DID MIKADO-KUN COME ALL THIS WAY TO SEE ME?
E-EITHER WAY......!!
UMM...
...COULD YOU...
...GIVE ME...
...SOME COOKIES?

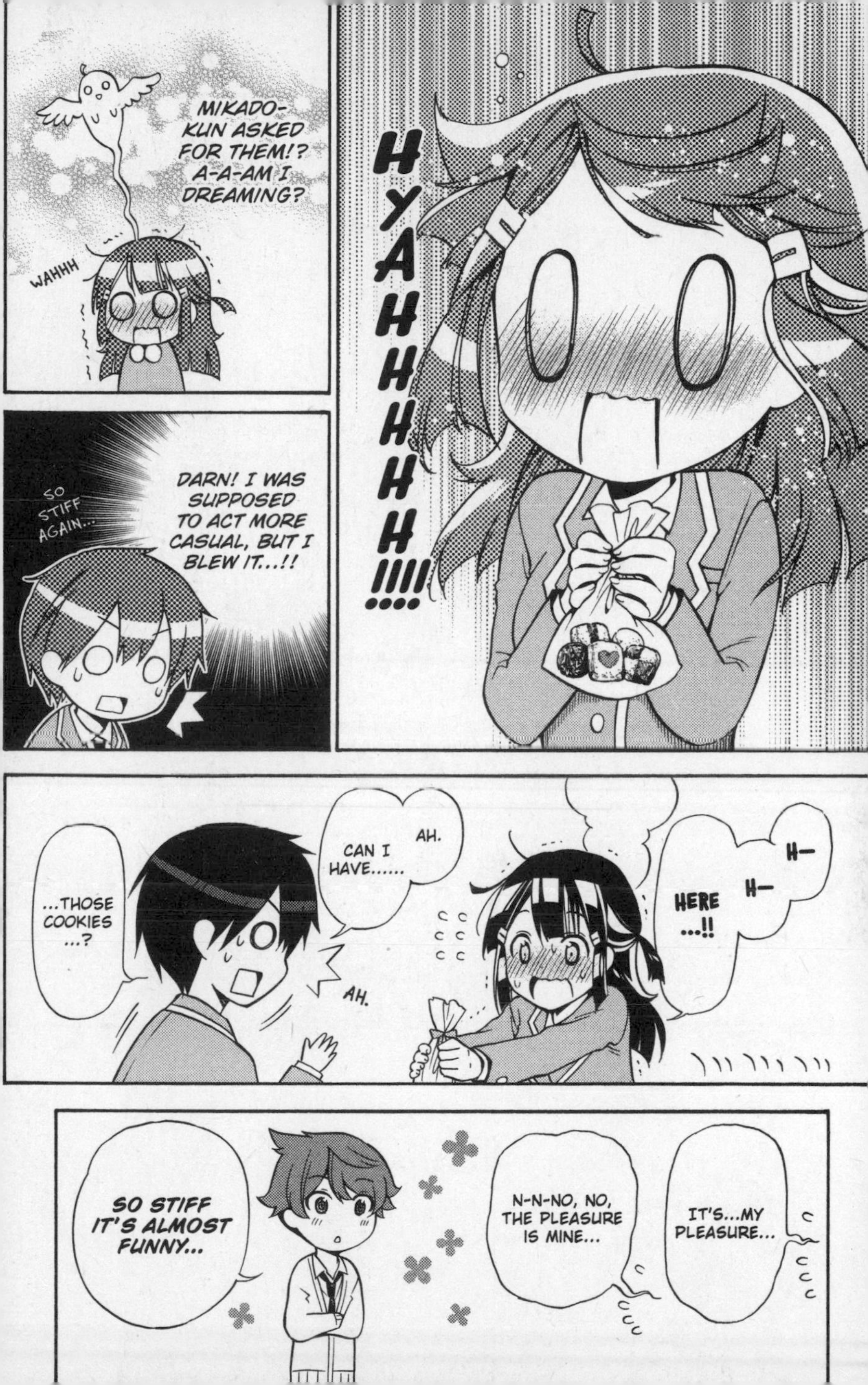
HYAHHHHH!!!!
MIKADO-KUN ASKED FOR THEM!? A-A-AM I DREAMING?
WAHHH
DARN! I WAS SUPPOSED TO ACT MORE CASUAL, BUT I BLEW IT...!!
SO STIFF AGAIN...
H— H— HERE...!!
AH. CAN I HAVE......
...THOSE COOKIES...?
AH.
IT'S...MY PLEASURE...
N-N-NO, NO, THE PLEASURE IS MINE...
SO STIFF IT'S ALMOST FUNNY...

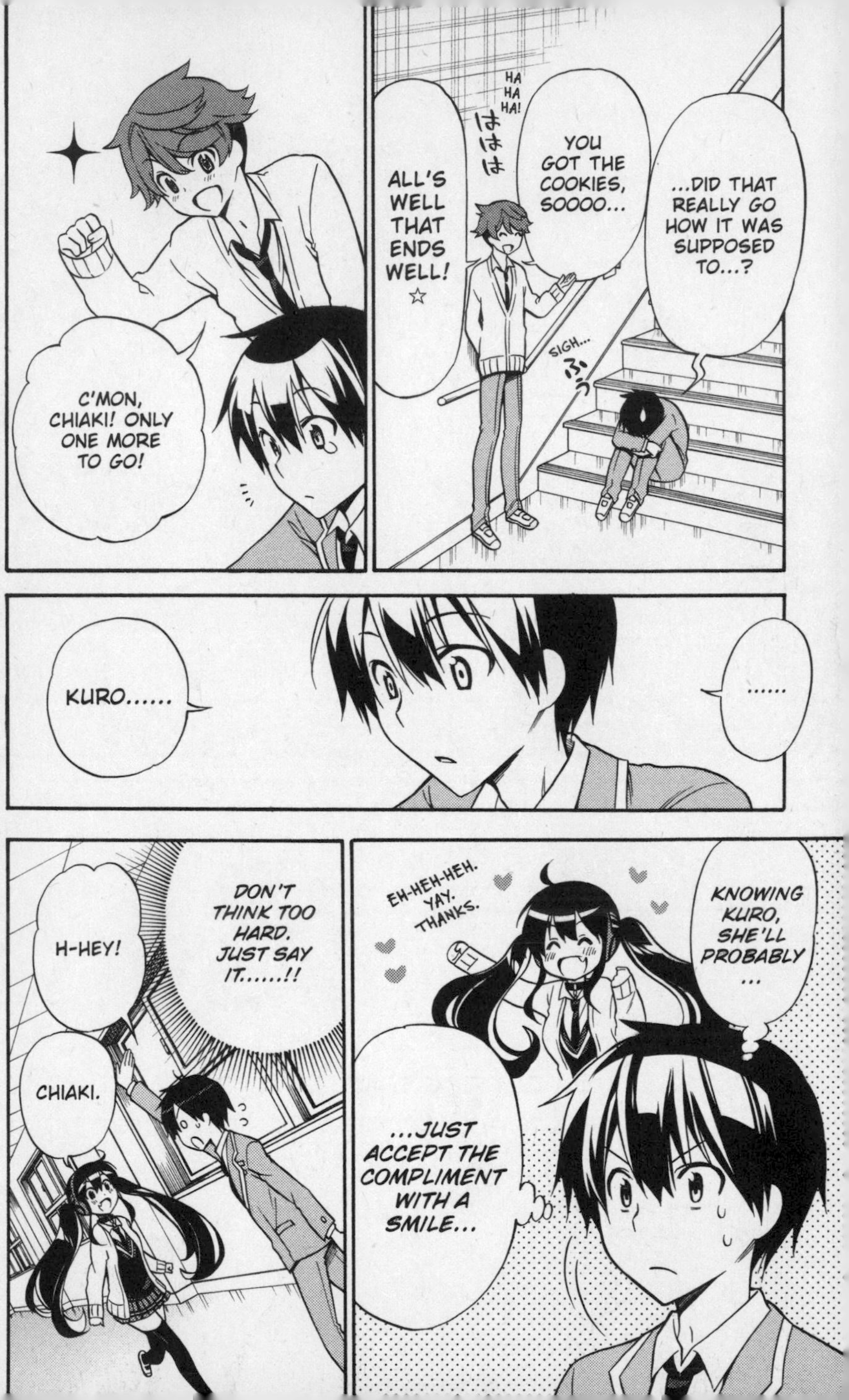
...DID THAT REALLY GO HOW IT WAS SUPPOSED TO...?
YOU GOT THE COOKIES, SOOOO...
HA HA HA!
ははは
ALL'S WELL THAT ENDS WELL! ☆
SIGH...
ふう
C'MON, CHIAKI! ONLY ONE MORE TO GO!
......
KURO......
KNOWING KURO, SHE'LL PROBABLY ...
EH-HEH-HEH. YAY. THANKS.
...JUST ACCEPT THE COMPLIMENT WITH A SMILE...
DON'T THINK TOO HARD. JUST SAY IT......!!
H-HEY!
CHIAKI.

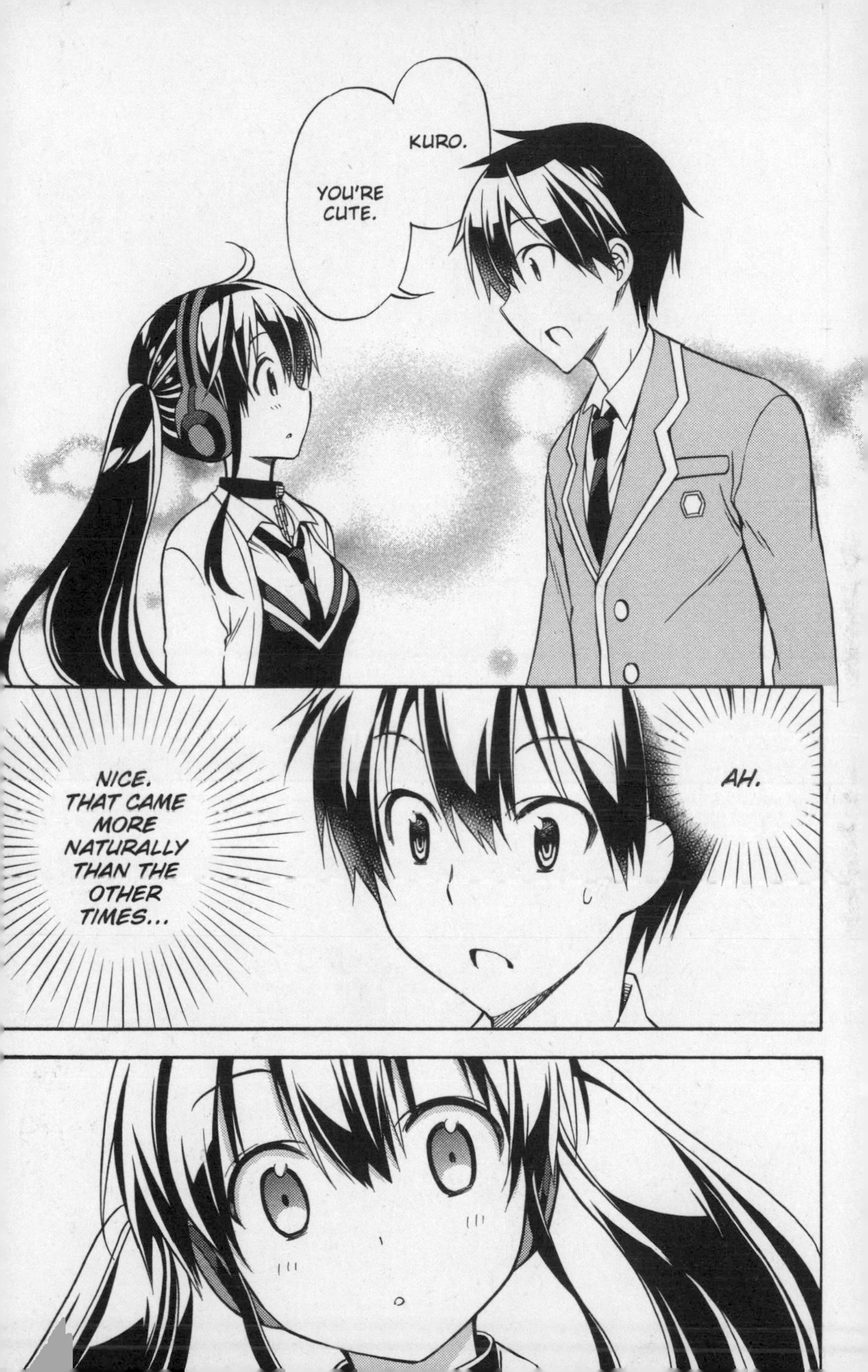
KURO.
YOU'RE CUTE.
AH.
NICE. THAT CAME MORE NATURALLY THAN THE OTHER TIMES...

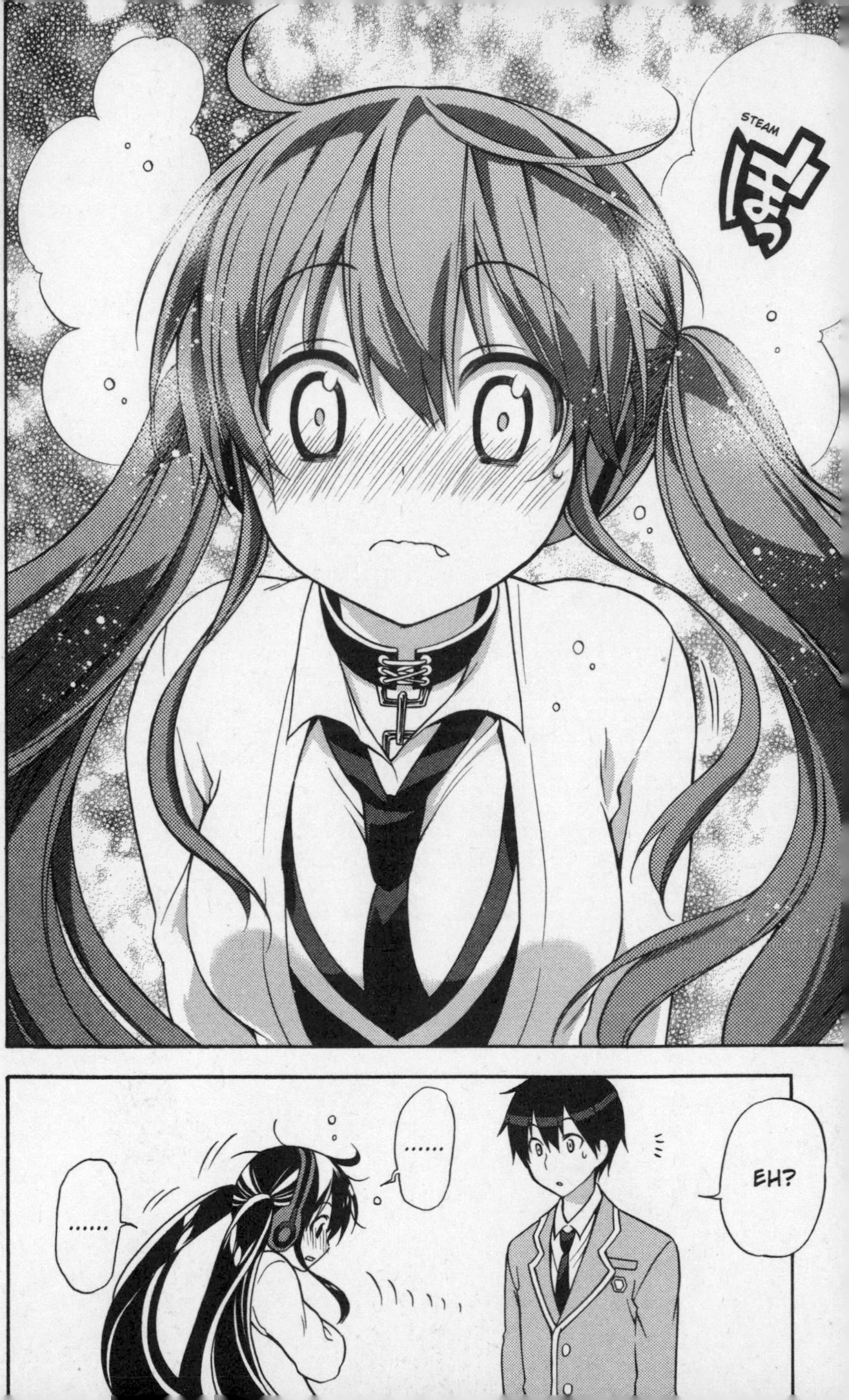
STEAM
ぼっ!
EH?
....
....

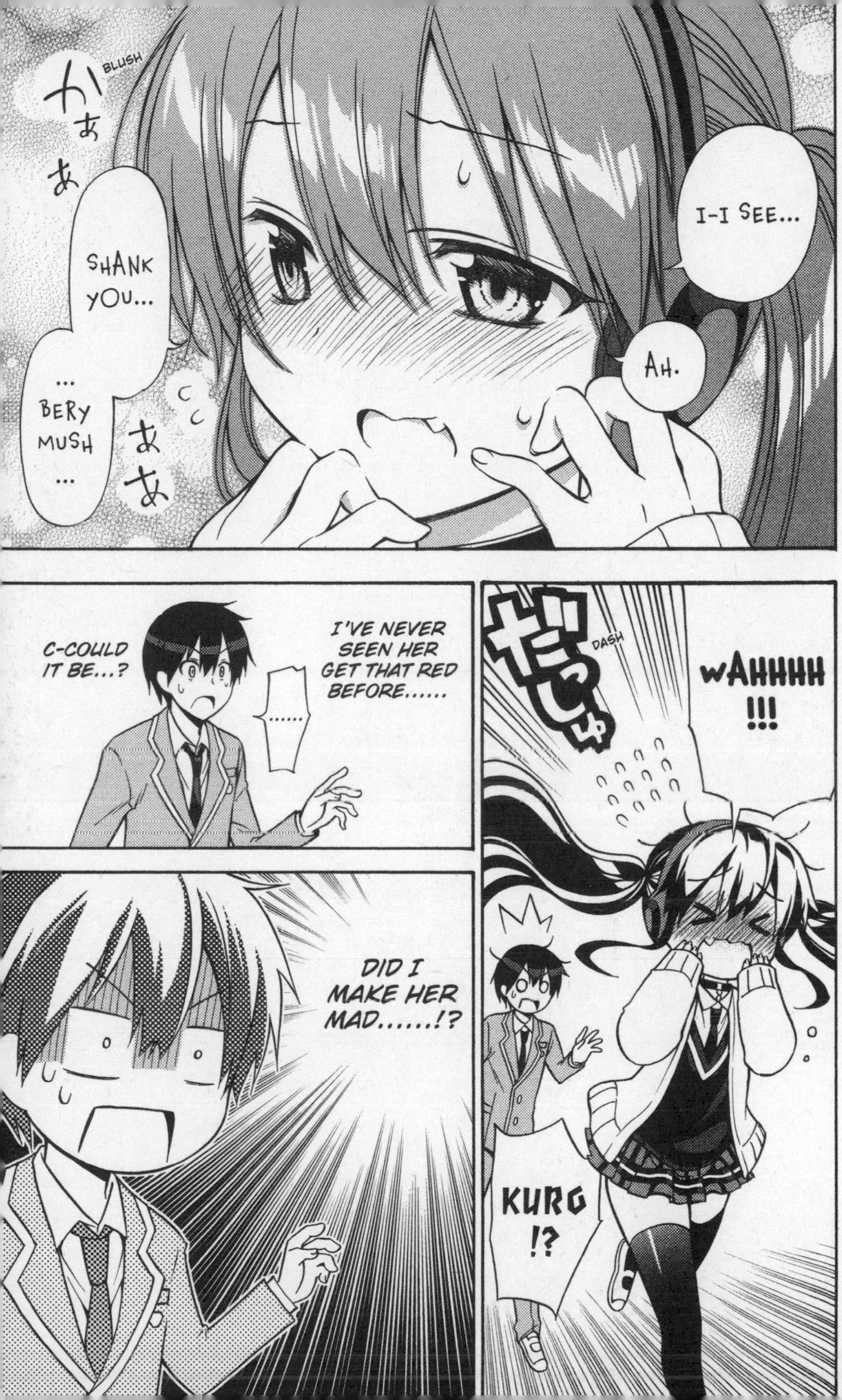
I-I SEE...
AH.
かぁぁぁぁ
BLUSH
SHANK YOU...
...BERY MUSH...
I'VE NEVER SEEN HER GET THAT RED BEFORE......
......
C-COULD IT BE...?
DID I MAKE HER MAD......!?
だっしゅ
DASH
WAHHHH!!!
KURG!?

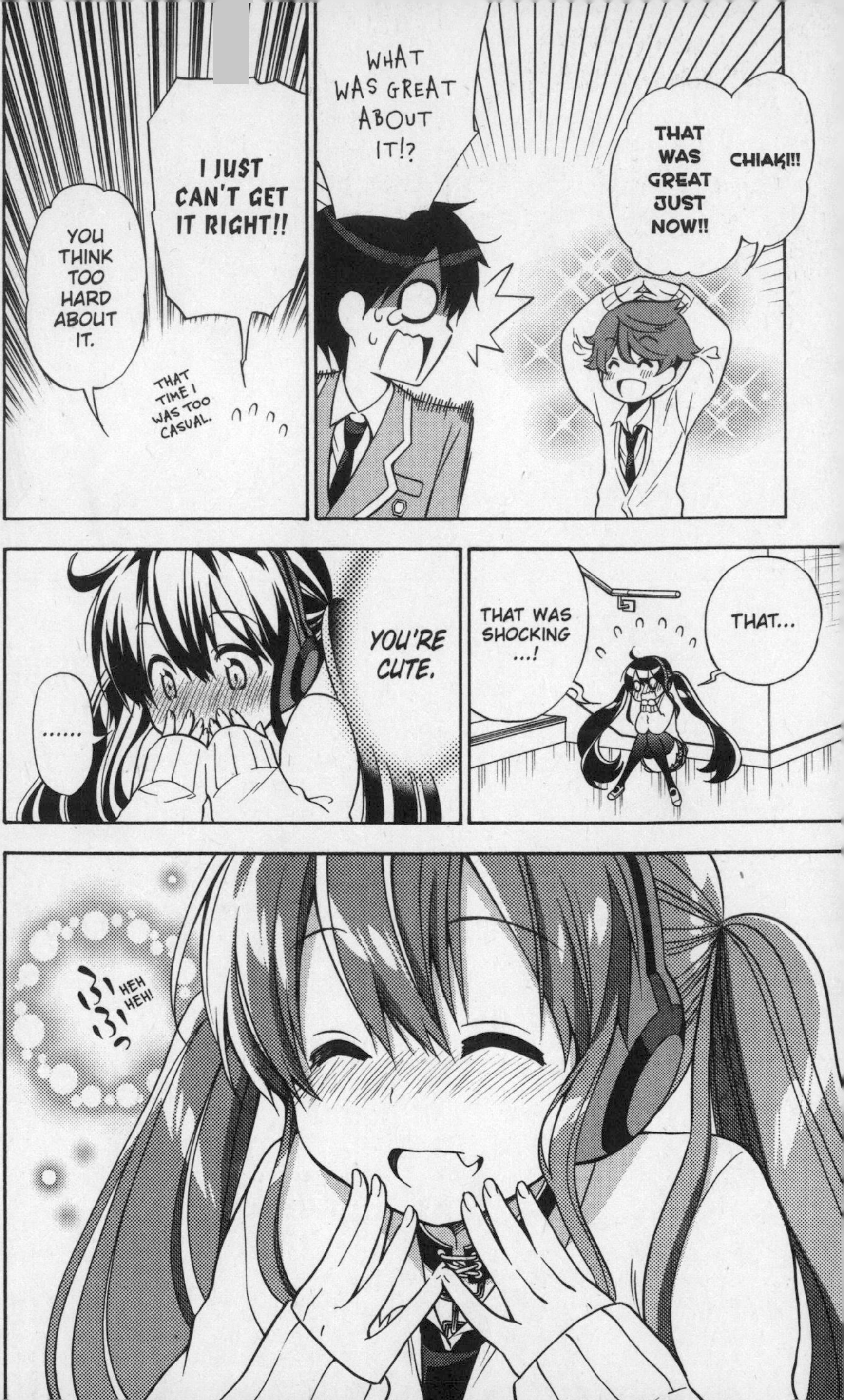
THAT WAS GREAT JUST NOW!! CHIAKI!!!
WHAT WAS GREAT ABOUT IT!?
I JUST CAN'T GET IT RIGHT!!
THAT TIME I WAS TOO CASUAL.
YOU THINK TOO HARD ABOUT IT.
THAT...
THAT WAS SHOCKING ...!
YOU'RE CUTE.
......
ふふっ
HEH HEH!

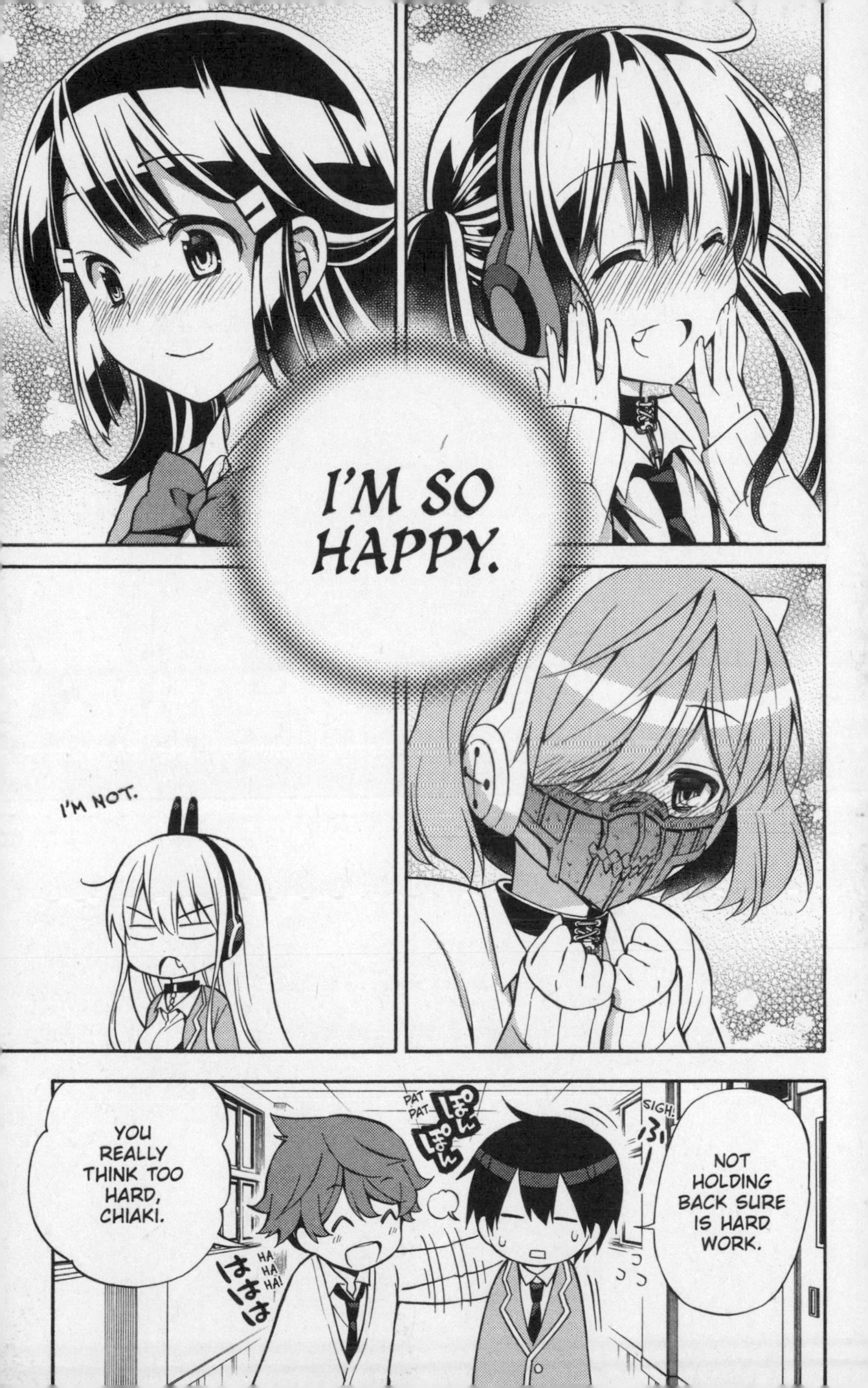
I'M SO HAPPY.
I'M NOT.
SIGH!
ふー
NOT HOLDING BACK SURE IS HARD WORK.
PAT PAT
ぽんぽん
HA HA HA!
ははは
YOU REALLY THINK TOO HARD, CHIAKI.

TODAY'S CERBERUS

CHIAKI CALLED ME CUTE? CUTE?
BLUSHING JUST REMEMBERING IT

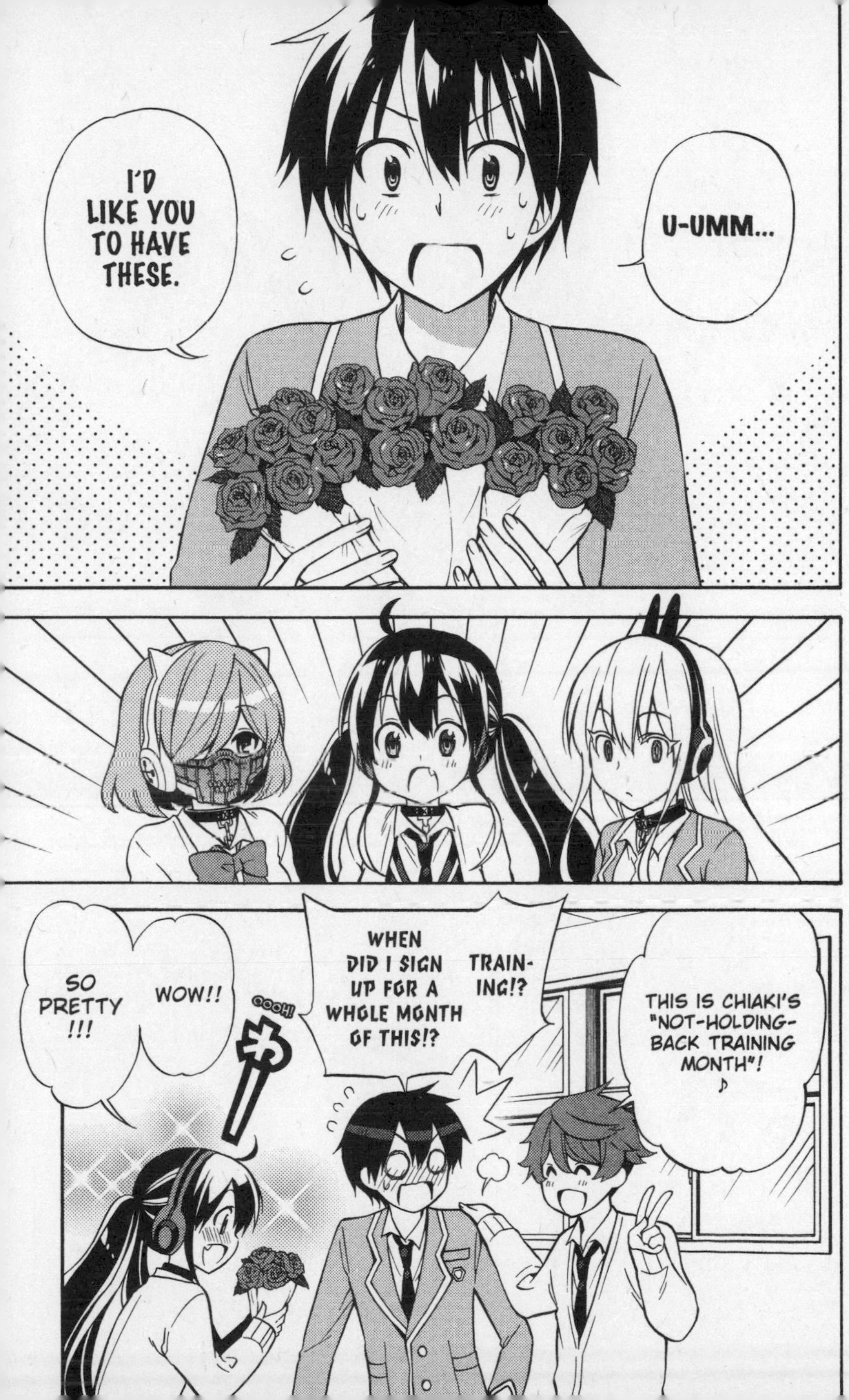
U-UMM...
I'D LIKE YOU TO HAVE THESE.
THIS IS CHIAKI'S "NOT-HOLDING-BACK TRAINING MONTH"! ♪
TRAIN-ING!?
WHEN DID I SIGN UP FOR A WHOLE MONTH OF THIS!?
OOOH!
WOW!!
SO PRETTY!!!

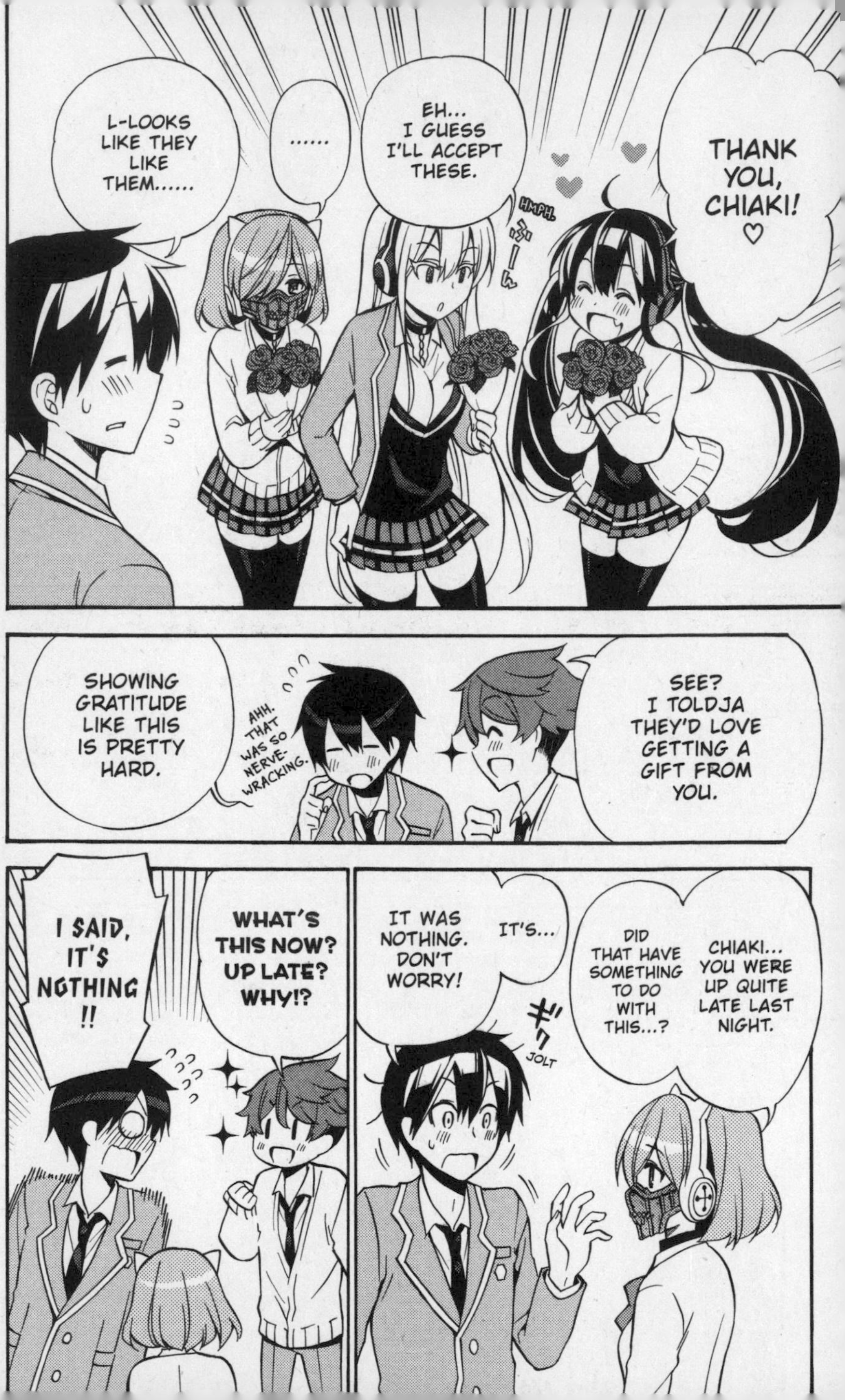
THANK YOU, CHIAKI! ♡
HMPH.
ふーん
EH... I GUESS I'LL ACCEPT THESE.
......
L-LOOKS LIKE THEY LIKE THEM......
SEE? I TOLDJA THEY'D LOVE GETTING A GIFT FROM YOU.
AHH. THAT WAS SO NERVE-WRACKING.
SHOWING GRATITUDE LIKE THIS IS PRETTY HARD.
CHIAKI... YOU WERE UP QUITE LATE LAST NIGHT.
DID THAT HAVE SOMETHING TO DO WITH THIS...?
ギク
JOLT
IT'S...
IT WAS NOTHING. DON'T WORRY!
WHAT'S THIS NOW? UP LATE? WHY!?
I SAID, IT'S NOTHING !!

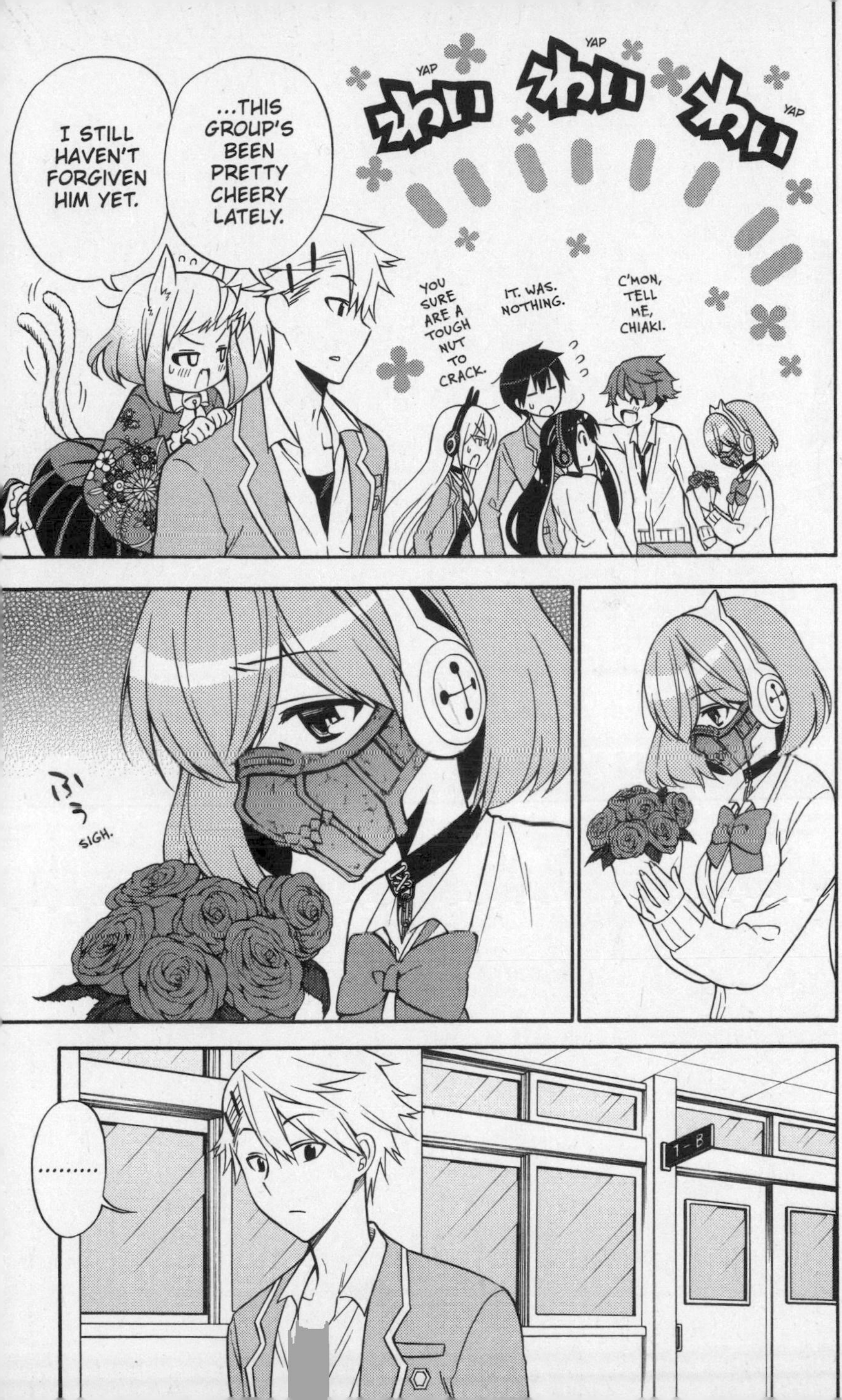
わい YAP
わい YAP
わい YAP
C'MON, TELL ME, CHIAKI.
IT. WAS. NOTHING.
YOU SURE ARE A TOUGH NUT TO CRACK.
...THIS GROUP'S BEEN PRETTY CHEERY LATELY.
I STILL HAVEN'T FORGIVEN HIM YET.
ふぅ SIGH.
....

CHAPTER 27: CLUMSY DOG

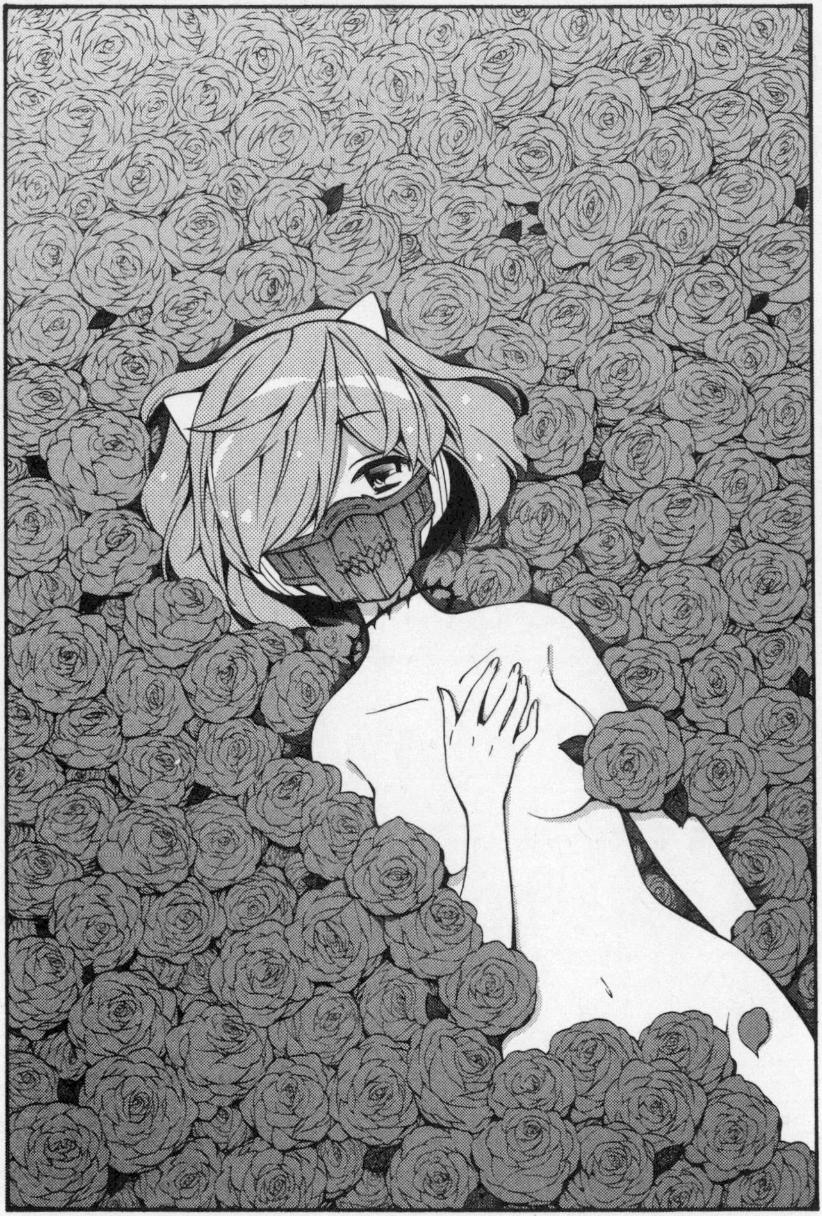

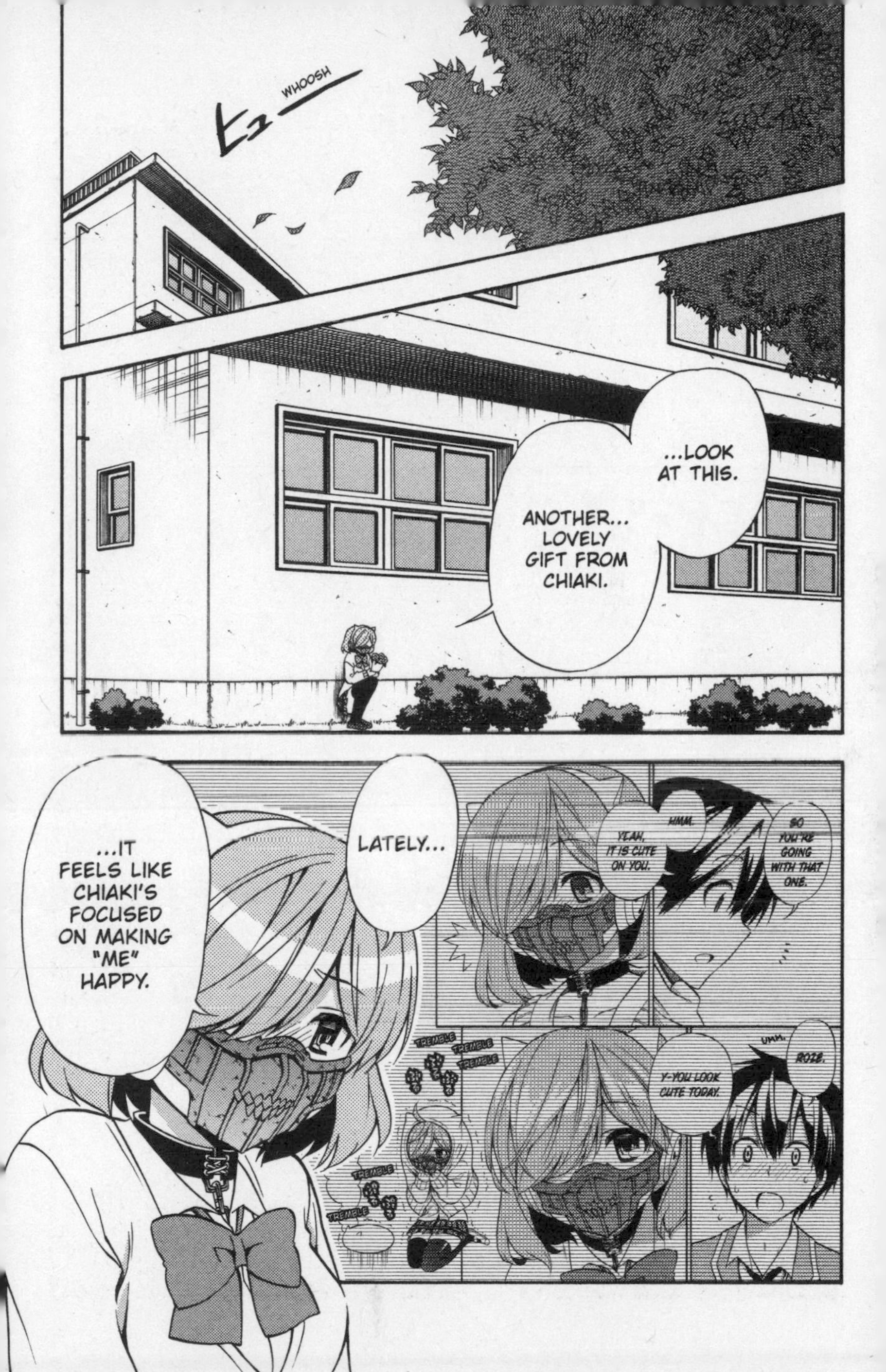
ヒュ
WHOOSH
...LOOK AT THIS.
ANOTHER... LOVELY GIFT FROM CHIAKI.
SO YOU'RE GOING WITH THAT ONE.
HMM.
YEAH, IT IS CUTE ON YOU.
UMM.
ROZE.
Y-YOU LOOK CUTE TODAY.
TREMBLE
TREMBLE
TREMBLE
TREMBLE
TREMBLE
LATELY...
...IT FEELS LIKE CHIAKI'S FOCUSED ON MAKING "ME" HAPPY.

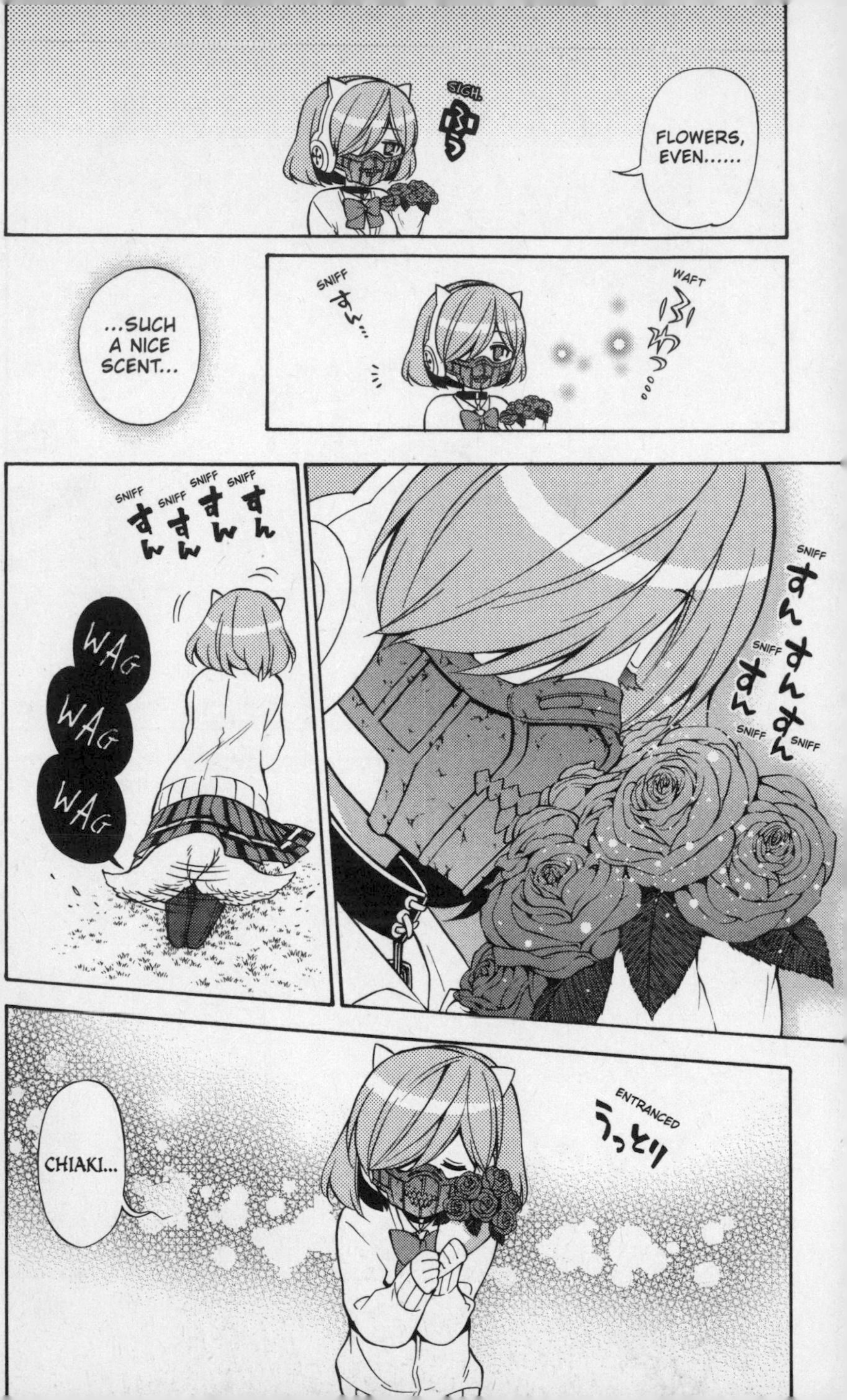

FLOWERS, EVEN......
SIGH.
WAFT
ふわっ...
SNIFF
すん...
...SUCH A NICE SCENT...
SNIFF
すん
SNIFF
すん
SNIFF
すん
SNIFF
すん
SNIFF SNIFF SNIFF SNIFF
すんすんすんすん
WAG
WAG
WAG
ENTRANCED
うっとり
CHIAKI...

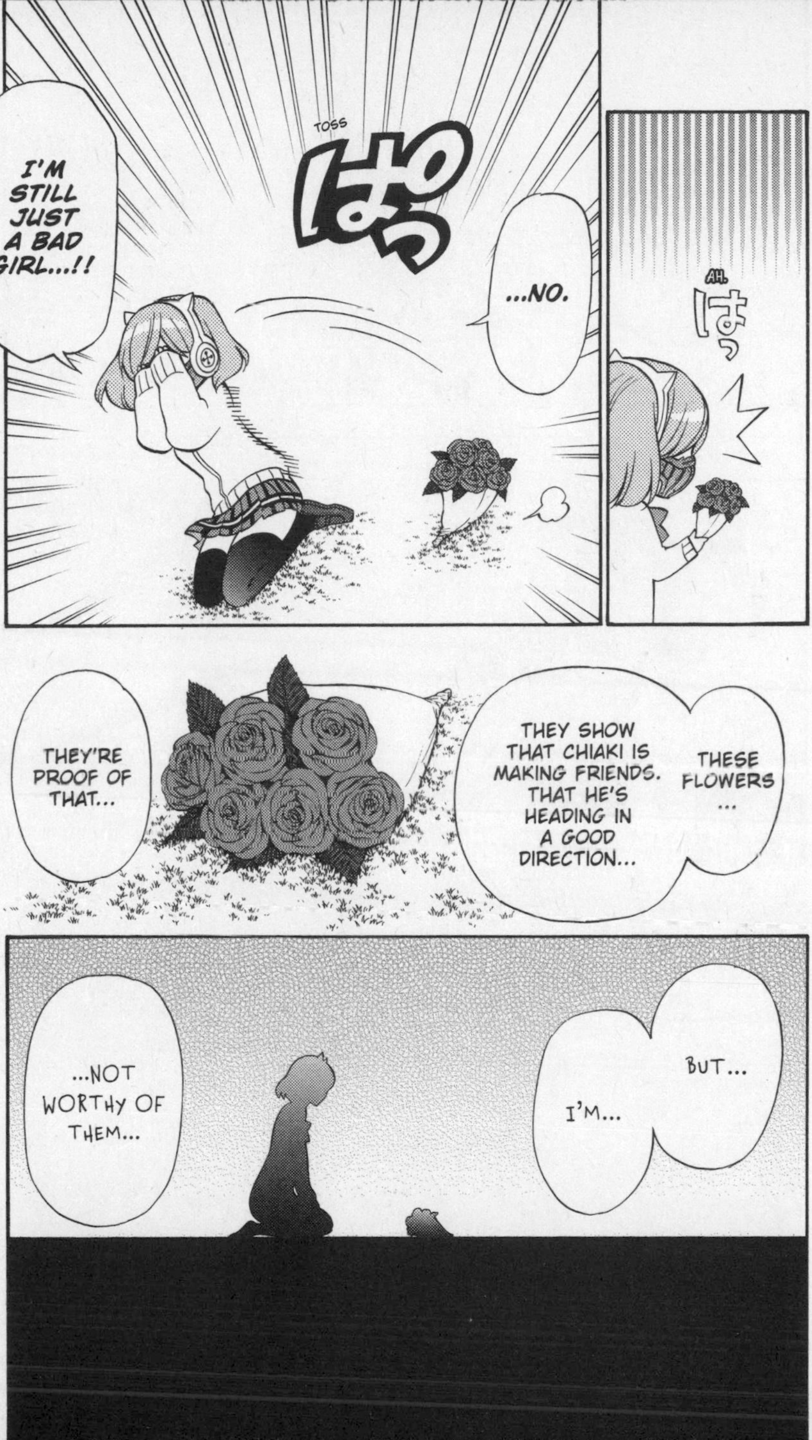
AH.
はっ
...NO.
TOSS
ぱっ
I'M STILL JUST A BAD GIRL...!!
THESE FLOWERS...
THEY SHOW THAT CHIAKI IS MAKING FRIENDS. THAT HE'S HEADING IN A GOOD DIRECTION...
THEY'RE PROOF OF THAT...
BUT...
I'M...
...NOT WORTHY OF THEM...

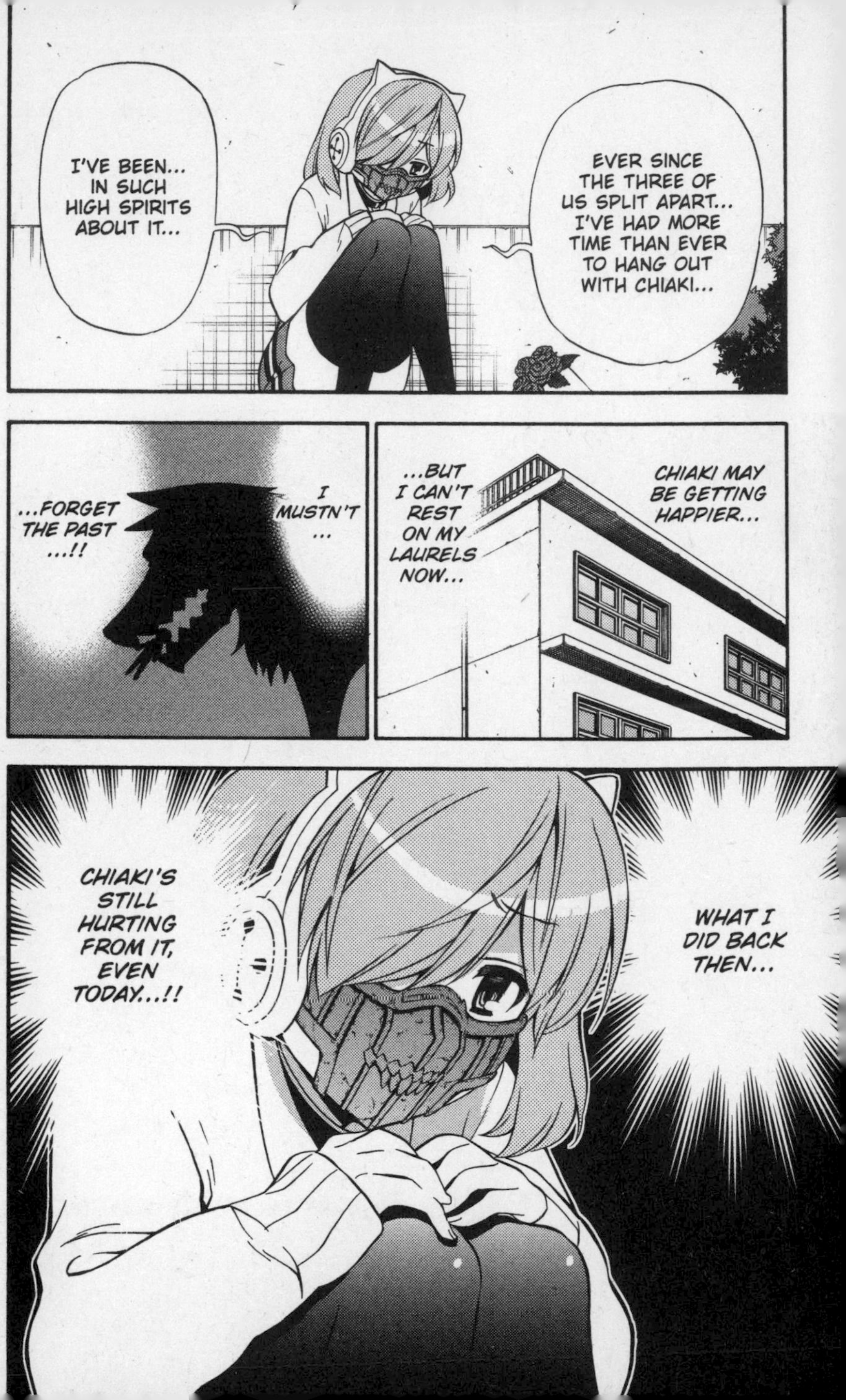
EVER SINCE THE THREE OF US SPLIT APART... I'VE HAD MORE TIME THAN EVER TO HANG OUT WITH CHIAKI...
I'VE BEEN... IN SUCH HIGH SPIRITS ABOUT IT...
CHIAKI MAY BE GETTING HAPPIER...
...BUT I CAN'T REST ON MY LAURELS NOW...
I MUSTN'T ...
...FORGET THE PAST ...!!
WHAT I DID BACK THEN...
CHIAKI'S STILL HURTING FROM IT, EVEN TODAY...!!

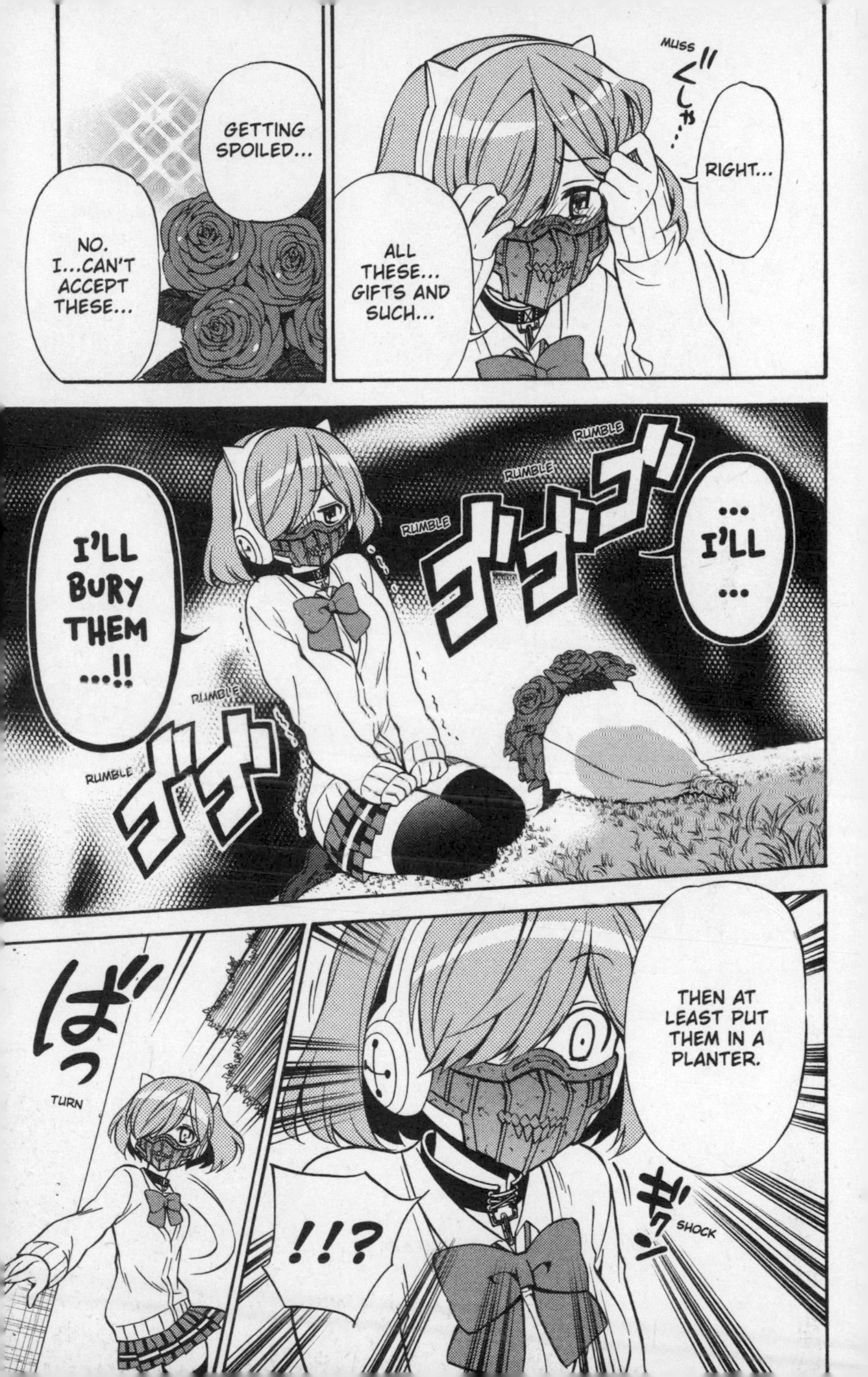
MUSS
くしゃ…
RIGHT…
ALL THESE… GIFTS AND SUCH…
GETTING SPOILED…
NO. I…CAN'T ACCEPT THESE…
RUMBLE
RUMBLE
RUMBLE
ゴゴゴ
…I'LL…
I'LL BURY THEM…!!
RUMBLE
RUMBLE
ゴゴ
THEN AT LEAST PUT THEM IN A PLANTER.
ギクン
SHOCK
!!?
ばっ
TURN

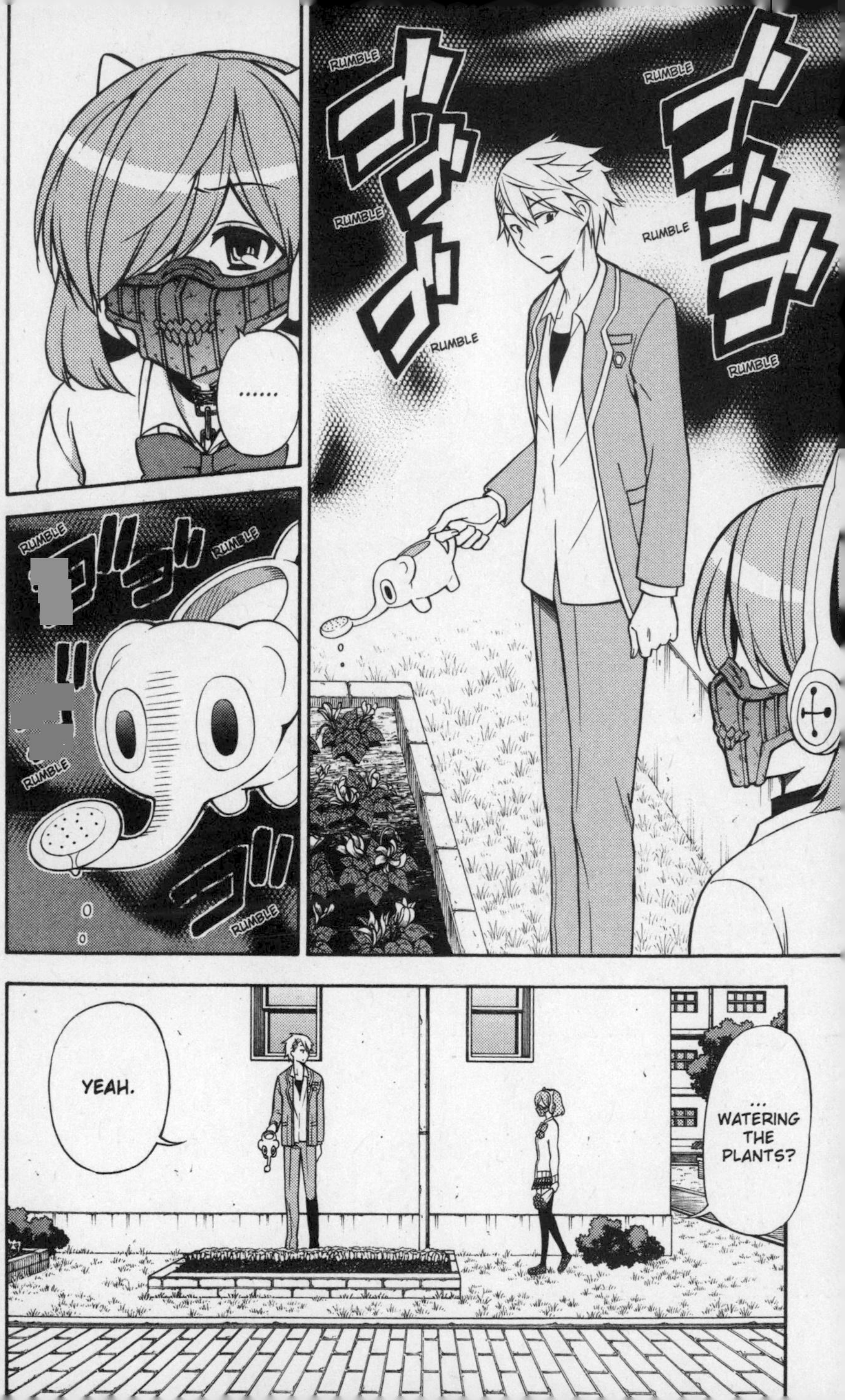
RUMBLE
RUMBLE
RUMBLE
RUMBLE
RUMBLE
RUMBLE
......
RUMBLE
RUMBLE
RUMBLE
RUMBLE
... WATERING THE PLANTS?
YEAH.

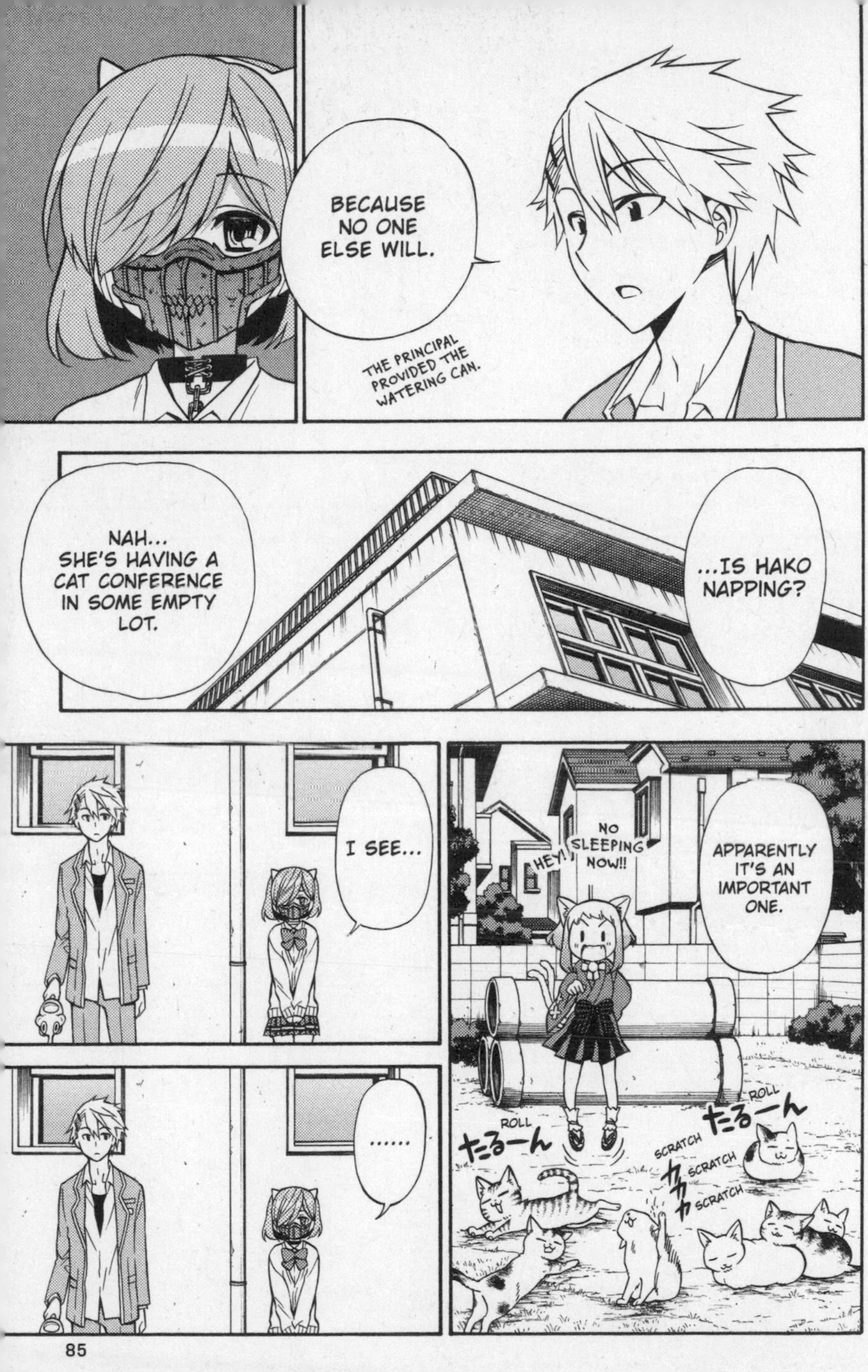
BECAUSE NO ONE ELSE WILL.
THE PRINCIPAL PROVIDED THE WATERING CAN.
...IS HAKO NAPPING?
NAH... SHE'S HAVING A CAT CONFERENCE IN SOME EMPTY LOT.
APPARENTLY IT'S AN IMPORTANT ONE.
NO SLEEPING NOW!!
HEY!
ROLL
たるーん
ROLL
たるーん
SCRATCH
カカカ
SCRATCH
SCRATCH
I SEE...
......

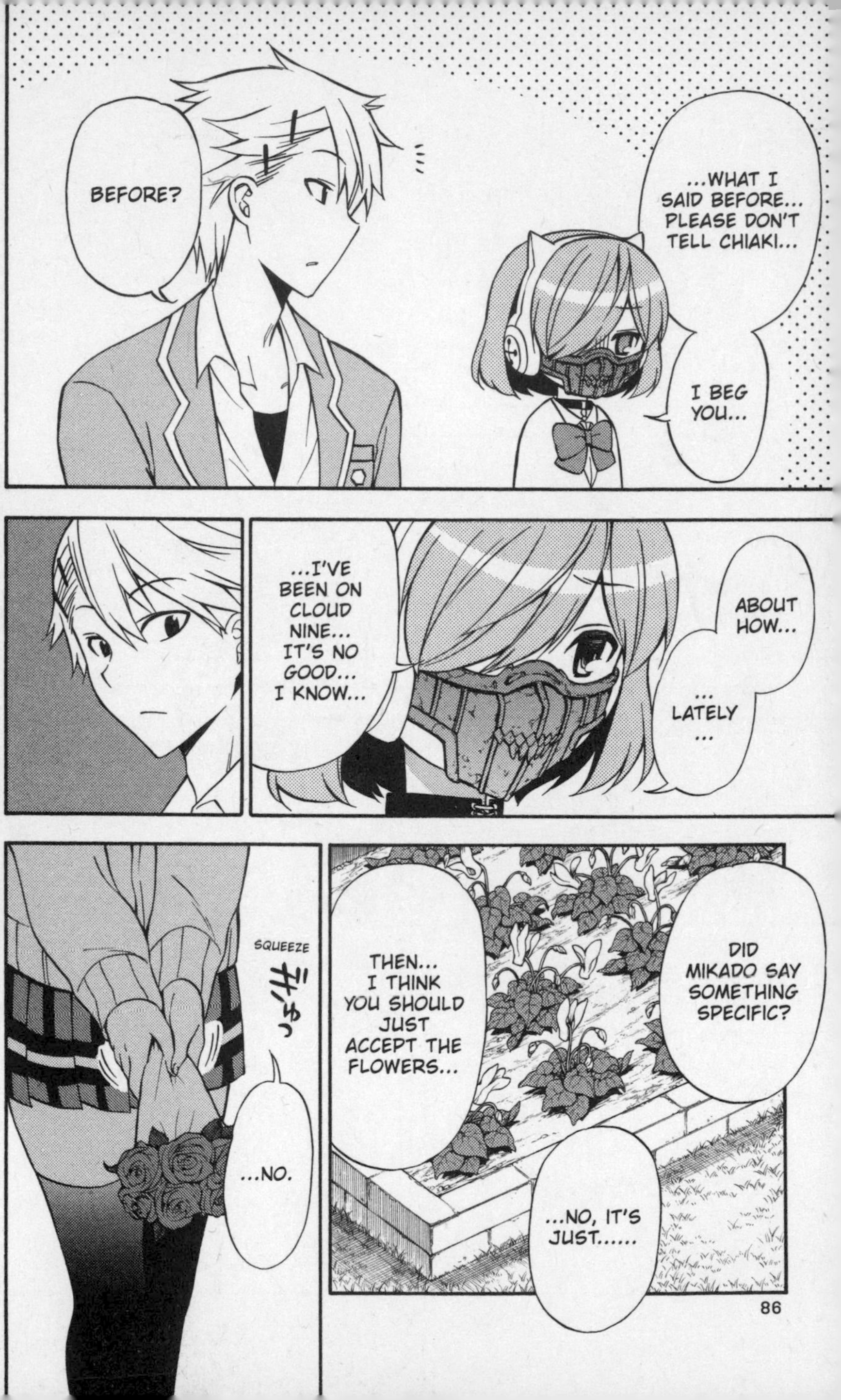
...WHAT I SAID BEFORE... PLEASE DON'T TELL CHIAKI...
I BEG YOU...
BEFORE?
ABOUT HOW...
... LATELY ...
...I'VE BEEN ON CLOUD NINE... IT'S NO GOOD... I KNOW...
DID MIKADO SAY SOMETHING SPECIFIC?
...NO, IT'S JUST......
THEN... I THINK YOU SHOULD JUST ACCEPT THE FLOWERS...
SQUEEZE
ギゅっ
...NO.

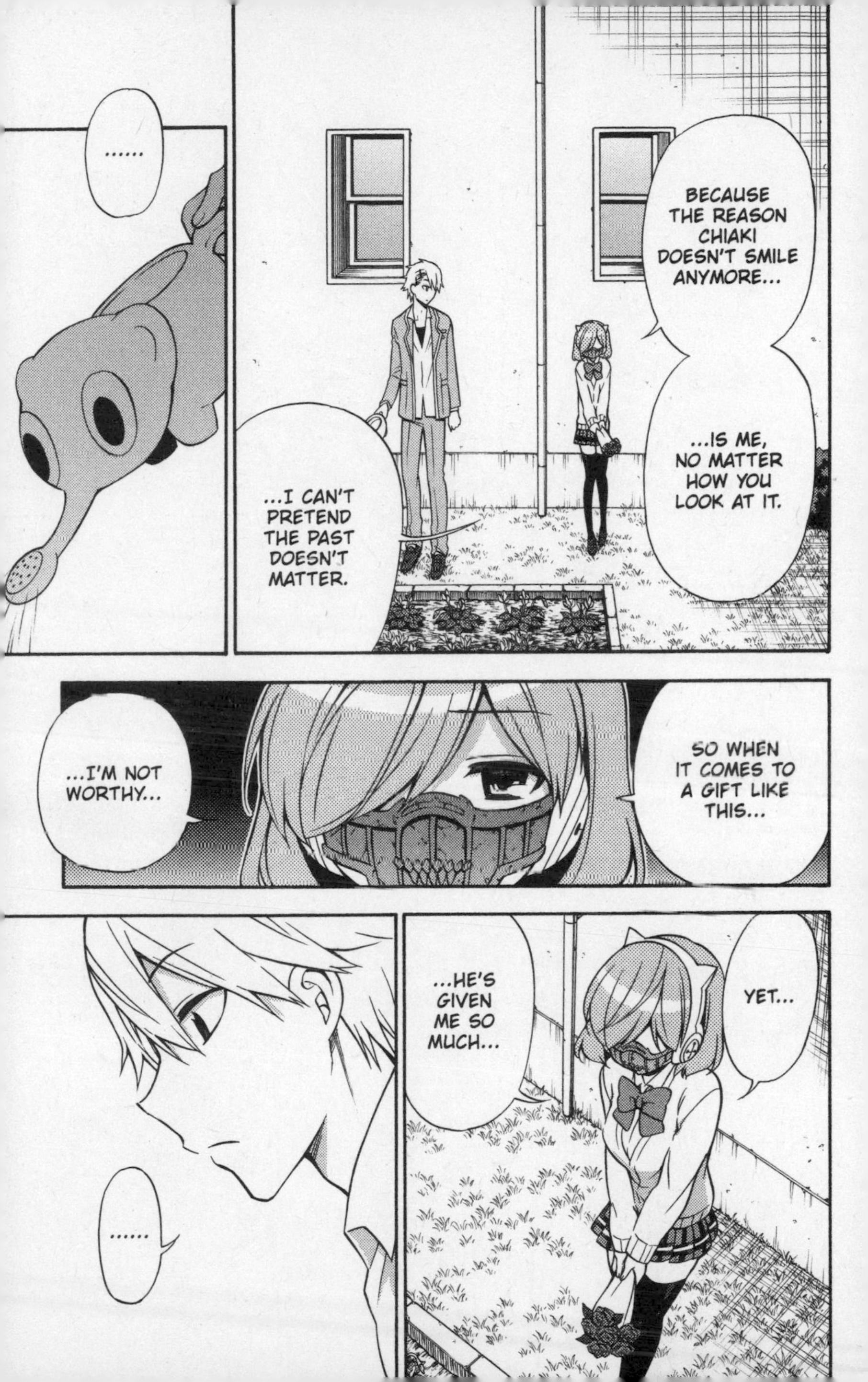
BECAUSE THE REASON CHIAKI DOESN'T SMILE ANYMORE...
...IS ME, NO MATTER HOW YOU LOOK AT IT.
...I CAN'T PRETEND THE PAST DOESN'T MATTER.
......
SO WHEN IT COMES TO A GIFT LIKE THIS...
...I'M NOT WORTHY...
YET...
...HE'S GIVEN ME SO MUCH...
......

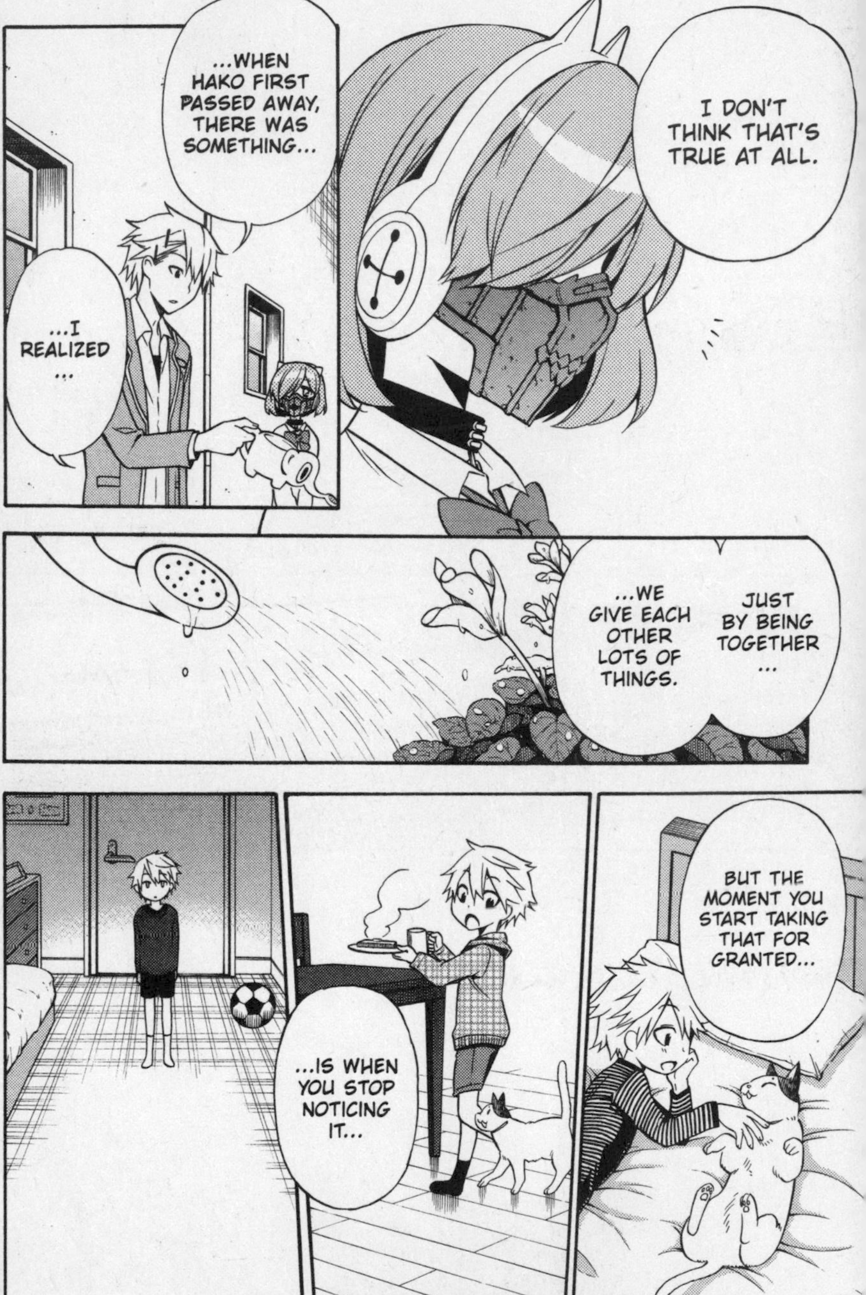
I DON'T THINK THAT'S TRUE AT ALL.
...WHEN HAKO FIRST PASSED AWAY, THERE WAS SOMETHING...
...I REALIZED ...
JUST BY BEING TOGETHER ...
...WE GIVE EACH OTHER LOTS OF THINGS.
BUT THE MOMENT YOU START TAKING THAT FOR GRANTED...
...IS WHEN YOU STOP NOTICING IT...

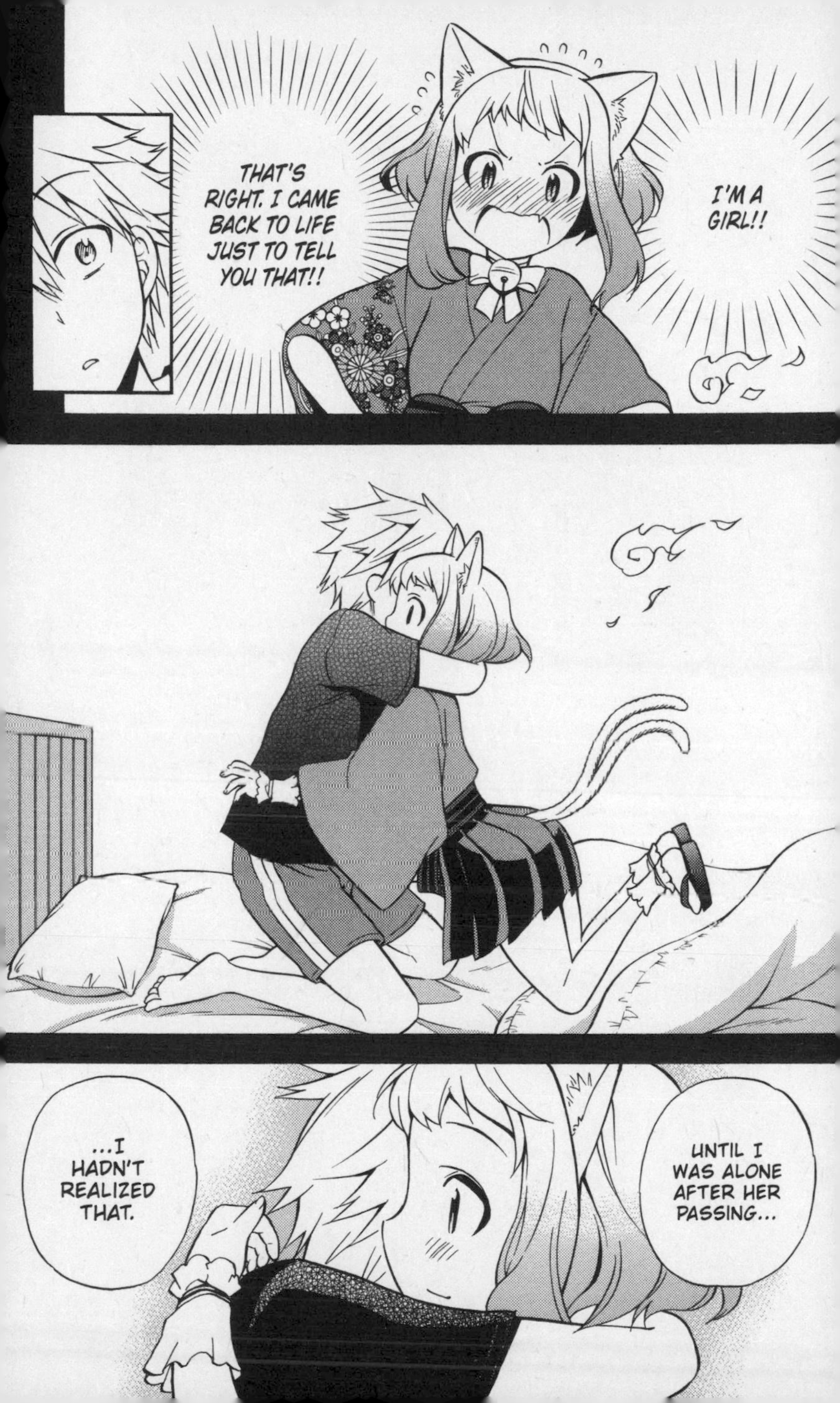
I'M A GIRL!!
THAT'S RIGHT. I CAME BACK TO LIFE JUST TO TELL YOU THAT!!
UNTIL I WAS ALONE AFTER HER PASSING...
...I HADN'T REALIZED THAT.

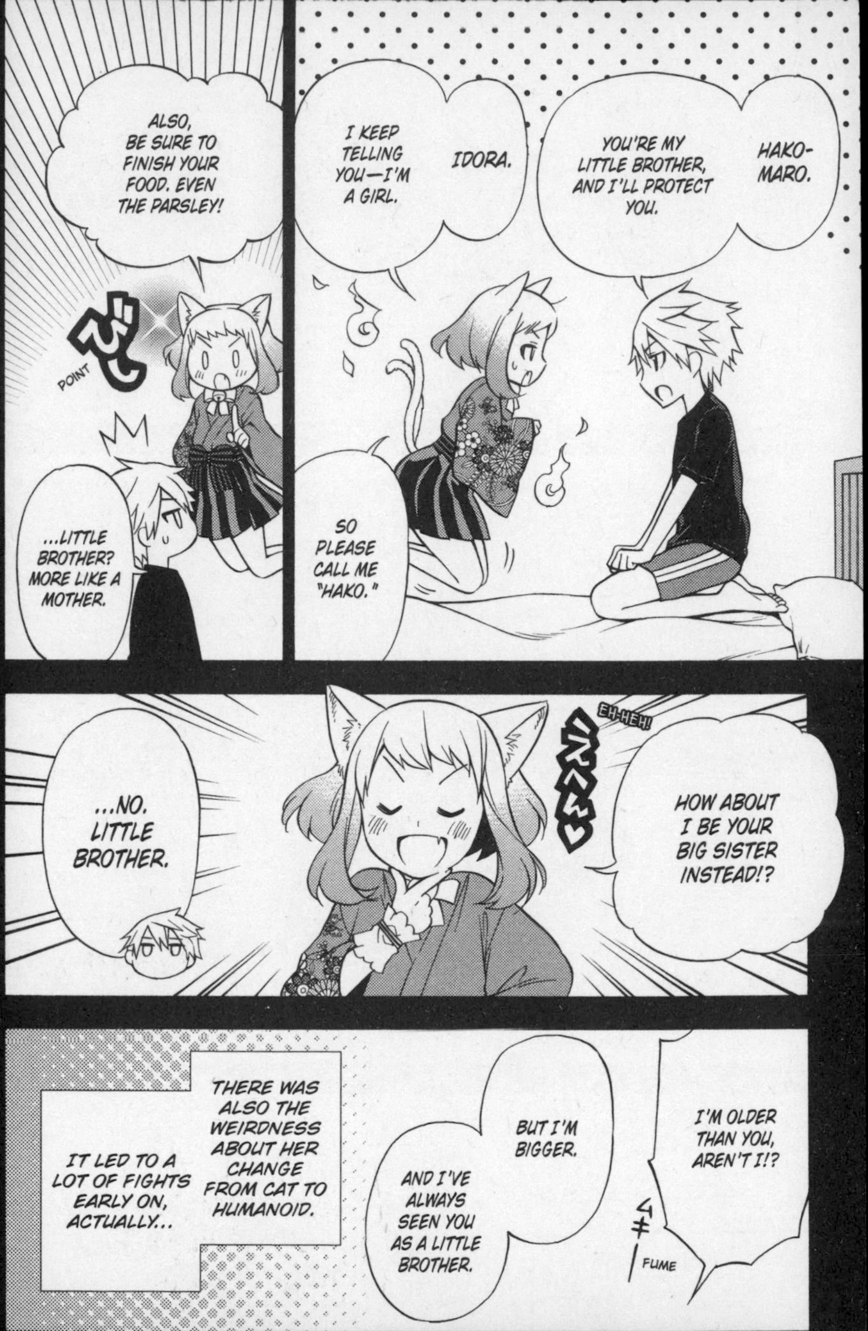
HAKO-MARO.
YOU'RE MY LITTLE BROTHER, AND I'LL PROTECT YOU.
IDORA.
I KEEP TELLING YOU—I'M A GIRL.
SO PLEASE CALL ME "HAKO."
ALSO, BE SURE TO FINISH YOUR FOOD. EVEN THE PARSLEY!
POINT
...LITTLE BROTHER? MORE LIKE A MOTHER.
EH-HEH!
HOW ABOUT I BE YOUR BIG SISTER INSTEAD!?
...NO. LITTLE BROTHER.
I'M OLDER THAN YOU, AREN'T I!?
FUME
BUT I'M BIGGER.
AND I'VE ALWAYS SEEN YOU AS A LITTLE BROTHER.
THERE WAS ALSO THE WEIRDNESS ABOUT HER CHANGE FROM CAT TO HUMANOID.
IT LED TO A LOT OF FIGHTS EARLY ON, ACTUALLY...

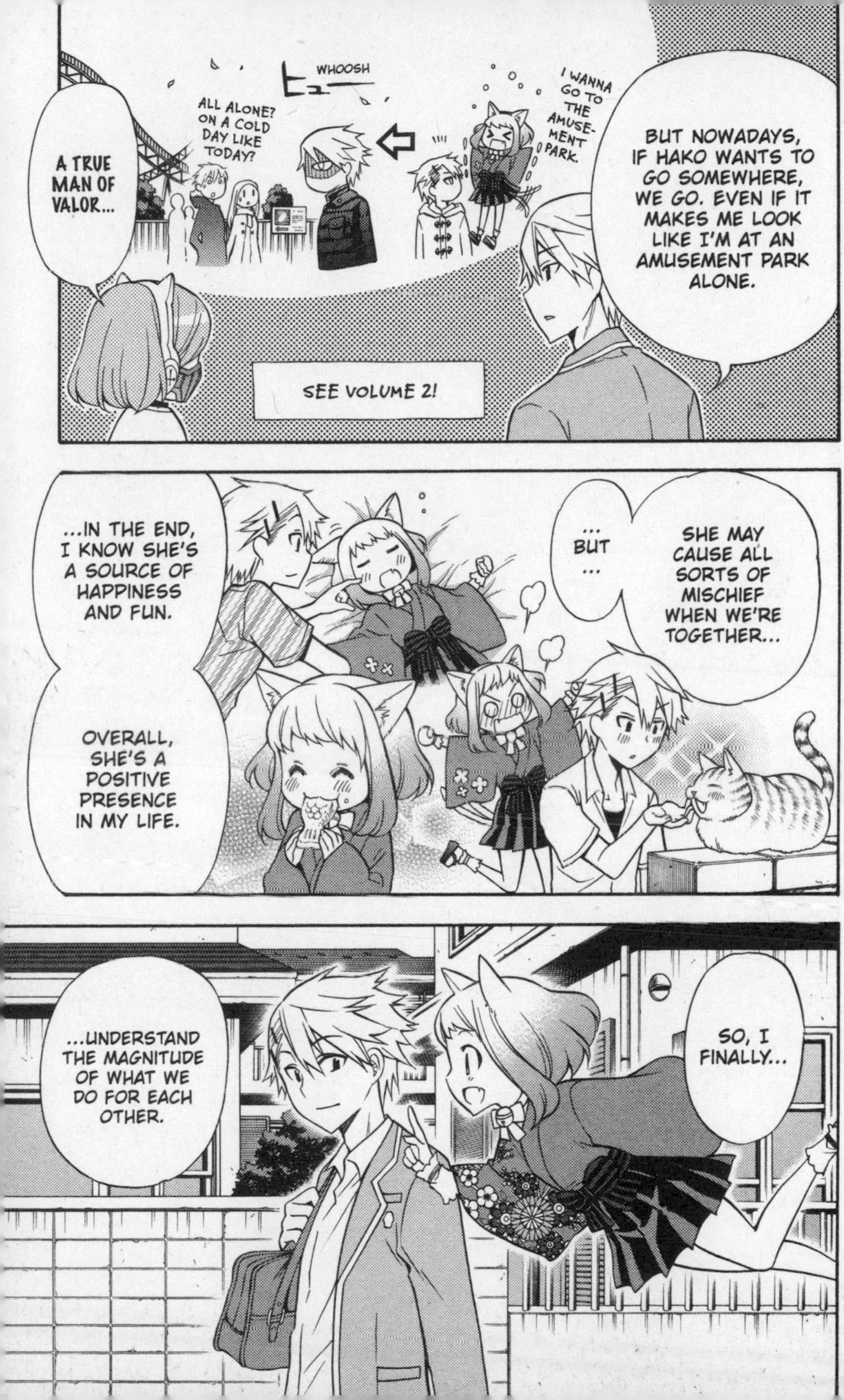
BUT NOWADAYS, IF HAKO WANTS TO GO SOMEWHERE, WE GO. EVEN IF IT MAKES ME LOOK LIKE I'M AT AN AMUSEMENT PARK ALONE.
I WANNA GO TO THE AMUSEMENT PARK.
WHOOSH
ALL ALONE? ON A COLD DAY LIKE TODAY?
A TRUE MAN OF VALOR...
SEE VOLUME 2!
SHE MAY CAUSE ALL SORTS OF MISCHIEF WHEN WE'RE TOGETHER...
...BUT...
...IN THE END, I KNOW SHE'S A SOURCE OF HAPPINESS AND FUN.
OVERALL, SHE'S A POSITIVE PRESENCE IN MY LIFE.
SO, I FINALLY...
...UNDERSTAND THE MAGNITUDE OF WHAT WE DO FOR EACH OTHER.

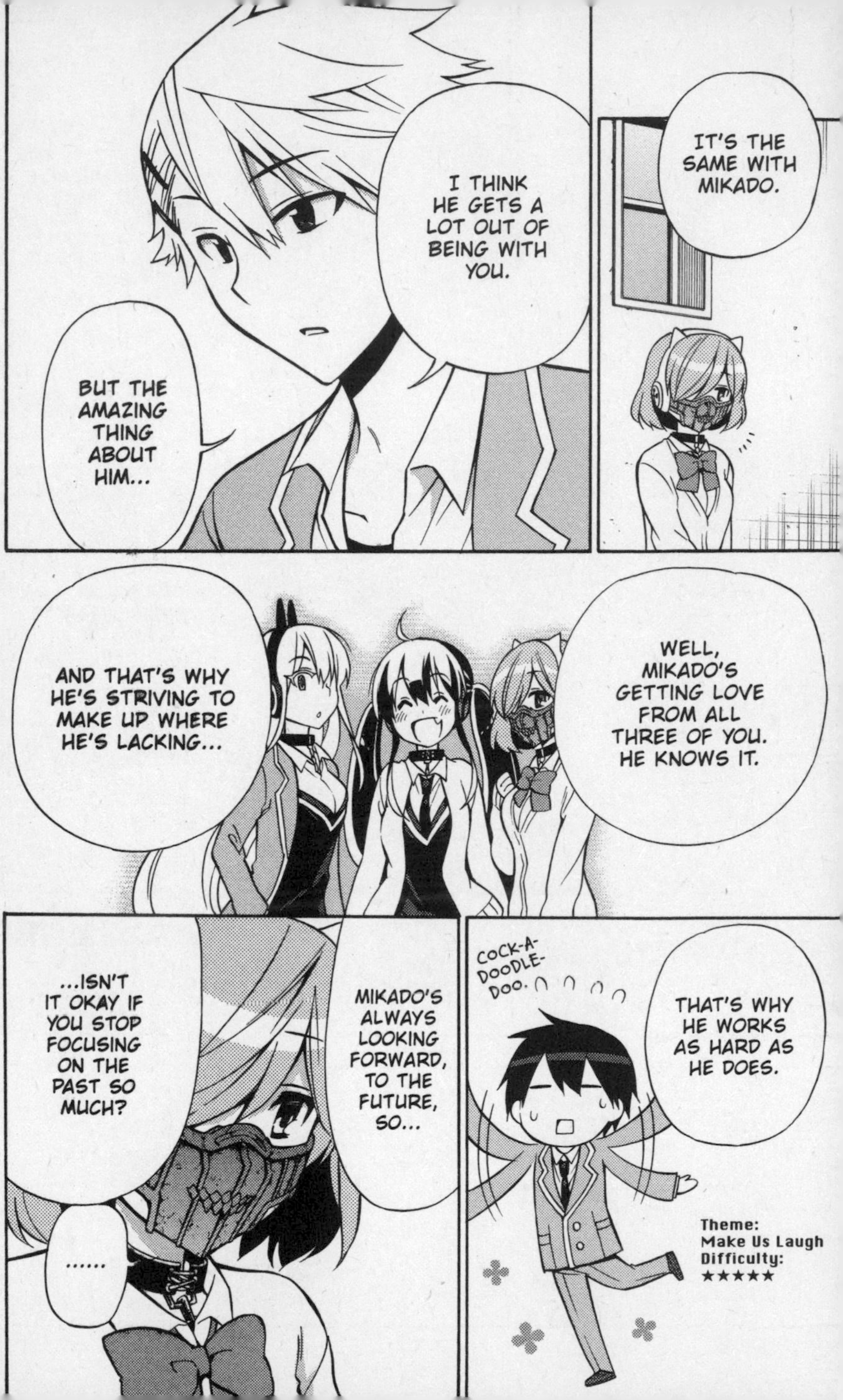
IT'S THE SAME WITH MIKADO.
I THINK HE GETS A LOT OUT OF BEING WITH YOU.
BUT THE AMAZING THING ABOUT HIM...
WELL, MIKADO'S GETTING LOVE FROM ALL THREE OF YOU. HE KNOWS IT.
AND THAT'S WHY HE'S STRIVING TO MAKE UP WHERE HE'S LACKING...
THAT'S WHY HE WORKS AS HARD AS HE DOES.
COCK-A-DOODLE-DOO.
Theme: Make Us Laugh
Difficulty: ★★★★★
MIKADO'S ALWAYS LOOKING FORWARD, TO THE FUTURE, SO...
...ISN'T IT OKAY IF YOU STOP FOCUSING ON THE PAST SO MUCH?
......

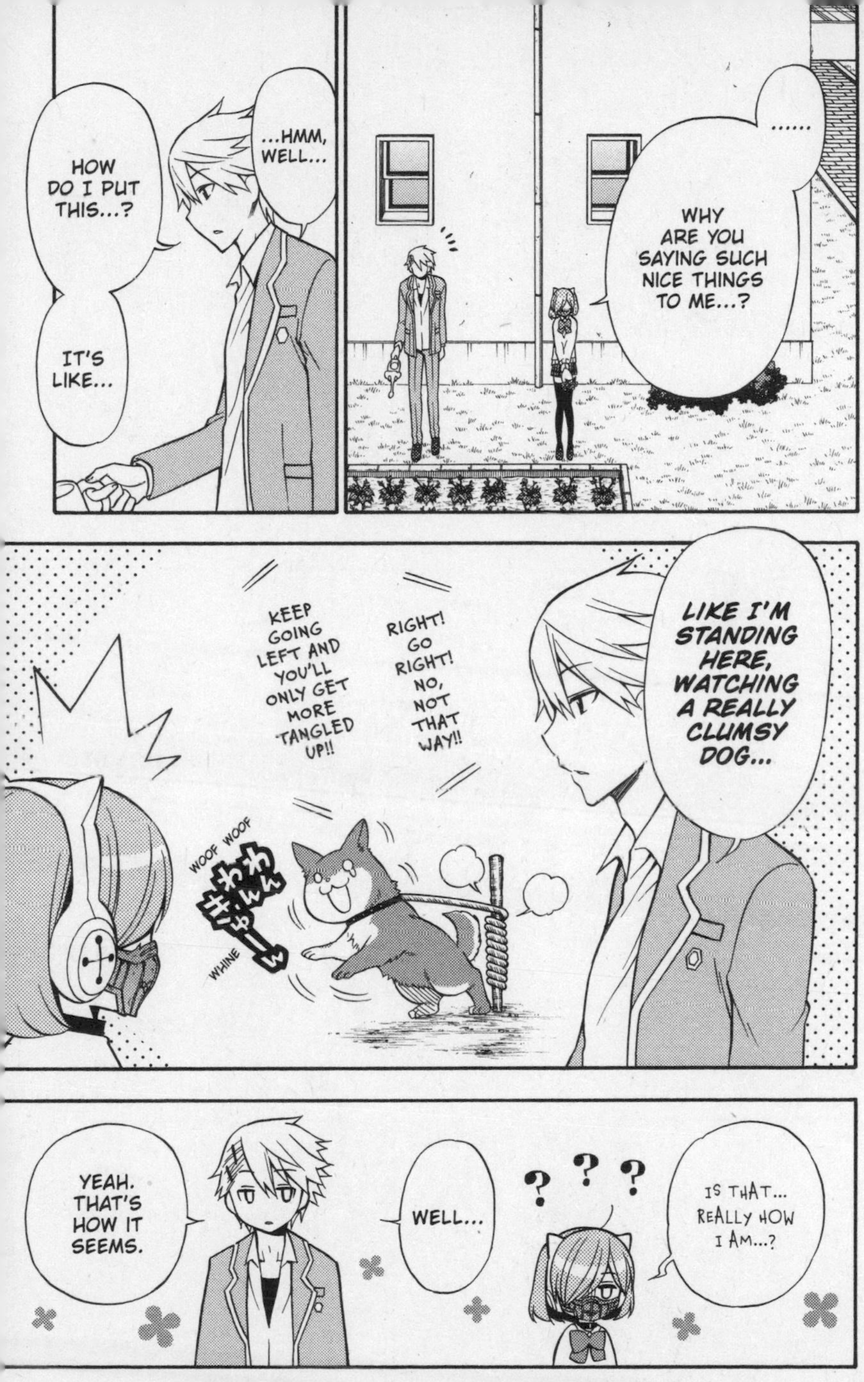
......
WHY ARE YOU SAYING SUCH NICE THINGS TO ME...?
...HMM, WELL...
HOW DO I PUT THIS...?
IT'S LIKE...
LIKE I'M STANDING HERE, WATCHING A REALLY CLUMSY DOG...
RIGHT! GO RIGHT! NO, NOT THAT WAY!!
KEEP GOING LEFT AND YOU'LL ONLY GET MORE TANGLED UP!!
WOOF WOOF
WHINE
IS THAT... REALLY HOW I AM...?
???
WELL...
YEAH. THAT'S HOW IT SEEMS.

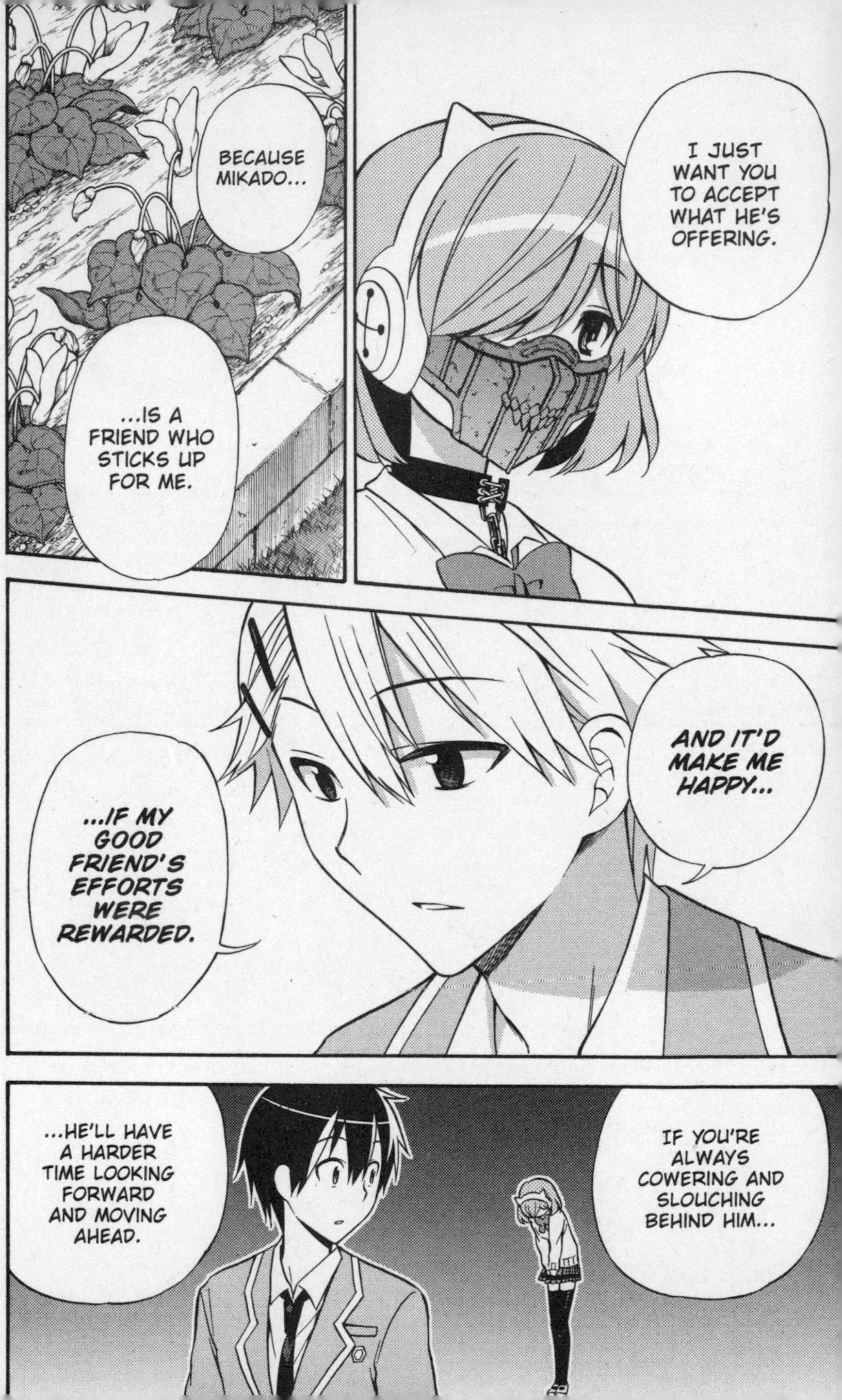
I JUST WANT YOU TO ACCEPT WHAT HE'S OFFERING.
BECAUSE MIKADO...
...IS A FRIEND WHO STICKS UP FOR ME.
AND IT'D MAKE ME HAPPY...
...IF MY GOOD FRIEND'S EFFORTS WERE REWARDED.
IF YOU'RE ALWAYS COWERING AND SLOUCHING BEHIND HIM...
...HE'LL HAVE A HARDER TIME LOOKING FORWARD AND MOVING AHEAD.

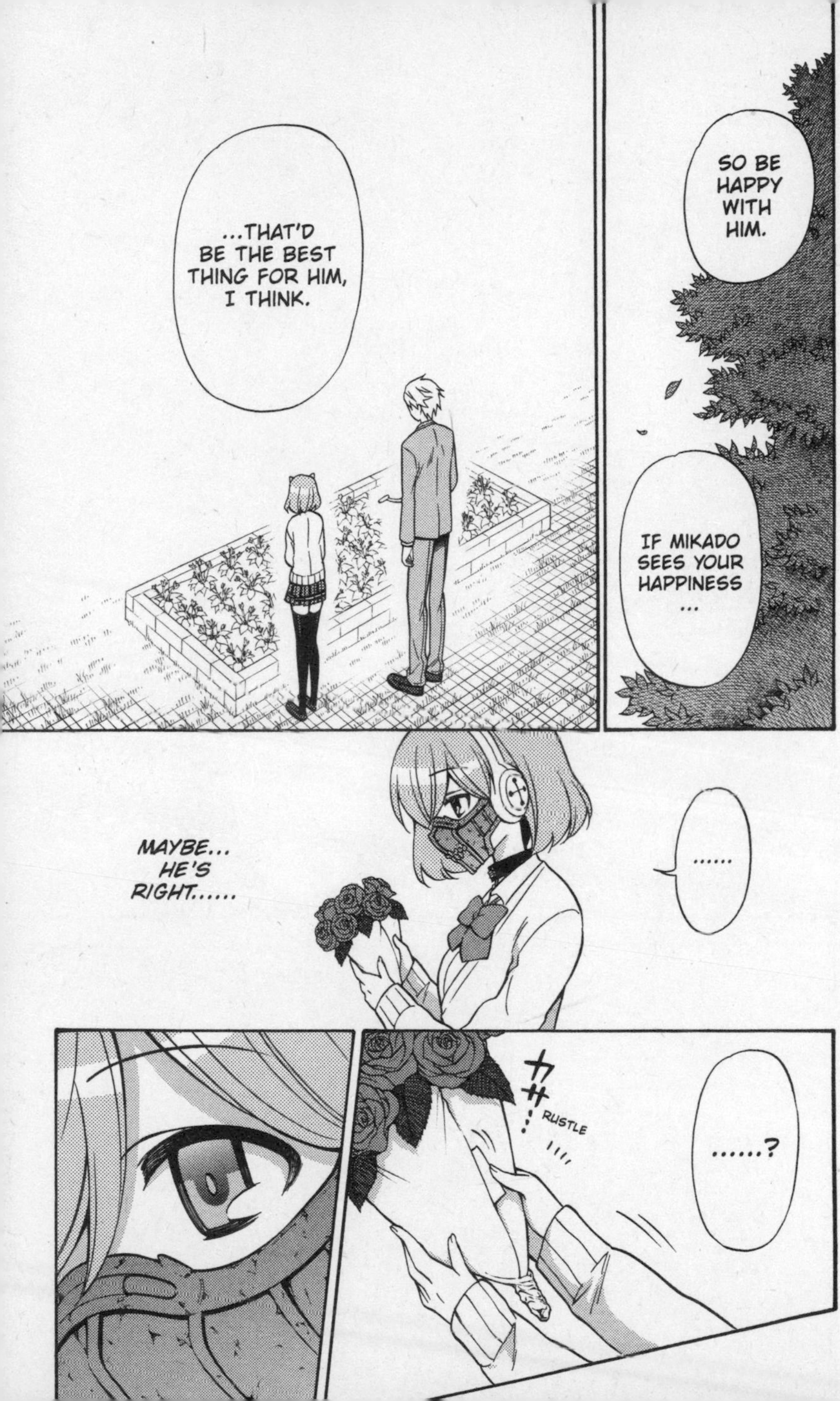
SO BE HAPPY WITH HIM.
IF MIKADO SEES YOUR HAPPINESS ...
...THAT'D BE THE BEST THING FOR HIM, I THINK.
......
MAYBE... HE'S RIGHT......
カサ
RUSTLE
......?

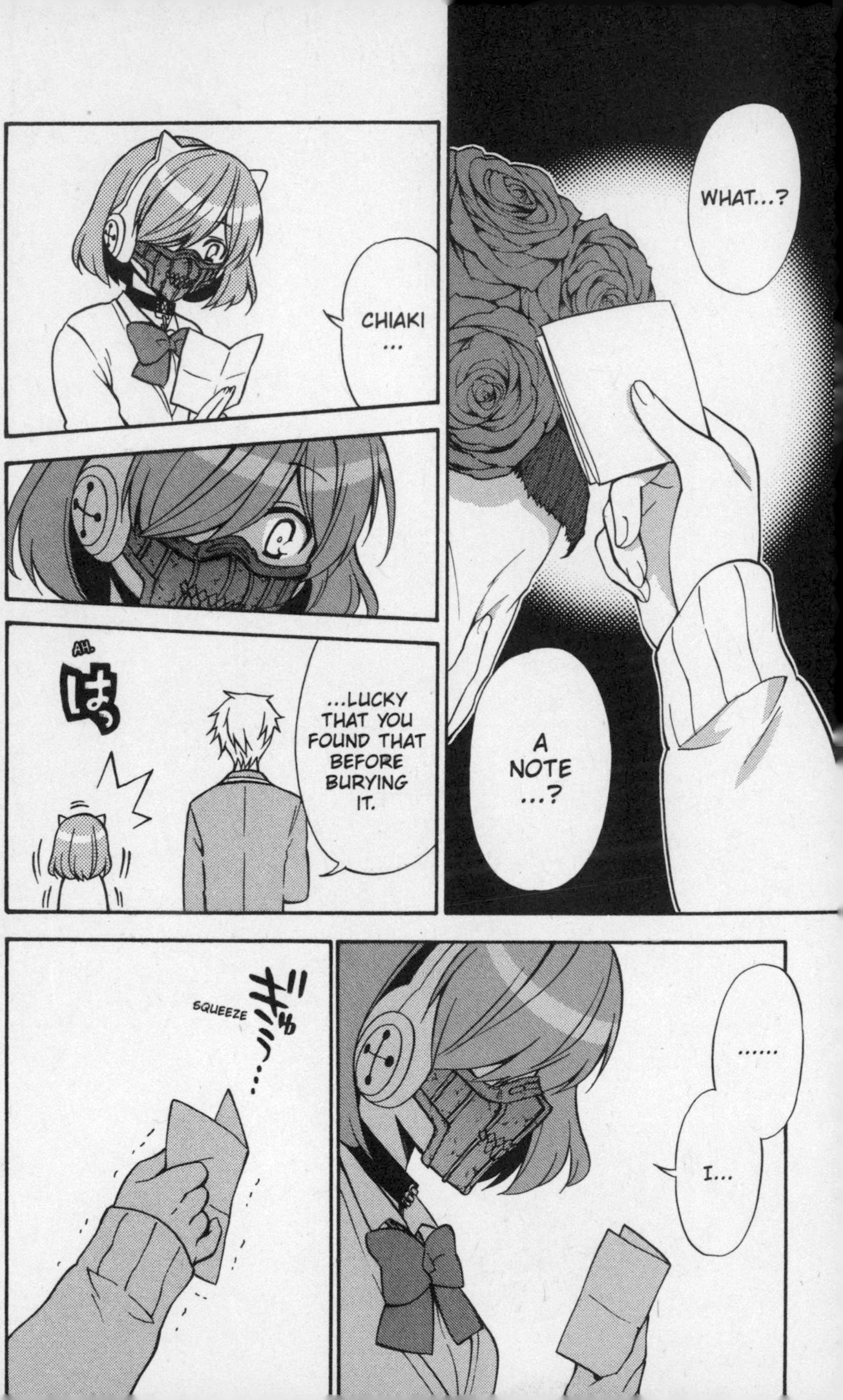
WHAT...?
A NOTE ...?
CHIAKI ...
...LUCKY THAT YOU FOUND THAT BEFORE BURYING IT.
AH.
はっ
......
I...
SQUEEZE

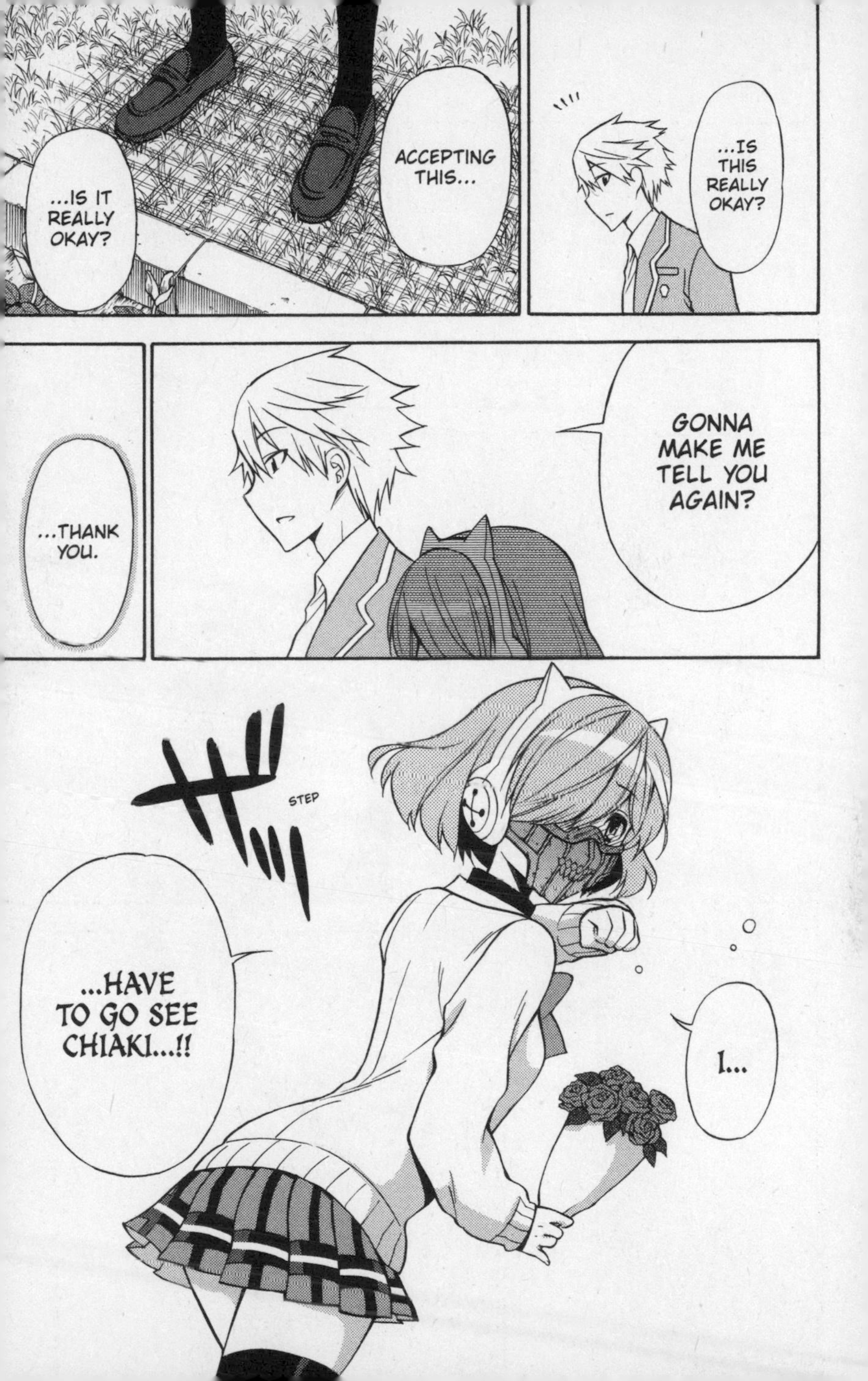
...IS THIS REALLY OKAY?
ACCEPTING THIS...
...IS IT REALLY OKAY?
GONNA MAKE ME TELL YOU AGAIN?
...THANK YOU.
STEP
I...
...HAVE TO GO SEE CHIAKI...!!

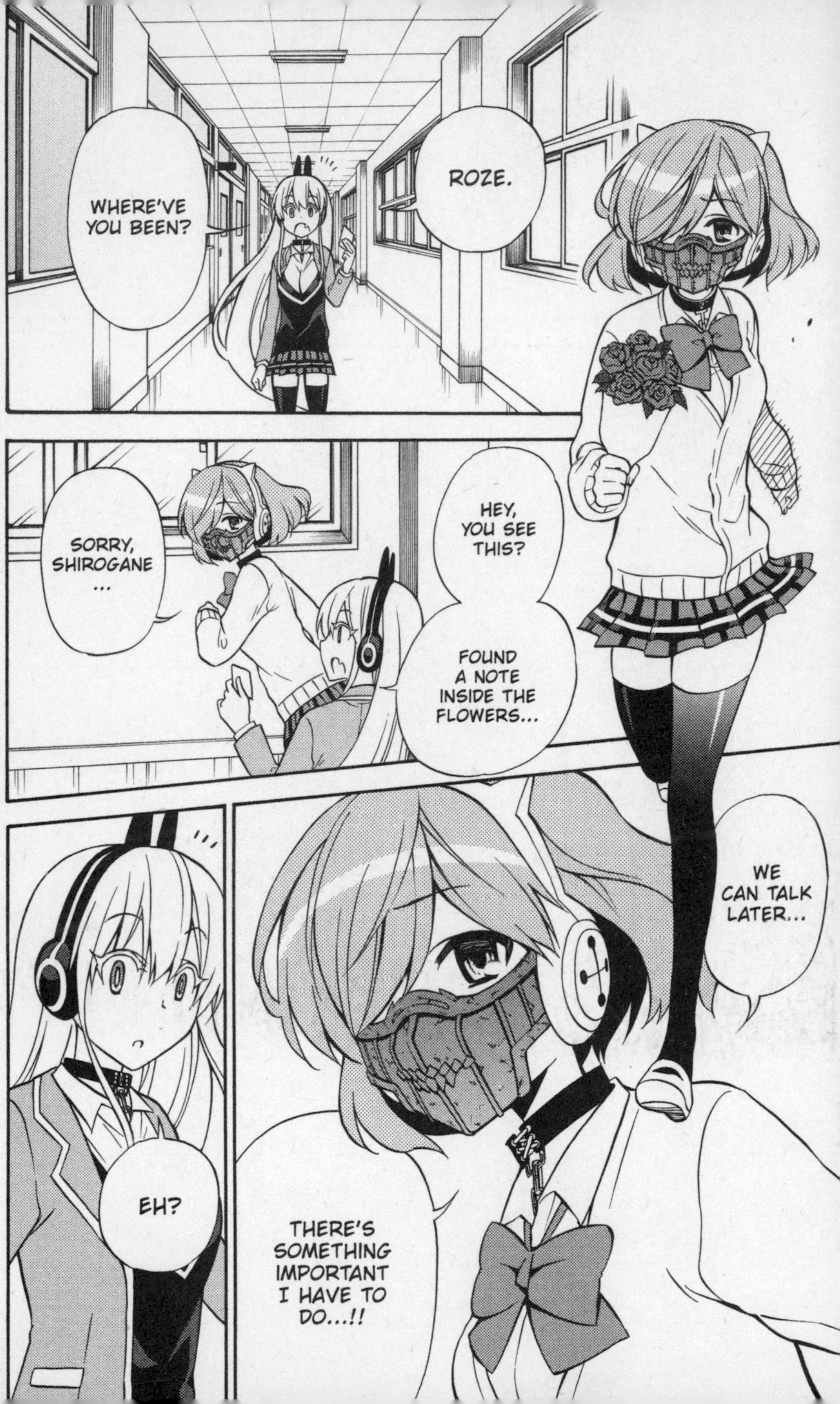
ROZE.
WHERE'VE YOU BEEN?
HEY, YOU SEE THIS?
FOUND A NOTE INSIDE THE FLOWERS...
SORRY, SHIROGANE ...
WE CAN TALK LATER...
THERE'S SOMETHING IMPORTANT I HAVE TO DO...!!
EH?

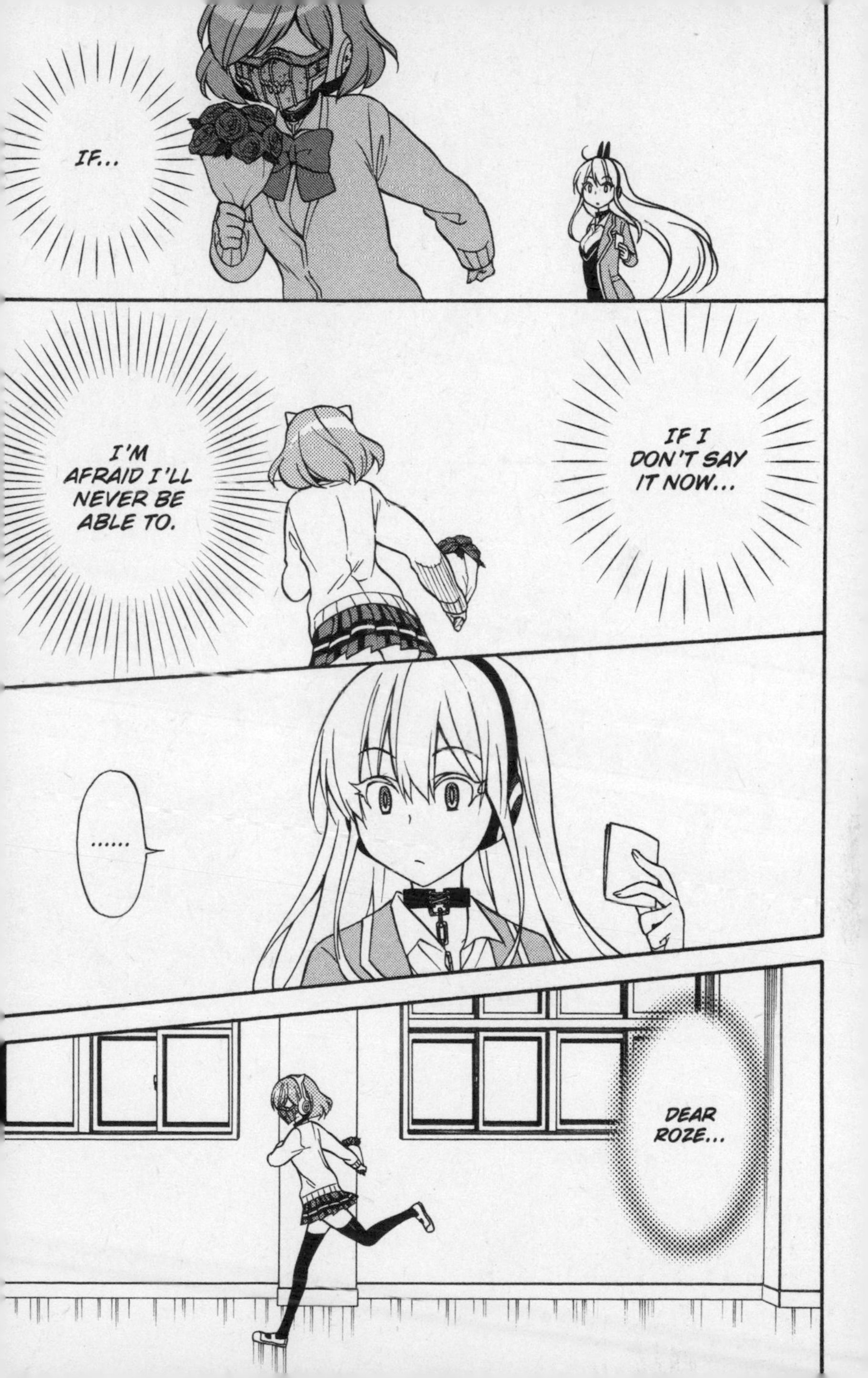
IF...
IF I DON'T SAY IT NOW...
I'M AFRAID I'LL NEVER BE ABLE TO.
......
DEAR ROZE...

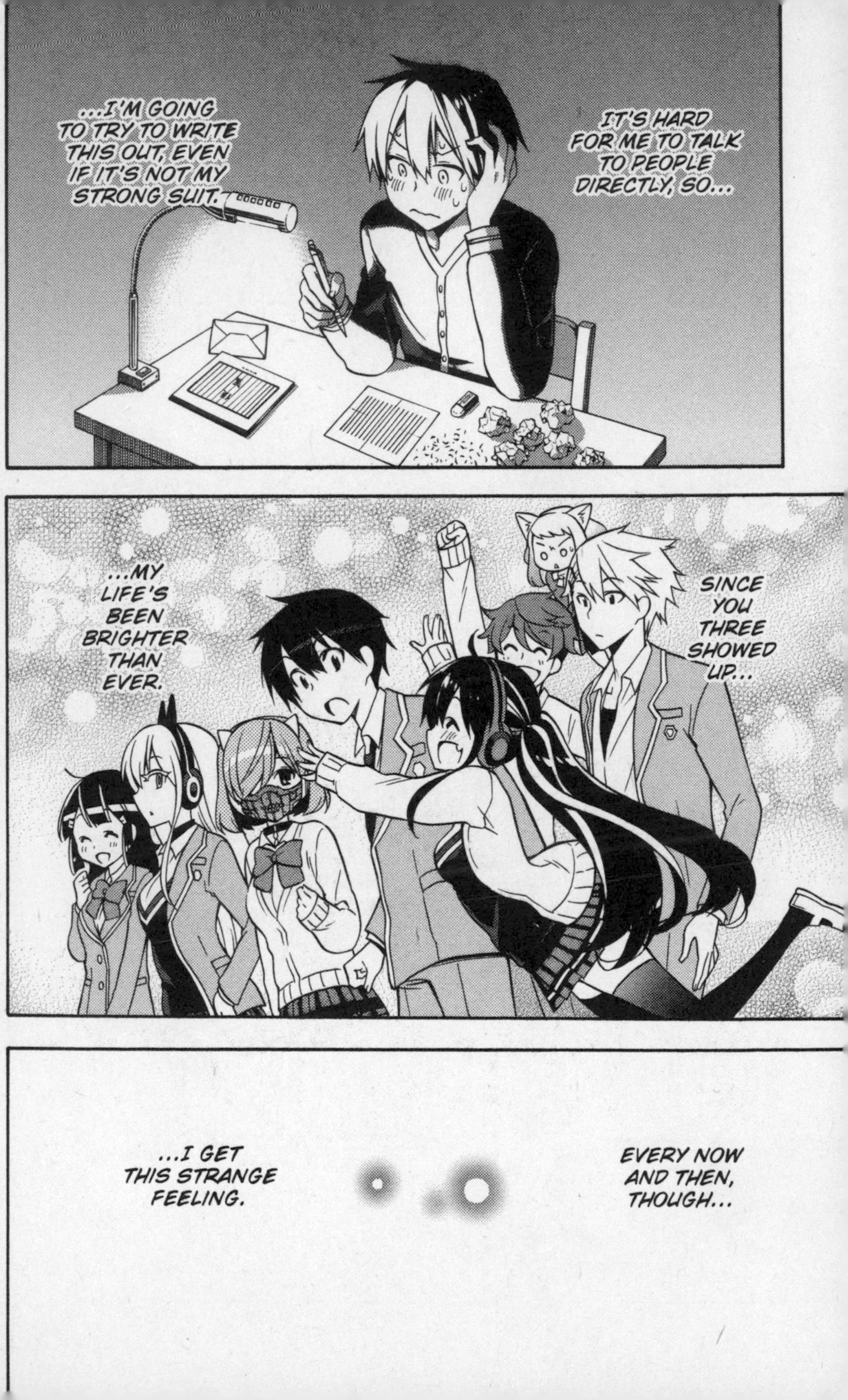
IT'S HARD FOR ME TO TALK TO PEOPLE DIRECTLY, SO...
...I'M GOING TO TRY TO WRITE THIS OUT, EVEN IF IT'S NOT MY STRONG SUIT.
SINCE YOU THREE SHOWED UP...
...MY LIFE'S BEEN BRIGHTER THAN EVER.
EVERY NOW AND THEN, THOUGH...
...I GET THIS STRANGE FEELING.

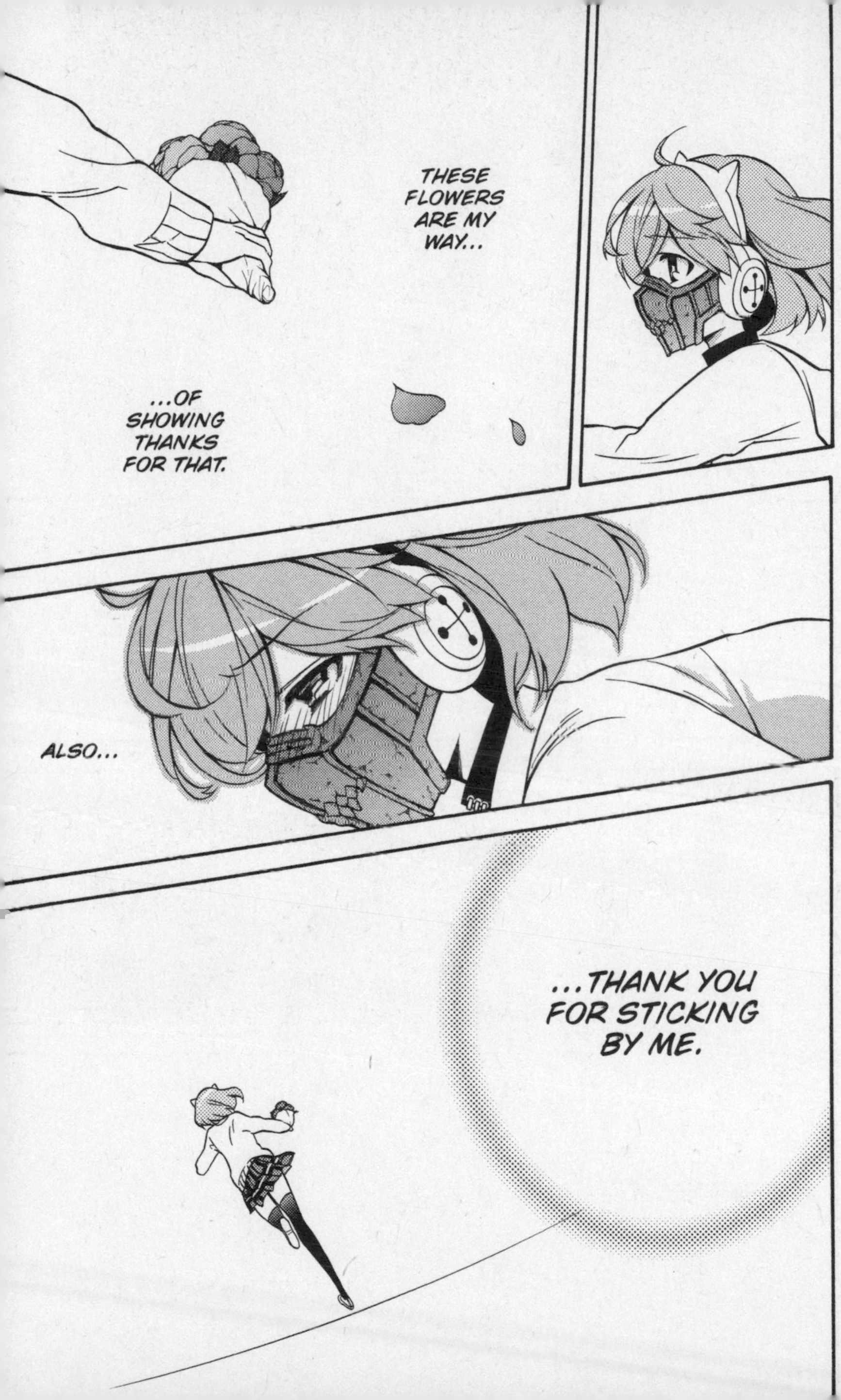
THESE FLOWERS ARE MY WAY...
...OF SHOWING THANKS FOR THAT.
ALSO...
...THANK YOU FOR STICKING BY ME.

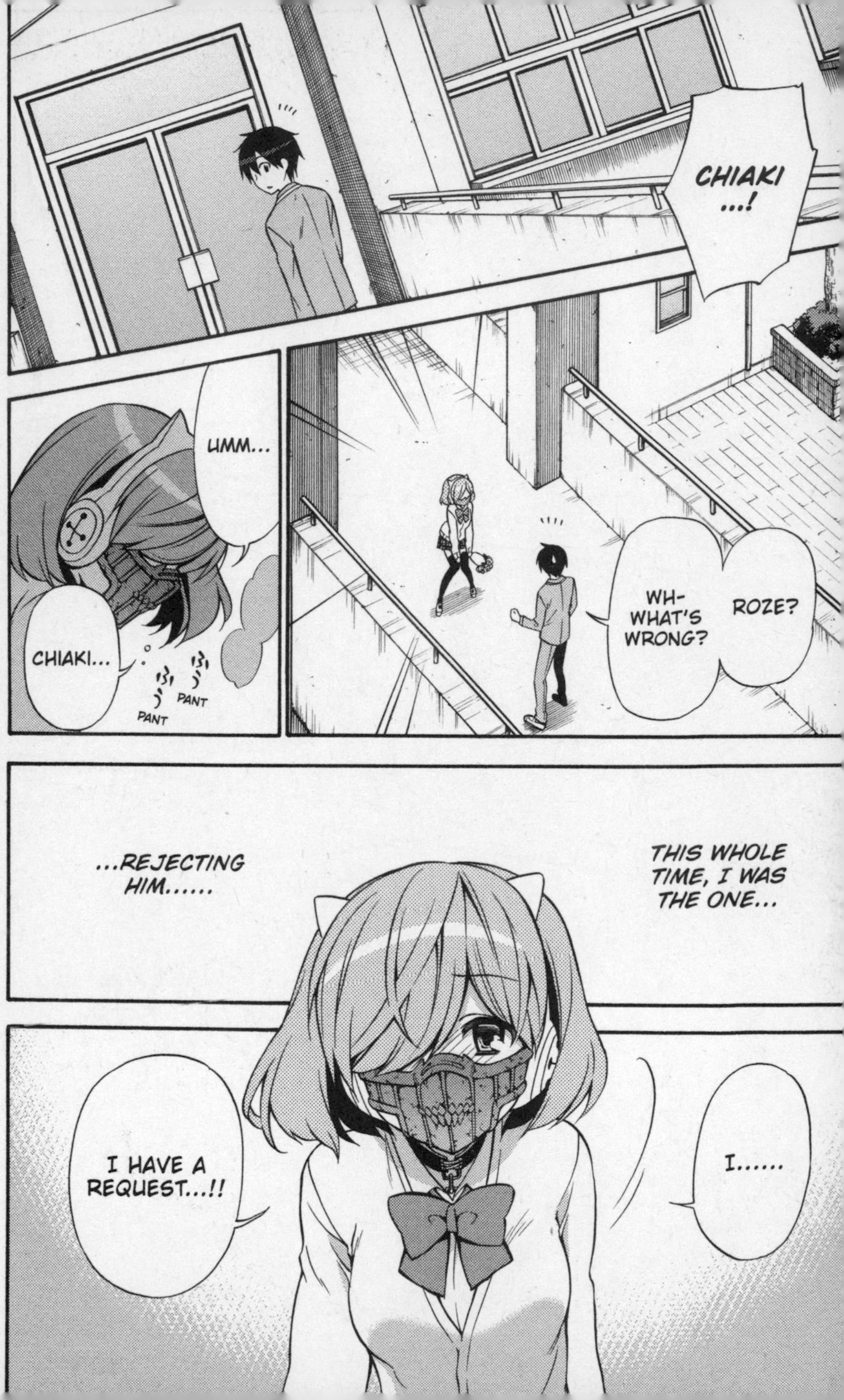
CHIAKI ...!
ROZE?
WH- WHAT'S WRONG?
UMM...
CHIAKI...
PANT
PANT
THIS WHOLE TIME, I WAS THE ONE...
...REJECTING HIM......
I......
I HAVE A REQUEST...!!

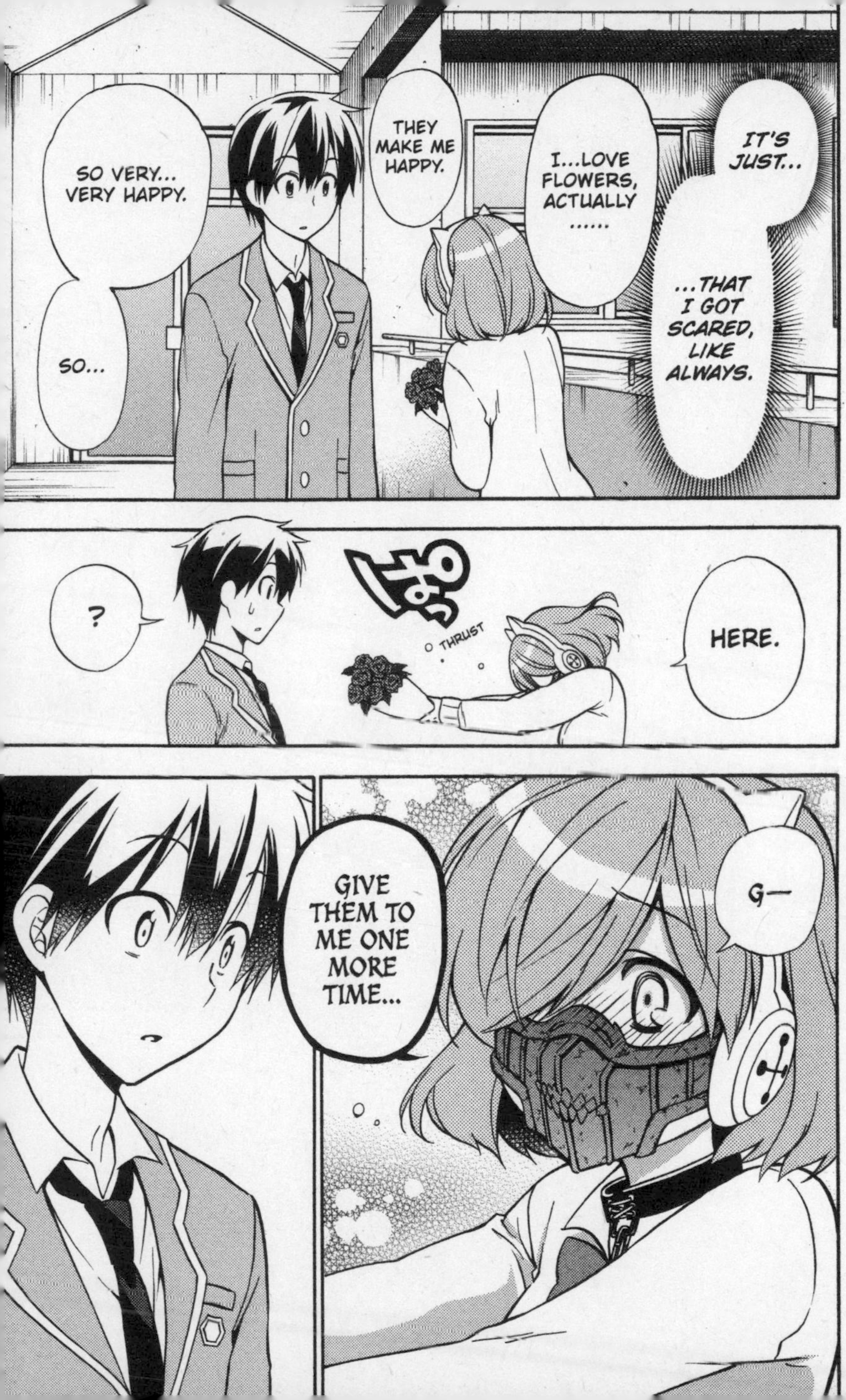
IT'S JUST...
...THAT I GOT SCARED, LIKE ALWAYS.
I...LOVE FLOWERS, ACTUALLY ......
THEY MAKE ME HAPPY.
SO VERY... VERY HAPPY.
SO...
HERE.
THRUST
?
G—
GIVE THEM TO ME ONE MORE TIME...

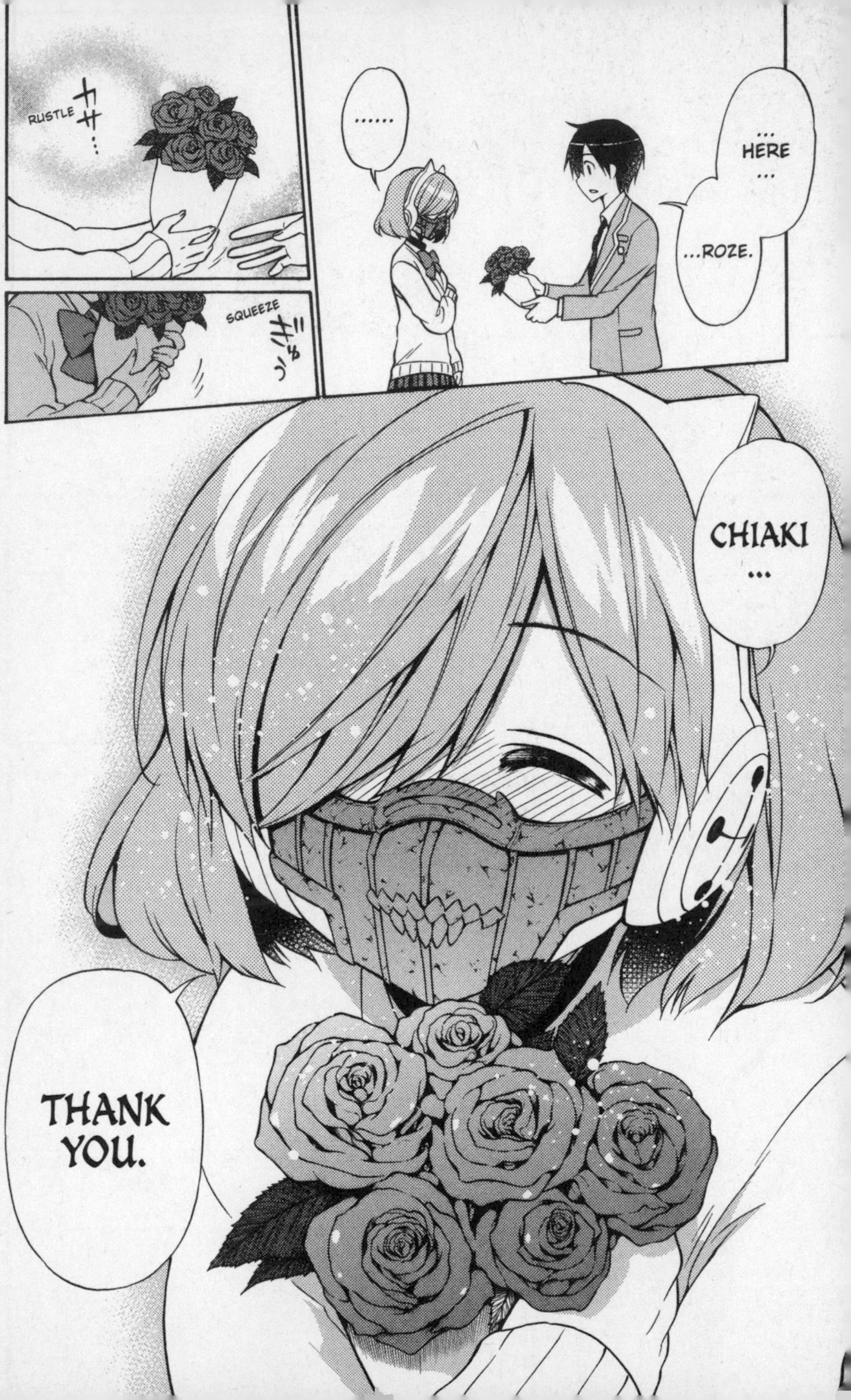
... HERE ...
...ROZE.
......
RUSTLE
SQUEEZE
CHIAKI ...
THANK YOU.

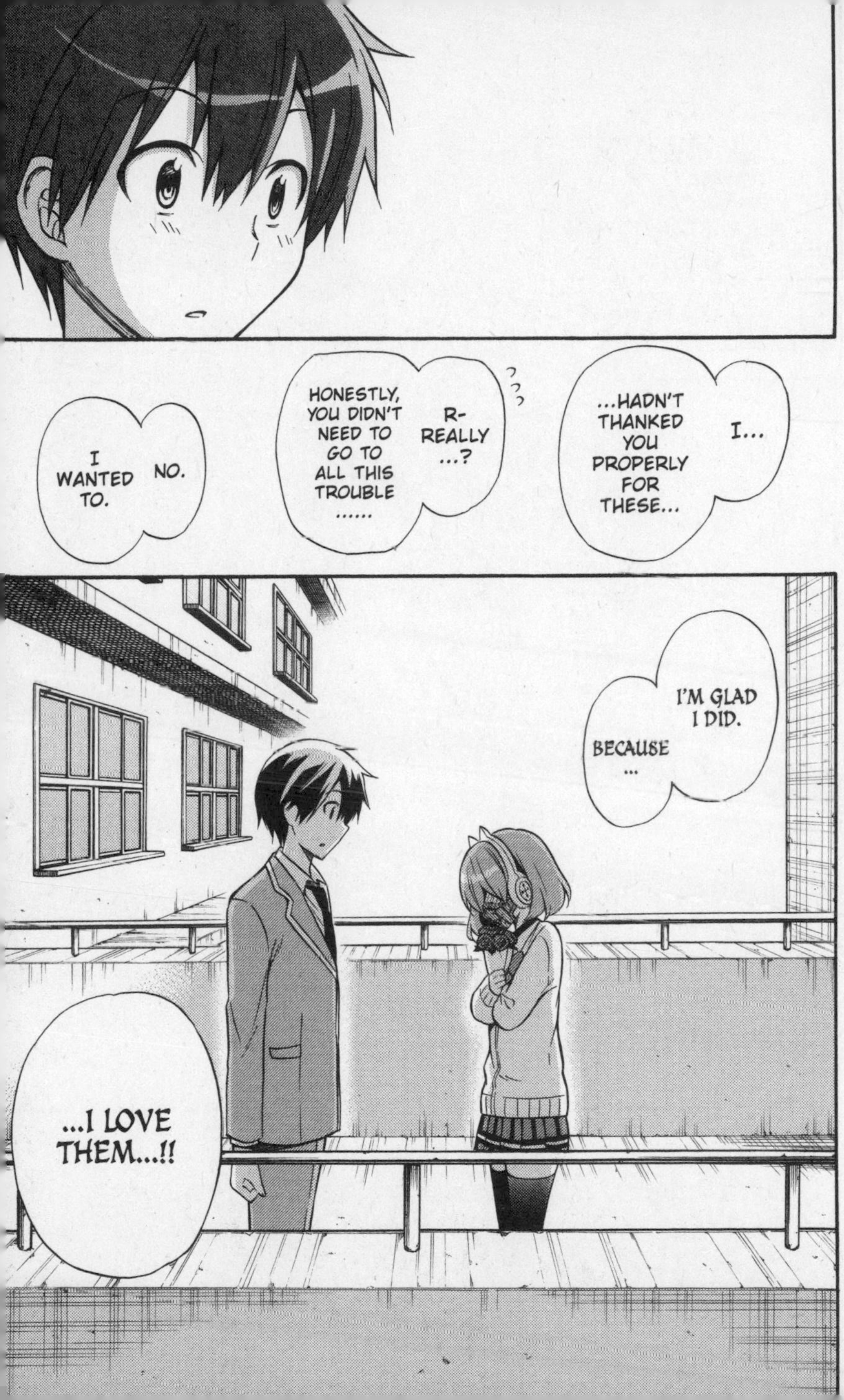
I...
...HADN'T THANKED YOU PROPERLY FOR THESE...
R-REALLY ...?
HONESTLY, YOU DIDN'T NEED TO GO TO ALL THIS TROUBLE ......
NO.
I WANTED TO.
I'M GLAD I DID.
BECAUSE ...
...I LOVE THEM...!!

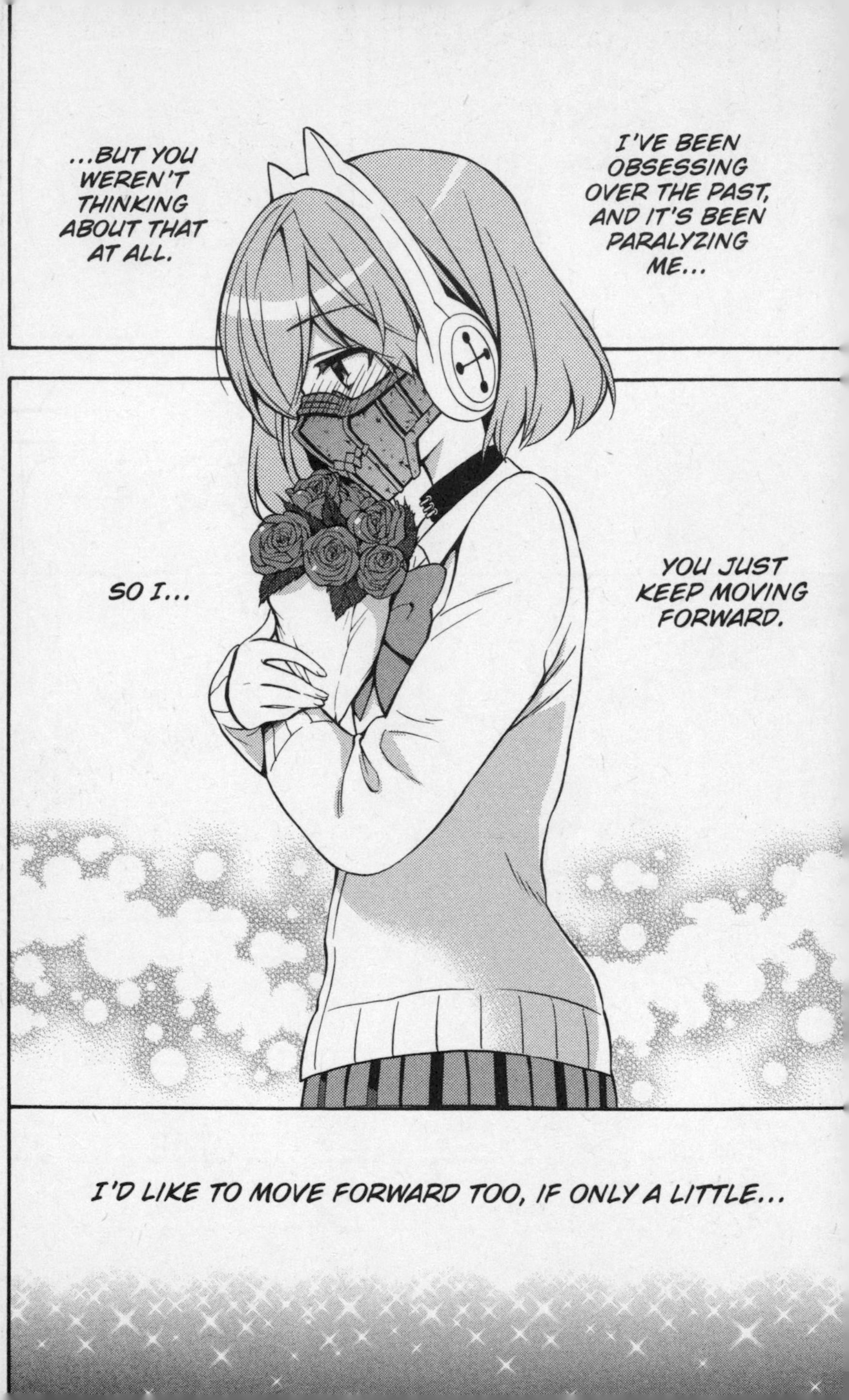
I'VE BEEN OBSESSING OVER THE PAST, AND IT'S BEEN PARALYZING ME...
...BUT YOU WEREN'T THINKING ABOUT THAT AT ALL.
YOU JUST KEEP MOVING FORWARD.
SO I...
I'D LIKE TO MOVE FORWARD TOO, IF ONLY A LITTLE...

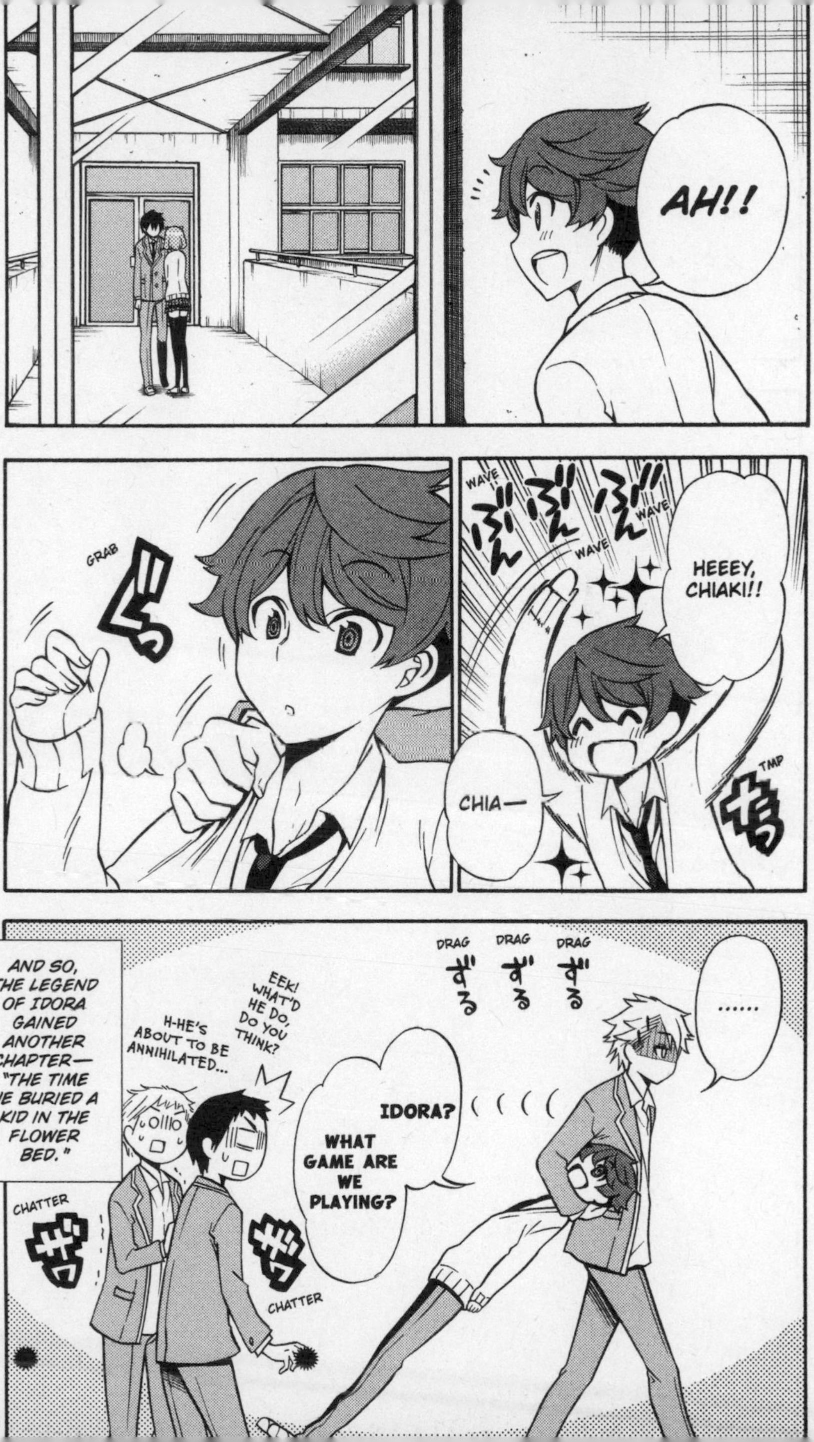
AH!!
WAVE WAVE WAVE
HEEEY, CHIAKI!!
CHIA—
TMP
GRAB
......
DRAG DRAG DRAG
ずる ずる ずる
IDORA?
WHAT GAME ARE WE PLAYING?
EEK! WHAT'D HE DO, DO YOU THINK?
H-HE'S ABOUT TO BE ANNIHILATED...
AND SO, THE LEGEND OF IDORA GAINED ANOTHER CHAPTER— "THE TIME HE BURIED A KID IN THE FLOWER BED."
CHATTER
CHATTER

TODAY'S CERBERUS 🐾

I SEE.

I RESEARCHED A WHOLE BUNCH OF FLOWER SYMBOLISM TO WRITE THIS CHAPTER BUT DIDN'T END UP USING ANY OF IT.

A WATERING CAN'S ANECDOTE

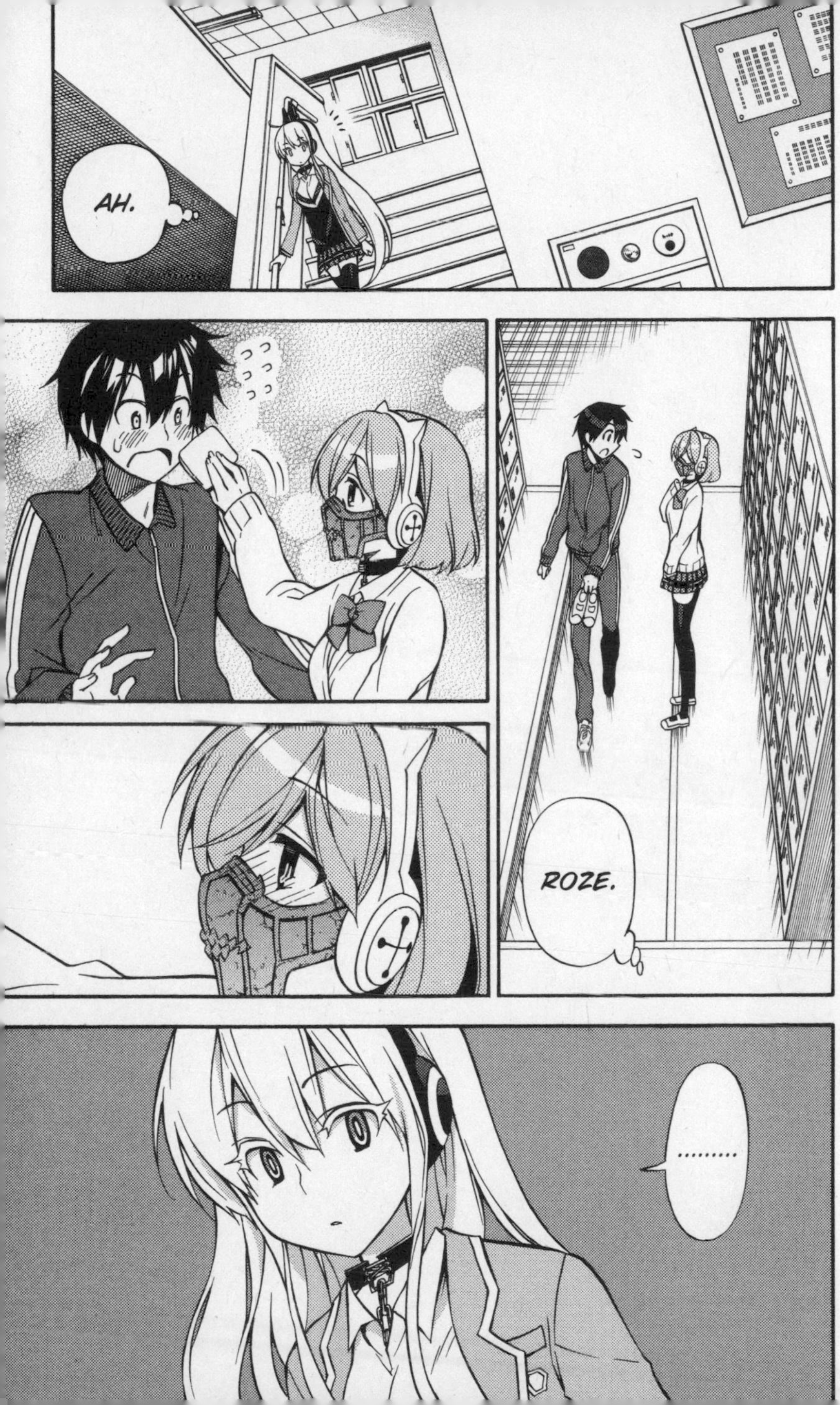
AH.
ROZE.
....

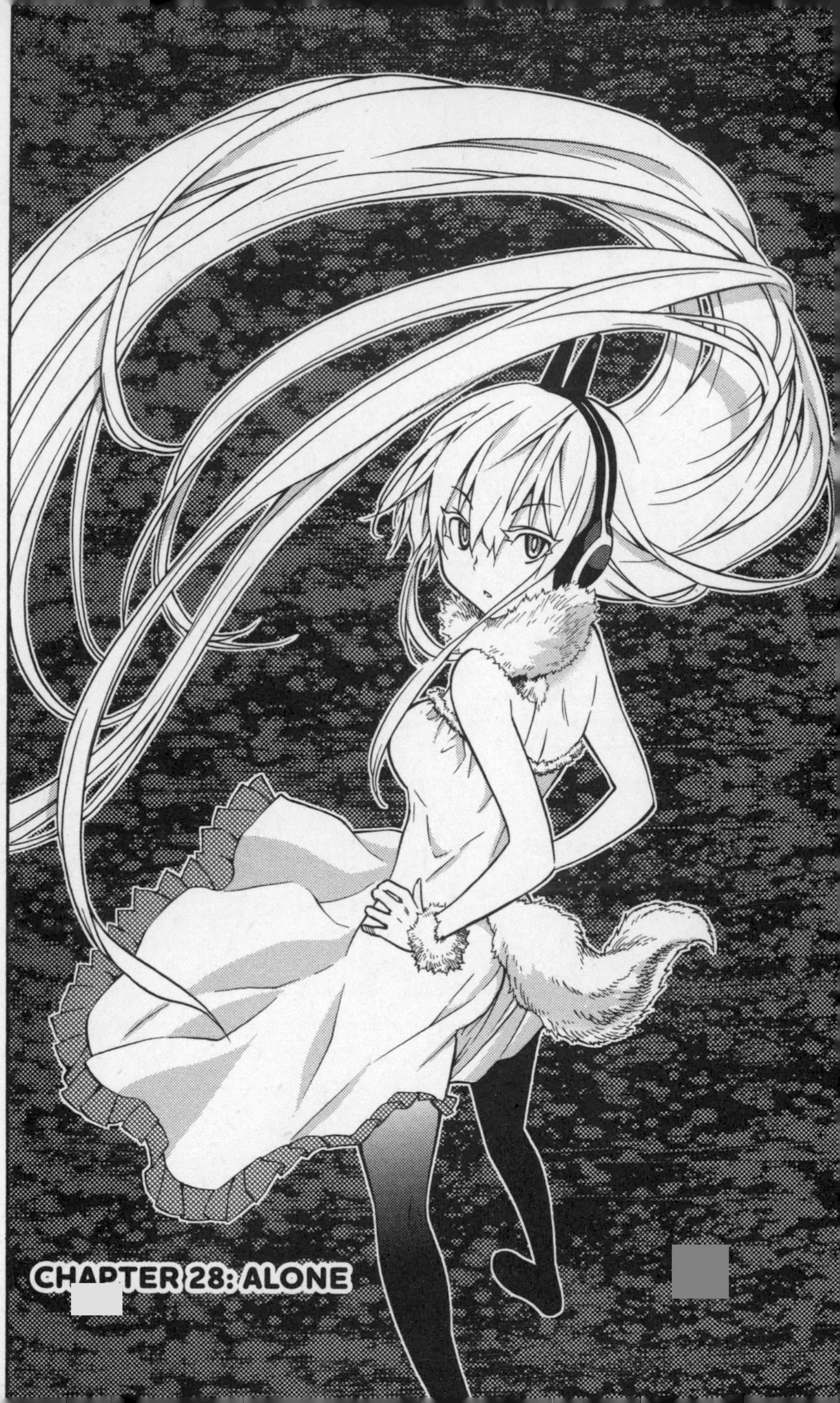
CHAPTER 28: ALONE

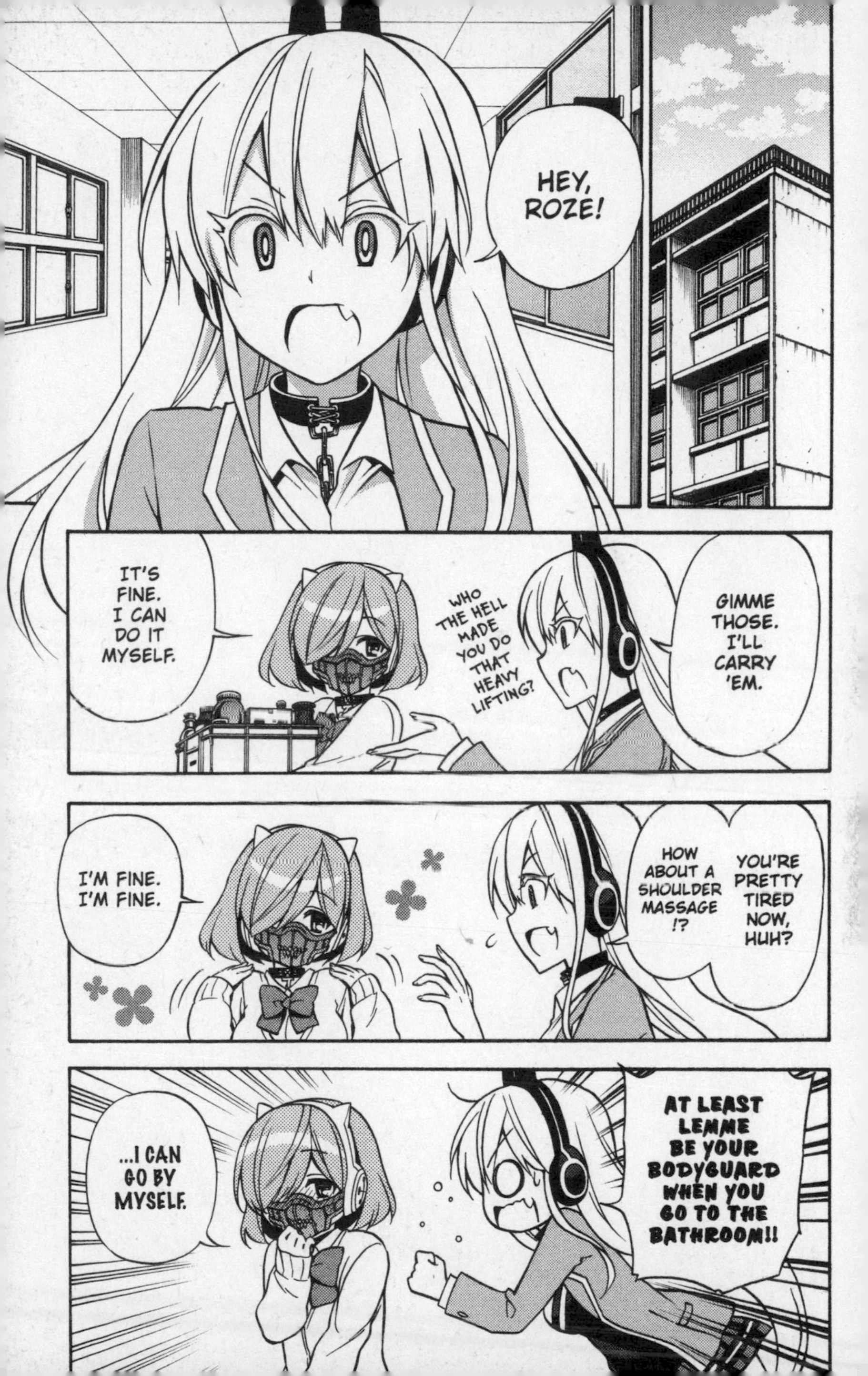
HEY, ROZE!
GIMME THOSE. I'LL CARRY 'EM.
WHO THE HELL MADE YOU DO THAT HEAVY LIFTING?
IT'S FINE. I CAN DO IT MYSELF.
YOU'RE PRETTY TIRED NOW, HUH?
HOW ABOUT A SHOULDER MASSAGE!?
I'M FINE. I'M FINE.
AT LEAST LEMME BE YOUR BODYGUARD WHEN YOU GO TO THE BATHROOM!!
...I CAN GO BY MYSELF.

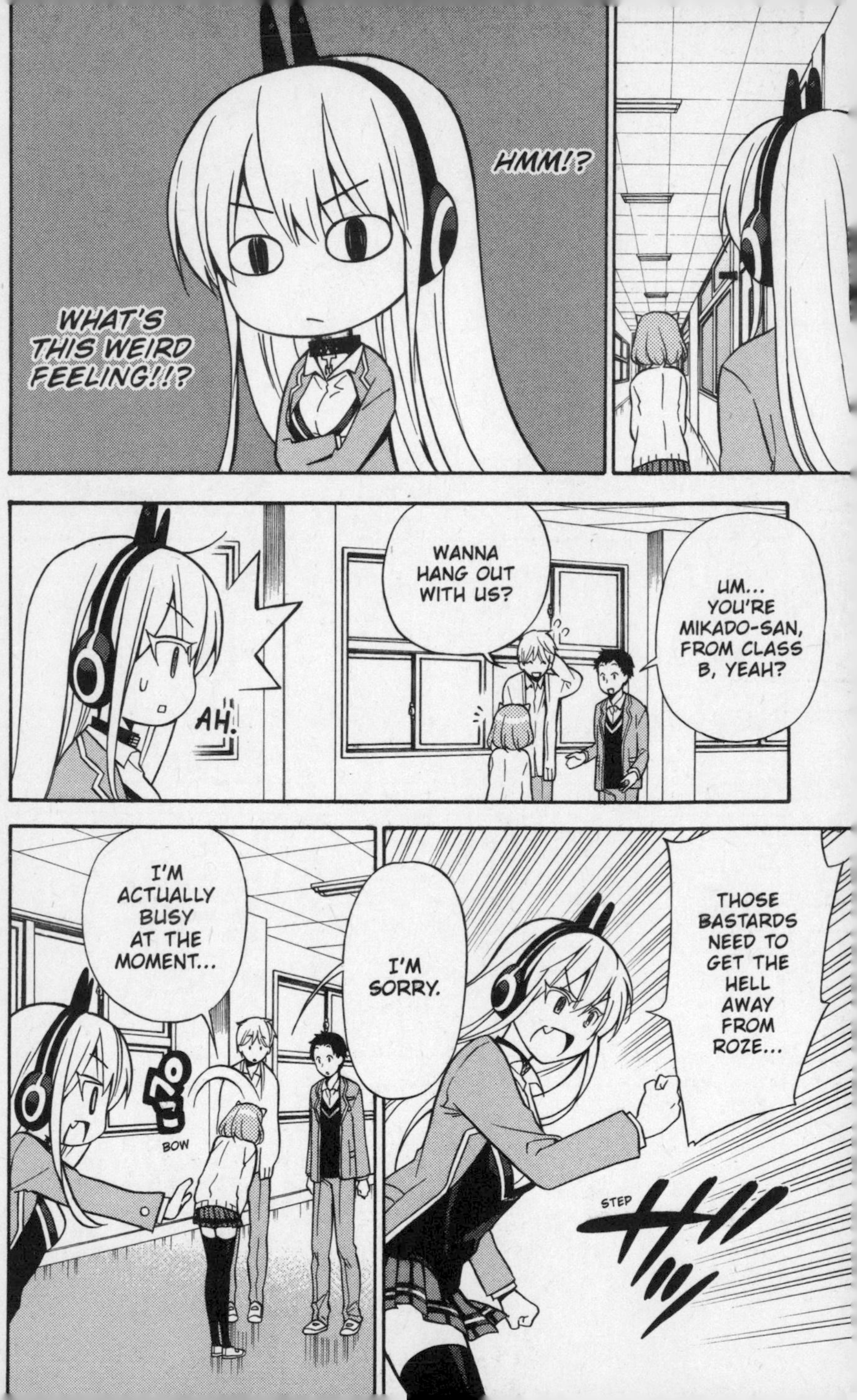
HMM!?
WHAT'S THIS WEIRD FEELING!!?
UM... YOU'RE MIKADO-SAN, FROM CLASS B, YEAH?
WANNA HANG OUT WITH US?
AH.
THOSE BASTARDS NEED TO GET THE HELL AWAY FROM ROZE...
STEP
I'M SORRY.
I'M ACTUALLY BUSY AT THE MOMENT...
BOW

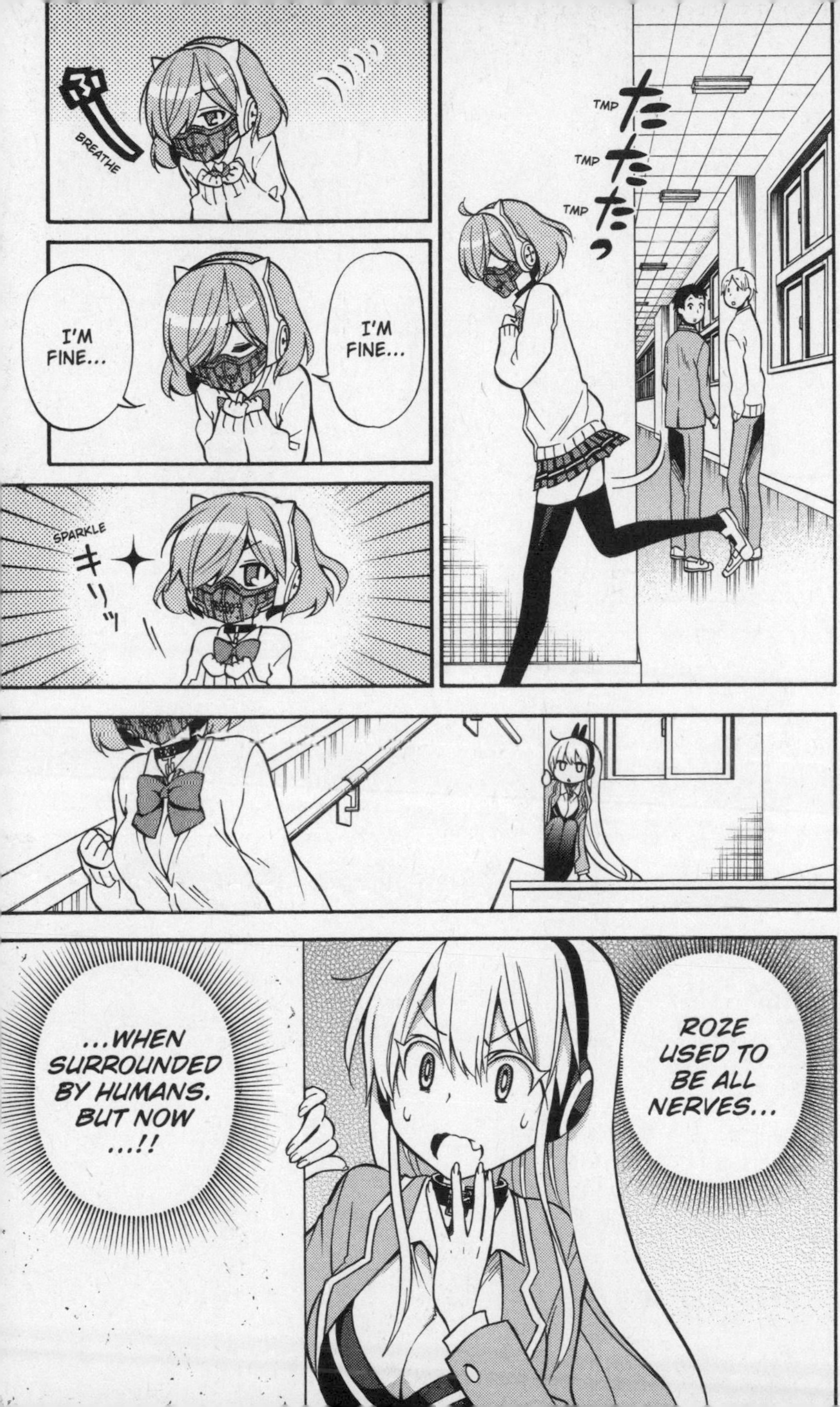
TMP
TMP
TMP
たたたっ
BREATHE
I'M FINE...
I'M FINE...
SPARKLE
キリッ
ROZE USED TO BE ALL NERVES...
...WHEN SURROUNDED BY HUMANS. BUT NOW ...!!

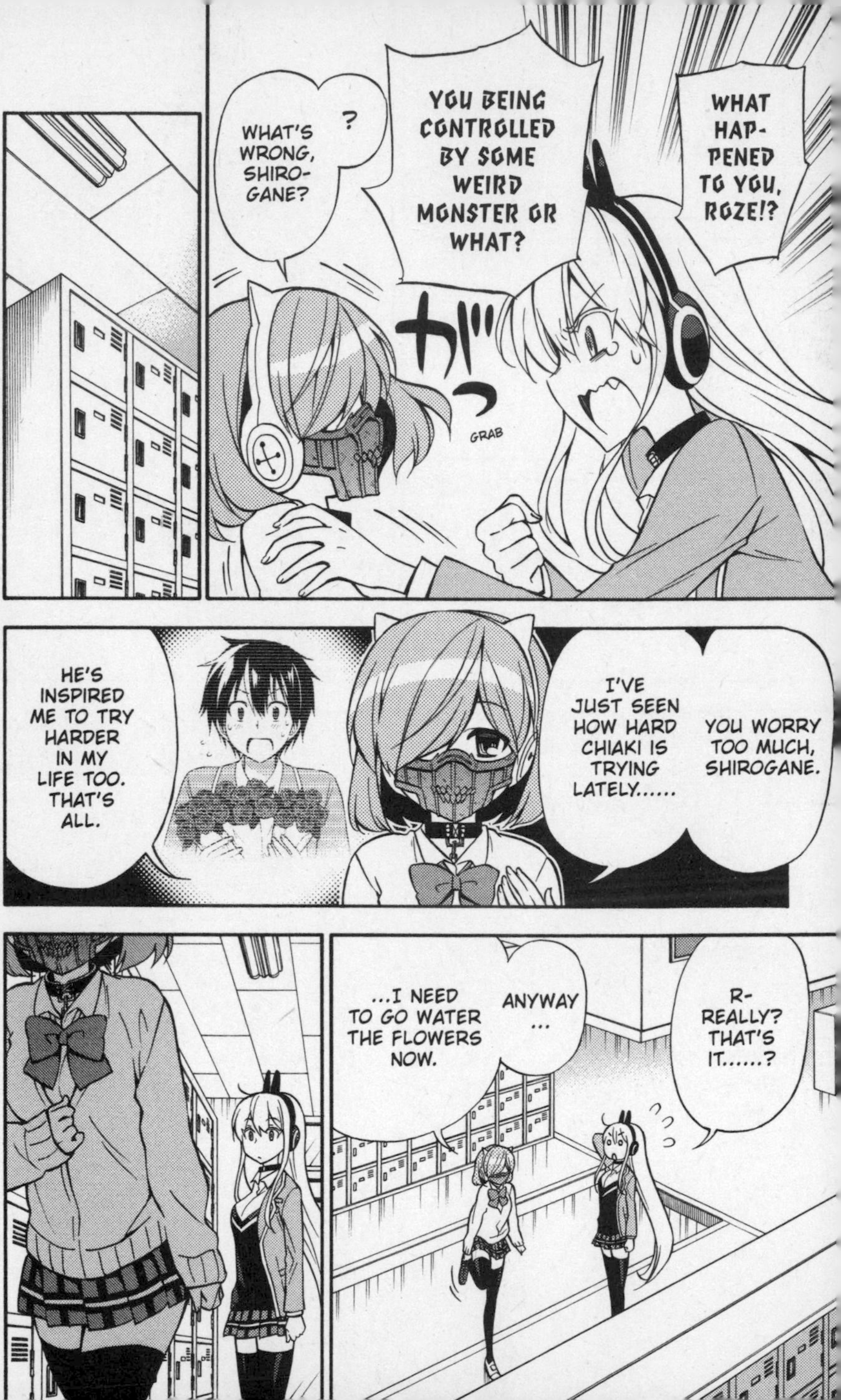
WHAT HAPPENED TO YOU, ROZE!?
YOU BEING CONTROLLED BY SOME WEIRD MONSTER OR WHAT?
GRAB
WHAT'S WRONG, SHIROGANE?
?
YOU WORRY TOO MUCH, SHIROGANE.
I'VE JUST SEEN HOW HARD CHIAKI IS TRYING LATELY......
HE'S INSPIRED ME TO TRY HARDER IN MY LIFE TOO. THAT'S ALL.
R-REALLY? THAT'S IT......?
ANYWAY ...
...I NEED TO GO WATER THE FLOWERS NOW.

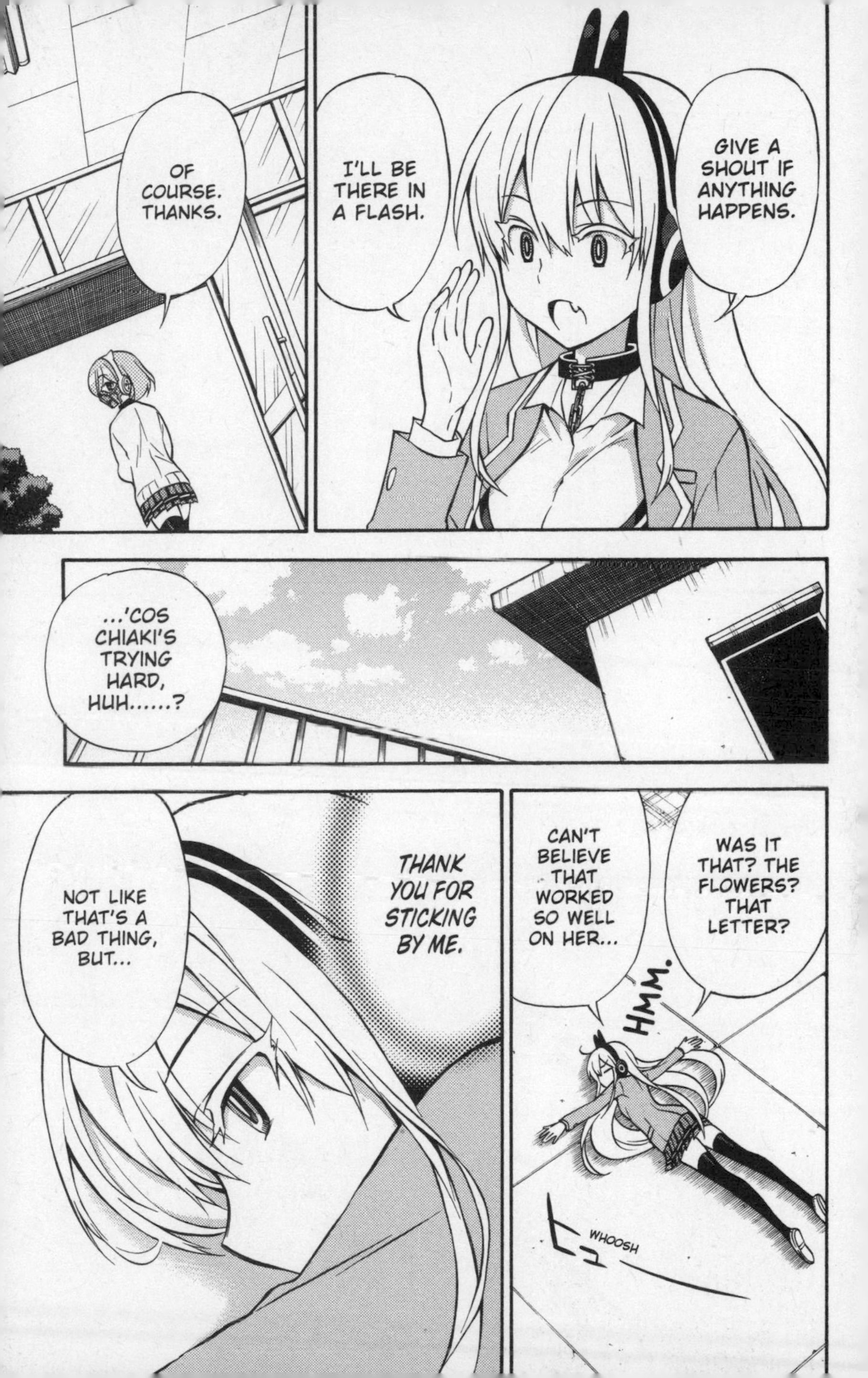
GIVE A SHOUT IF ANYTHING HAPPENS.
I'LL BE THERE IN A FLASH.
OF COURSE. THANKS.
...'COS CHIAKI'S TRYING HARD, HUH......?
WAS IT THAT? THE FLOWERS? THAT LETTER?
HMM.
CAN'T BELIEVE THAT WORKED SO WELL ON HER...
WHOOSH
THANK YOU FOR STICKING BY ME.
NOT LIKE THAT'S A BAD THING, BUT...

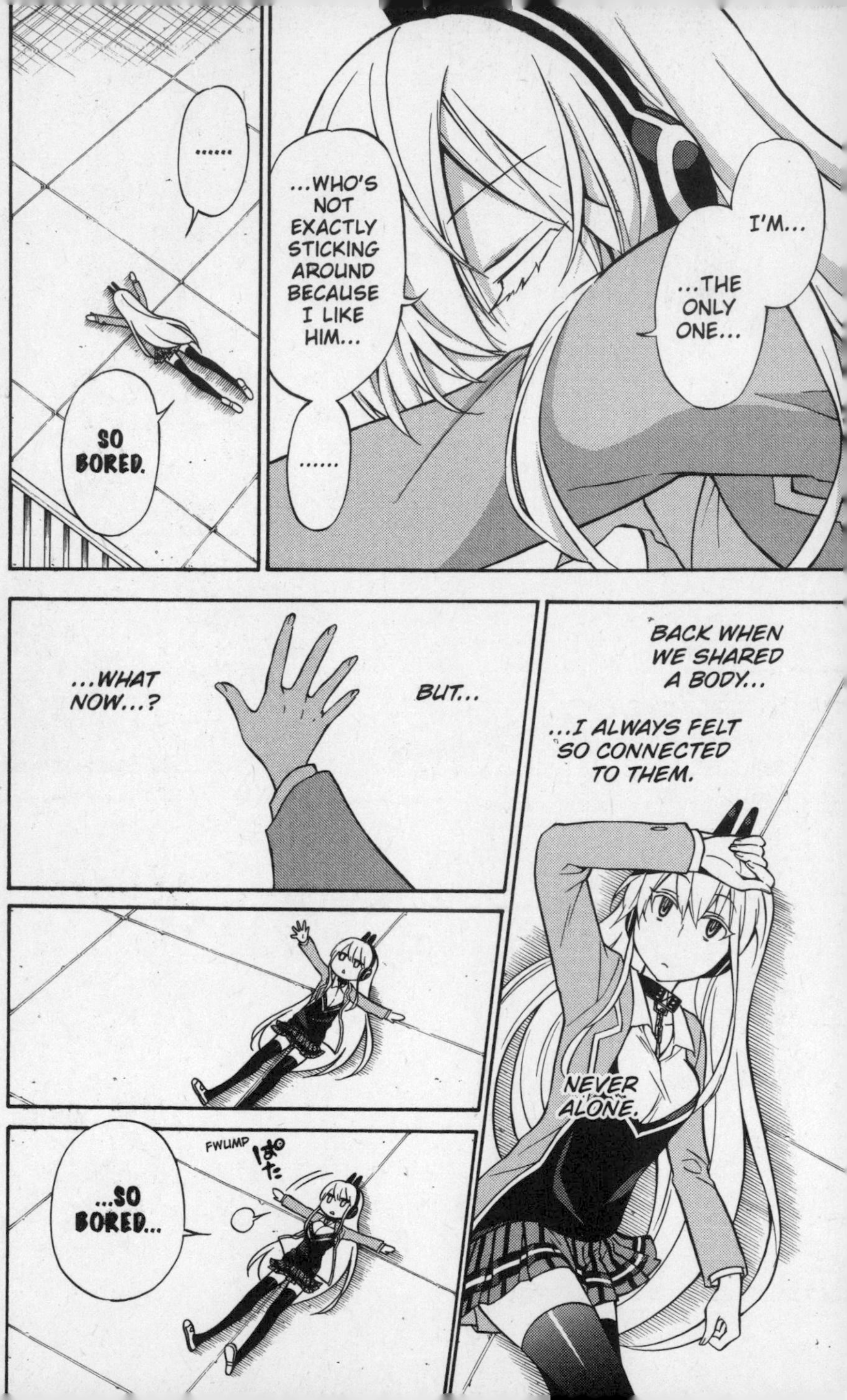

I'M...
...THE ONLY ONE...
...WHO'S NOT EXACTLY STICKING AROUND BECAUSE I LIKE HIM...
......
......
SO BORED.
BACK WHEN WE SHARED A BODY...
...I ALWAYS FELT SO CONNECTED TO THEM.
NEVER ALONE.
BUT...
...WHAT NOW...?
FWUMP
ぱた
...SO BORED...

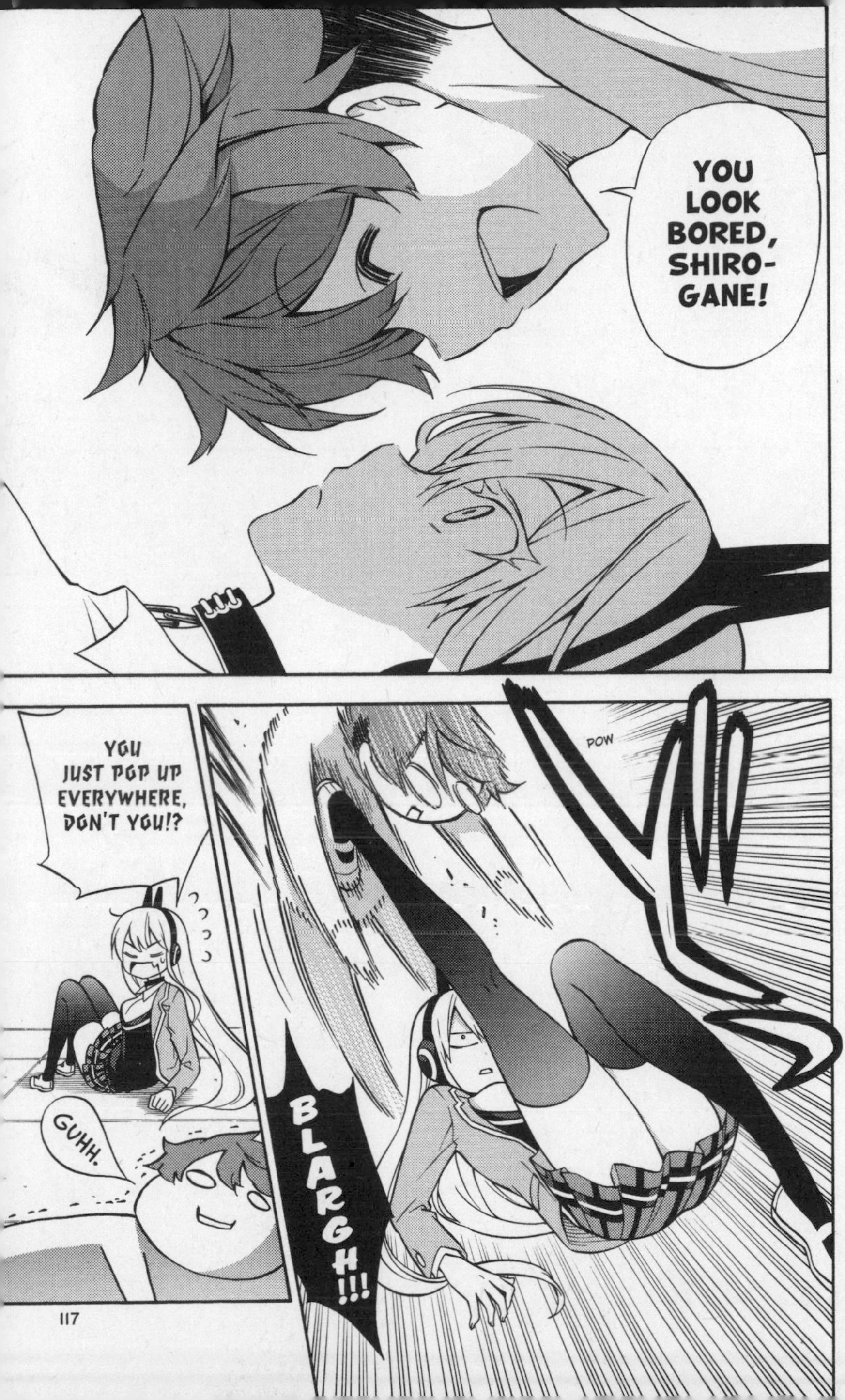
YOU LOOK BORED, SHIRO-GANE!
POW
BLARGH!!!
YOU JUST POP UP EVERYWHERE, DON'T YOU!?
GUHH.

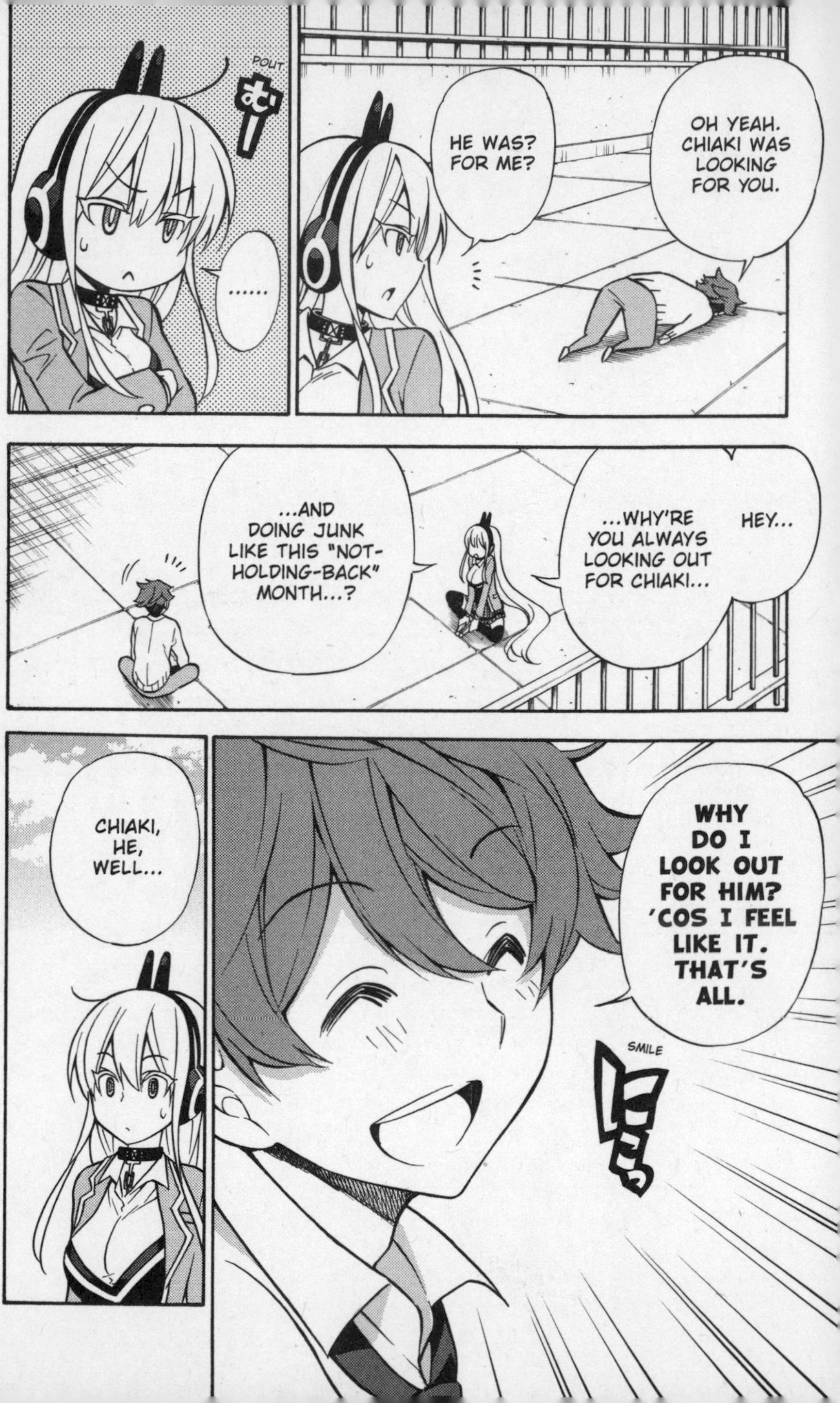
OH YEAH. CHIAKI WAS LOOKING FOR YOU.
HE WAS? FOR ME?
POUT
......
HEY...
...WHY'RE YOU ALWAYS LOOKING OUT FOR CHIAKI...
...AND DOING JUNK LIKE THIS "NOT-HOLDING-BACK" MONTH...?
WHY DO I LOOK OUT FOR HIM? 'COS I FEEL LIKE IT. THAT'S ALL.
SMILE
CHIAKI, HE, WELL...

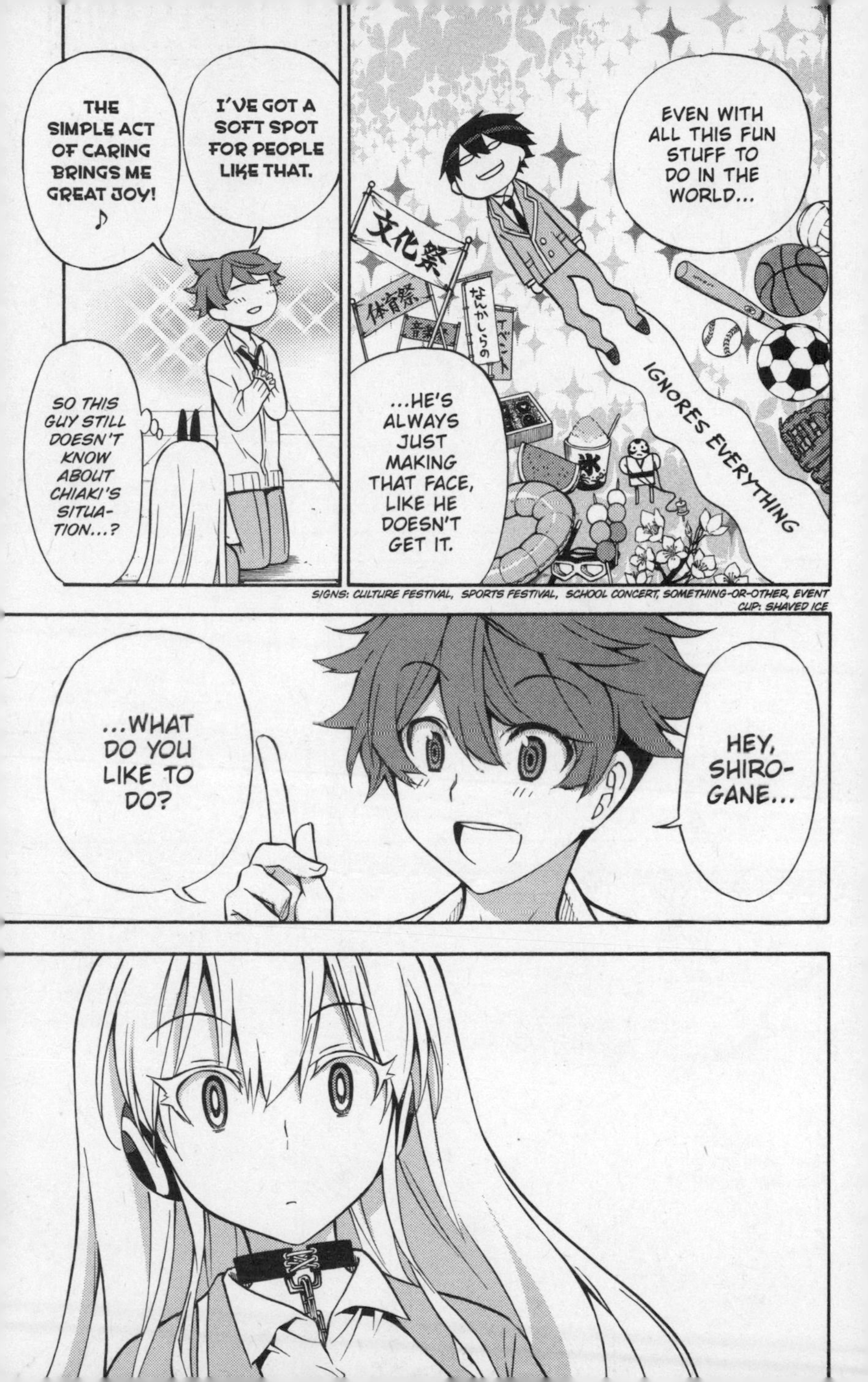
EVEN WITH ALL THIS FUN STUFF TO DO IN THE WORLD...
文化祭
体育祭
なんかしらの
氷
...HE'S ALWAYS JUST MAKING THAT FACE, LIKE HE DOESN'T GET IT.
IGNORES EVERYTHING
I'VE GOT A SOFT SPOT FOR PEOPLE LIKE THAT.
THE SIMPLE ACT OF CARING BRINGS ME GREAT JOY! ♪
SO THIS GUY STILL DOESN'T KNOW ABOUT CHIAKI'S SITUATION...?
SIGNS: CULTURE FESTIVAL, SPORTS FESTIVAL, SCHOOL CONCERT, SOMETHING-OR-OTHER, EVENT
CUP: SHAVED ICE
HEY, SHIROGANE...
...WHAT DO YOU LIKE TO DO?

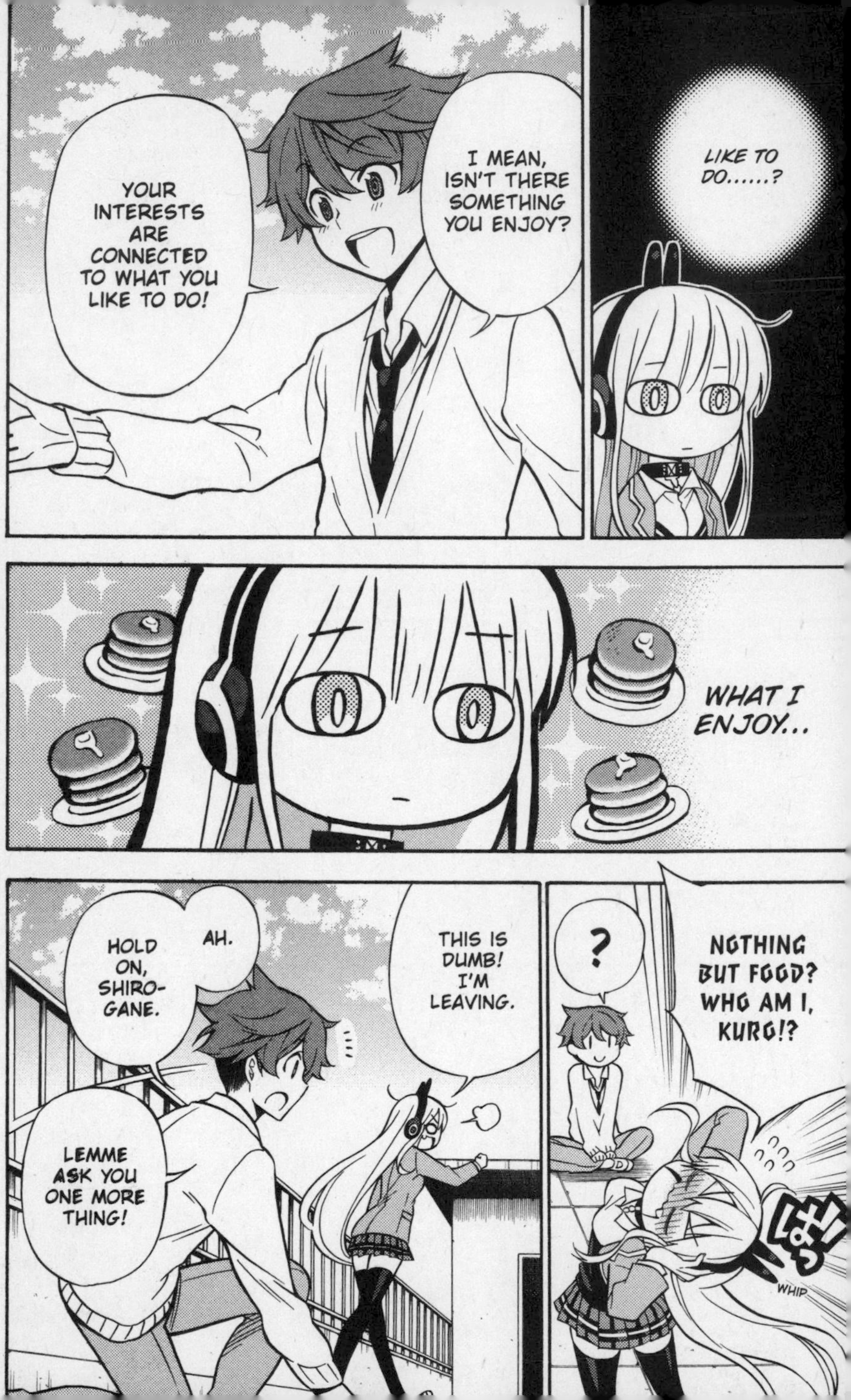
LIKE TO DO......?
I MEAN, ISN'T THERE SOMETHING YOU ENJOY?
YOUR INTERESTS ARE CONNECTED TO WHAT YOU LIKE TO DO!
WHAT I ENJOY...
NOTHING BUT FOOD? WHO AM I, KURO!?
?
WHIP
THIS IS DUMB! I'M LEAVING.
AH.
HOLD ON, SHIRO-GANE.
LEMME ASK YOU ONE MORE THING!

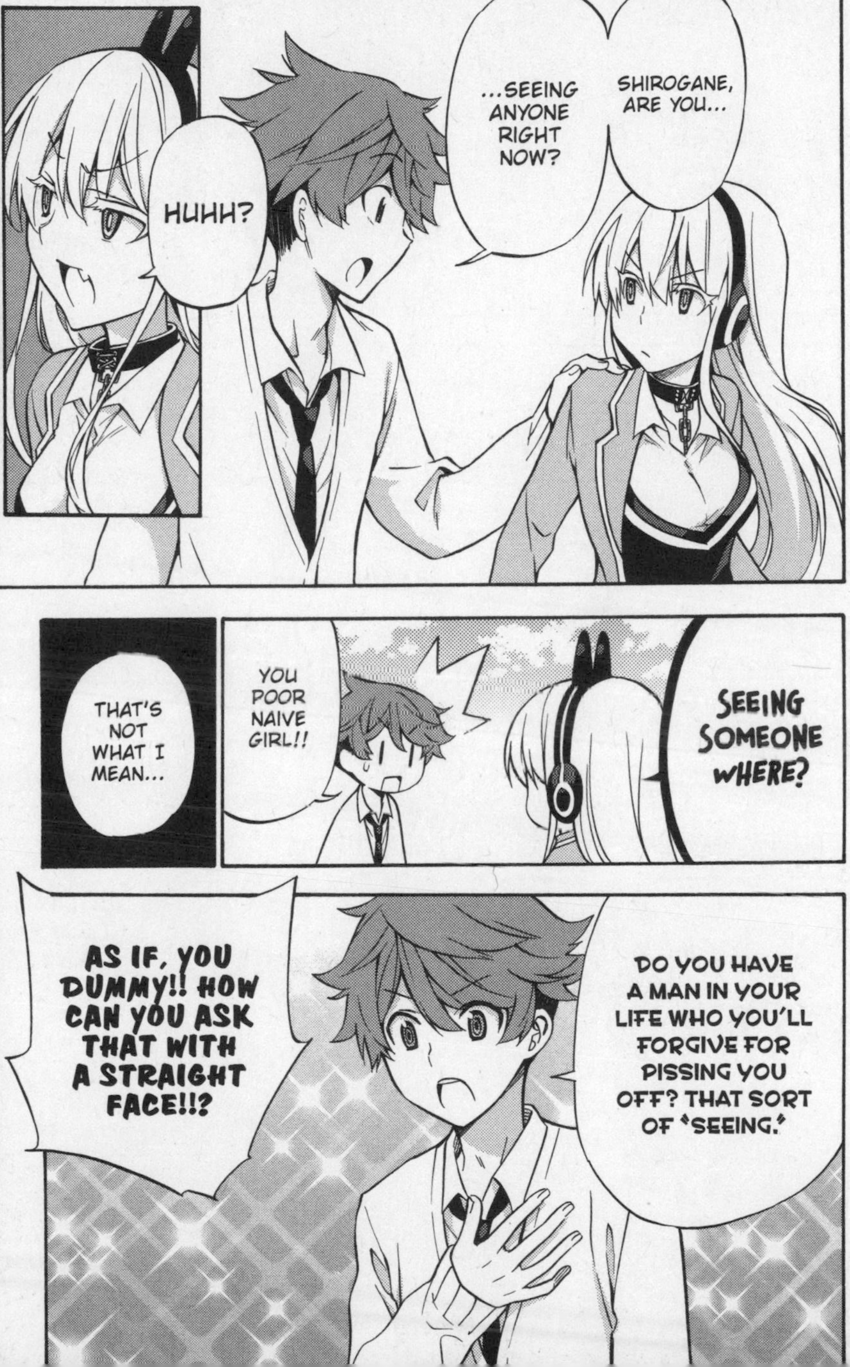
SHIROGANE, ARE YOU...
...SEEING ANYONE RIGHT NOW?
HUHH?
SEEING SOMEONE WHERE?
YOU POOR NAIVE GIRL!!
THAT'S NOT WHAT I MEAN...
DO YOU HAVE A MAN IN YOUR LIFE WHO YOU'LL FORGIVE FOR PISSING YOU OFF? THAT SORT OF "SEEING."
AS IF, YOU DUMMY!! HOW CAN YOU ASK THAT WITH A STRAIGHT FACE!!?

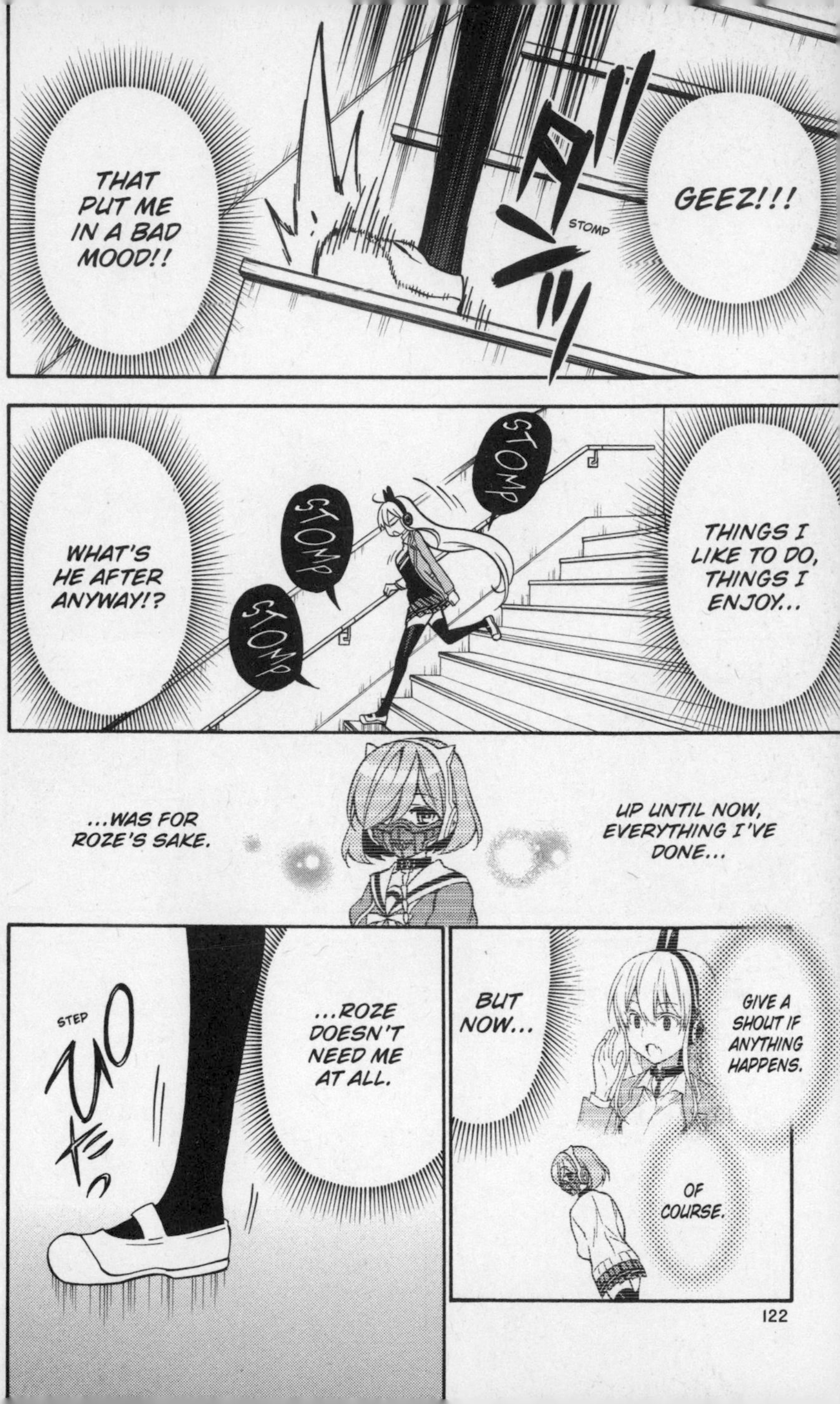
GEEZ!!!
STOMP
THAT PUT ME IN A BAD MOOD!!
THINGS I LIKE TO DO, THINGS I ENJOY...
STOMP
STOMP
STOMP
WHAT'S HE AFTER ANYWAY!?
UP UNTIL NOW, EVERYTHING I'VE DONE...
...WAS FOR ROZE'S SAKE.
GIVE A SHOUT IF ANYTHING HAPPENS.
OF COURSE.
BUT NOW...
...ROZE DOESN'T NEED ME AT ALL.
STEP

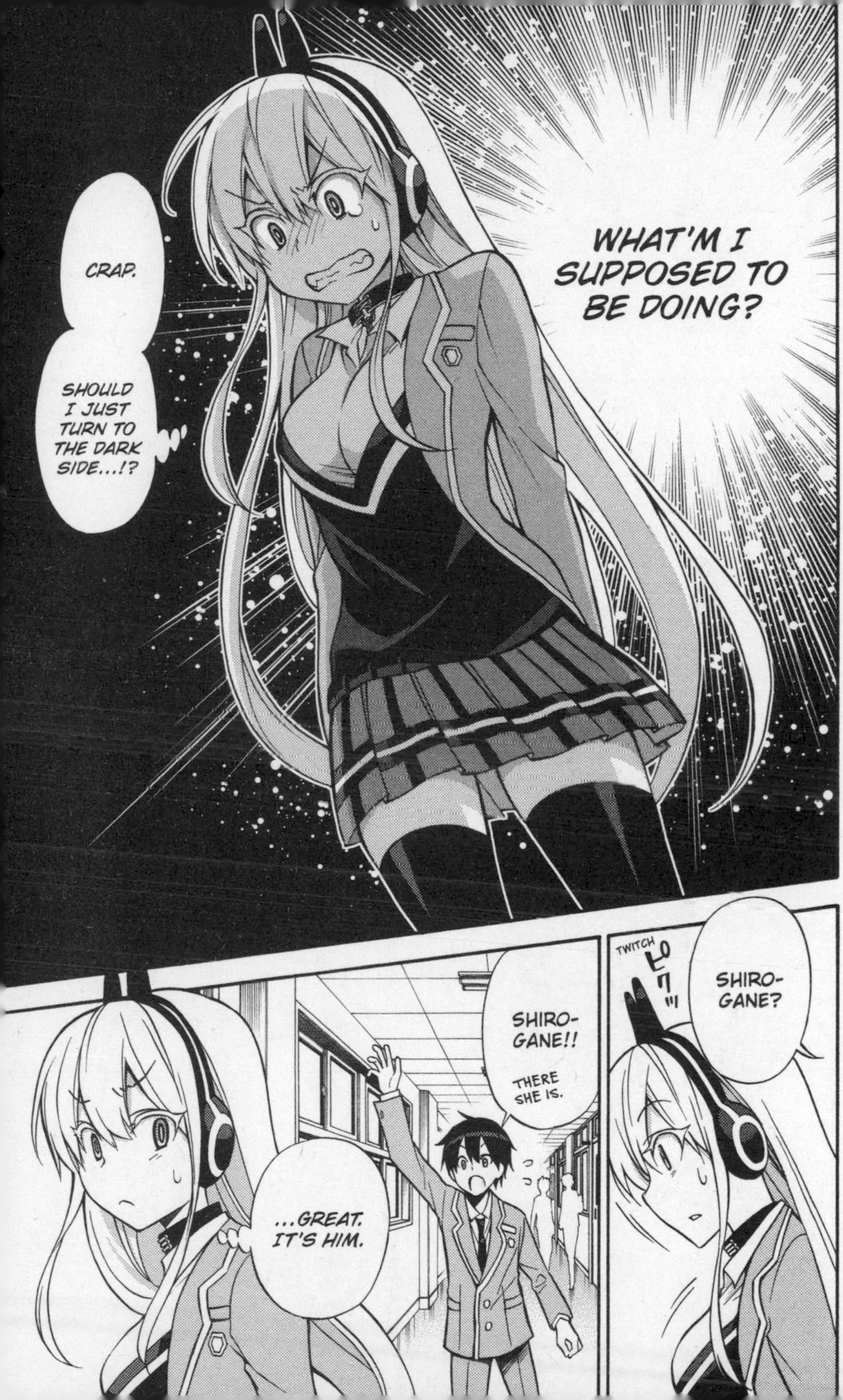
WHAT'M I SUPPOSED TO BE DOING?
CRAP.
SHOULD I JUST TURN TO THE DARK SIDE...!?
TWITCH
SHIRO-GANE?
SHIRO-GANE!!
THERE SHE IS.
...GREAT. IT'S HIM.

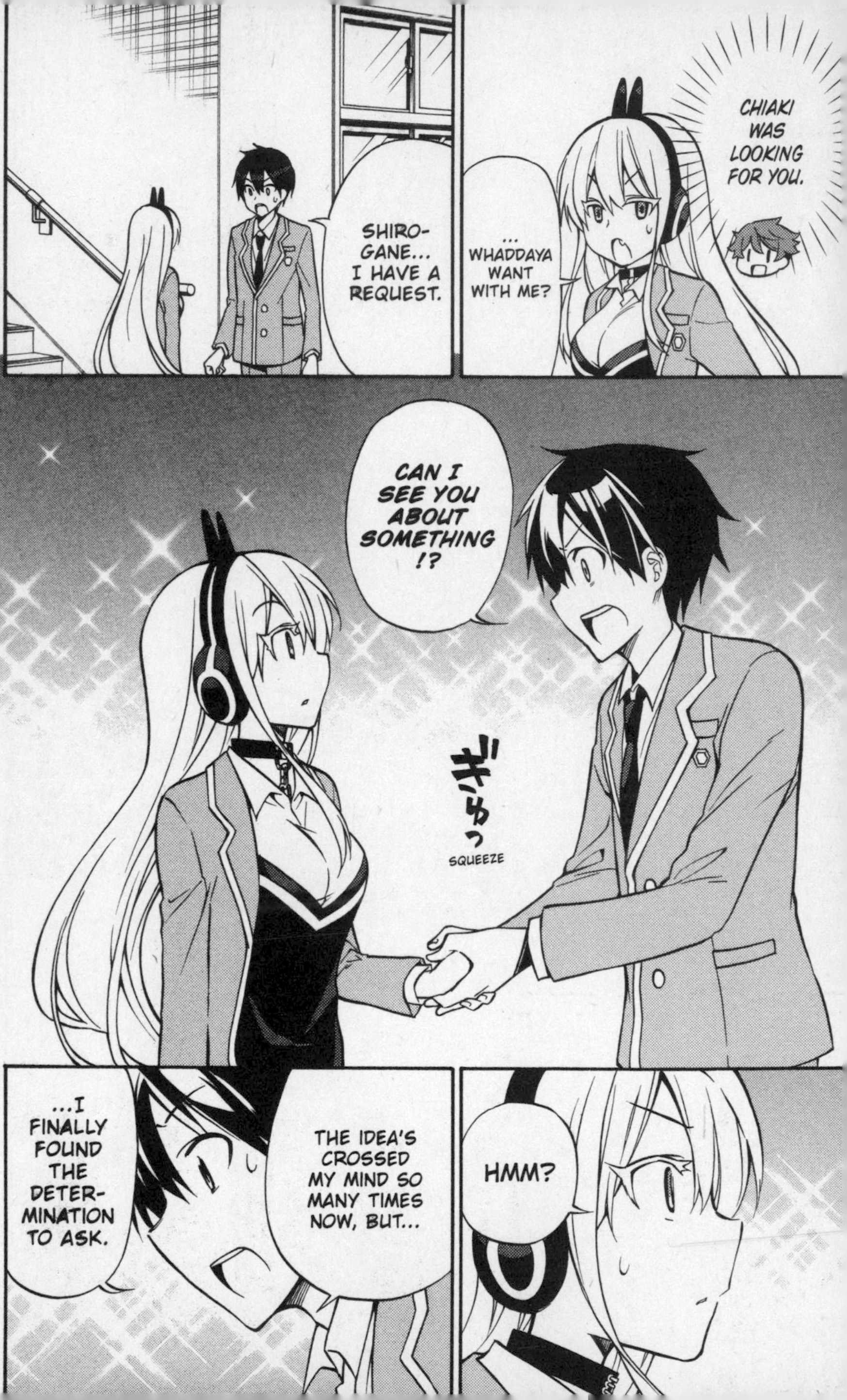
CHIAKI WAS LOOKING FOR YOU.
...WHADDAYA WANT WITH ME?
SHIRO-GANE... I HAVE A REQUEST.
CAN I SEE YOU ABOUT SOMETHING!?
ぎゅっ
SQUEEZE
HMM?
THE IDEA'S CROSSED MY MIND SO MANY TIMES NOW, BUT...
...I FINALLY FOUND THE DETER-MINATION TO ASK.

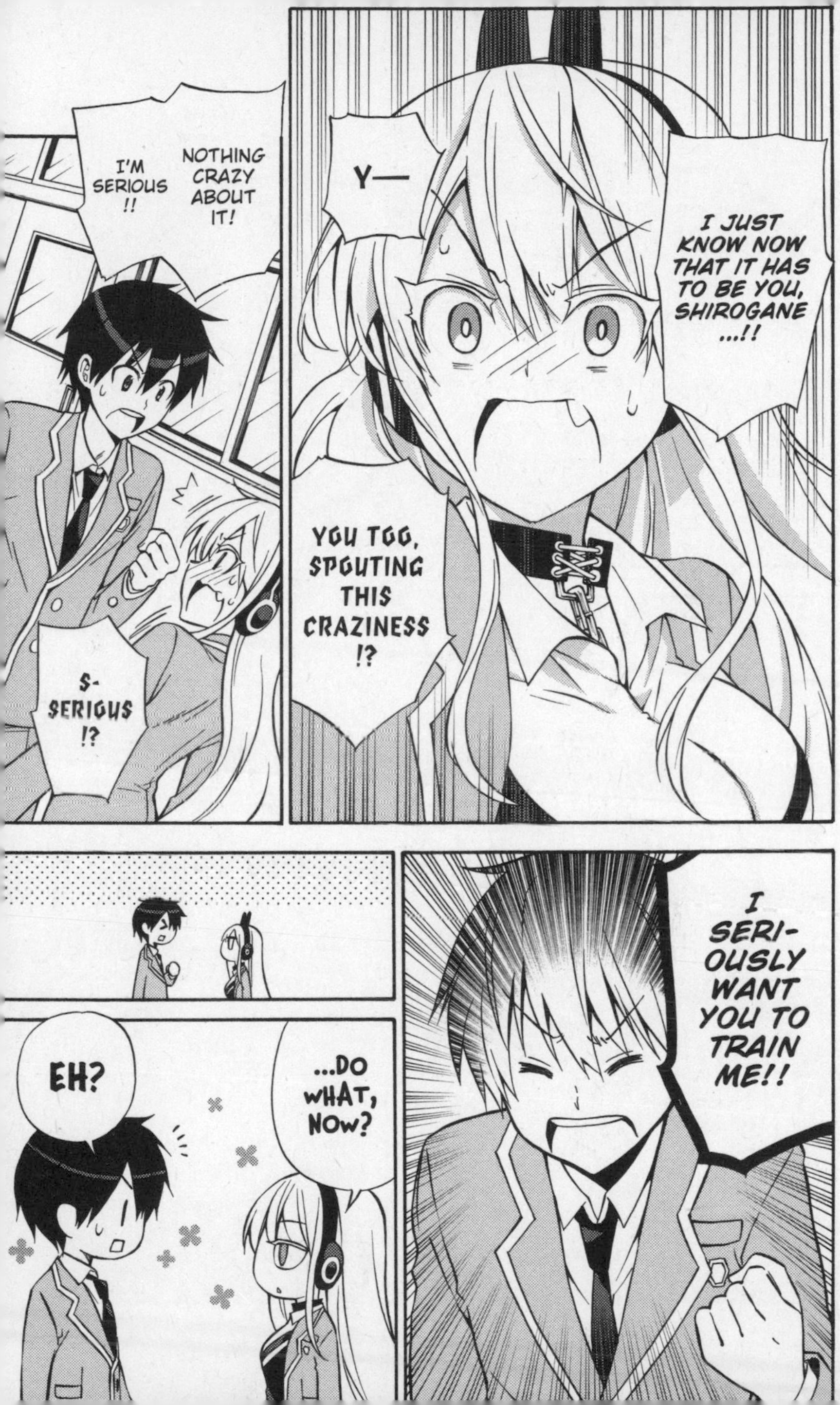
I JUST KNOW NOW THAT IT HAS TO BE YOU, SHIROGANE ...!!
Y—
YOU TOO, SPOUTING THIS CRAZINESS !?
I'M SERIOUS !!
NOTHING CRAZY ABOUT IT!
S-SERIOUS !?
I SERI-OUSLY WANT YOU TO TRAIN ME!!
...DO WHAT, NOW?
EH?

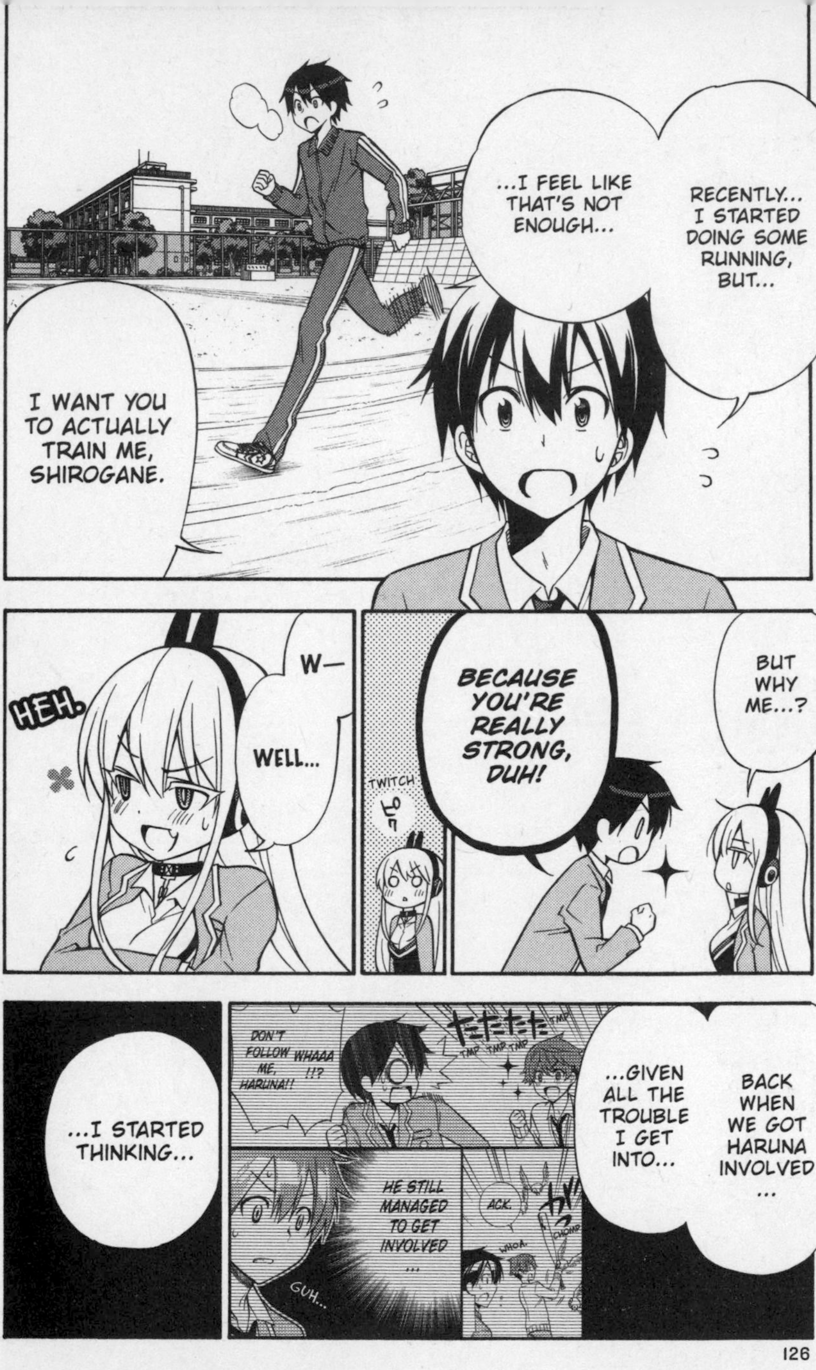
RECENTLY... I STARTED DOING SOME RUNNING, BUT...
...I FEEL LIKE THAT'S NOT ENOUGH...
I WANT YOU TO ACTUALLY TRAIN ME, SHIROGANE.
BUT WHY ME...?
BECAUSE YOU'RE REALLY STRONG, DUH!
TWITCH
W—
WELL...
HEH.
BACK WHEN WE GOT HARUNA INVOLVED ...
...GIVEN ALL THE TROUBLE I GET INTO...
TMP TMP TMP TMP
WHAAA !!?
DON'T FOLLOW ME, HARUNA!!
WHOA.
CHOMP
ACK.
HE STILL MANAGED TO GET INVOLVED ...
GUH...
...I STARTED THINKING...

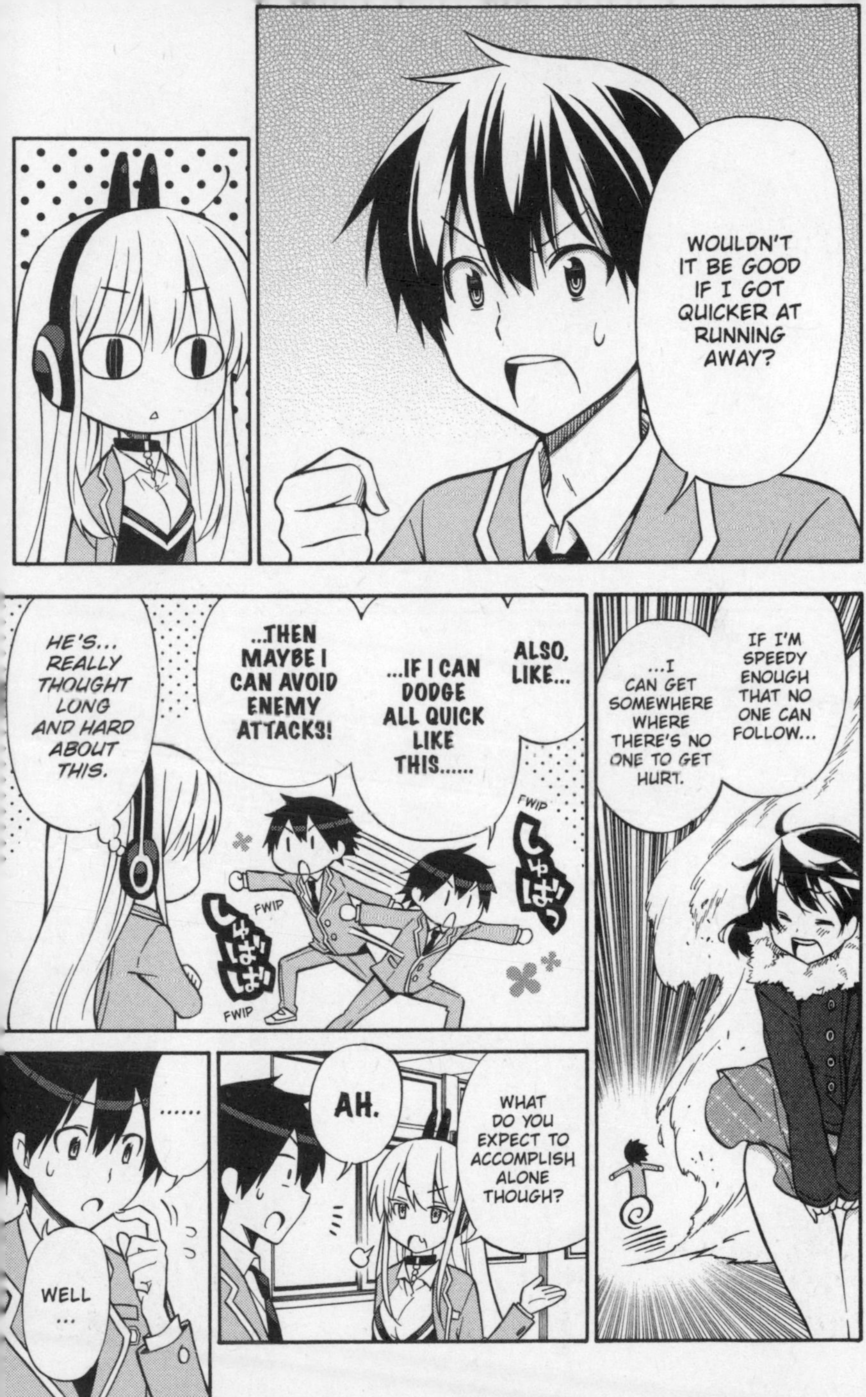
WOULDN'T IT BE GOOD IF I GOT QUICKER AT RUNNING AWAY?
IF I'M SPEEDY ENOUGH THAT NO ONE CAN FOLLOW...
...I CAN GET SOMEWHERE WHERE THERE'S NO ONE TO GET HURT.
ALSO, LIKE...
...IF I CAN DODGE ALL QUICK LIKE THIS......
FWIP
しゅばっ
FWIP
FWIP
...THEN MAYBE I CAN AVOID ENEMY ATTACKS!
HE'S... REALLY THOUGHT LONG AND HARD ABOUT THIS.
WHAT DO YOU EXPECT TO ACCOMPLISH ALONE THOUGH?
AH.
......
WELL ...

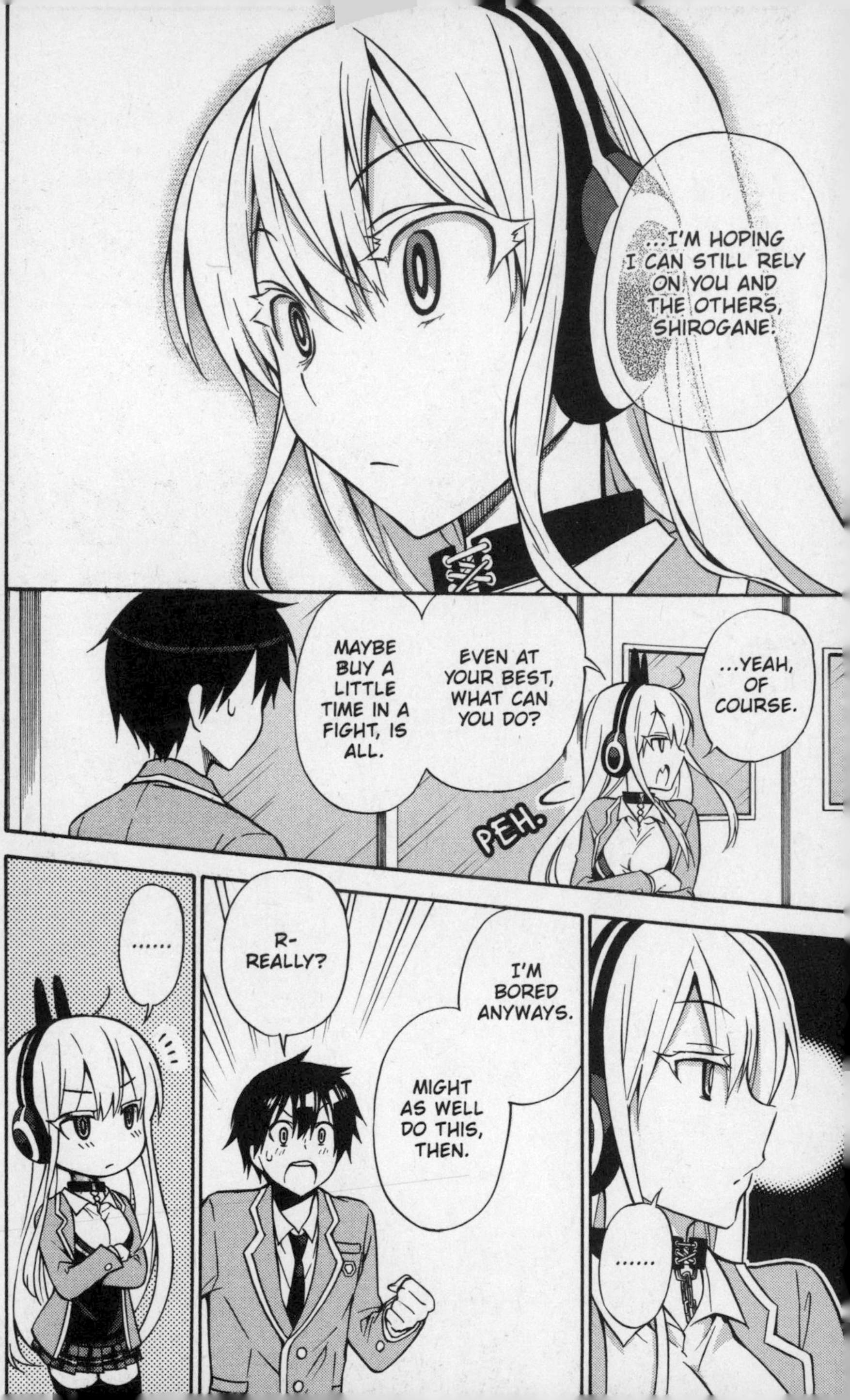
...I'M HOPING I CAN STILL RELY ON YOU AND THE OTHERS, SHIROGANE.
...YEAH, OF COURSE.
PEH.
EVEN AT YOUR BEST, WHAT CAN YOU DO?
MAYBE BUY A LITTLE TIME IN A FIGHT, IS ALL.
......
I'M BORED ANYWAYS.
MIGHT AS WELL DO THIS, THEN.
R-REALLY?
......

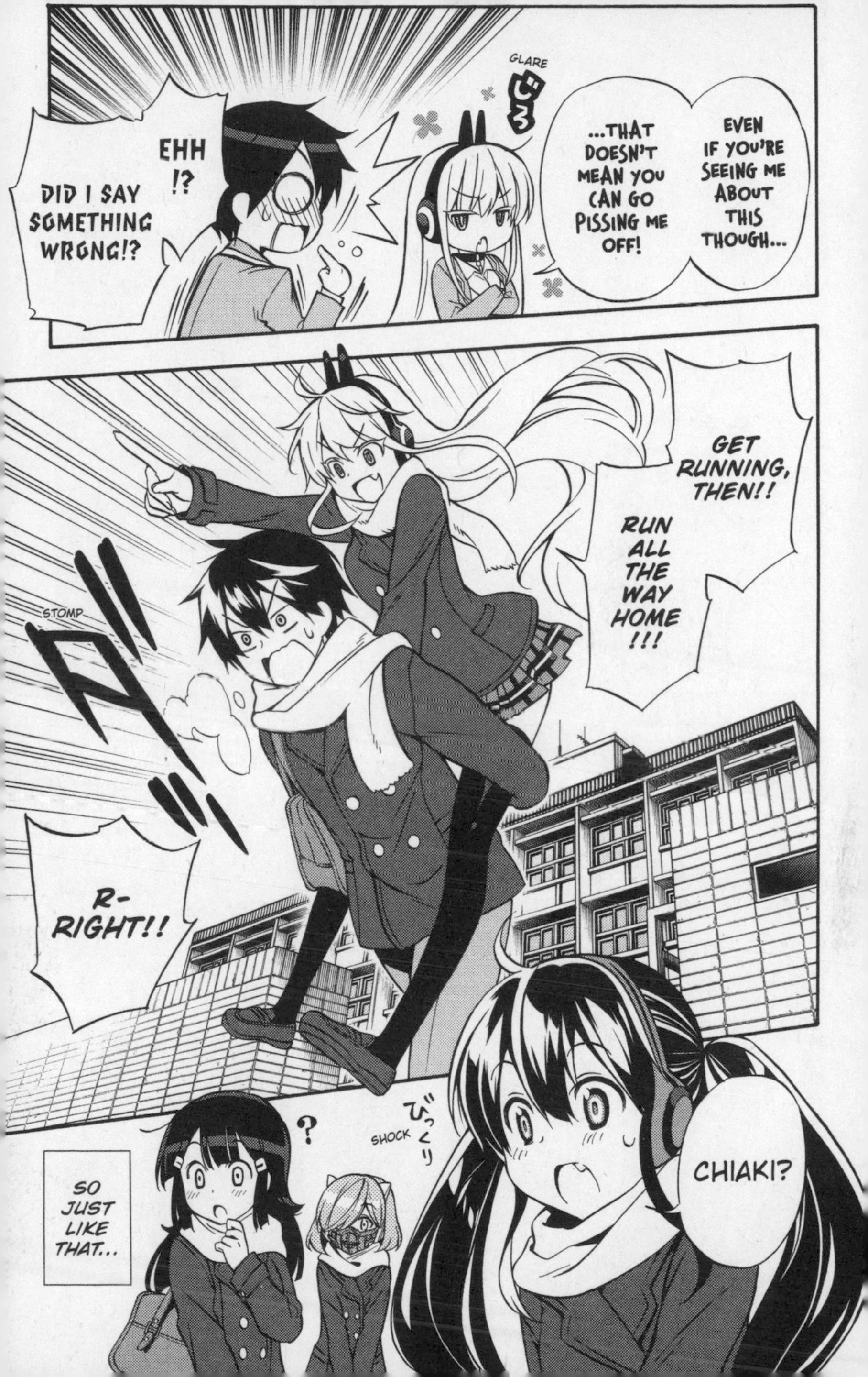
GLARE
じろ
EVEN IF YOU'RE SEEING ME ABOUT THIS THOUGH...
...THAT DOESN'T MEAN YOU CAN GO PISSING ME OFF!
EHH !?
DID I SAY SOMETHING WRONG!?
GET RUNNING, THEN!!
RUN ALL THE WAY HOME!!!
STOMP
R-RIGHT!!
CHIAKI?
びっくり
SHOCK
?
SO JUST LIKE THAT...

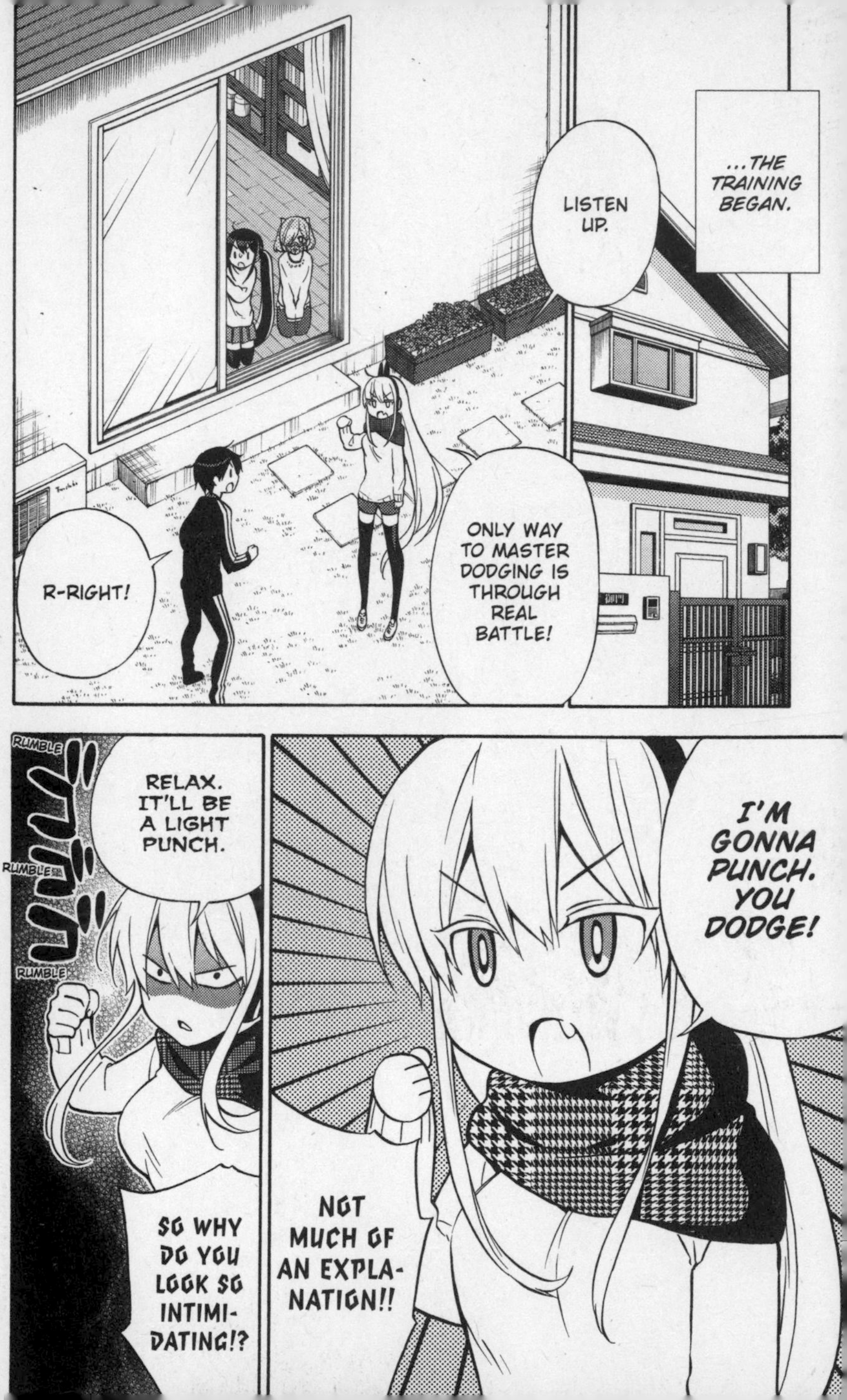
...THE TRAINING BEGAN.
LISTEN UP.
ONLY WAY TO MASTER DODGING IS THROUGH REAL BATTLE!
R-RIGHT!
I'M GONNA PUNCH. YOU DODGE!
NOT MUCH OF AN EXPLA-NATION!!
RELAX. IT'LL BE A LIGHT PUNCH.
RUMBLE
RUMBLE
RUMBLE
SO WHY DO YOU LOOK SO INTIMI-DATING!?

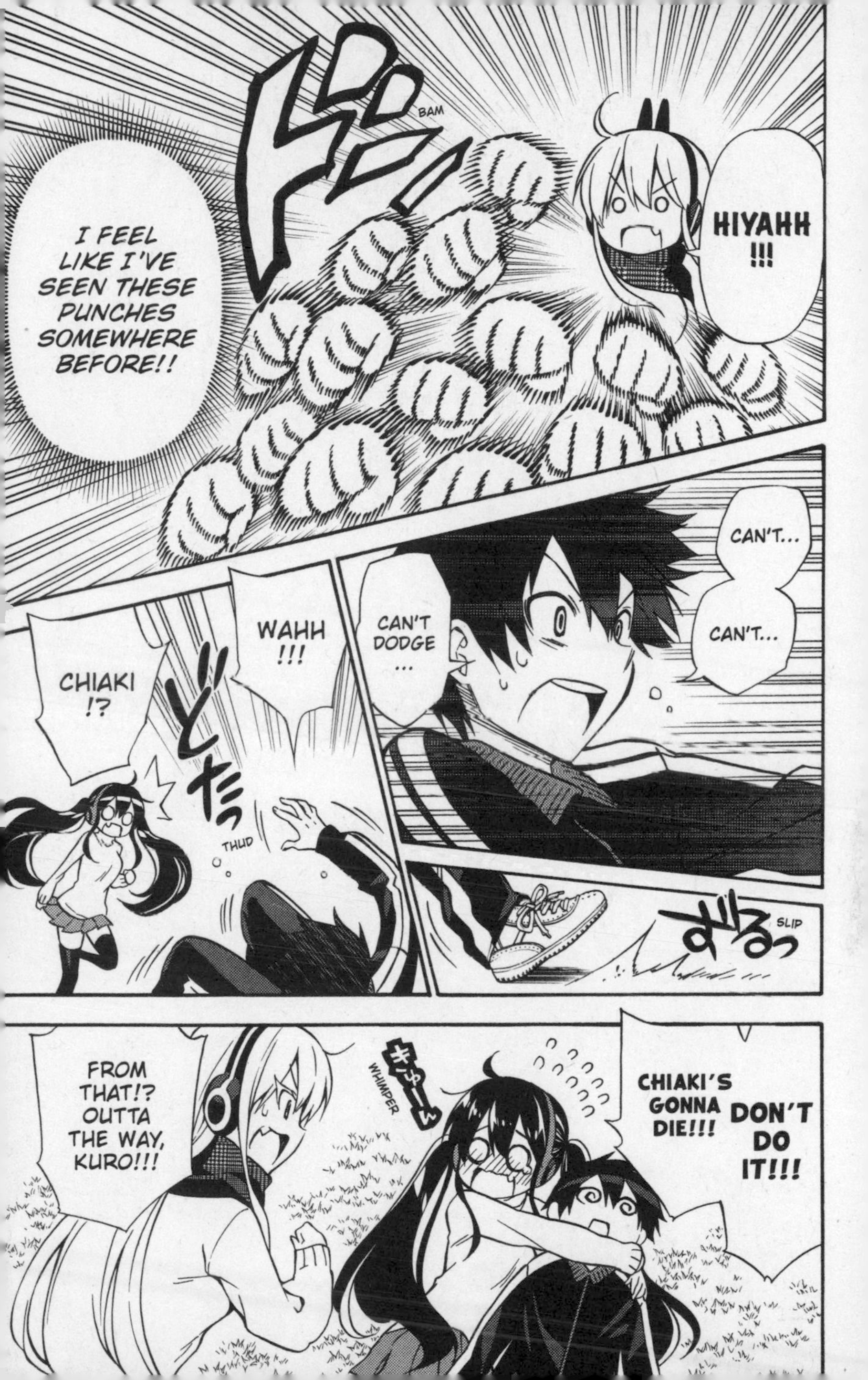
HIYAHH!!!
BAM
I FEEL LIKE I'VE SEEN THESE PUNCHES SOMEWHERE BEFORE!!
CAN'T...
CAN'T...
CAN'T DODGE...
SLIP
WAHH!!!
CHIAKI!?
THUD
CHIAKI'S GONNA DIE!!!
DON'T DO IT!!!
WHIMPER
FROM THAT!? OUTTA THE WAY, KURO!!!

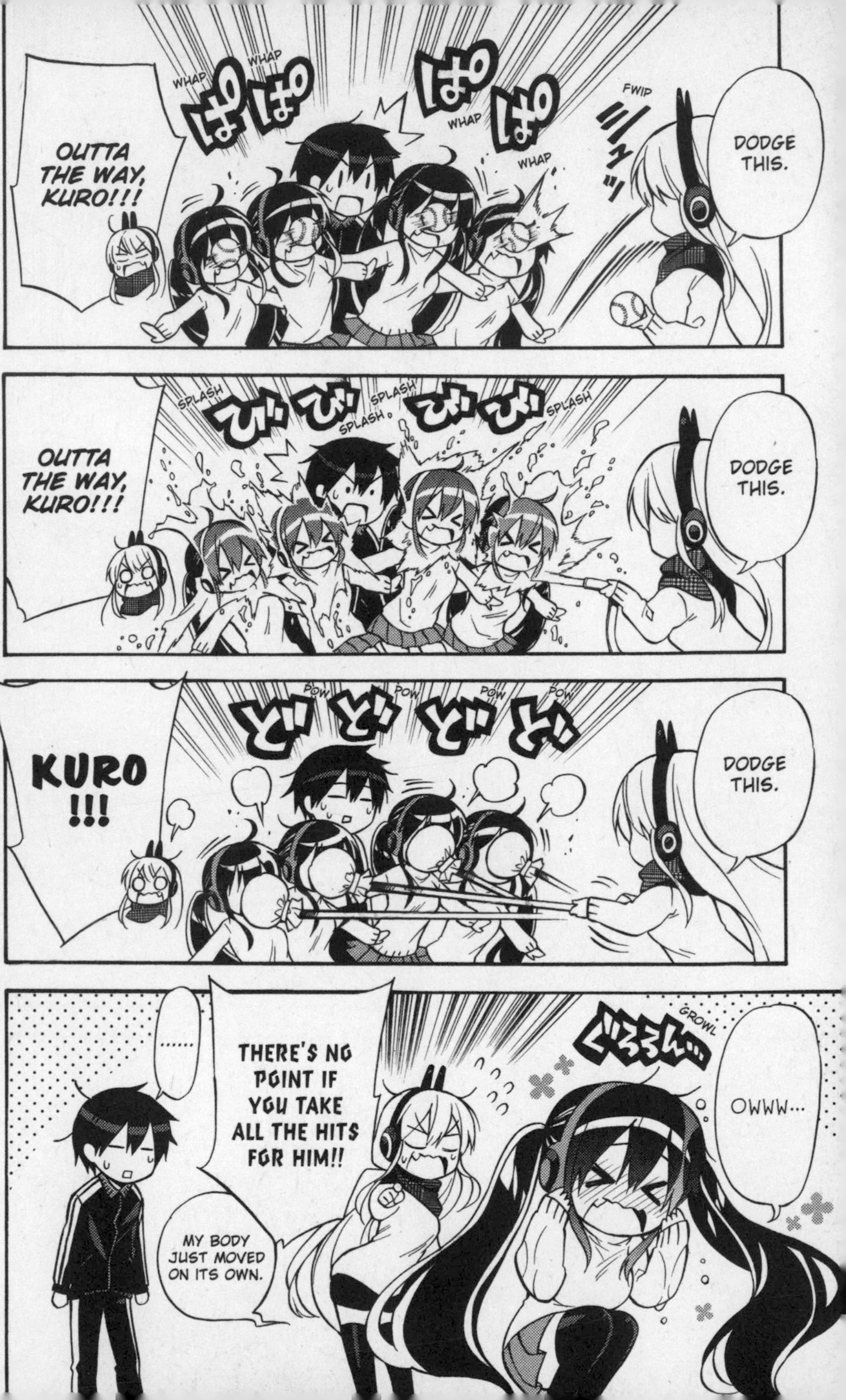
DODGE THIS.
FWIP
WHAP
WHAP
WHAP
WHAP
OUTTA THE WAY, KURO!!!
DODGE THIS.
SPLASH
SPLASH
SPLASH
SPLASH
OUTTA THE WAY, KURO!!!
DODGE THIS.
POW
POW
POW
POW
KURO !!!
GROWL
OWWW...
THERE'S NO POINT IF YOU TAKE ALL THE HITS FOR HIM!!
......
MY BODY JUST MOVED ON ITS OWN.

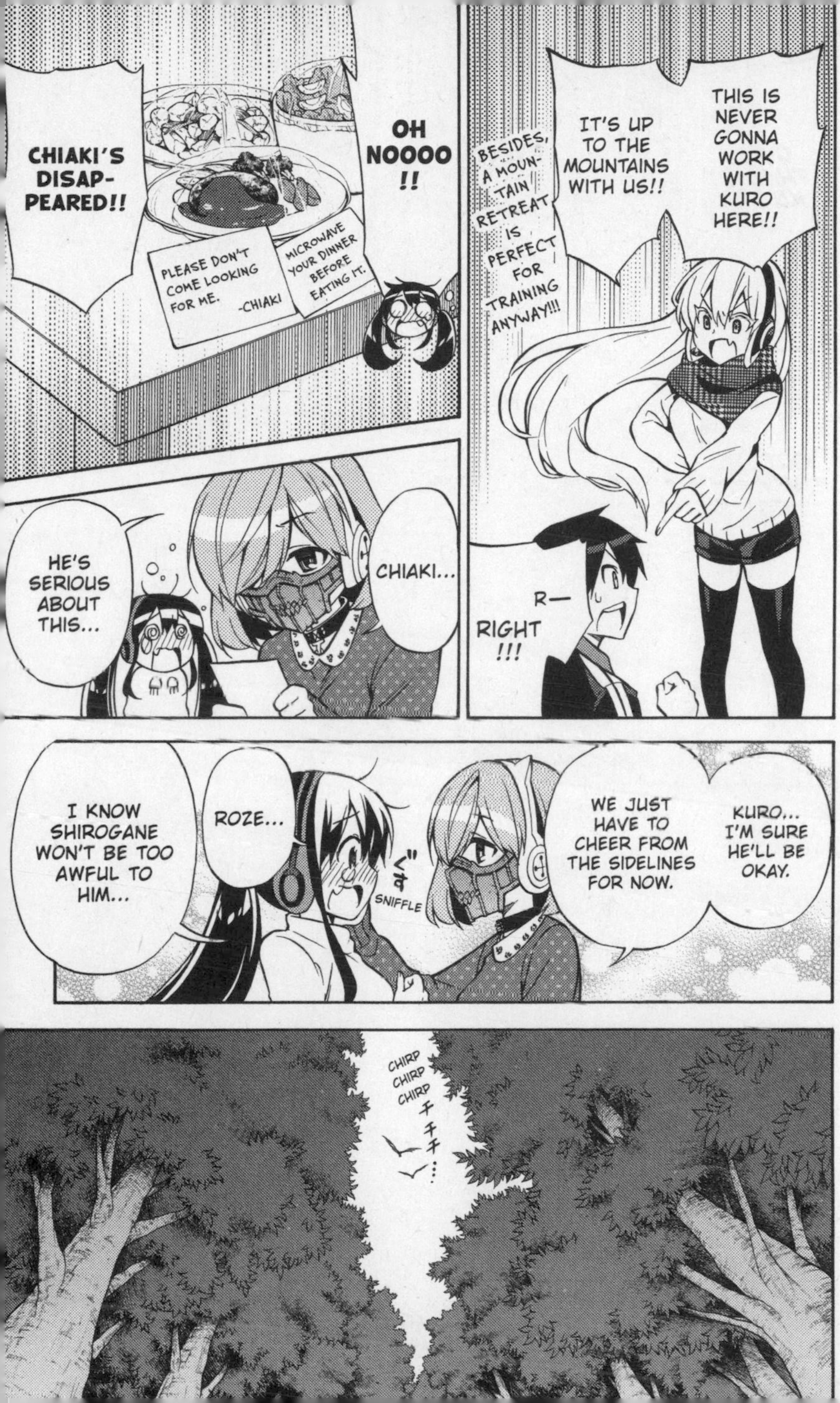
THIS IS NEVER GONNA WORK WITH KURO HERE!!
IT'S UP TO THE MOUNTAINS WITH US!!
BESIDES, A MOUN-TAIN RETREAT IS PERFECT FOR TRAINING ANYWAY!!!
R— RIGHT!!!
OH NOOOO!!
CHIAKI'S DISAP-PEARED!!
MICROWAVE YOUR DINNER BEFORE EATING IT.
PLEASE DON'T COME LOOKING FOR ME. -CHIAKI
CHIAKI...
HE'S SERIOUS ABOUT THIS...
KURO... I'M SURE HE'LL BE OKAY.
WE JUST HAVE TO CHEER FROM THE SIDELINES FOR NOW.
ぐす
SNIFFLE
ROZE...
I KNOW SHIROGANE WON'T BE TOO AWFUL TO HIM...
CHIRP CHIRP CHIRP
チチチ…

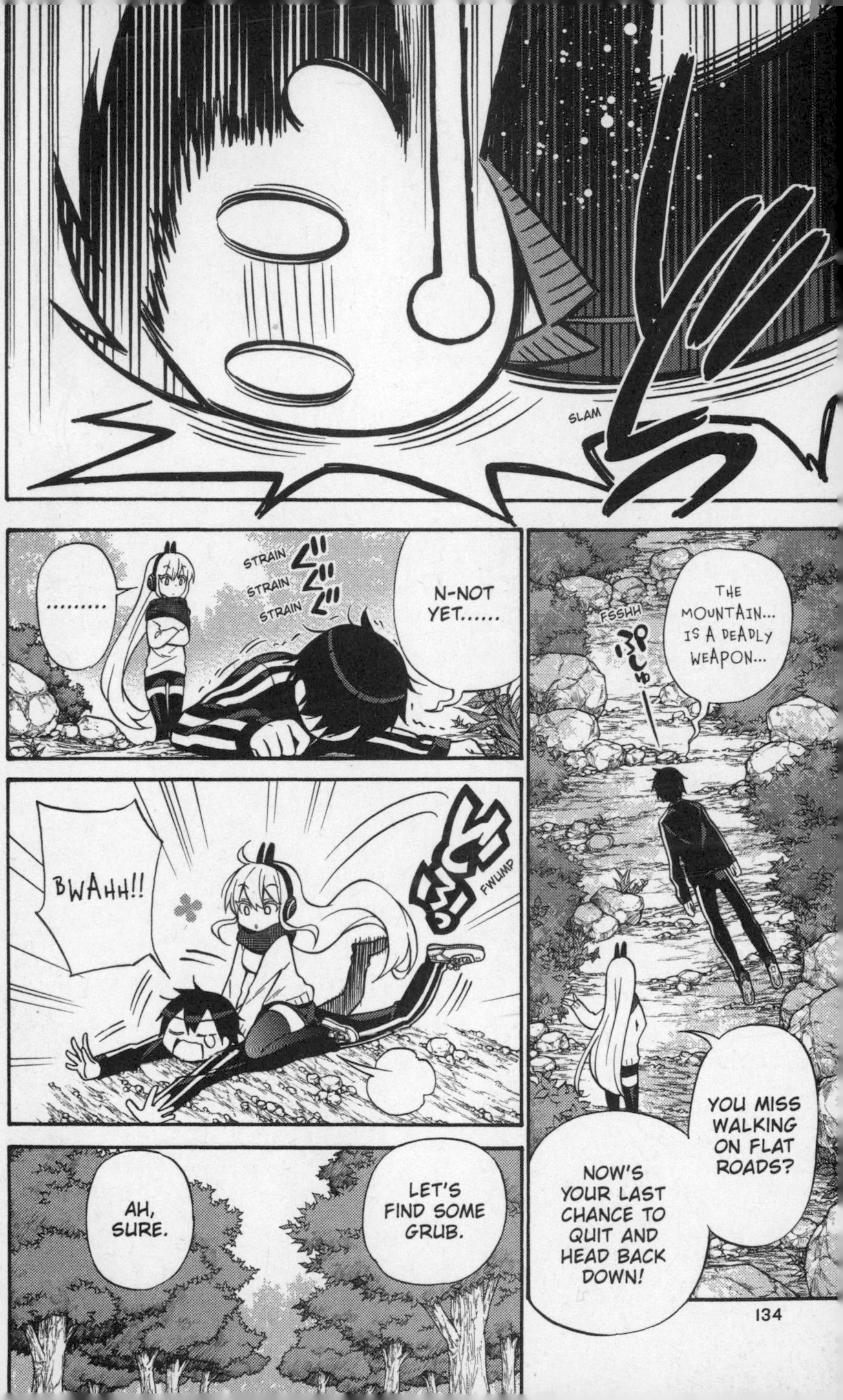
SLAM
THE MOUNTAIN... IS A DEADLY WEAPON...
FSSHH
YOU MISS WALKING ON FLAT ROADS?
NOW'S YOUR LAST CHANCE TO QUIT AND HEAD BACK DOWN!
N-NOT YET......
STRAIN
STRAIN
STRAIN
....
FWUMP
BWAHH!!
LET'S FIND SOME GRUB.
AH, SURE.

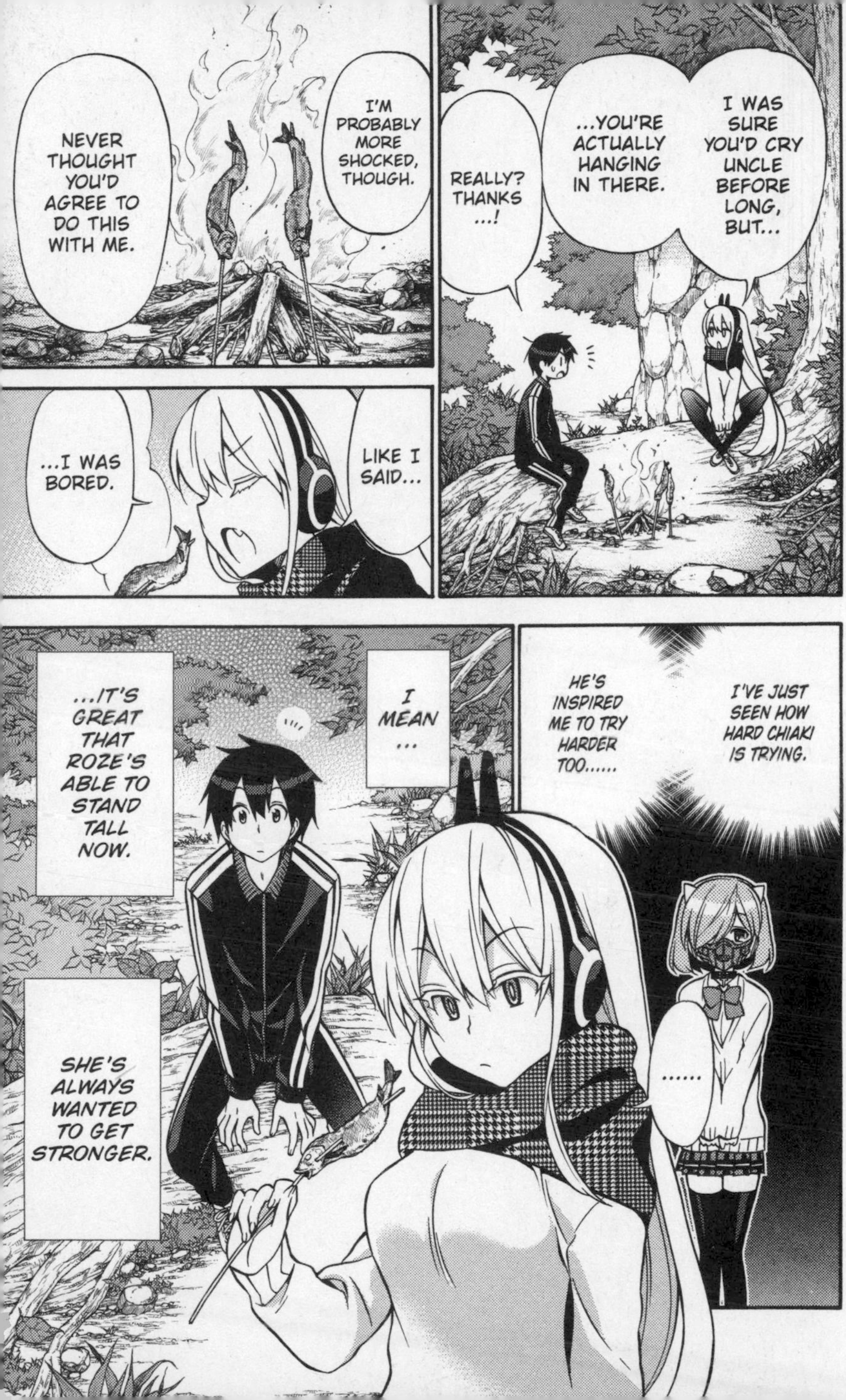
I WAS SURE YOU'D CRY UNCLE BEFORE LONG, BUT...
...YOU'RE ACTUALLY HANGING IN THERE.
REALLY? THANKS ...!
I'M PROBABLY MORE SHOCKED, THOUGH.
NEVER THOUGHT YOU'D AGREE TO DO THIS WITH ME.
LIKE I SAID...
...I WAS BORED.
I'VE JUST SEEN HOW HARD CHIAKI IS TRYING.
HE'S INSPIRED ME TO TRY HARDER TOO......
......
I MEAN ...
...IT'S GREAT THAT ROZE'S ABLE TO STAND TALL NOW.
SHE'S ALWAYS WANTED TO GET STRONGER.

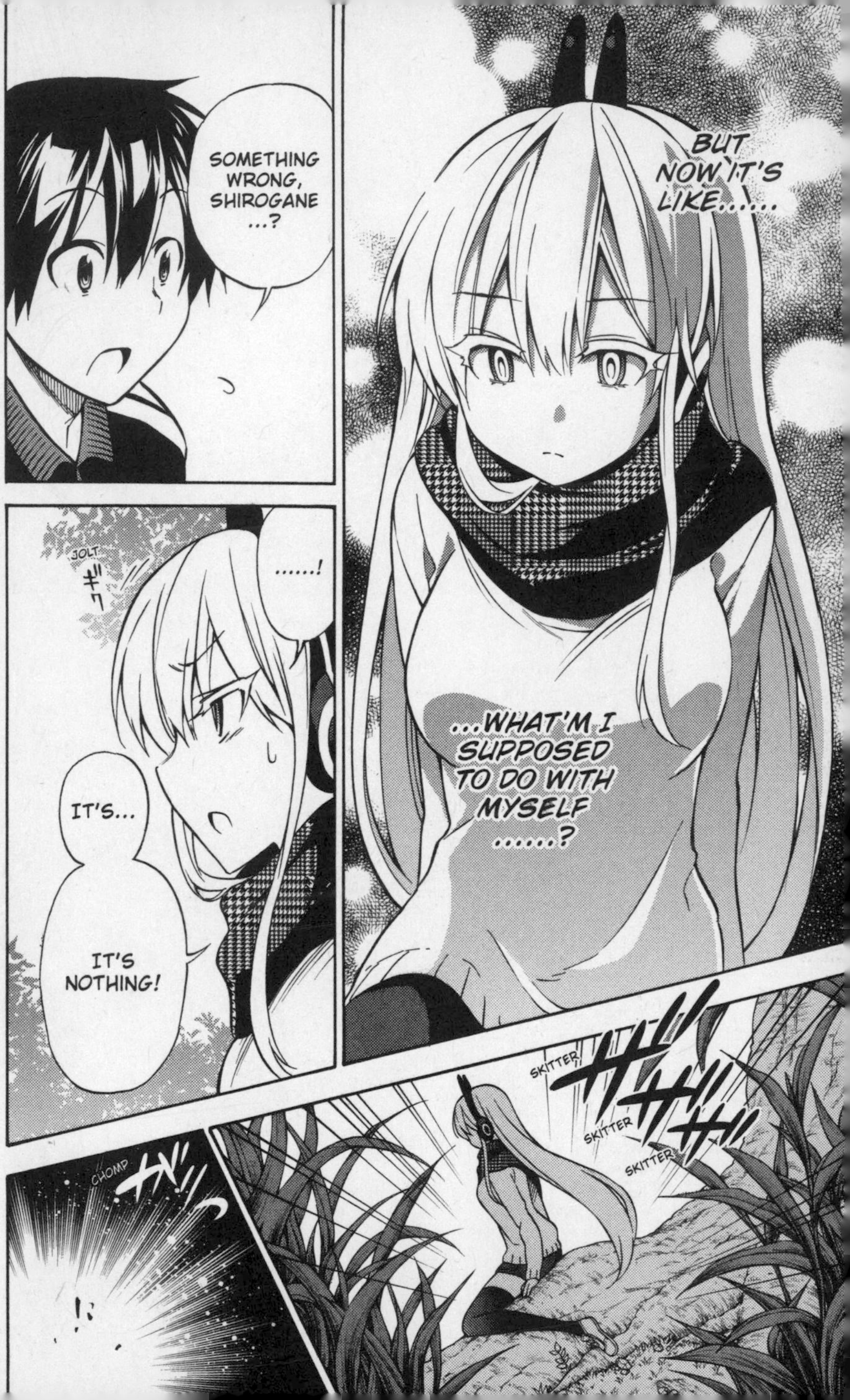
BUT NOW IT'S LIKE......
...WHAT'M I SUPPOSED TO DO WITH MYSELF ......?
SOMETHING WRONG, SHIROGANE ...?
JOLT
ギク
......!
IT'S...
IT'S NOTHING!
SKITTER
SKITTER
SKITTER
CHOMP

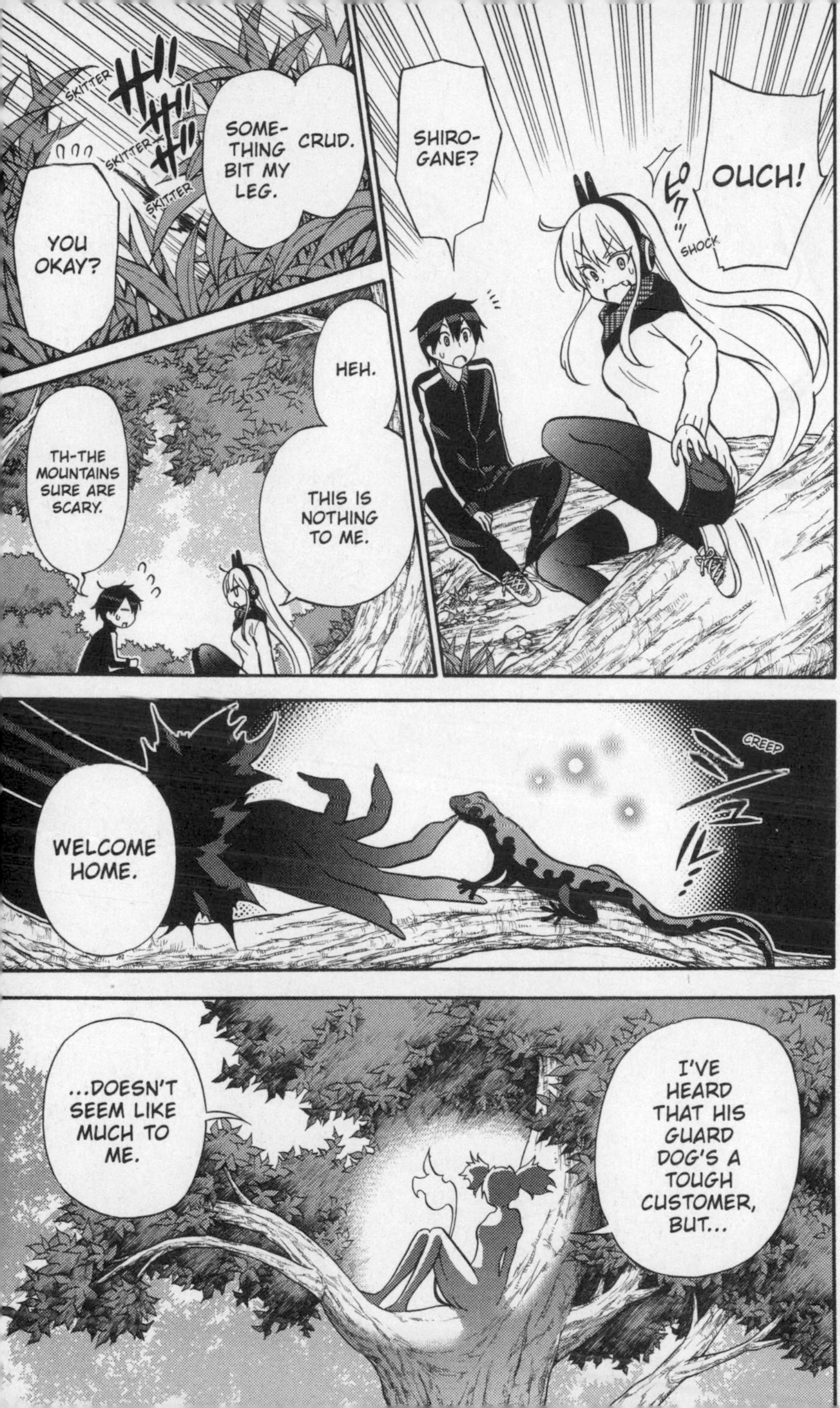
OUCH!
SHOCK
SHIRO-GANE?
CRUD.
SOME-THING BIT MY LEG.
SKITTER
SKITTER
SKITTER
YOU OKAY?
HEH.
THIS IS NOTHING TO ME.
TH-THE MOUNTAINS SURE ARE SCARY.
CREEP
WELCOME HOME.
I'VE HEARD THAT HIS GUARD DOG'S A TOUGH CUSTOMER, BUT...
...DOESN'T SEEM LIKE MUCH TO ME.

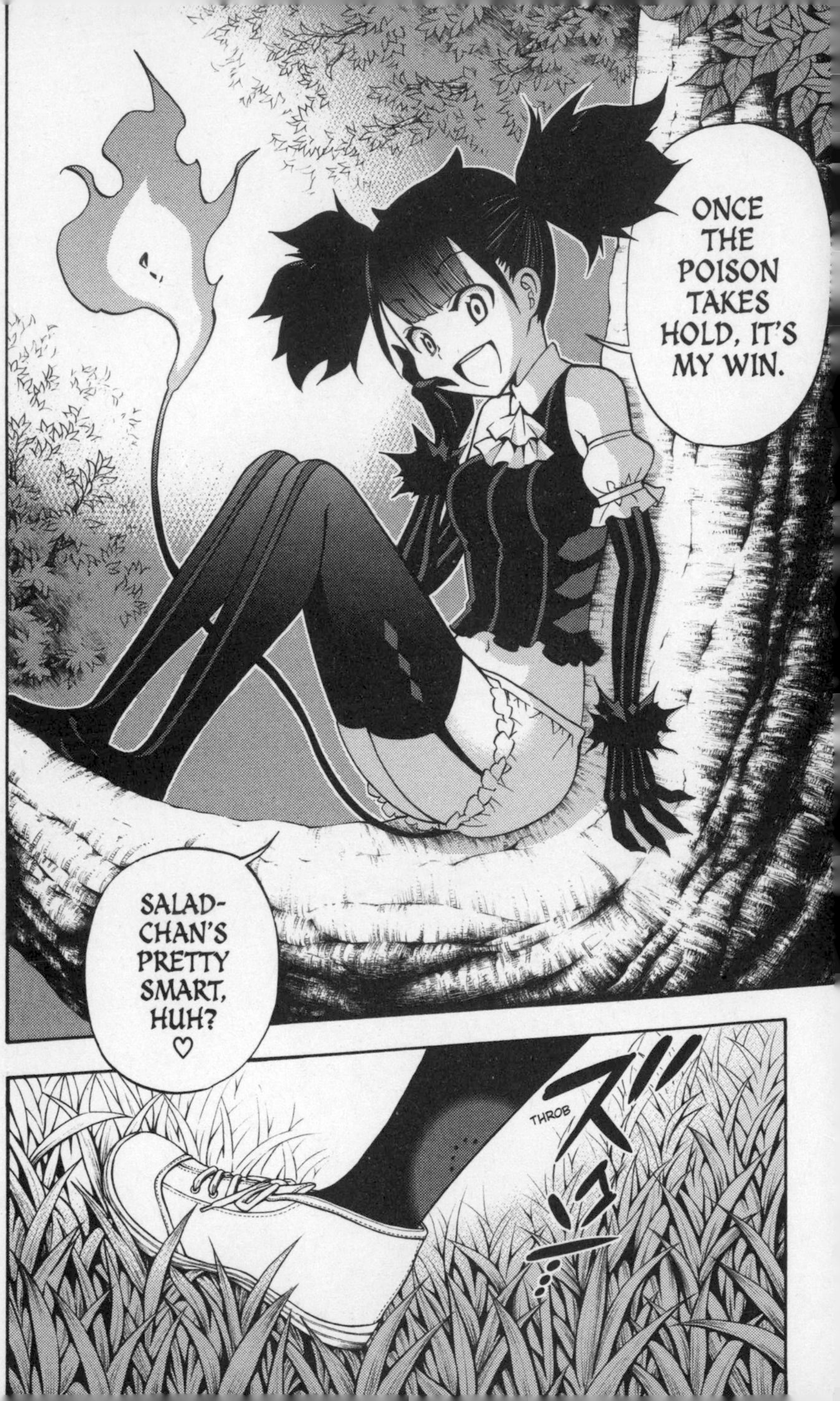
ONCE THE POISON TAKES HOLD, IT'S MY WIN.
SALAD-CHAN'S PRETTY SMART, HUH? ♡
THROB

🐾 TODAY'S CERBERUS

CHIAKI.

IS IT TASTY, KURO?

MUNCH もぐ
MUNCH もぐ
SNIFFLE ぐ
ぐ ず
SNIFFLE ぐ ず

TODAY'S CERBERUS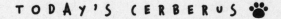

I'M
GONNA...

...BE THE
KING OF THE
DODGERS!

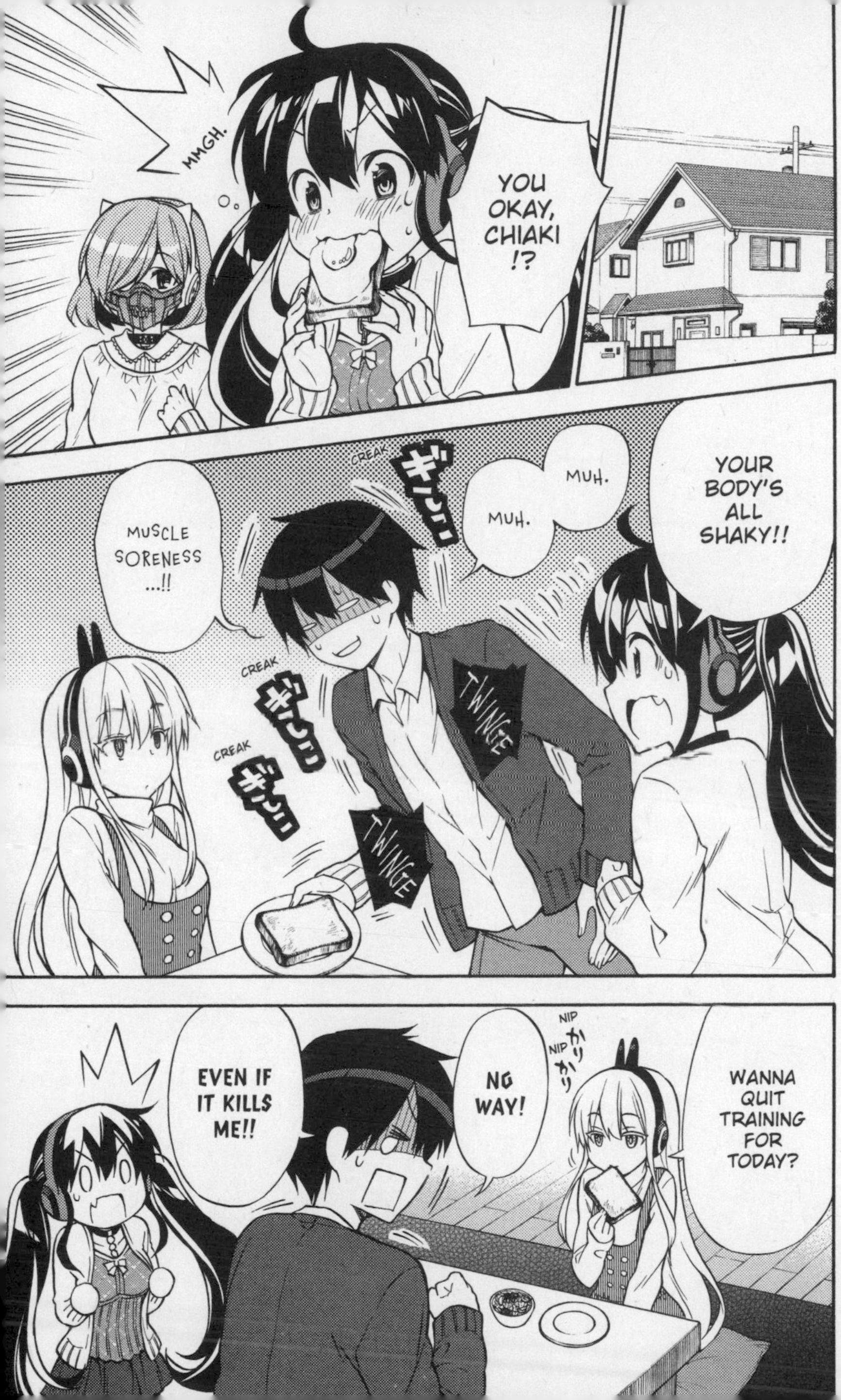
YOU OKAY, CHIAKI !?
MMGH.
YOUR BODY'S ALL SHAKY!!
MUH.
MUH.
CREAK
CREAK
CREAK
MUSCLE SORENESS ...!!
TWINGE
TWINGE
WANNA QUIT TRAINING FOR TODAY?
NIP
NIP
NO WAY!
EVEN IF IT KILLS ME!!

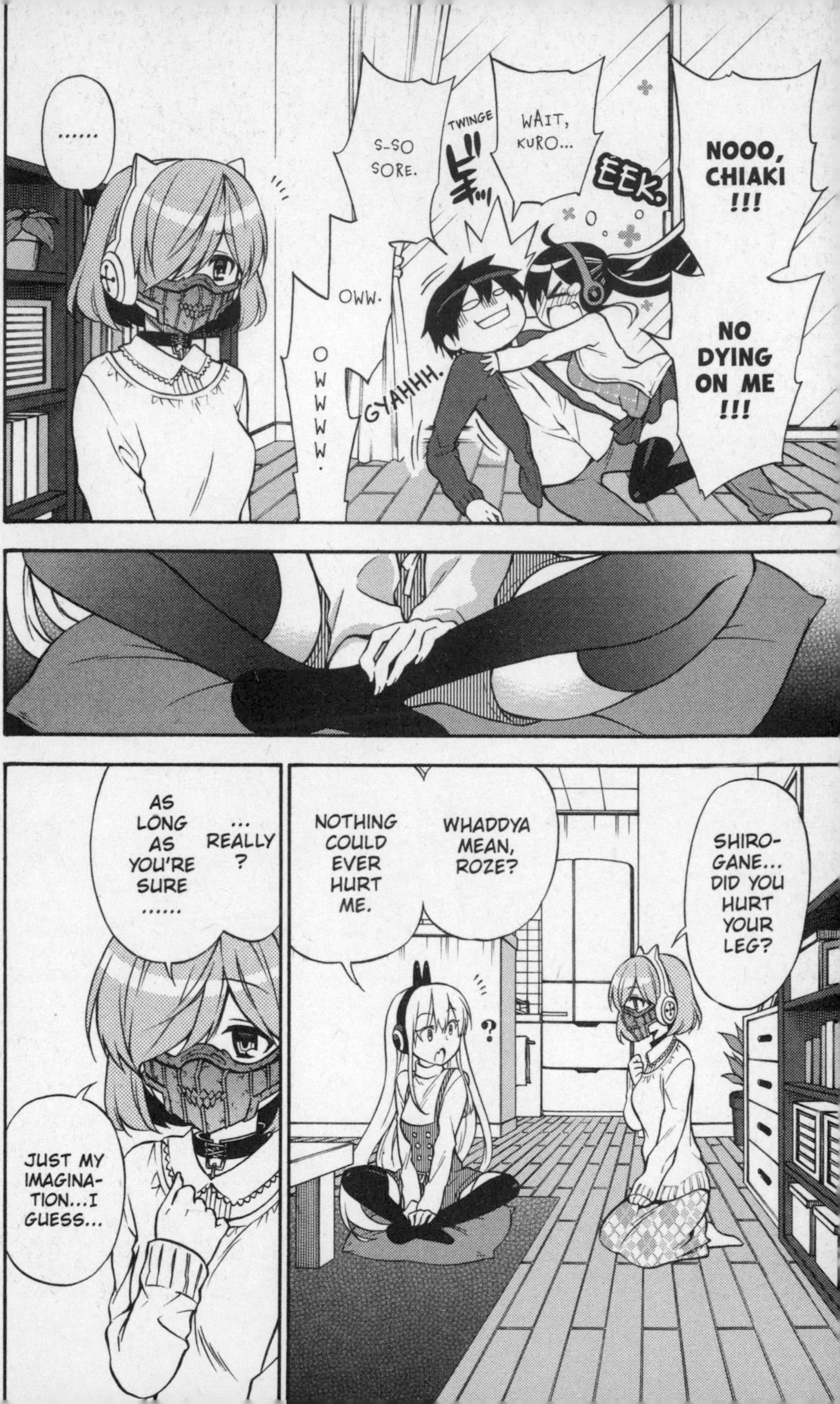
NOOO, CHIAKI !!!
NO DYING ON ME !!!
EEK.
WAIT, KURO...
TWINGE
S-SO SORE.
OWW.
OWWWWW.
GYAHHH.
......
SHIRO-GANE... DID YOU HURT YOUR LEG?
WHADDYA MEAN, ROZE?
NOTHING COULD EVER HURT ME.
...REALLY?
AS LONG AS YOU'RE SURE ......
JUST MY IMAGINATION...I GUESS...

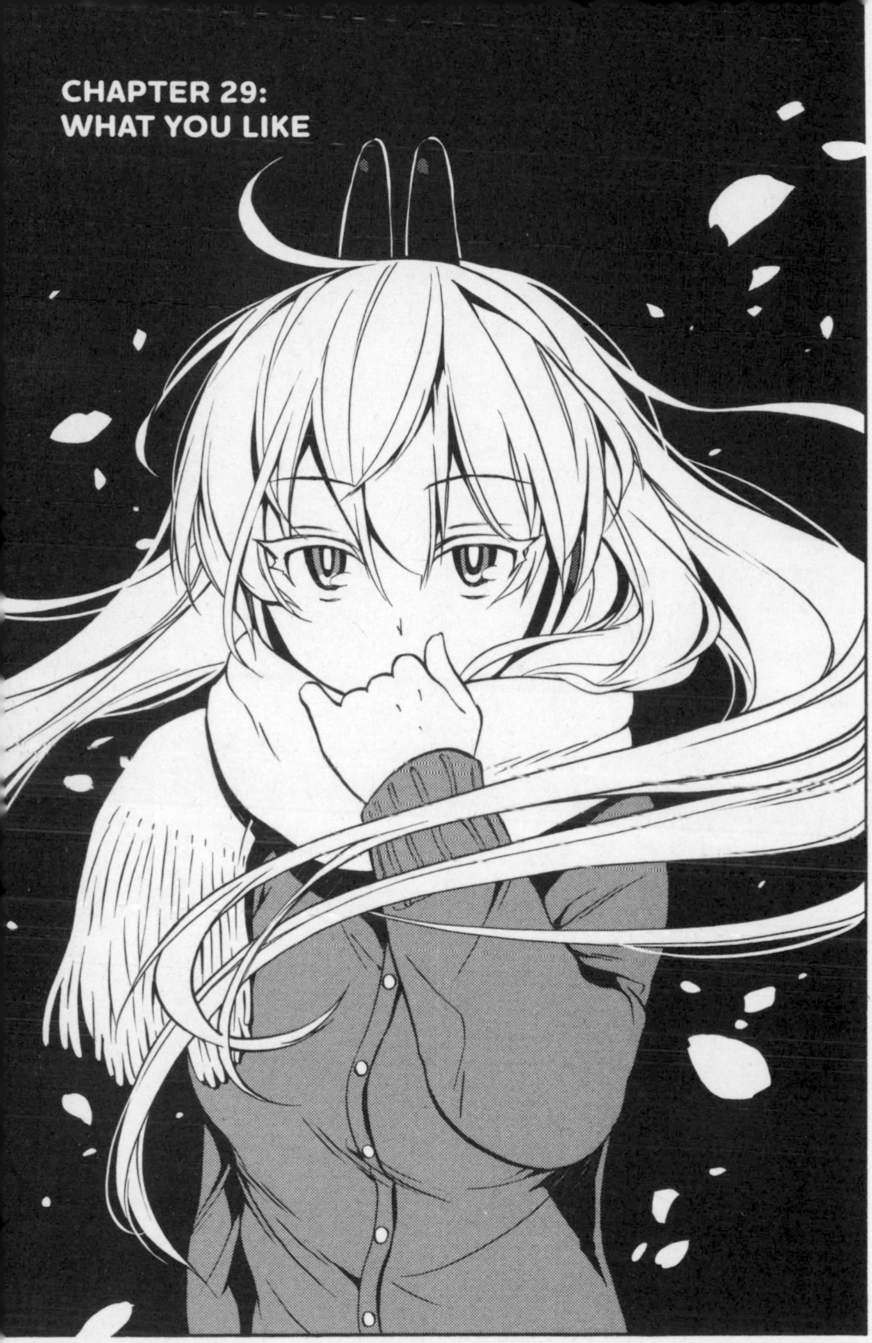
CHAPTER 29:
WHAT YOU LIKE

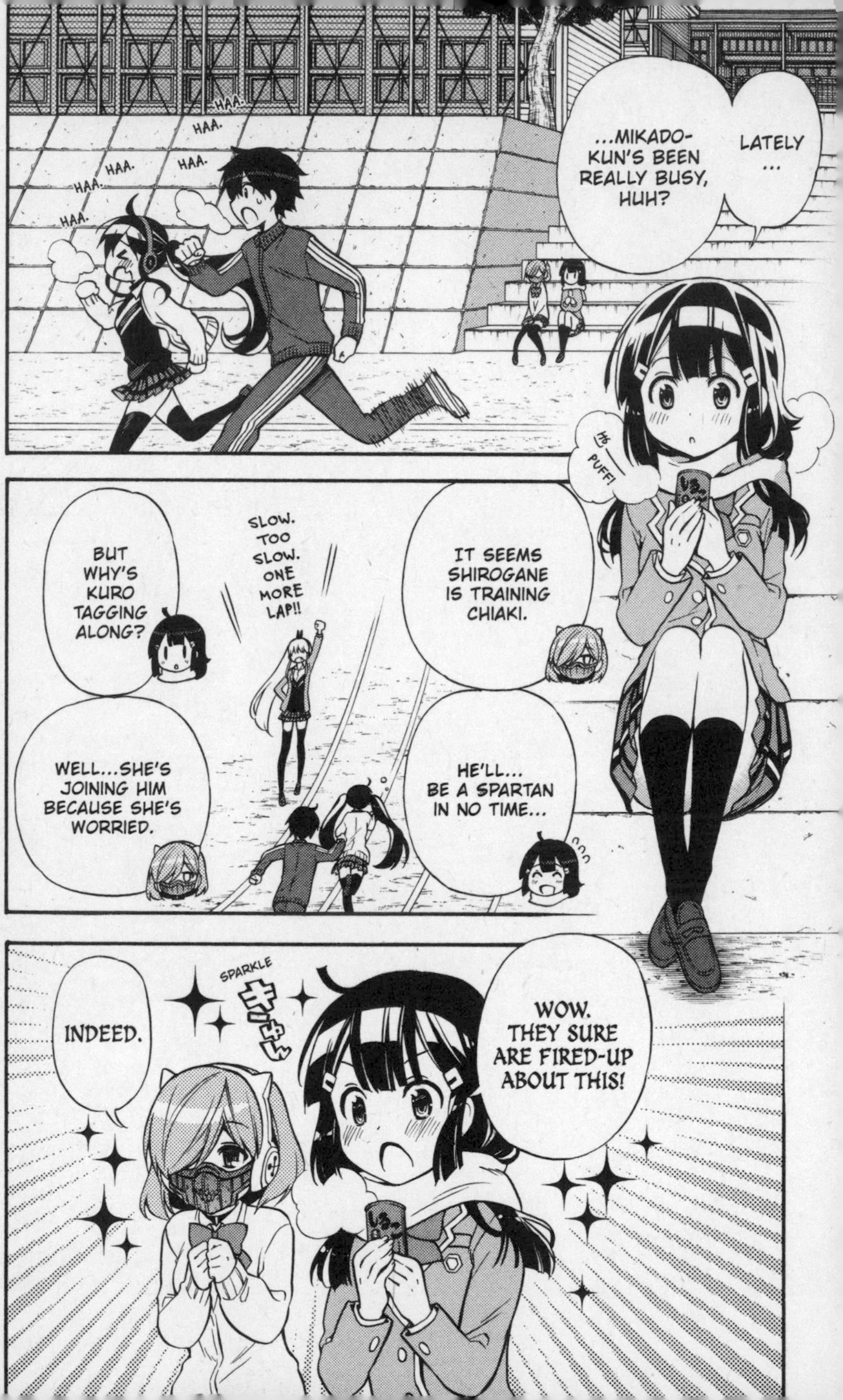
LATELY...
...MIKADO-KUN'S BEEN REALLY BUSY, HUH?
HAA. HAA. HAA. HAA. HAA. HAA.
PUFF!
IT SEEMS SHIROGANE IS TRAINING CHIAKI.
HE'LL... BE A SPARTAN IN NO TIME...
SLOW. TOO SLOW. ONE MORE LAP!!
BUT WHY'S KURO TAGGING ALONG?
WELL...SHE'S JOINING HIM BECAUSE SHE'S WORRIED.
WOW. THEY SURE ARE FIRED-UP ABOUT THIS!
SPARKLE
INDEED.

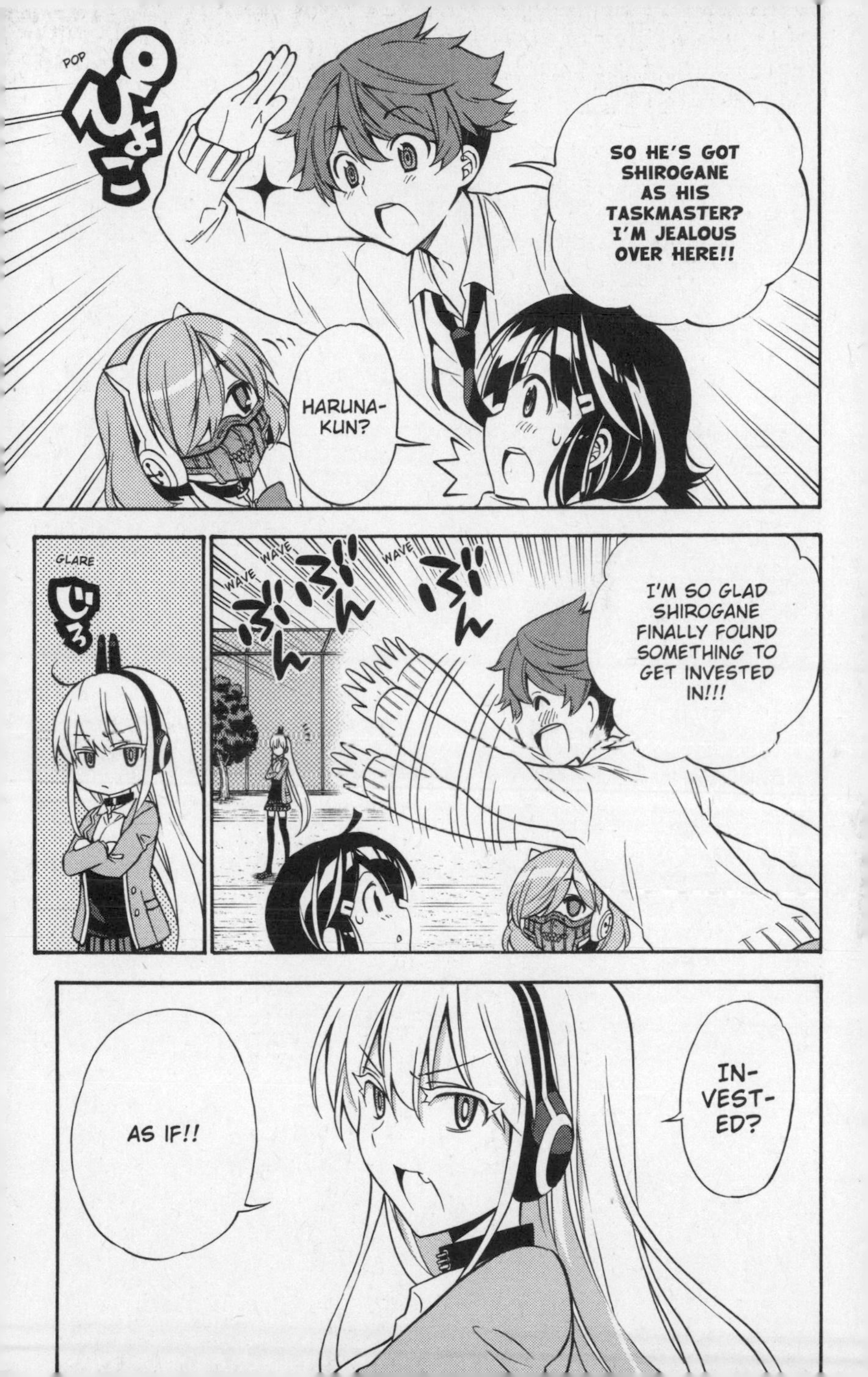
POP
ぴょこ
SO HE'S GOT SHIROGANE AS HIS TASKMASTER? I'M JEALOUS OVER HERE!!
HARUNA-KUN?
I'M SO GLAD SHIROGANE FINALLY FOUND SOMETHING TO GET INVESTED IN!!!
WAVE
ぶん
WAVE
ぶん
WAVE
ぶん
GLARE
じろ
IN-VEST-ED?
AS IF!!

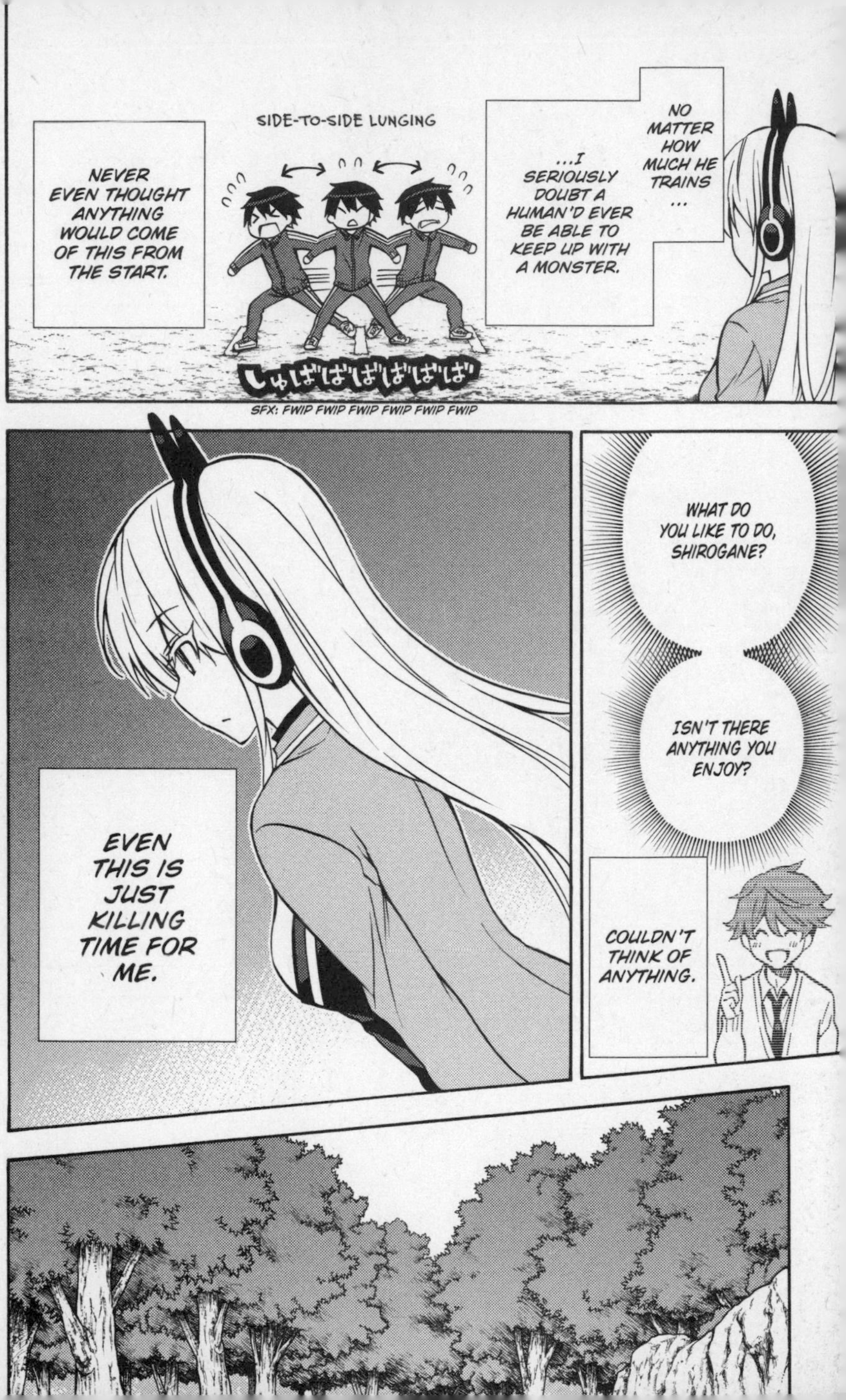
NO MATTER HOW MUCH HE TRAINS ...
...I SERIOUSLY DOUBT A HUMAN'D EVER BE ABLE TO KEEP UP WITH A MONSTER.
SIDE-TO-SIDE LUNGING
NEVER EVEN THOUGHT ANYTHING WOULD COME OF THIS FROM THE START.
しゅばばばばばば
SFX: FWIP FWIP FWIP FWIP FWIP FWIP
WHAT DO YOU LIKE TO DO, SHIROGANE?
ISN'T THERE ANYTHING YOU ENJOY?
COULDN'T THINK OF ANYTHING.
EVEN THIS IS JUST KILLING TIME FOR ME.

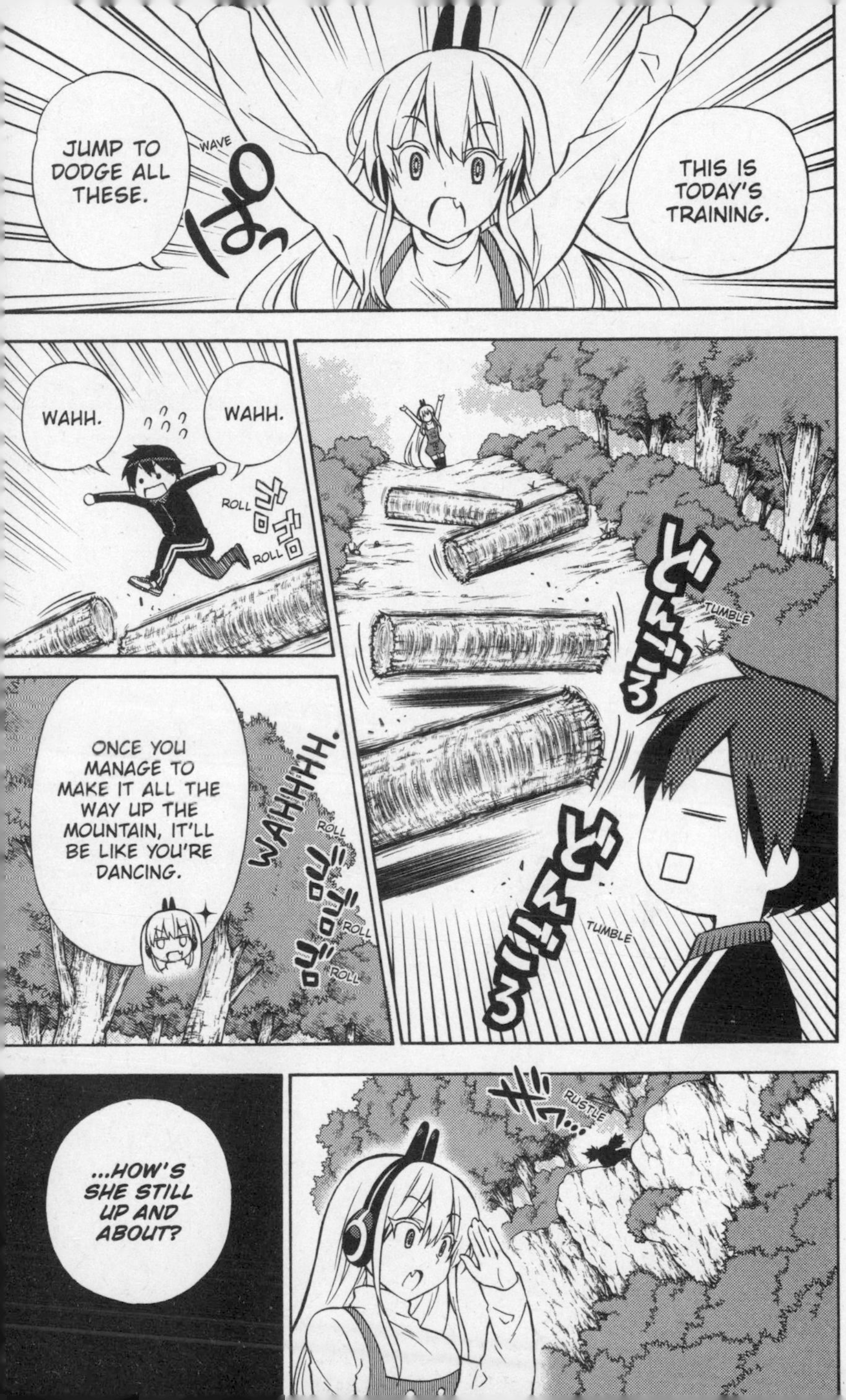
THIS IS TODAY'S TRAINING.
WAVE
JUMP TO DODGE ALL THESE.
TUMBLE
TUMBLE
WAHH.
WAHH.
ROLL
ROLL
WAHHHHH.
ROLL
ROLL
ROLL
ONCE YOU MANAGE TO MAKE IT ALL THE WAY UP THE MOUNTAIN, IT'LL BE LIKE YOU'RE DANCING.
RUSTLE
...HOW'S SHE STILL UP AND ABOUT?

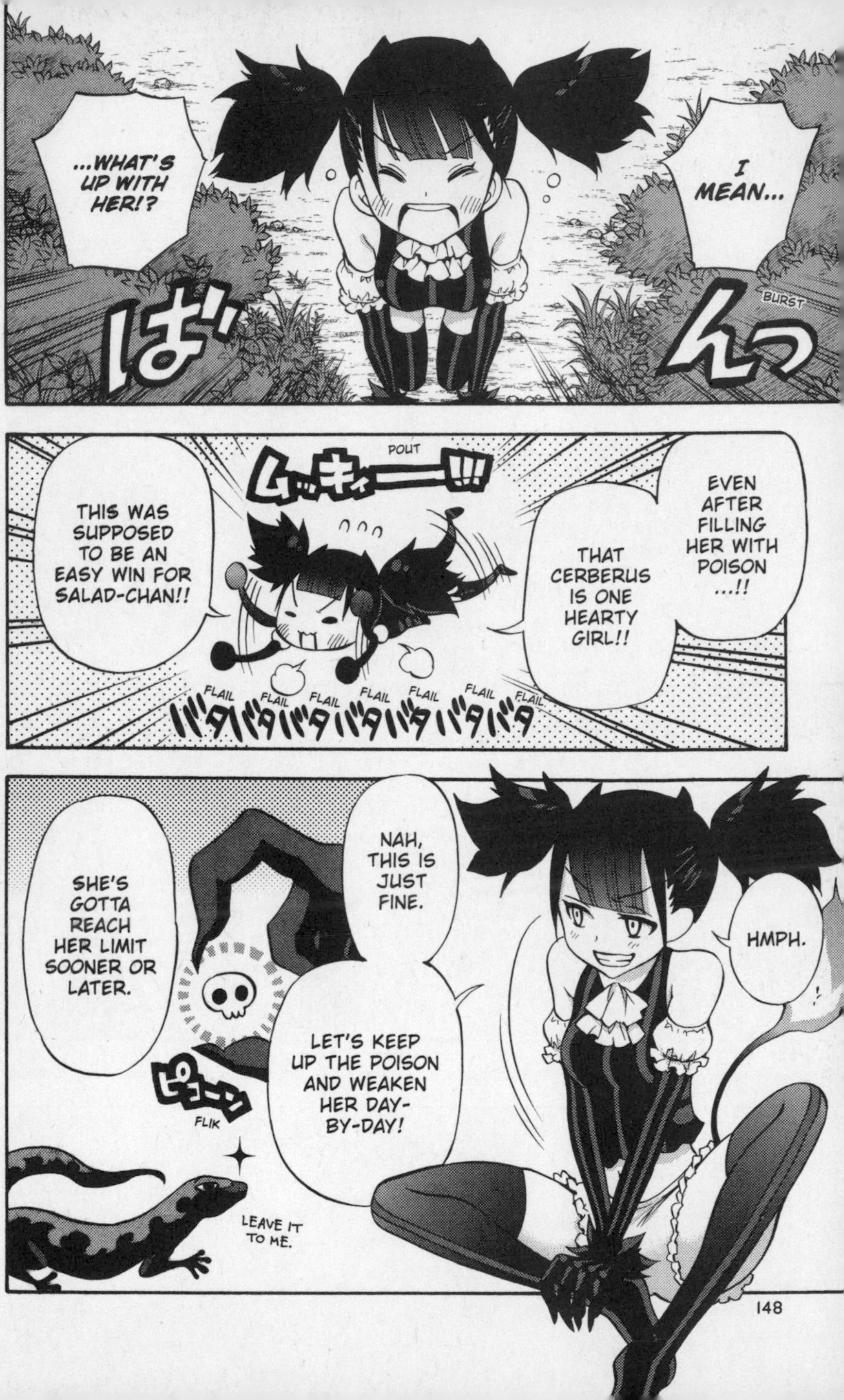
I MEAN...
...WHAT'S UP WITH HER!?
ばんっ
BURST
EVEN AFTER FILLING HER WITH POISON ...!!
THAT CERBERUS IS ONE HEARTY GIRL!!
ムッキィー!!!
POUT
THIS WAS SUPPOSED TO BE AN EASY WIN FOR SALAD-CHAN!!
バタバタバタバタバタバタバタ
FLAIL FLAIL FLAIL FLAIL FLAIL FLAIL FLAIL
HMPH.
NAH, THIS IS JUST FINE.
LET'S KEEP UP THE POISON AND WEAKEN HER DAY-BY-DAY!
SHE'S GOTTA REACH HER LIMIT SOONER OR LATER.
ピコーン
FLIK
LEAVE IT TO ME.

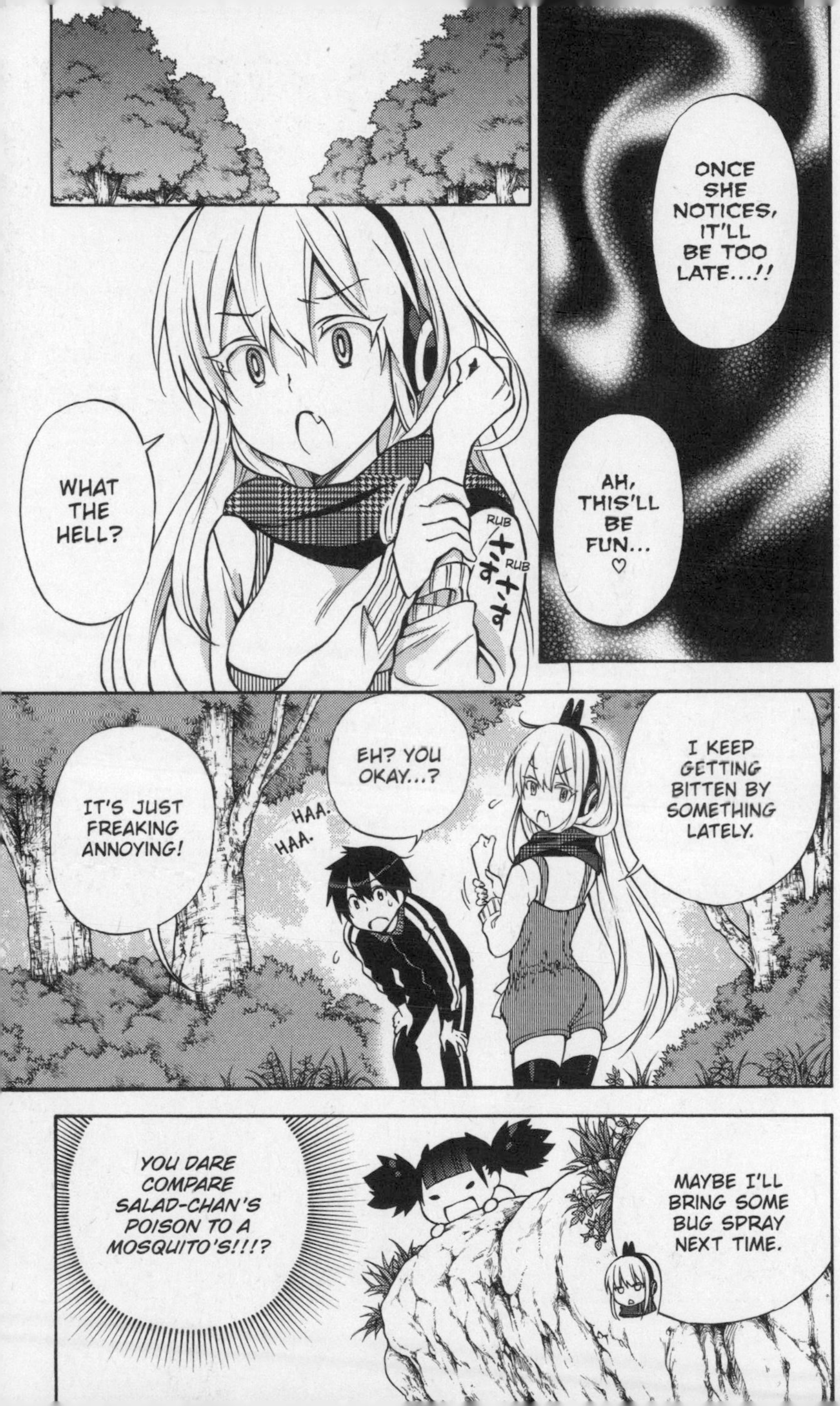
ONCE SHE NOTICES, IT'LL BE TOO LATE...!!
AH, THIS'LL BE FUN... ♡
WHAT THE HELL?
RUB RUB
さすさす
I KEEP GETTING BITTEN BY SOMETHING LATELY.
EH? YOU OKAY...?
HAA. HAA.
IT'S JUST FREAKING ANNOYING!
MAYBE I'LL BRING SOME BUG SPRAY NEXT TIME.
YOU DARE COMPARE SALAD-CHAN'S POISON TO A MOSQUITO'S!!!?

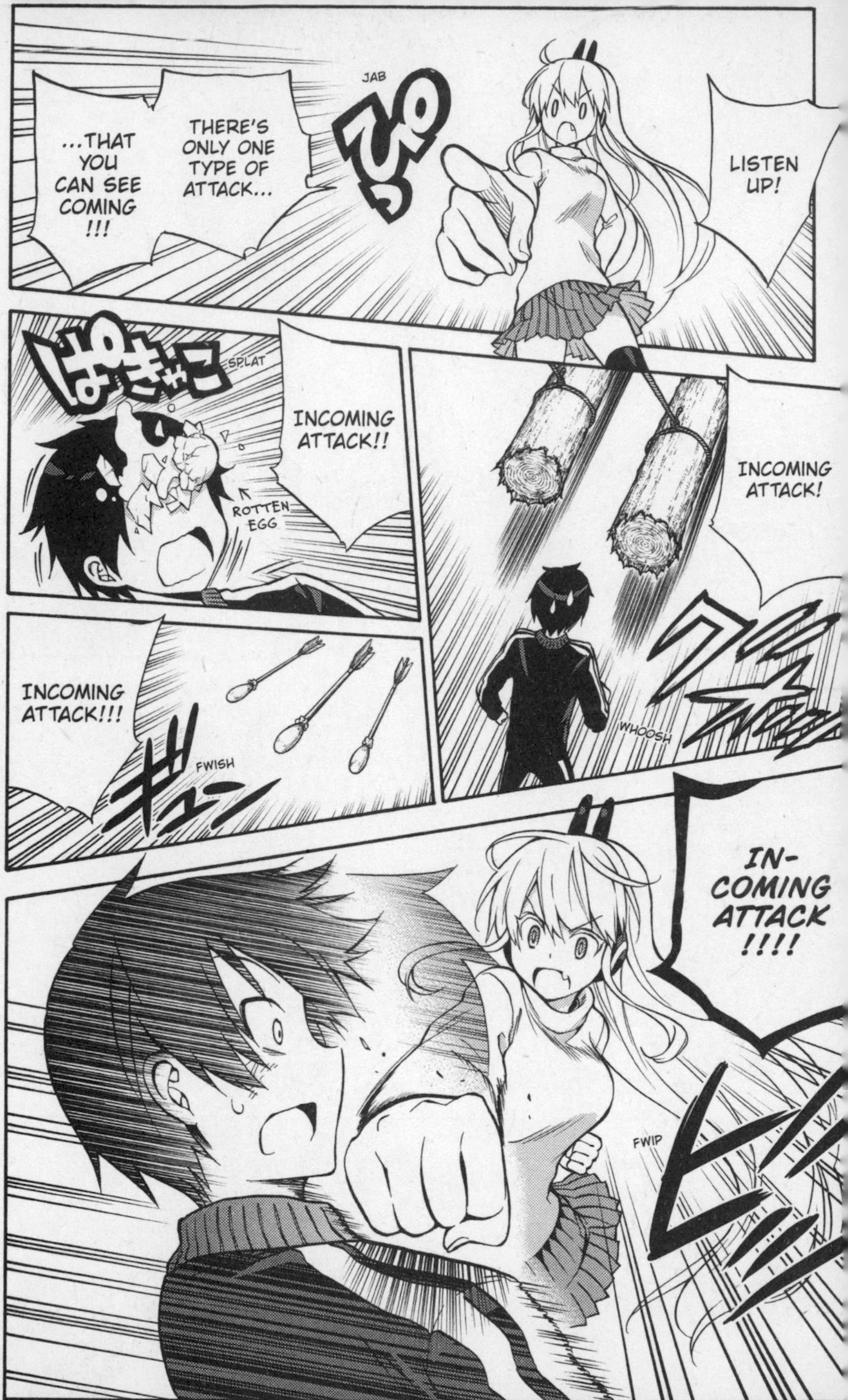
LISTEN UP!
JAB
THERE'S ONLY ONE TYPE OF ATTACK...
...THAT YOU CAN SEE COMING!!!
INCOMING ATTACK!
WHOOSH
INCOMING ATTACK!!
SPLAT
ROTTEN EGG
INCOMING ATTACK!!!
FWISH
IN-COMING ATTACK!!!!
FWIP

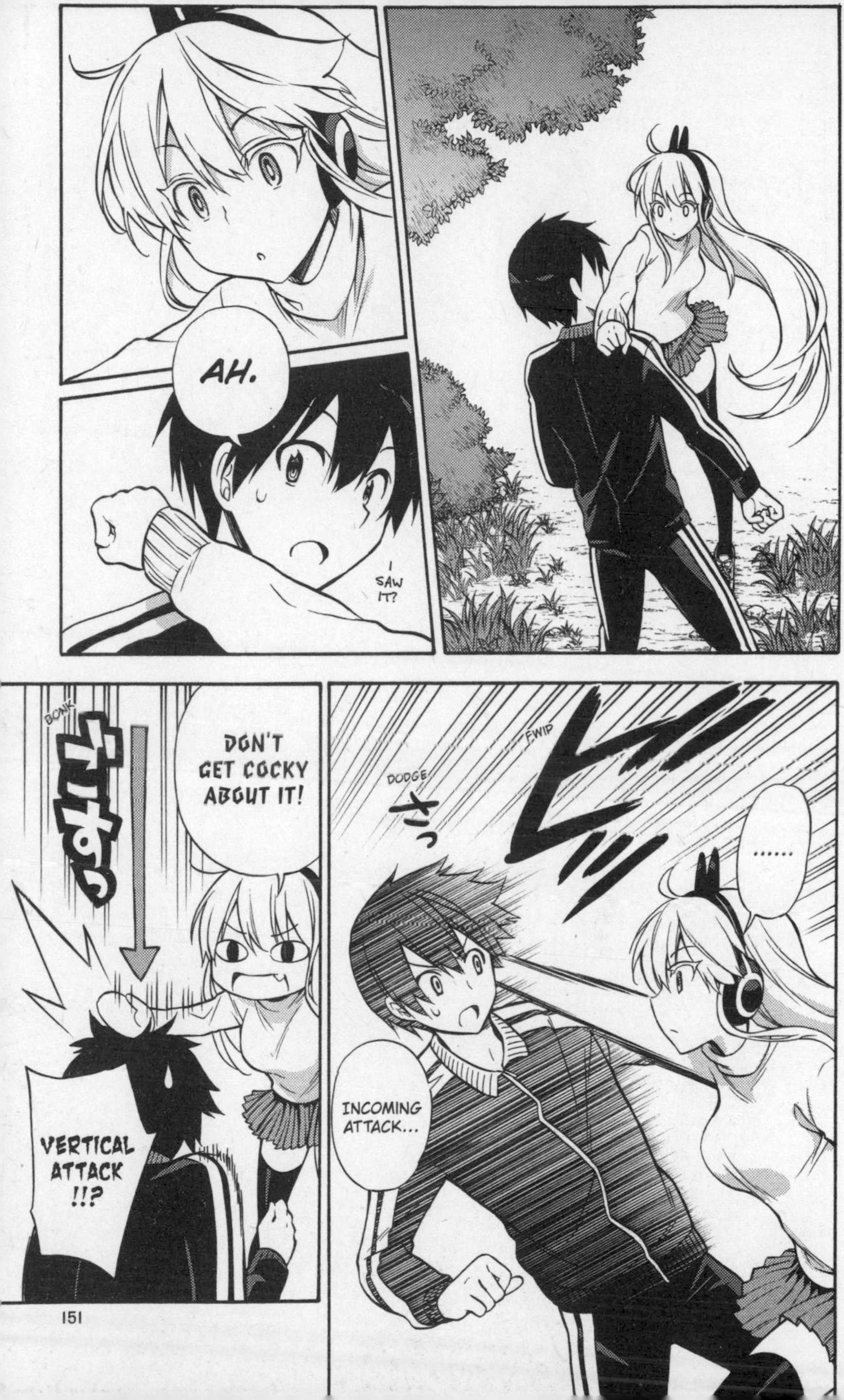
AH.
I SAW IT?
DODGE
さっ
FWIP
......
INCOMING ATTACK...
BONK
DON'T GET COCKY ABOUT IT!
VERTICAL ATTACK !!?

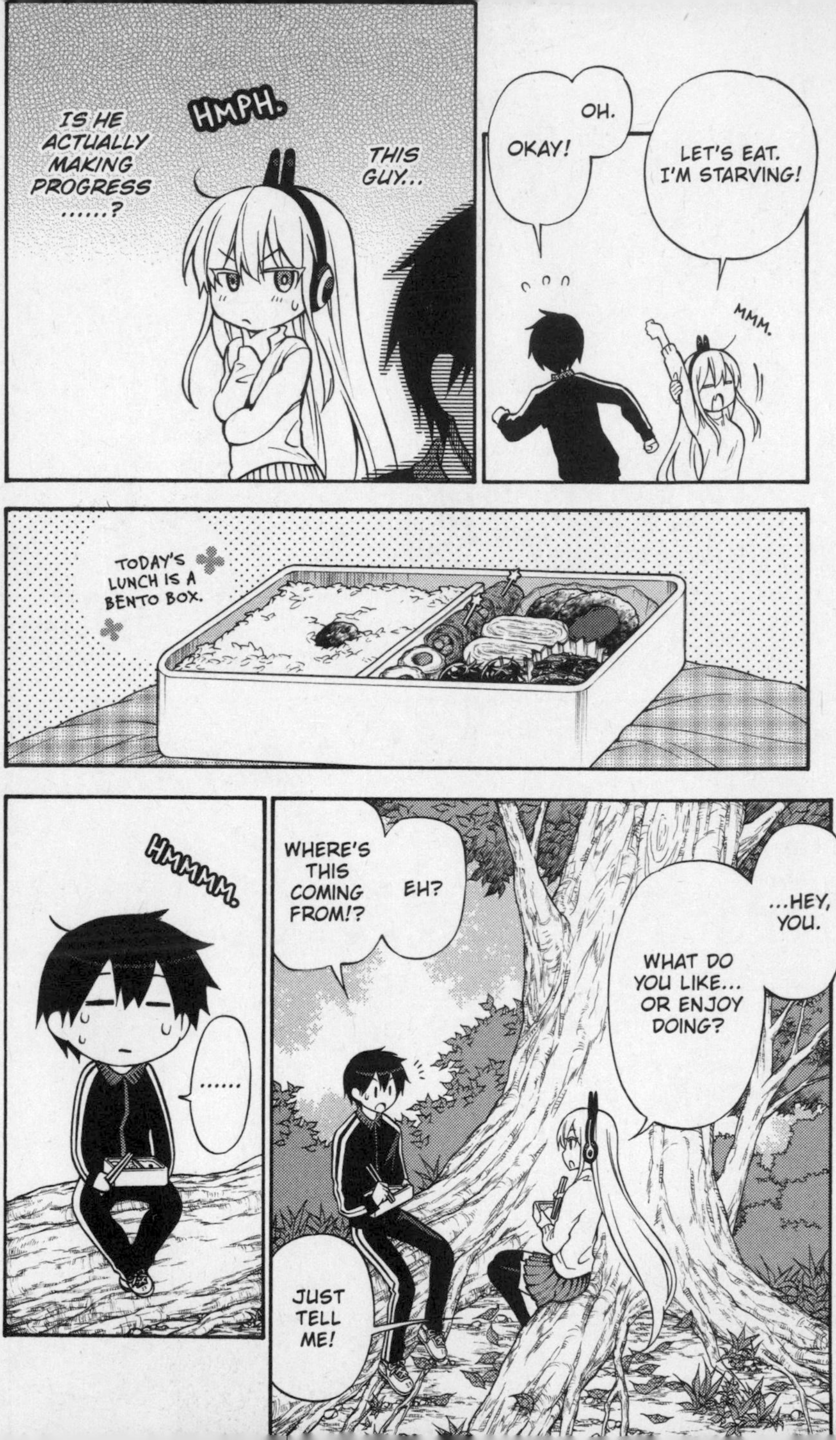
LET'S EAT. I'M STARVING!
OH.
OKAY!
MMM.
THIS GUY...
HMPH.
IS HE ACTUALLY MAKING PROGRESS ......?
TODAY'S LUNCH IS A BENTO BOX.
...HEY, YOU.
WHAT DO YOU LIKE... OR ENJOY DOING?
EH?
WHERE'S THIS COMING FROM!?
JUST TELL ME!
HMMMM.
......

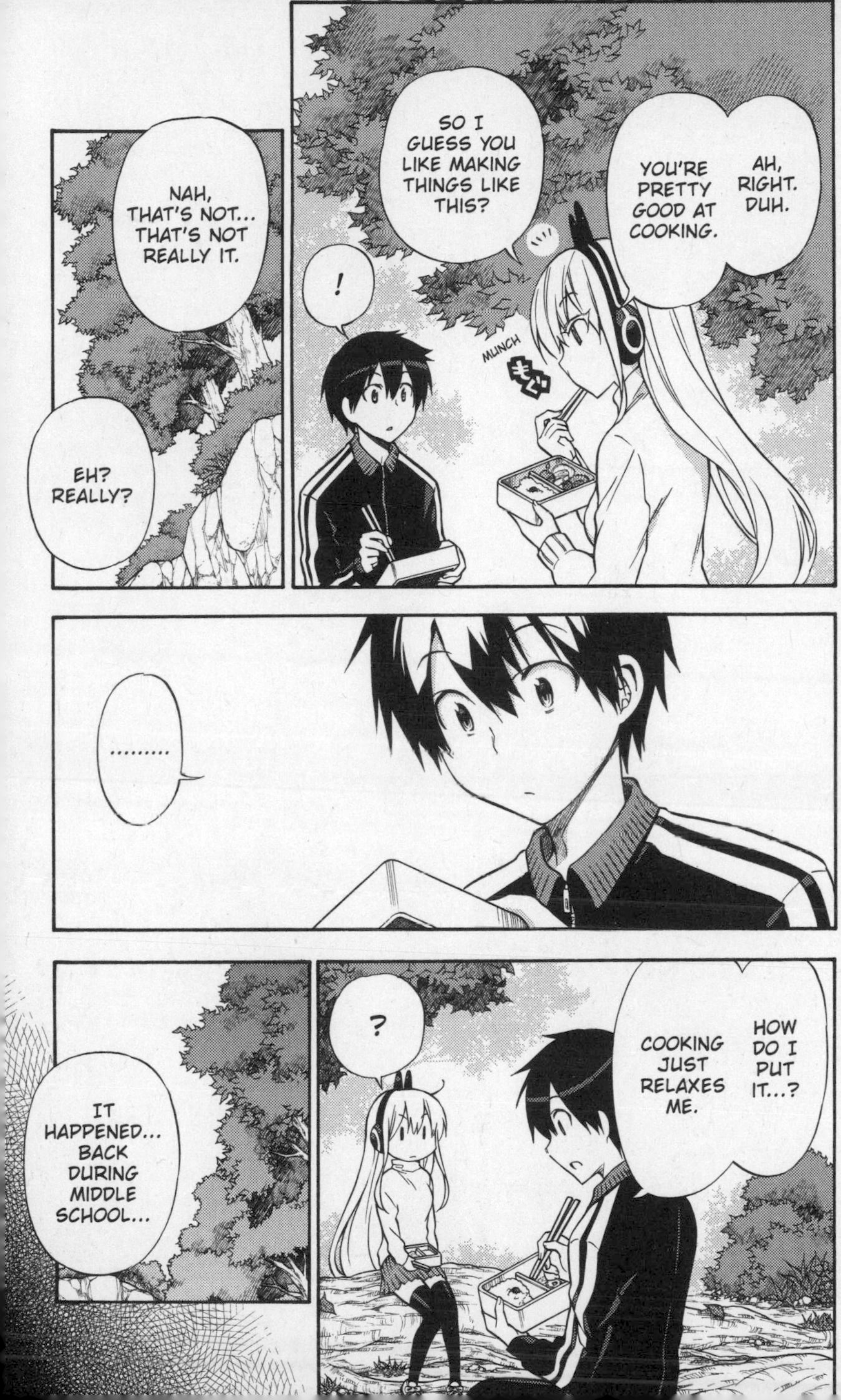
AH, RIGHT. DUH.
YOU'RE PRETTY GOOD AT COOKING.
SO I GUESS YOU LIKE MAKING THINGS LIKE THIS?
MUNCH
!
NAH, THAT'S NOT... THAT'S NOT REALLY IT.
EH? REALLY?
....
HOW DO I PUT IT...?
COOKING JUST RELAXES ME.
?
IT HAPPENED... BACK DURING MIDDLE SCHOOL...

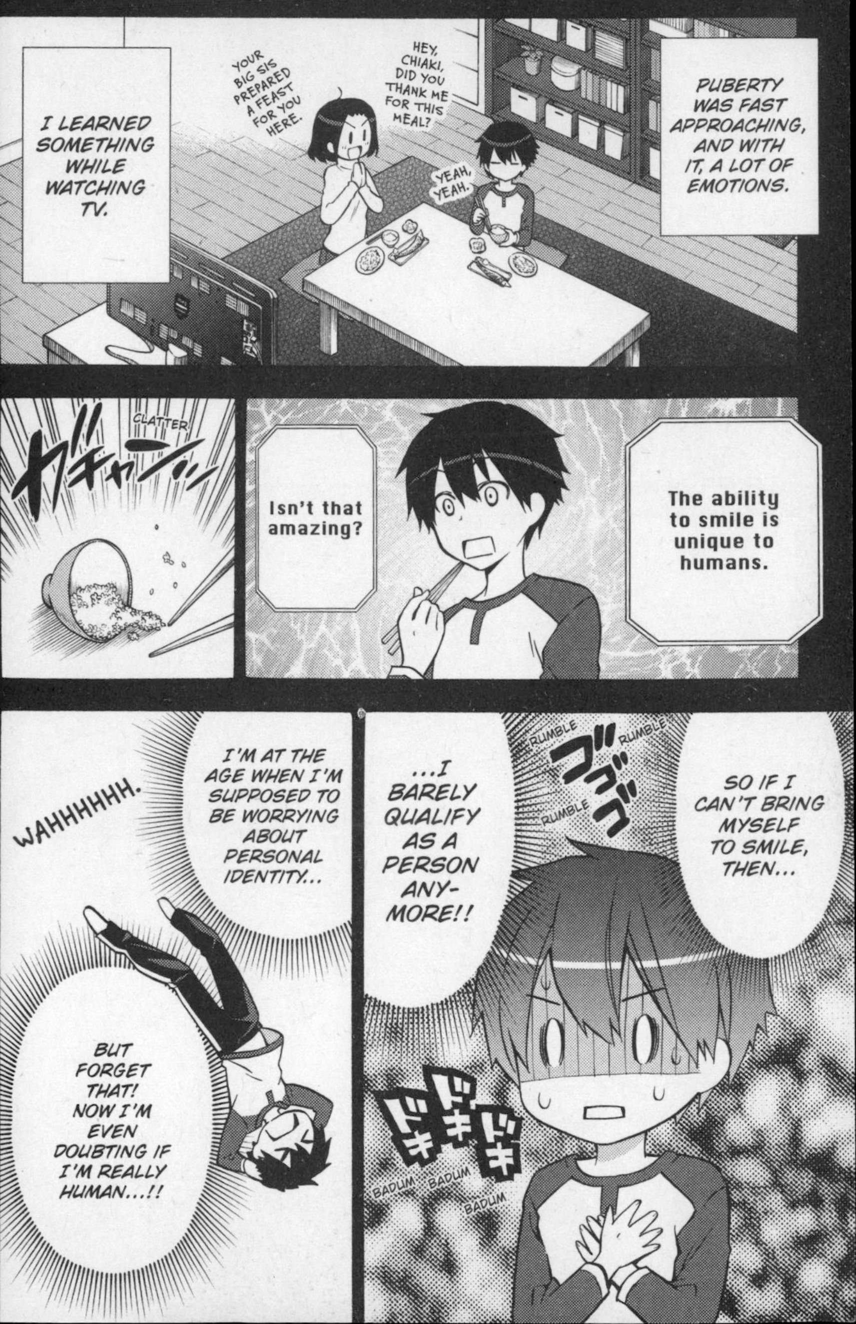
PUBERTY WAS FAST APPROACHING, AND WITH IT, A LOT OF EMOTIONS.
HEY, CHIAKI, DID YOU THANK ME FOR THIS MEAL?
YOUR BIG SIS PREPARED A FEAST FOR YOU HERE.
YEAH, YEAH.
I LEARNED SOMETHING WHILE WATCHING TV.
The ability to smile is unique to humans.
Isn't that amazing?
CLATTER
SO IF I CAN'T BRING MYSELF TO SMILE, THEN...
RUMBLE
RUMBLE
RUMBLE
...I BARELY QUALIFY AS A PERSON ANYMORE!!
BADUM
BADUM
BADUM
I'M AT THE AGE WHEN I'M SUPPOSED TO BE WORRYING ABOUT PERSONAL IDENTITY...
WAHHHHHH.
BUT FORGET THAT! NOW I'M EVEN DOUBTING IF I'M REALLY HUMAN...!!

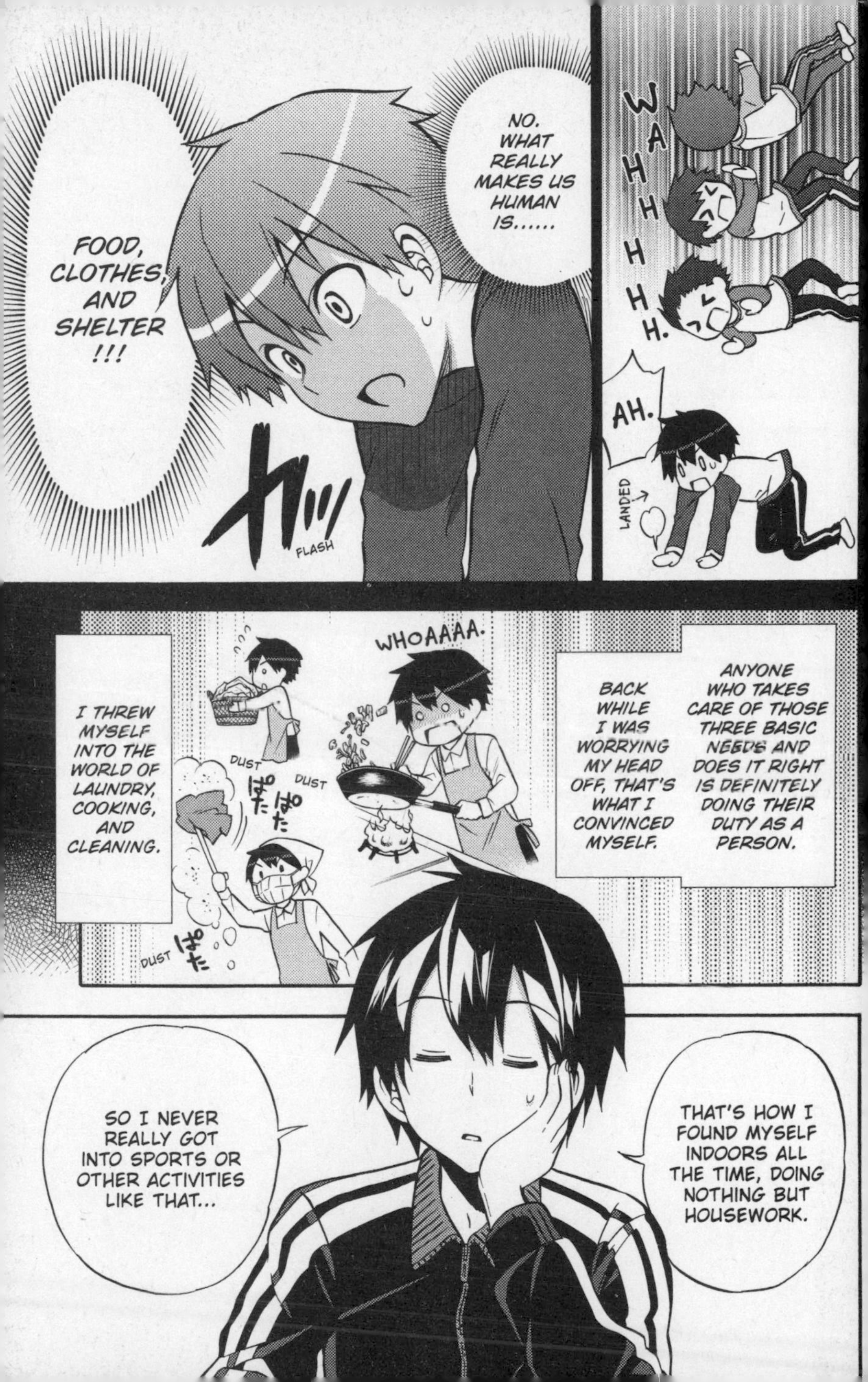
WAHHHHH.
AH.
LANDED
NO. WHAT REALLY MAKES US HUMAN IS......
FOOD, CLOTHES, AND SHELTER !!!
FLASH
ANYONE WHO TAKES CARE OF THOSE THREE BASIC NEEDS AND DOES IT RIGHT IS DEFINITELY DOING THEIR DUTY AS A PERSON.
BACK WHILE I WAS WORRYING MY HEAD OFF, THAT'S WHAT I CONVINCED MYSELF.
WHOAAAA.
DUST
ぱたぱた
DUST
I THREW MYSELF INTO THE WORLD OF LAUNDRY, COOKING, AND CLEANING.
DUST
ぱた
THAT'S HOW I FOUND MYSELF INDOORS ALL THE TIME, DOING NOTHING BUT HOUSEWORK.
SO I NEVER REALLY GOT INTO SPORTS OR OTHER ACTIVITIES LIKE THAT...

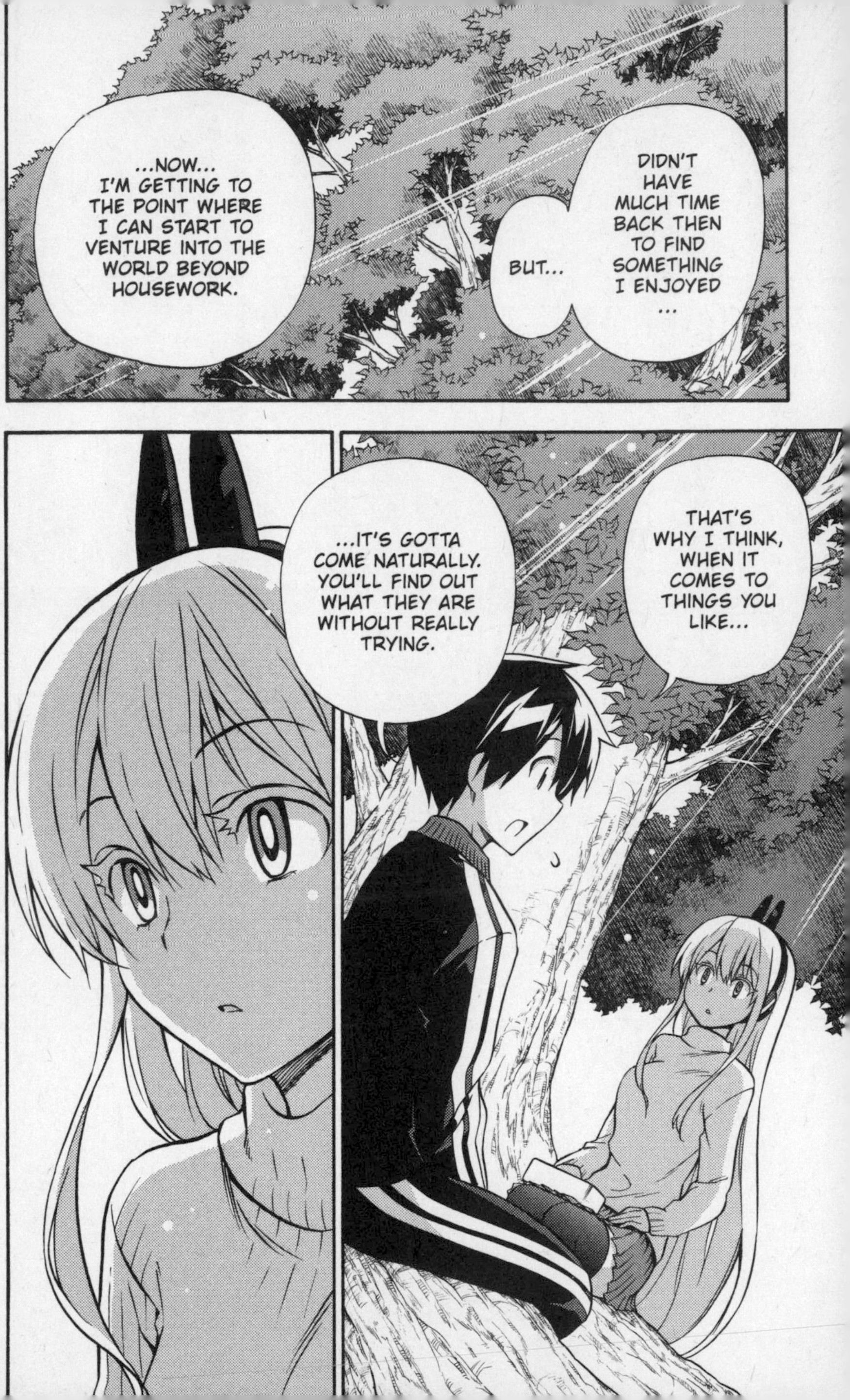
DIDN'T HAVE MUCH TIME BACK THEN TO FIND SOMETHING I ENJOYED ...
BUT...
...NOW... I'M GETTING TO THE POINT WHERE I CAN START TO VENTURE INTO THE WORLD BEYOND HOUSEWORK.
THAT'S WHY I THINK, WHEN IT COMES TO THINGS YOU LIKE...
...IT'S GOTTA COME NATURALLY. YOU'LL FIND OUT WHAT THEY ARE WITHOUT REALLY TRYING.

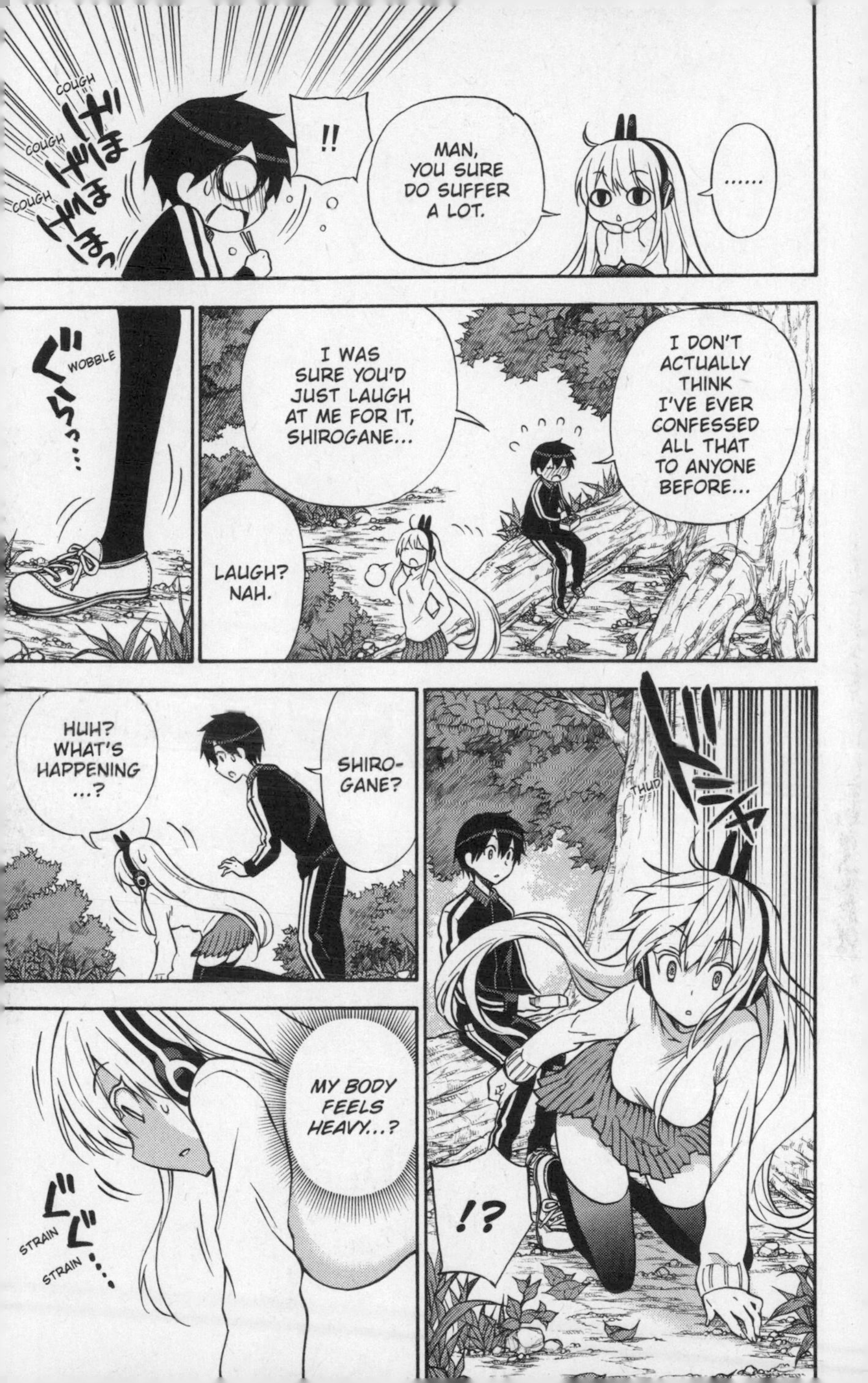
......
MAN, YOU SURE DO SUFFER A LOT.
!!
げほ COUGH
げほ COUGH
げほっ COUGH
I DON'T ACTUALLY THINK I'VE EVER CONFESSED ALL THAT TO ANYONE BEFORE...
I WAS SURE YOU'D JUST LAUGH AT ME FOR IT, SHIROGANE...
LAUGH? NAH.
ぐらっ… WOBBLE
ドシャ THUD
!?
SHIRO-GANE?
HUH? WHAT'S HAPPENING...?
MY BODY FEELS HEAVY...?
ぐぐ… STRAIN STRAIN

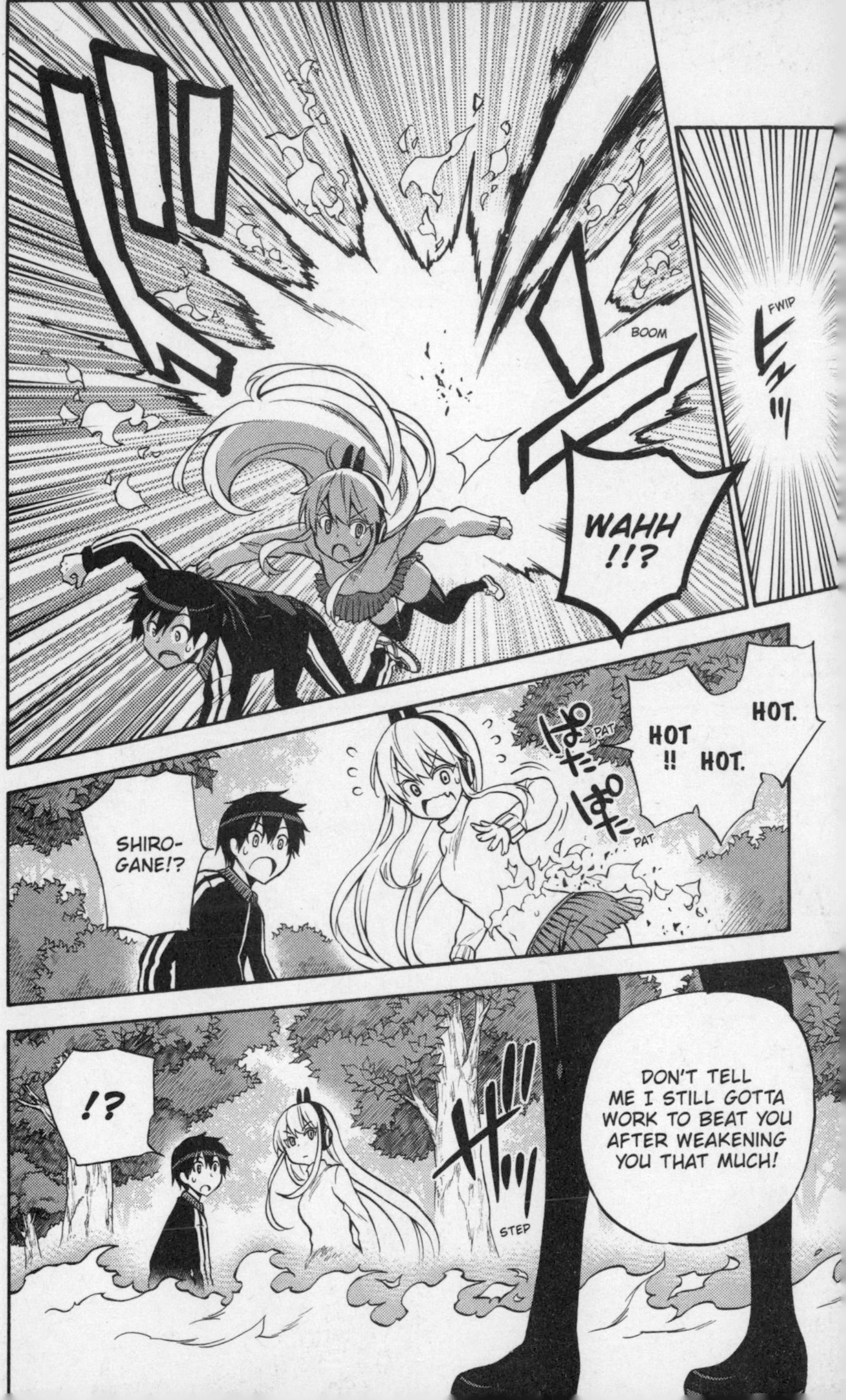
FWIP
BOOM
WAHH !!?
HOT.
HOT !!
HOT.
PAT
PAT
SHIRO-GANE!?
DON'T TELL ME I STILL GOTTA WORK TO BEAT YOU AFTER WEAKENING YOU THAT MUCH!
STEP
!?

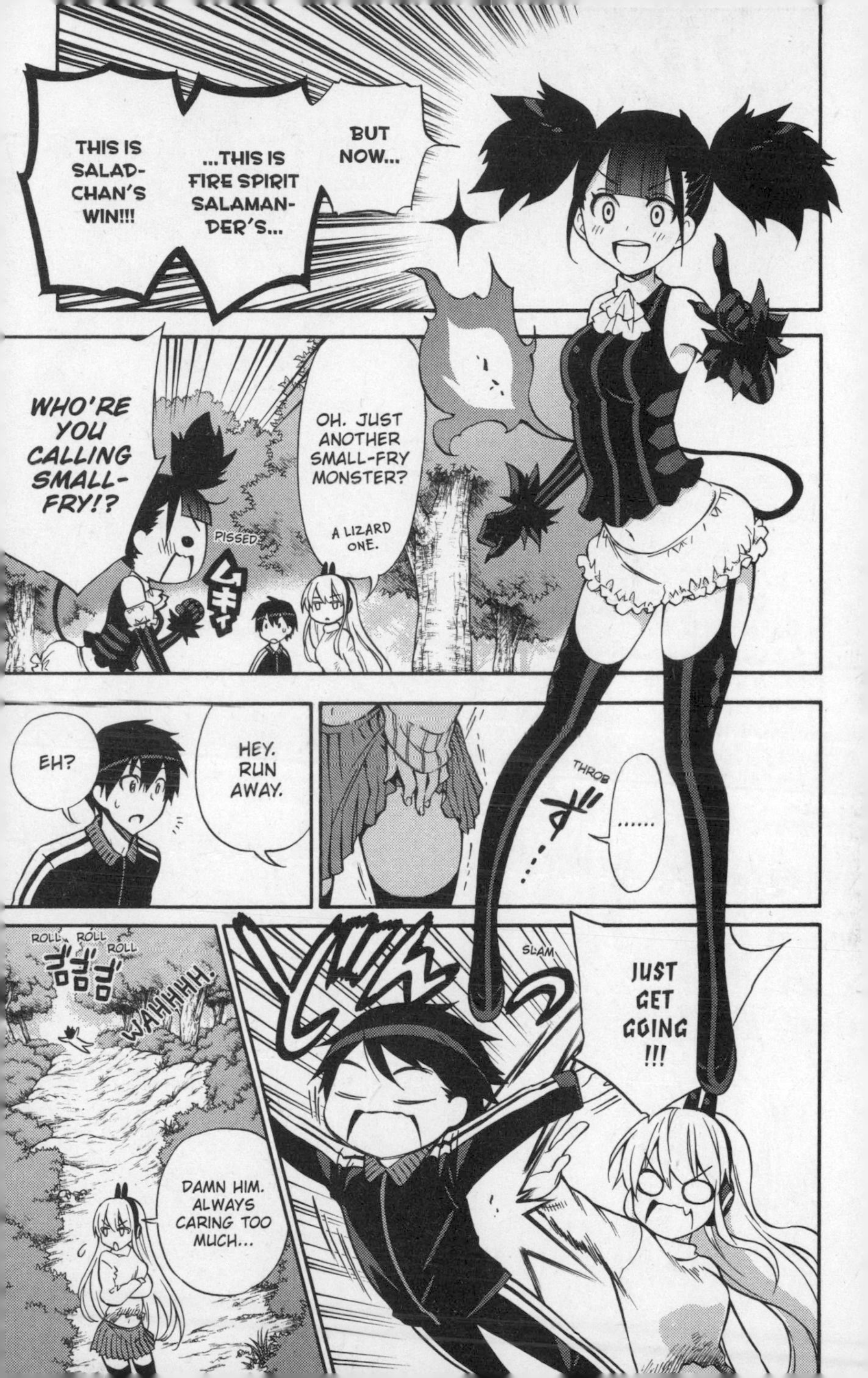
BUT NOW...
...THIS IS FIRE SPIRIT SALAMANDER'S...
THIS IS SALAD-CHAN'S WIN!!!
OH. JUST ANOTHER SMALL-FRY MONSTER?
A LIZARD ONE.
WHO'RE YOU CALLING SMALL-FRY!?
PISSED
ムキィ
THROB
ず...
......
HEY. RUN AWAY.
EH?
JUST GET GOING!!!
SLAM
ROLL ROLL ROLL
ゴロゴロ
WAHHHH.
DAMN HIM. ALWAYS CARING TOO MUCH...

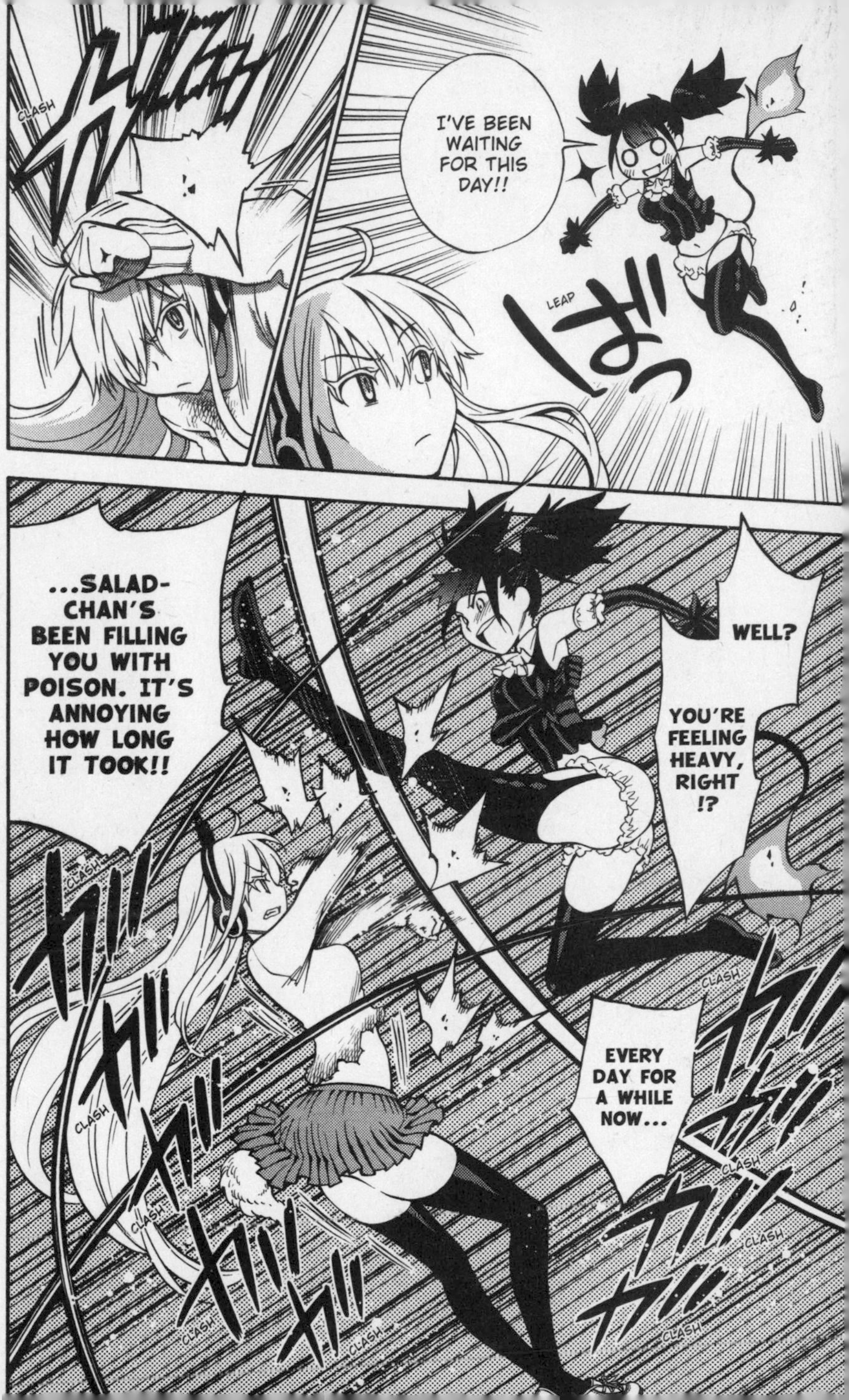
I'VE BEEN WAITING FOR THIS DAY!!
LEAP
CLASH
WELL?
YOU'RE FEELING HEAVY, RIGHT!?
EVERY DAY FOR A WHILE NOW...
...SALAD-CHAN'S BEEN FILLING YOU WITH POISON. IT'S ANNOYING HOW LONG IT TOOK!!
CLASH
CLASH
CLASH
CLASH
CLASH
CLASH
CLASH
CLASH
CLASH

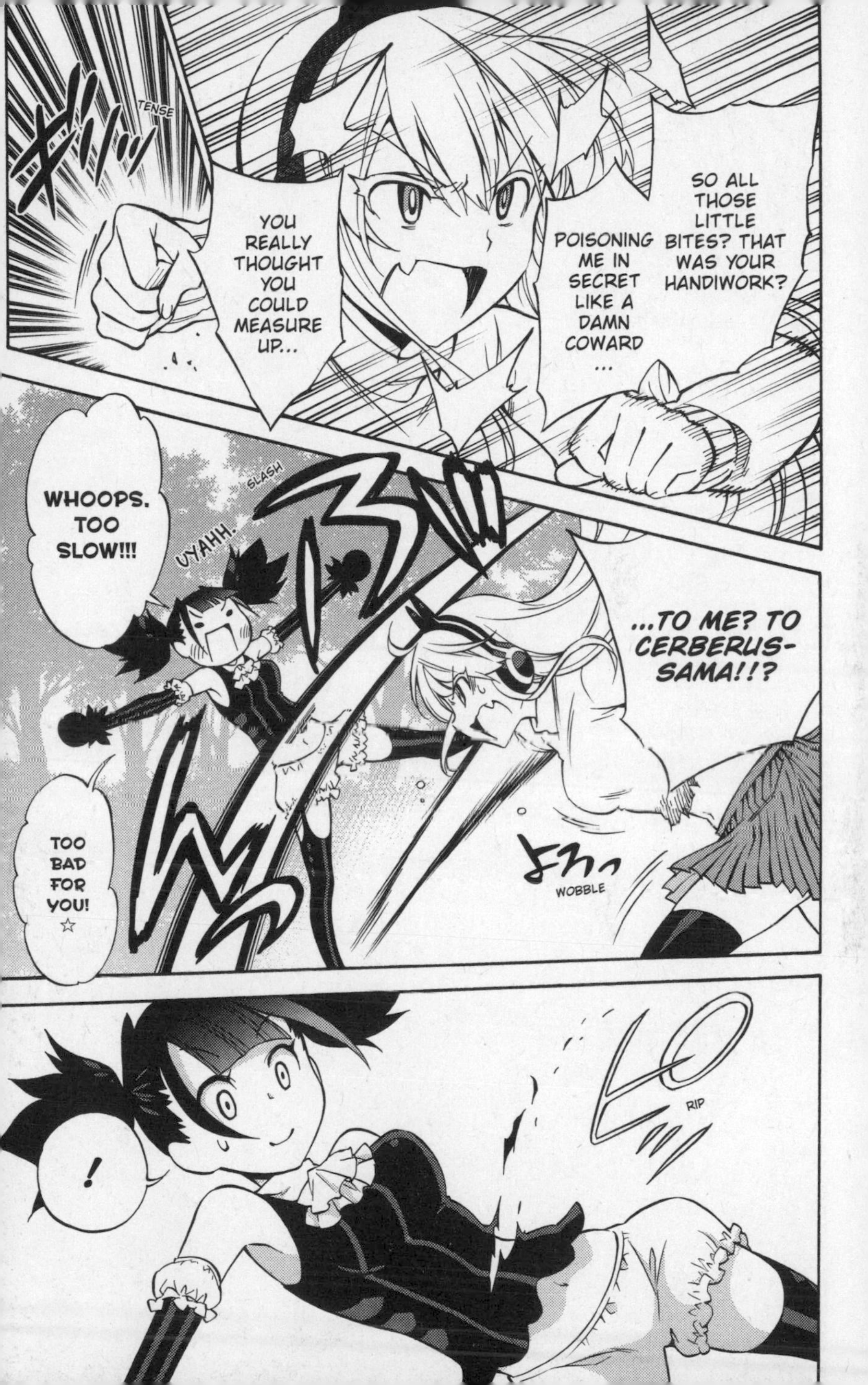
SO ALL THOSE LITTLE BITES? THAT WAS YOUR HANDIWORK?
POISONING ME IN SECRET LIKE A DAMN COWARD ...
YOU REALLY THOUGHT YOU COULD MEASURE UP...
TENSE
...TO ME? TO CERBERUS-SAMA!!?
よろっ
WOBBLE
SLASH
UYAHH.
WHOOPS. TOO SLOW!!!
TOO BAD FOR YOU! ☆
RIP
!

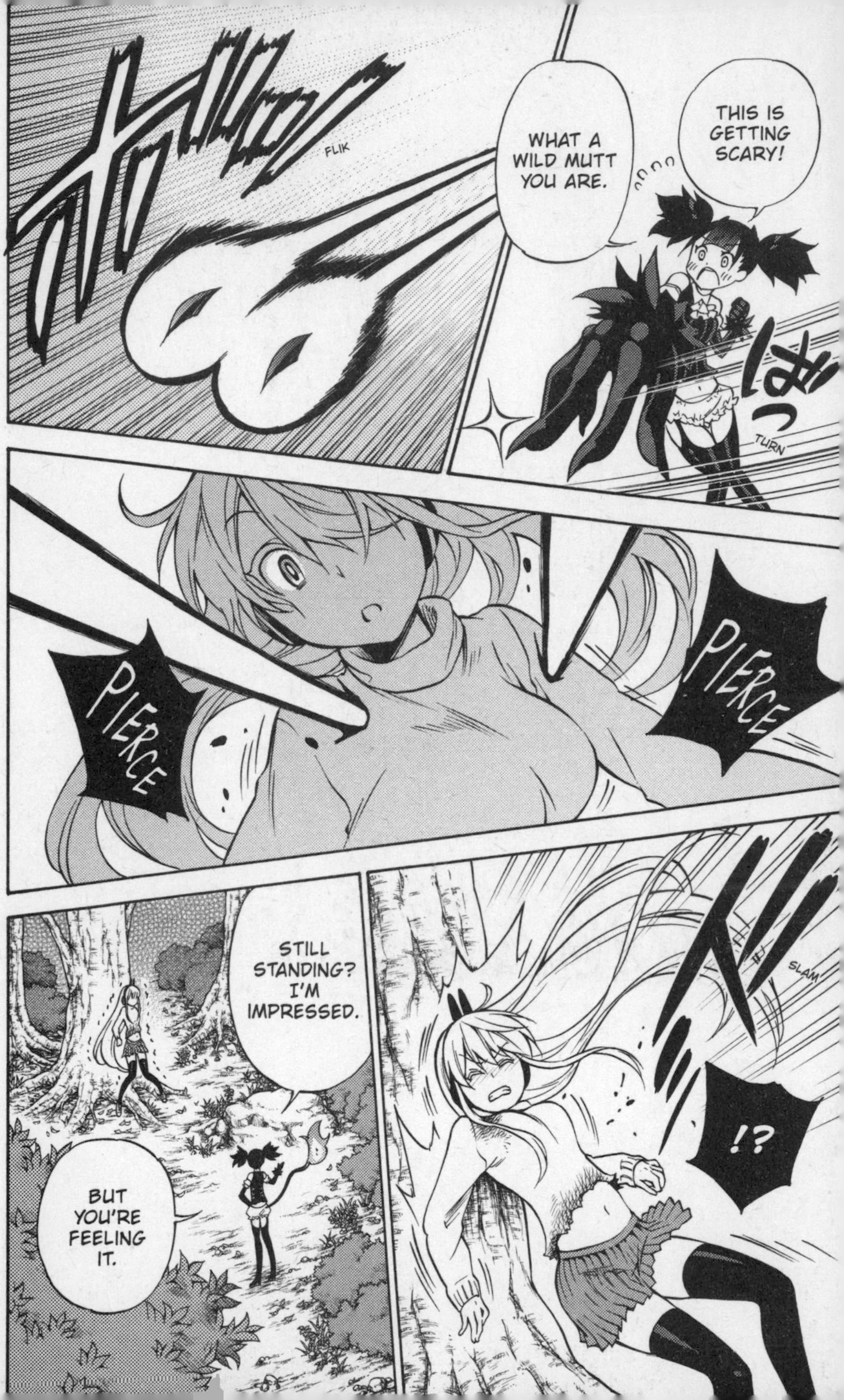

THIS IS GETTING SCARY!
WHAT A WILD MUTT YOU ARE.
ぱっ
TURN
FLIK
PIERCE
PIERCE
SLAM
!?
STILL STANDING? I'M IMPRESSED.
BUT YOU'RE FEELING IT.

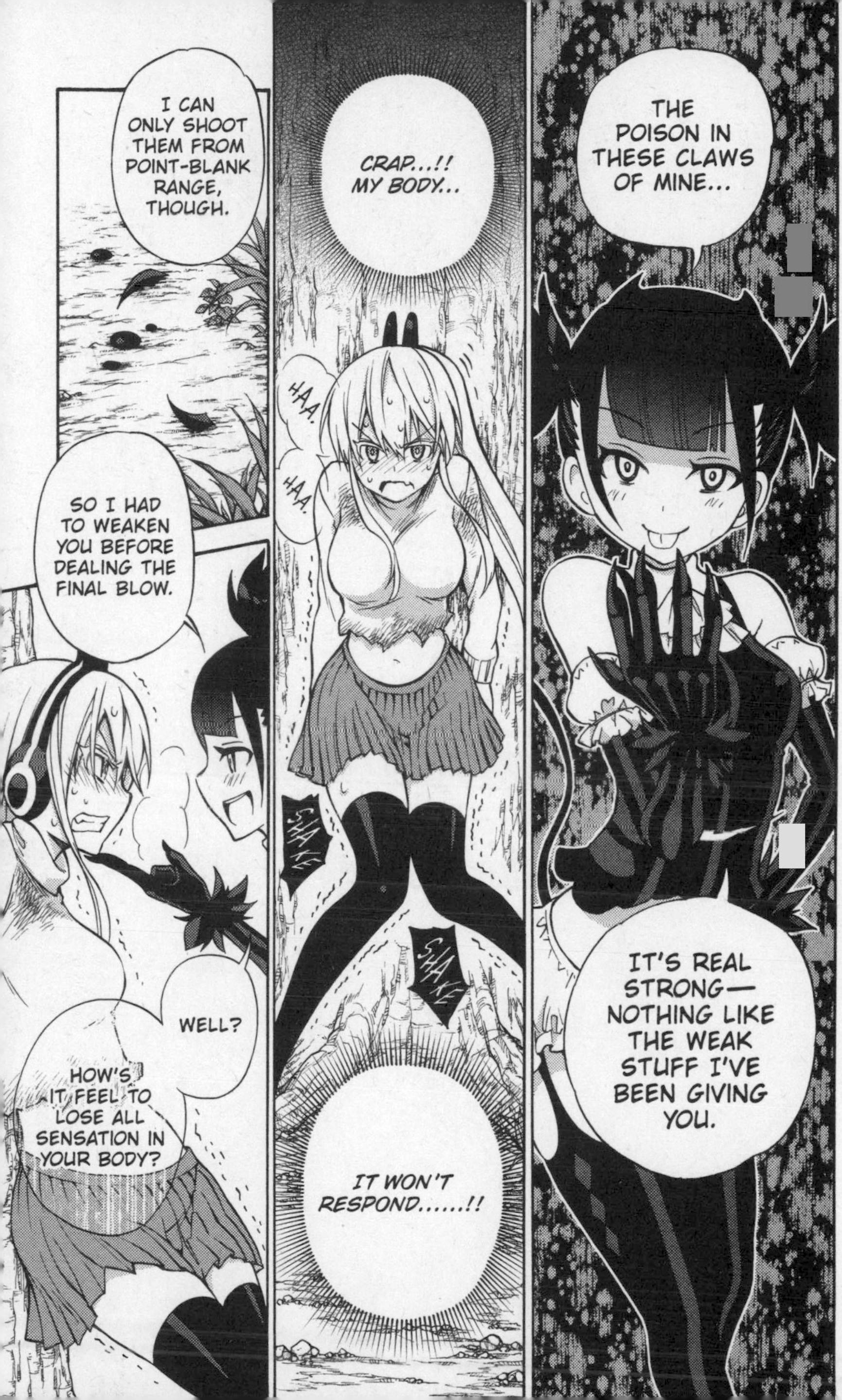
THE POISON IN THESE CLAWS OF MINE...
IT'S REAL STRONG—NOTHING LIKE THE WEAK STUFF I'VE BEEN GIVING YOU.
CRAP...!! MY BODY...
HAA
HAA
SHAKE
SHAKE
IT WON'T RESPOND......!!
I CAN ONLY SHOOT THEM FROM POINT-BLANK RANGE, THOUGH.
SO I HAD TO WEAKEN YOU BEFORE DEALING THE FINAL BLOW.
WELL?
HOW'S IT FEEL TO LOSE ALL SENSATION IN YOUR BODY?

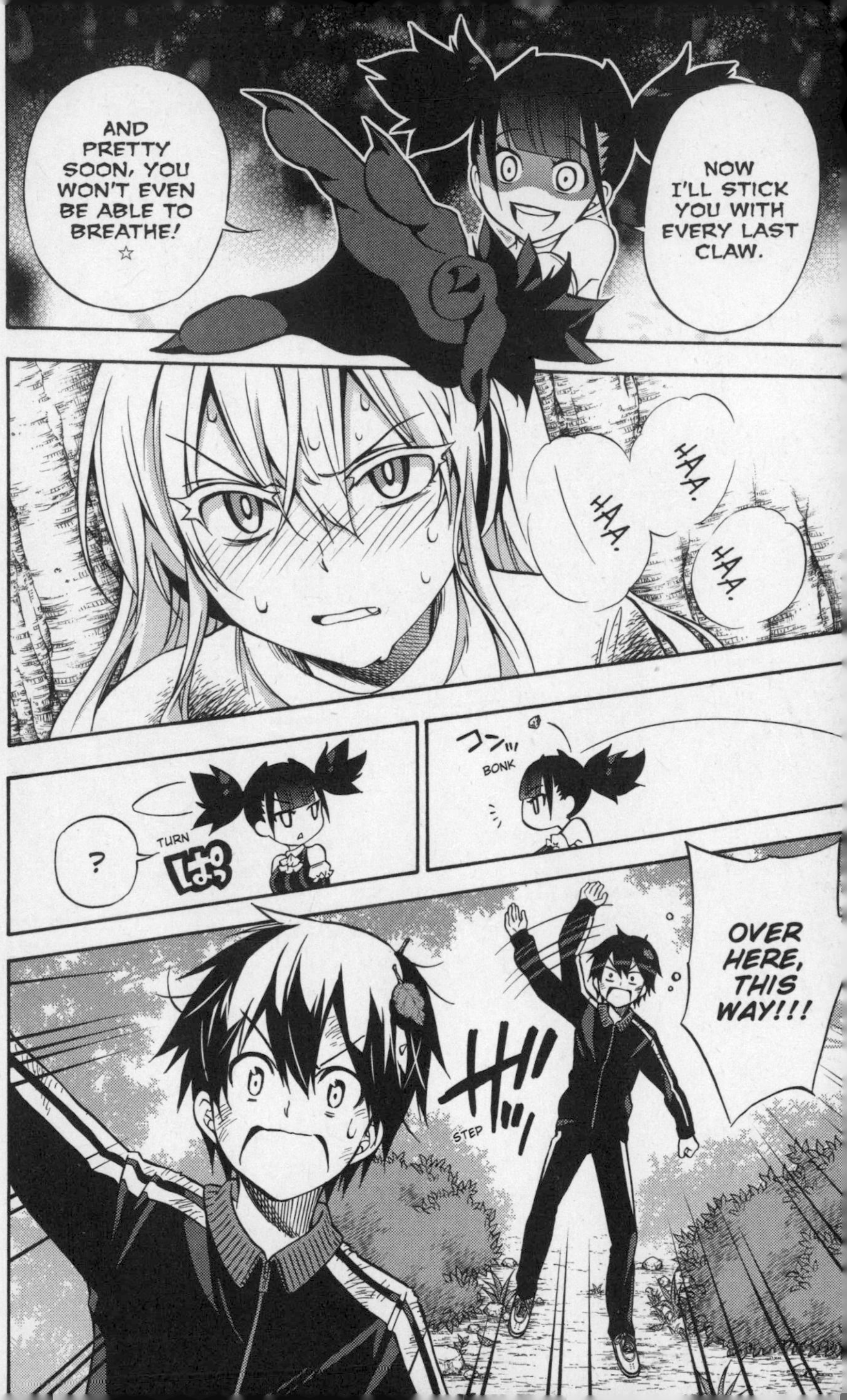
NOW I'LL STICK YOU WITH EVERY LAST CLAW.
AND PRETTY SOON, YOU WON'T EVEN BE ABLE TO BREATHE! ☆
HAA.
HAA.
HAA.
コンッ
BONK
?
TURN
OVER HERE, THIS WAY!!!
STEP

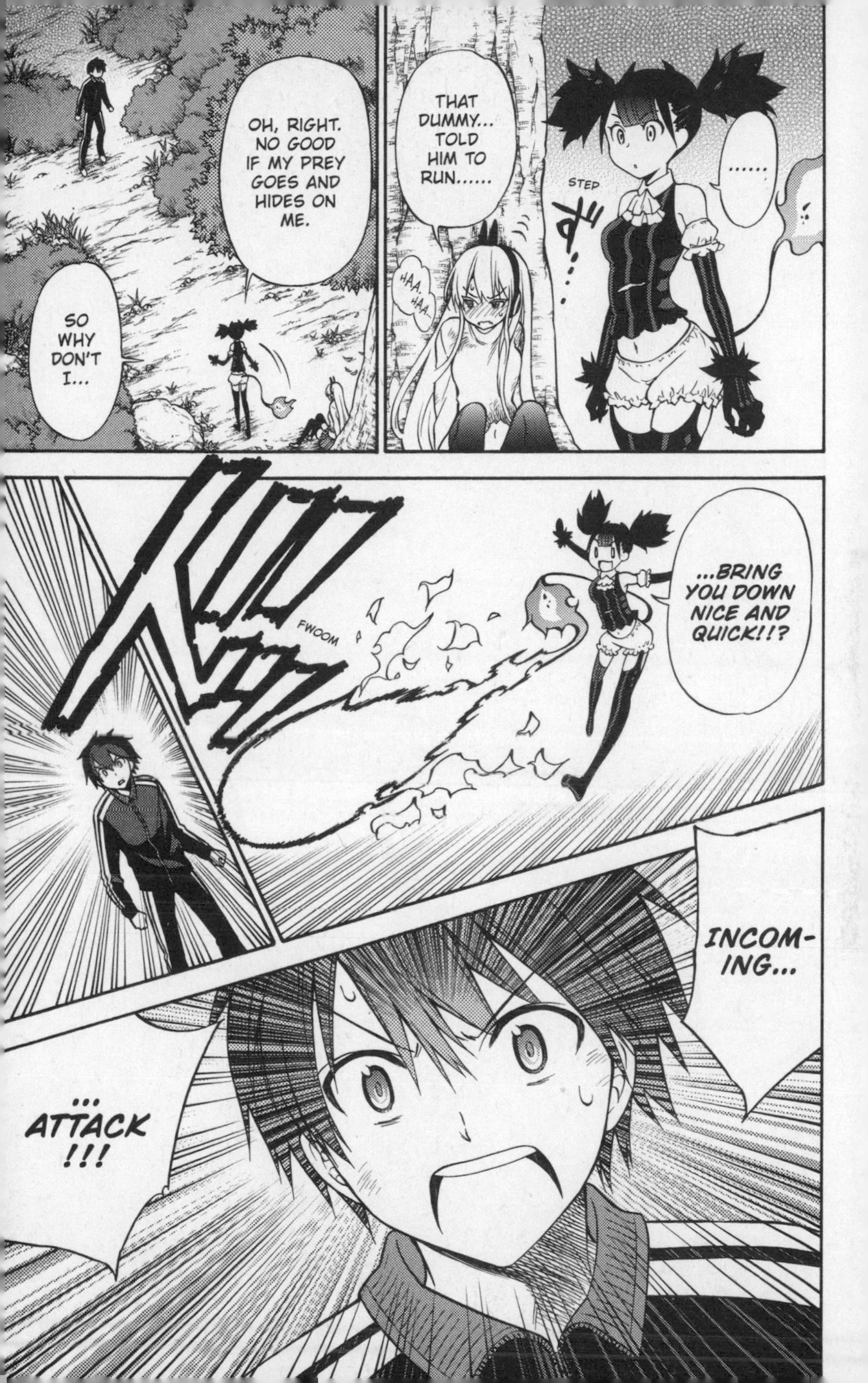
......
STEP
THAT DUMMY... TOLD HIM TO RUN......
HAA. HAA...
OH, RIGHT. NO GOOD IF MY PREY GOES AND HIDES ON ME.
SO WHY DON'T I...
...BRING YOU DOWN NICE AND QUICK!!?
FWOOM
INCOM-ING...
...ATTACK!!!

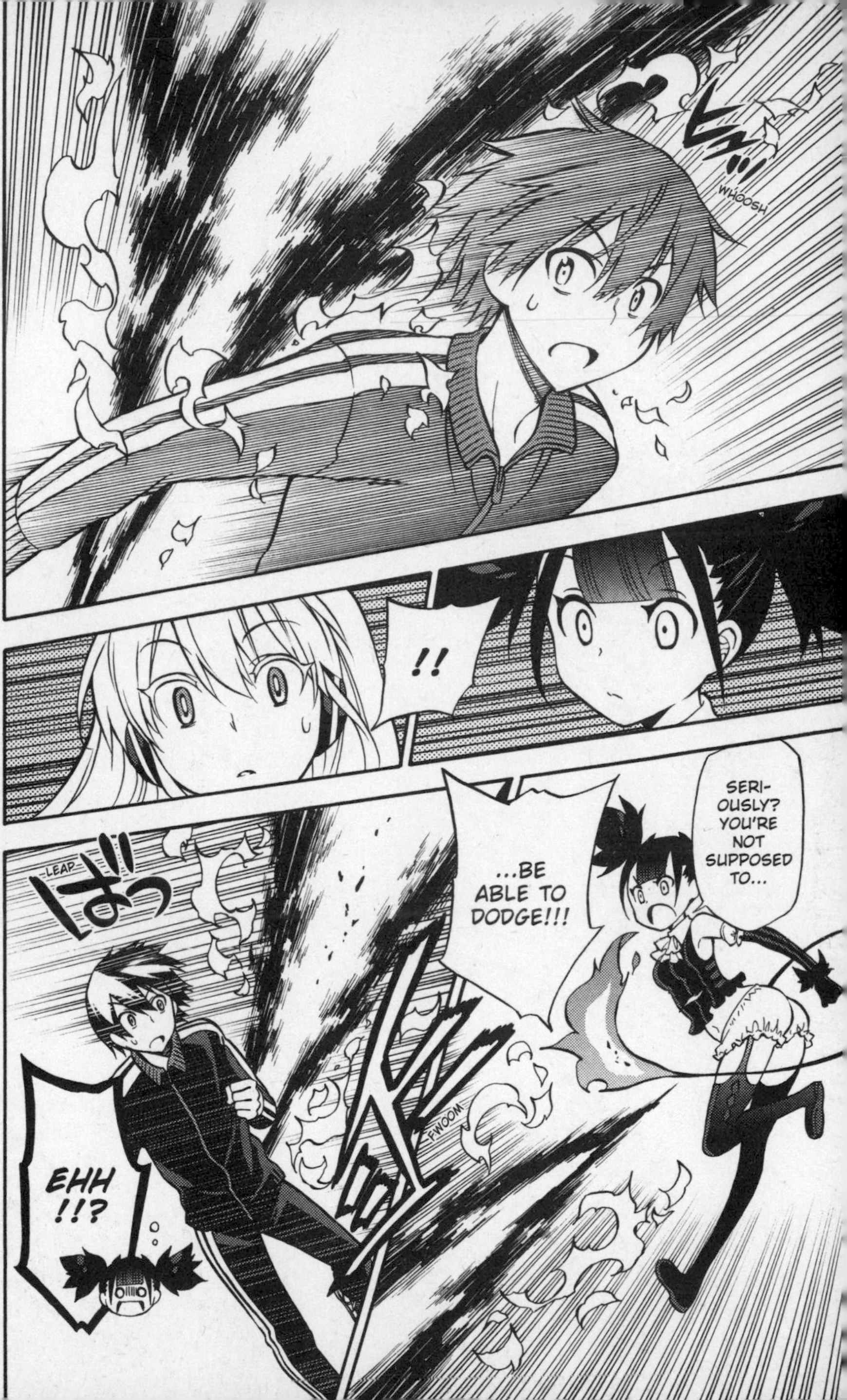
WHOOSH
!!
SERI-OUSLY? YOU'RE NOT SUPPOSED TO...
...BE ABLE TO DODGE!!!
FWOOM
LEAP
EHH!!?

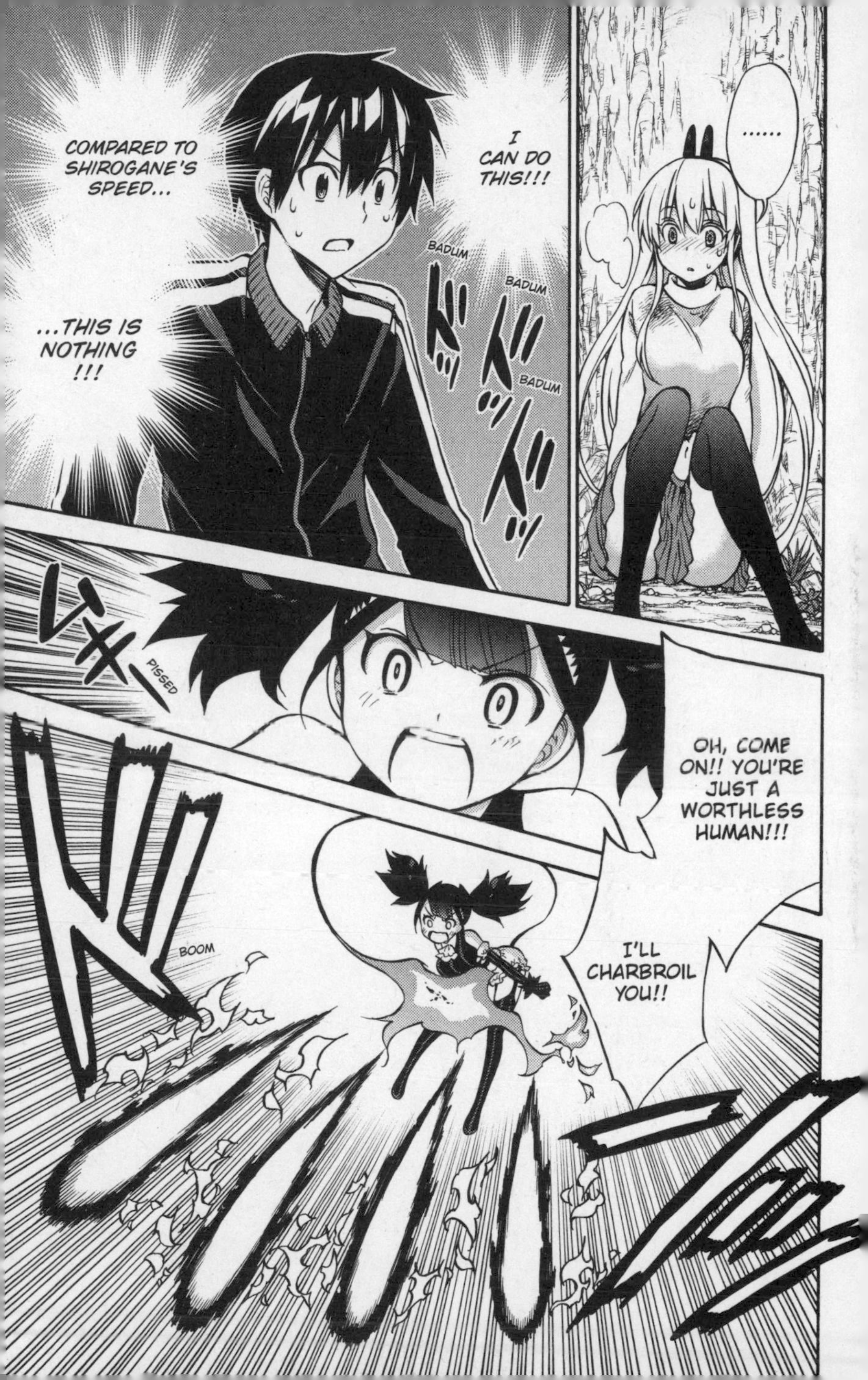
......
I CAN DO THIS!!!
COMPARED TO SHIROGANE'S SPEED...
BADUM
BADUM
BADUM
...THIS IS NOTHING !!!
PISSED
OH, COME ON!! YOU'RE JUST A WORTHLESS HUMAN!!!
I'LL CHARBROIL YOU!!
BOOM

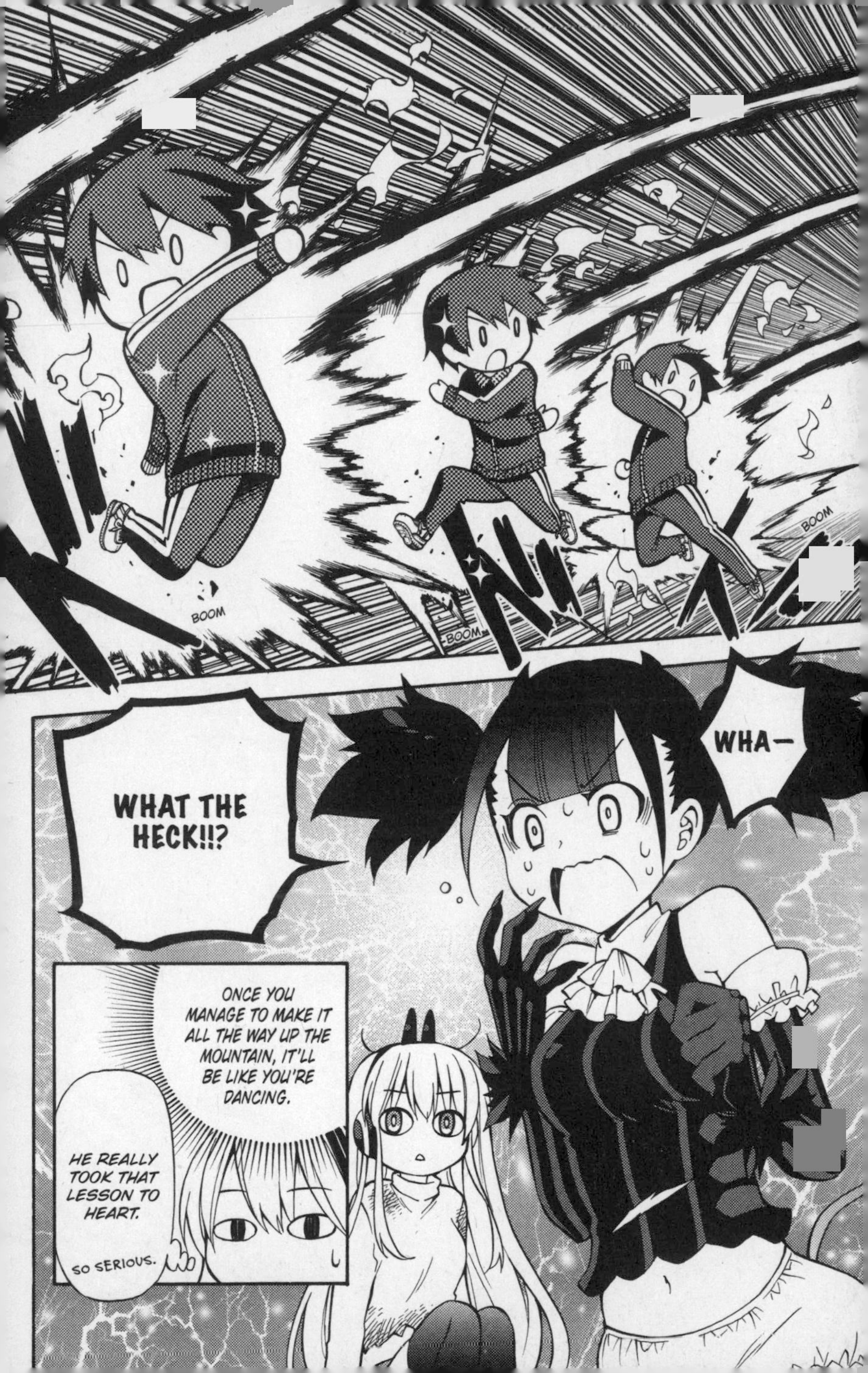
BOOM
BOOM
BOOM
WHA—
WHAT THE HECK!!?
ONCE YOU MANAGE TO MAKE IT ALL THE WAY UP THE MOUNTAIN, IT'LL BE LIKE YOU'RE DANCING.
HE REALLY TOOK THAT LESSON TO HEART.
SO SERIOUS.

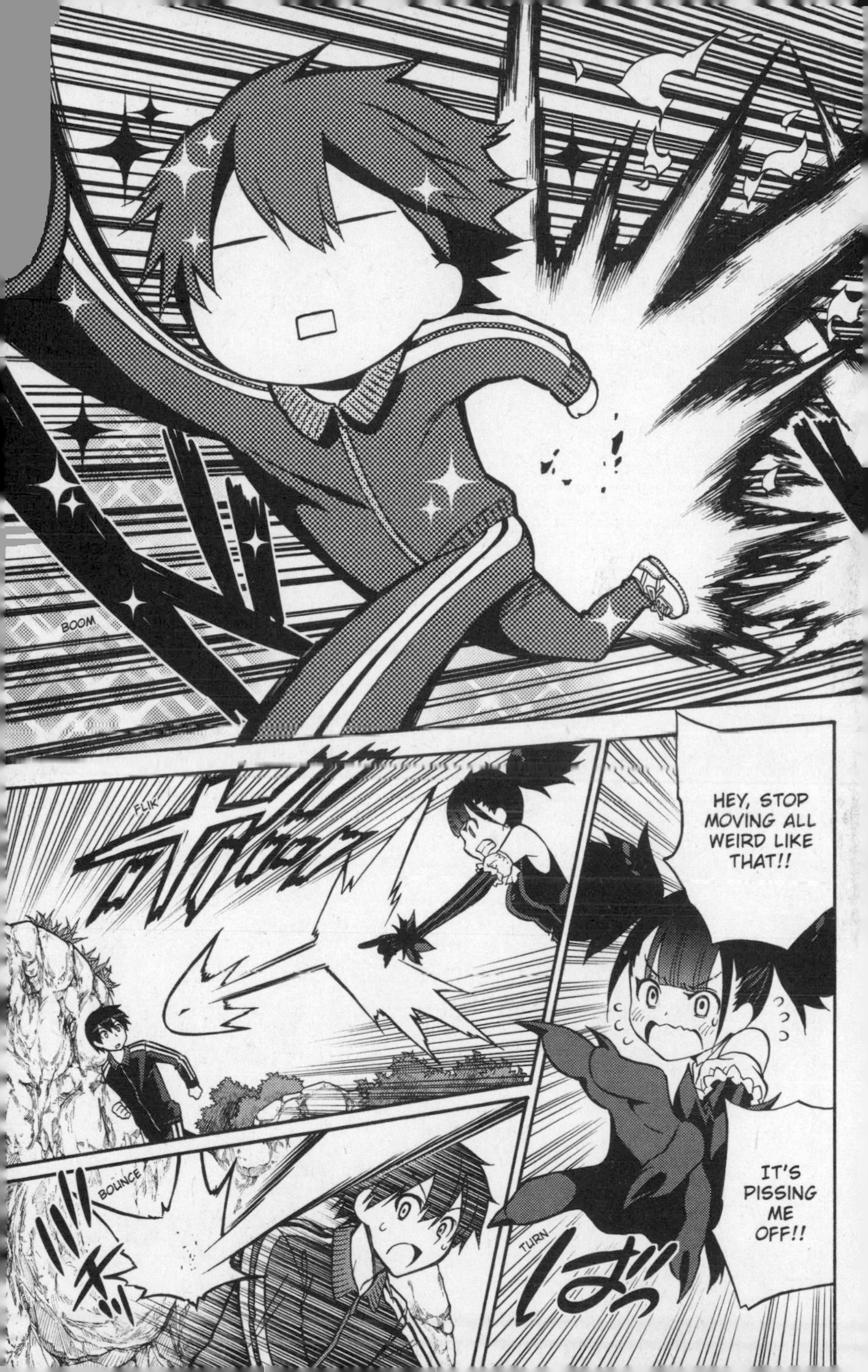
BOOM
HEY, STOP MOVING ALL WEIRD LIKE THAT!!
IT'S PISSING ME OFF!!
TURN
FLIK
BOUNCE

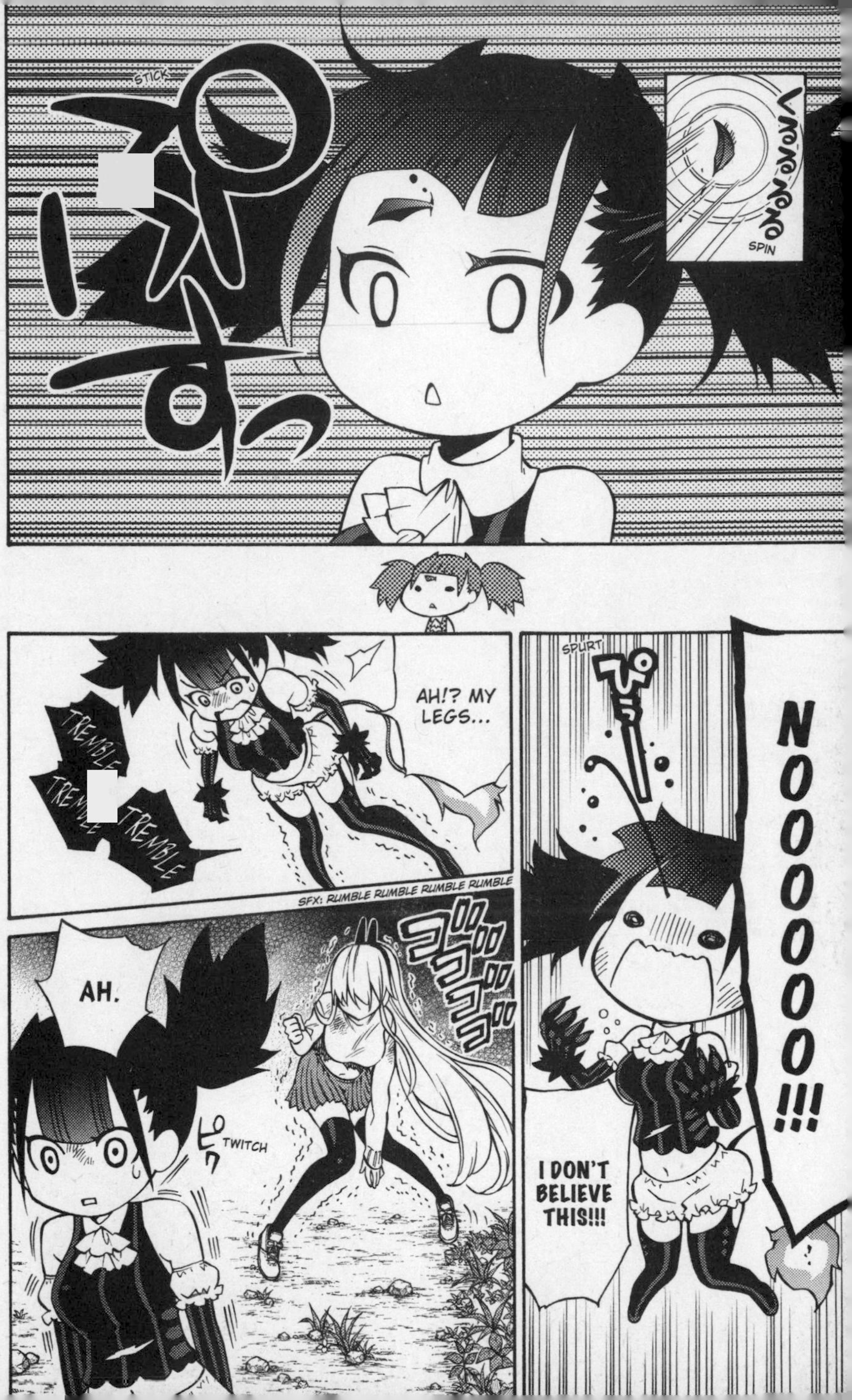
STICK
SPIN
SPURT
NOOOOOOO!!!
I DON'T BELIEVE THIS!!!
AH!? MY LEGS...
TREMBLE TREMBLE TREMBLE
SFX: RUMBLE RUMBLE RUMBLE RUMBLE
AH.
TWITCH

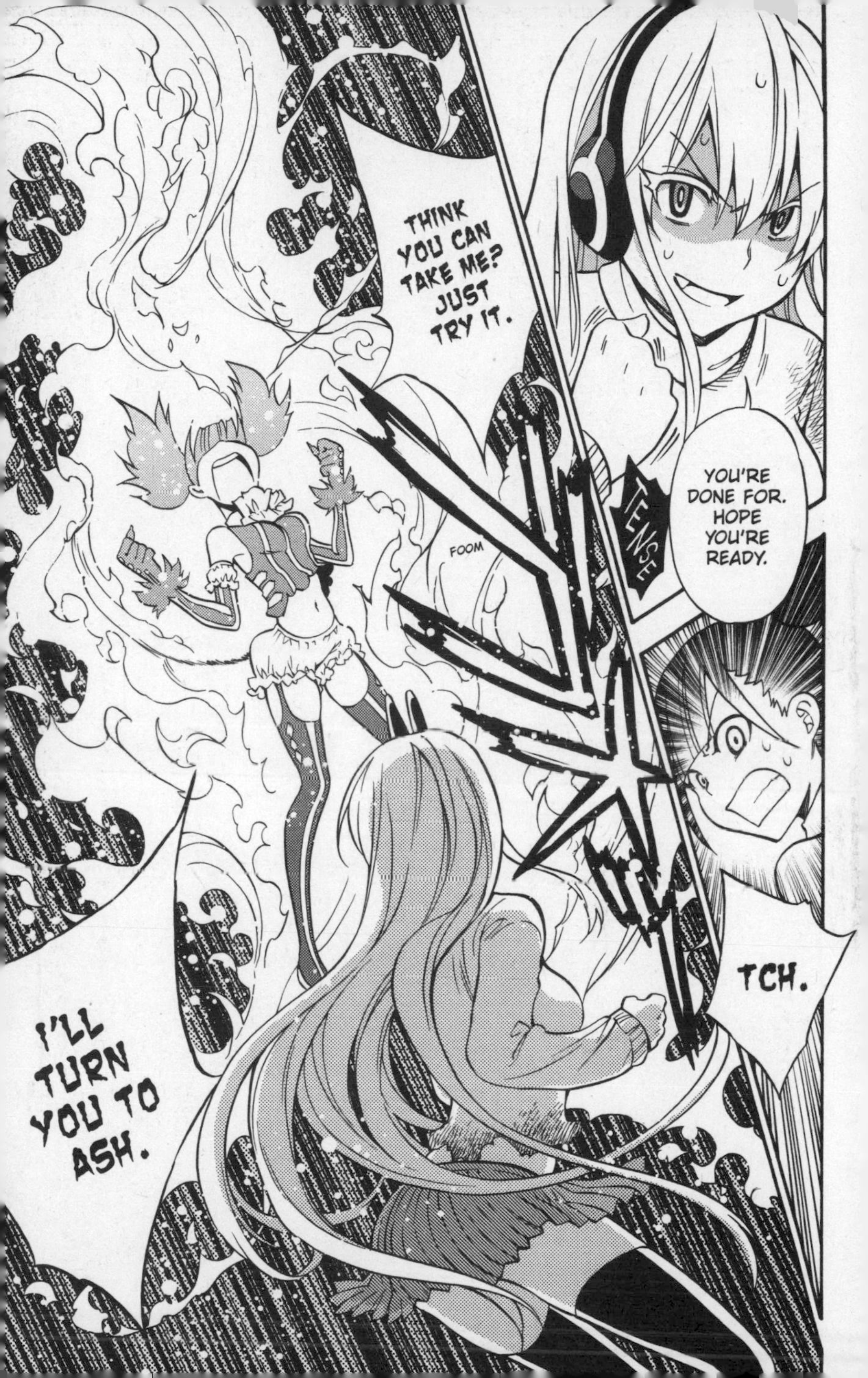
THINK YOU CAN TAKE ME? JUST TRY IT.
YOU'RE DONE FOR. HOPE YOU'RE READY.
TENSE
FOOM
TCH.
I'LL TURN YOU TO ASH.

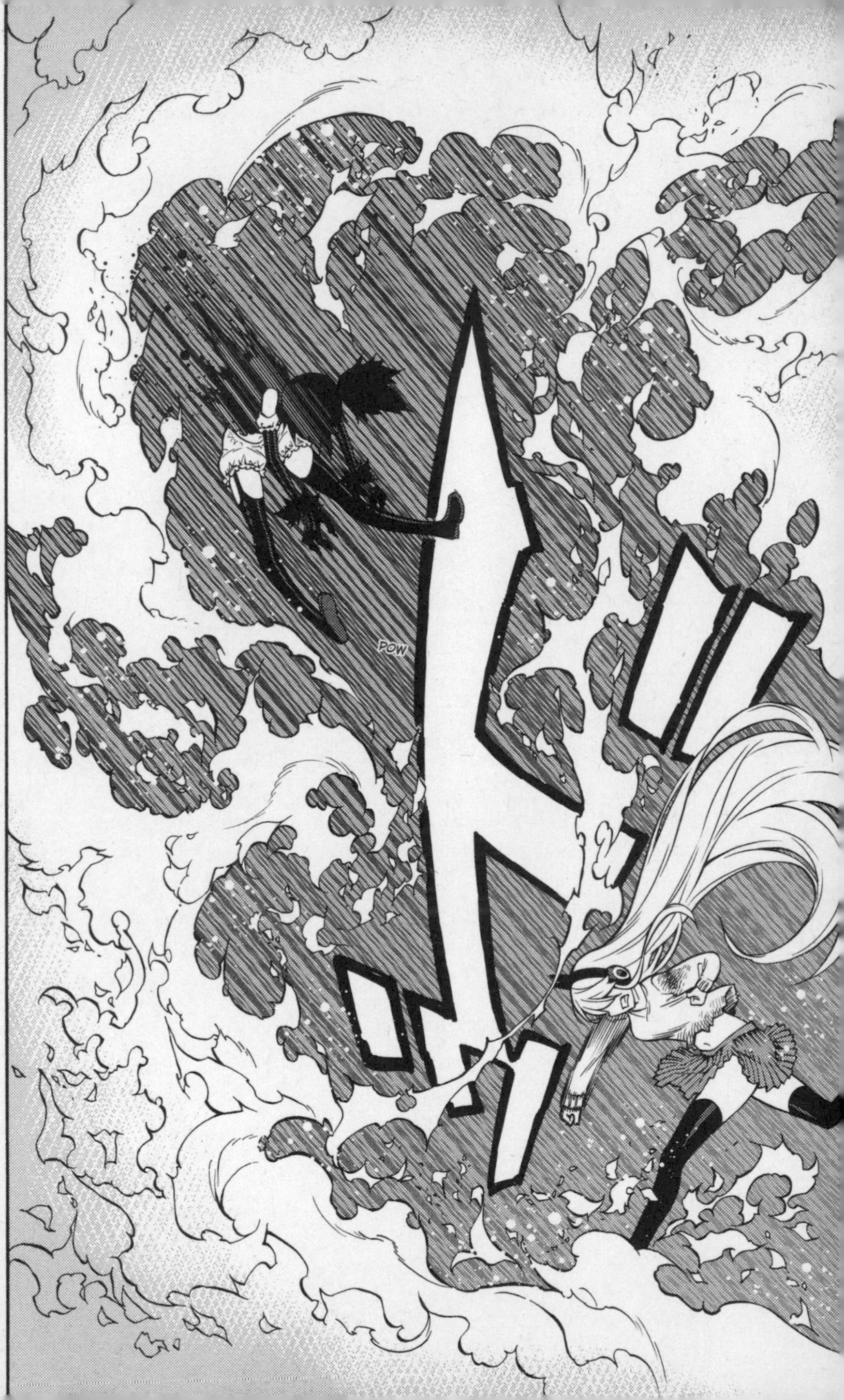
POW

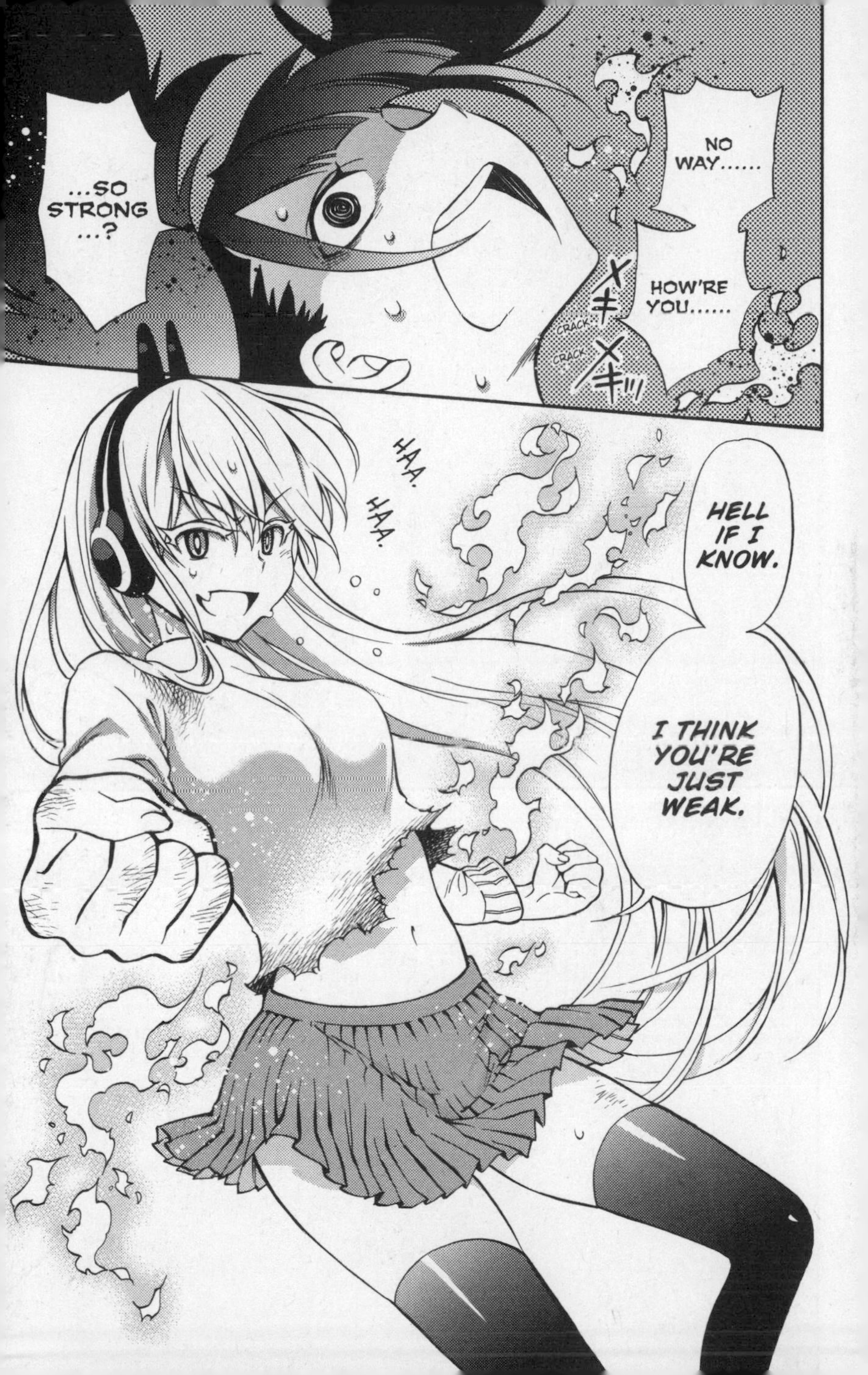
NO WAY......
HOW'RE YOU......
CRACK
CRACK
...SO STRONG ...?
HAA. HAA.
HELL IF I KNOW.
I THINK YOU'RE JUST WEAK.

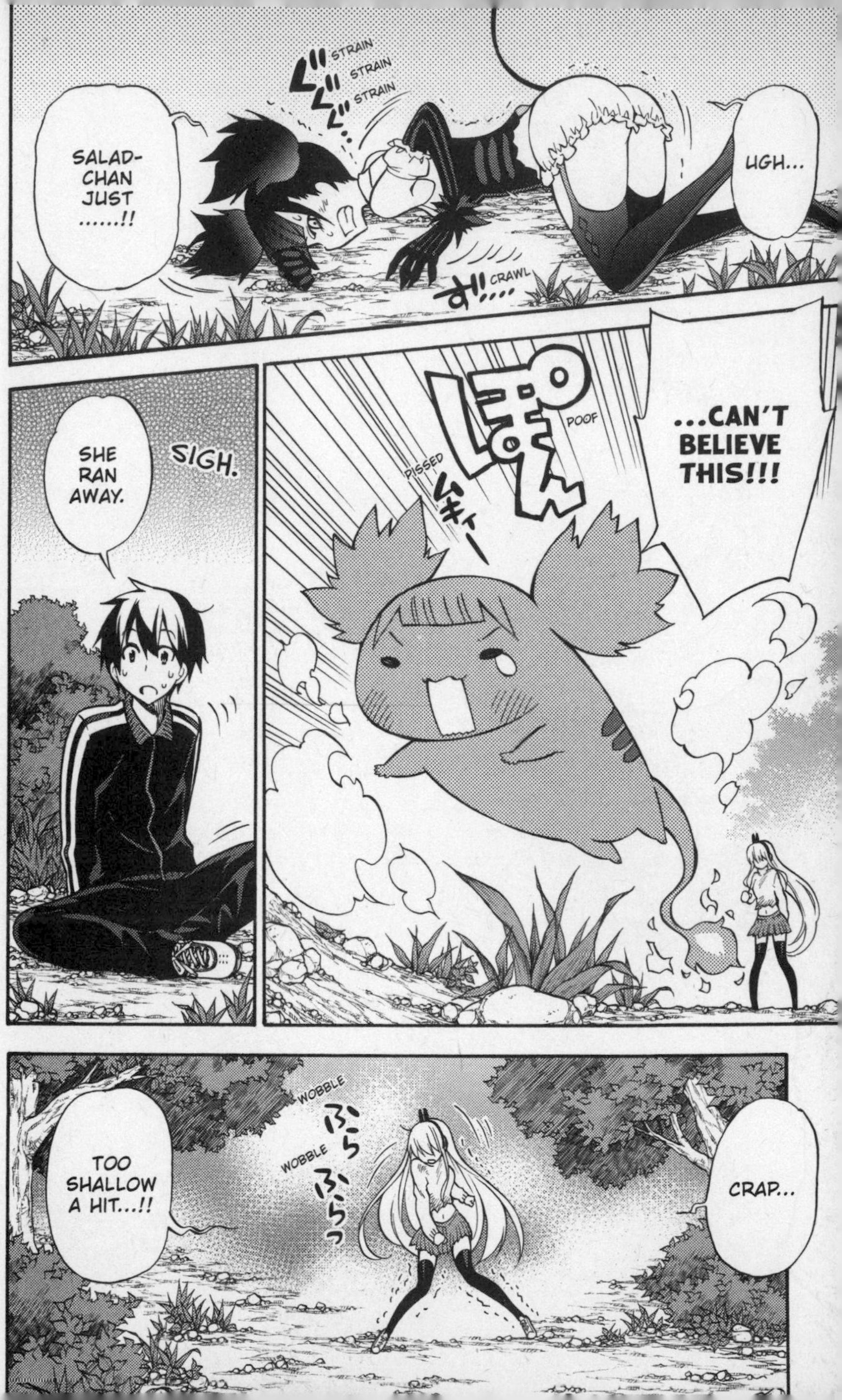
UGH...
STRAIN
STRAIN
STRAIN
SALAD-CHAN JUST ......!!
CRAWL
...CAN'T BELIEVE THIS!!!
POOF
PISSED
SIGH.
SHE RAN AWAY.
CRAP...
WOBBLE
WOBBLE
TOO SHALLOW A HIT...!!

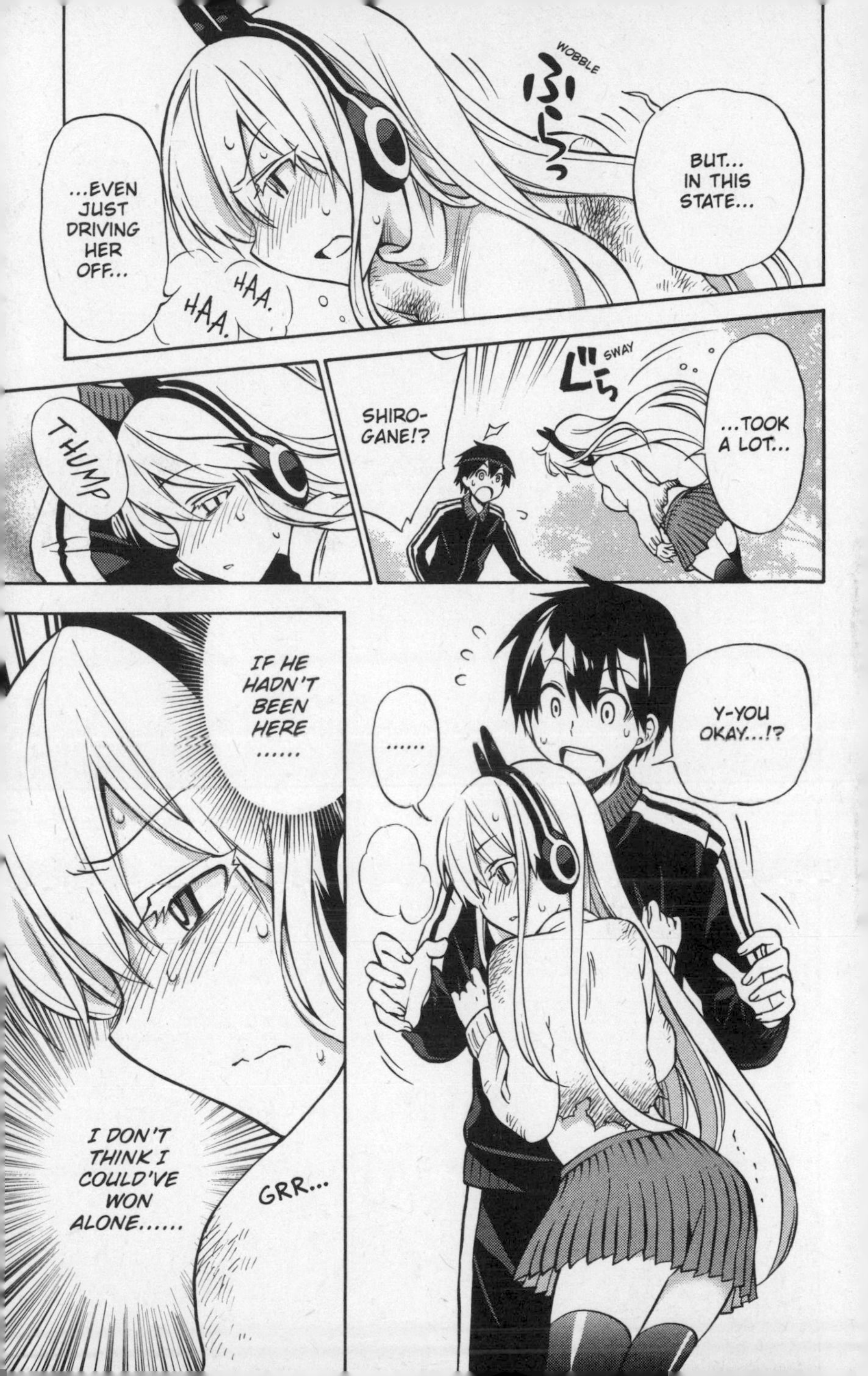
WOBBLE
ふらっ
BUT... IN THIS STATE...
...EVEN JUST DRIVING HER OFF...
HAA. HAA.
...TOOK A LOT...
SWAY
ぐら
SHIRO-GANE!?
THUMP
Y-YOU OKAY...!?
......
IF HE HADN'T BEEN HERE ......
I DON'T THINK I COULD'VE WON ALONE......
GRR...

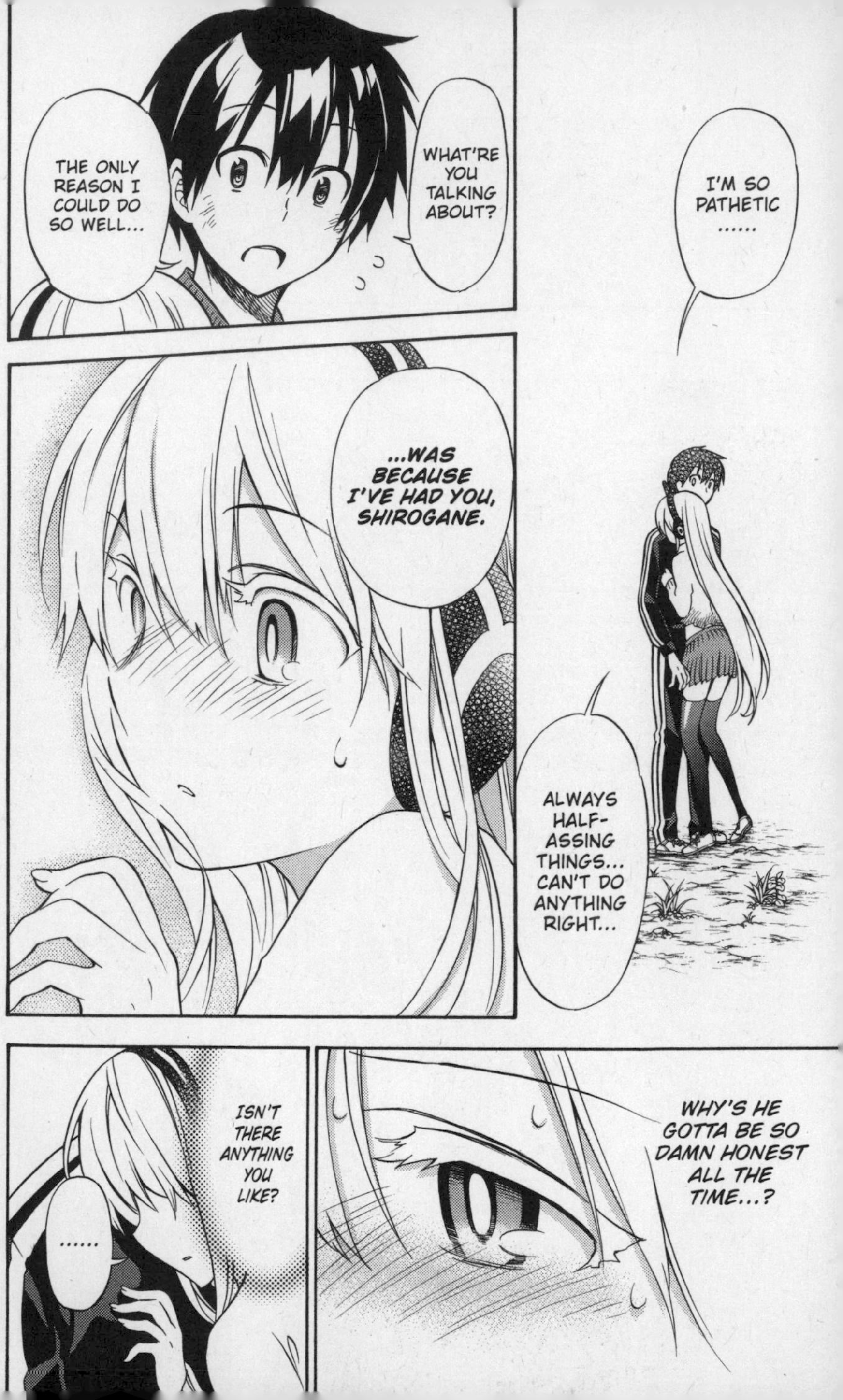
I'M SO PATHETIC ......
ALWAYS HALF-ASSING THINGS... CAN'T DO ANYTHING RIGHT...
WHAT'RE YOU TALKING ABOUT?
THE ONLY REASON I COULD DO SO WELL...
...WAS BECAUSE I'VE HAD YOU, SHIROGANE.
WHY'S HE GOTTA BE SO DAMN HONEST ALL THE TIME...?
ISN'T THERE ANYTHING YOU LIKE?
......

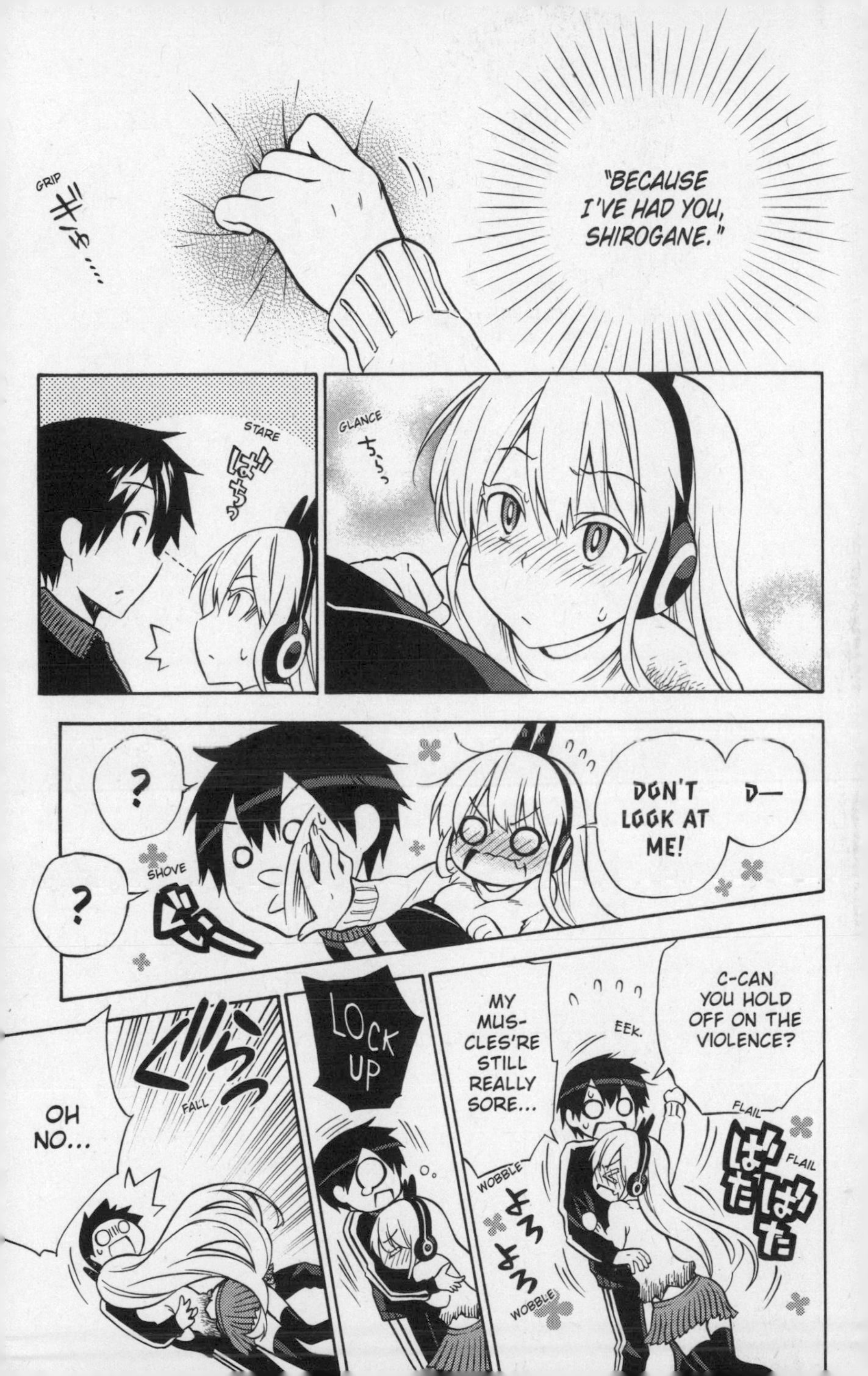
"BECAUSE I'VE HAD YOU, SHIROGANE."
GRIP
ギュ…
GLANCE
ちらっ
STARE
ぱちっ
D— DON'T LOOK AT ME!
SHOVE
?
?
C-CAN YOU HOLD OFF ON THE VIOLENCE?
EEK.
FLAIL
FLAIL
ぱたぱた
MY MUSCLES'RE STILL REALLY SORE...
WOBBLE
よろよろ
WOBBLE
LOCK UP
ぐらっ
FALL
OH NO...

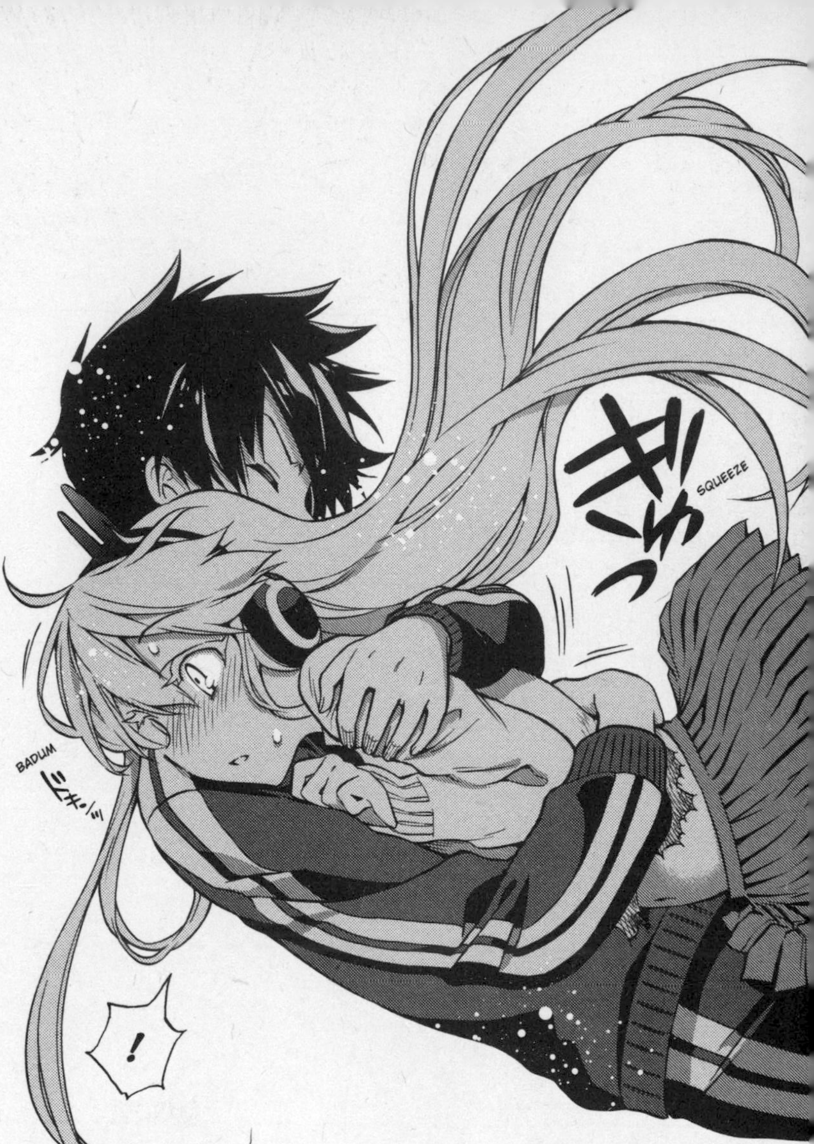
ぎゅっ
SQUEEZE
BADUM
!

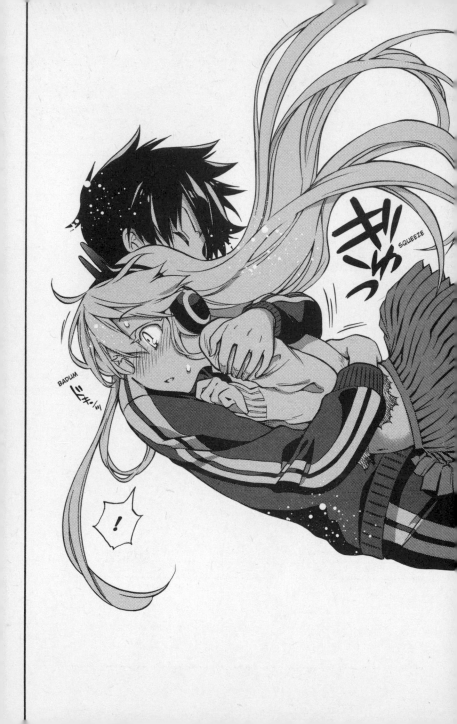

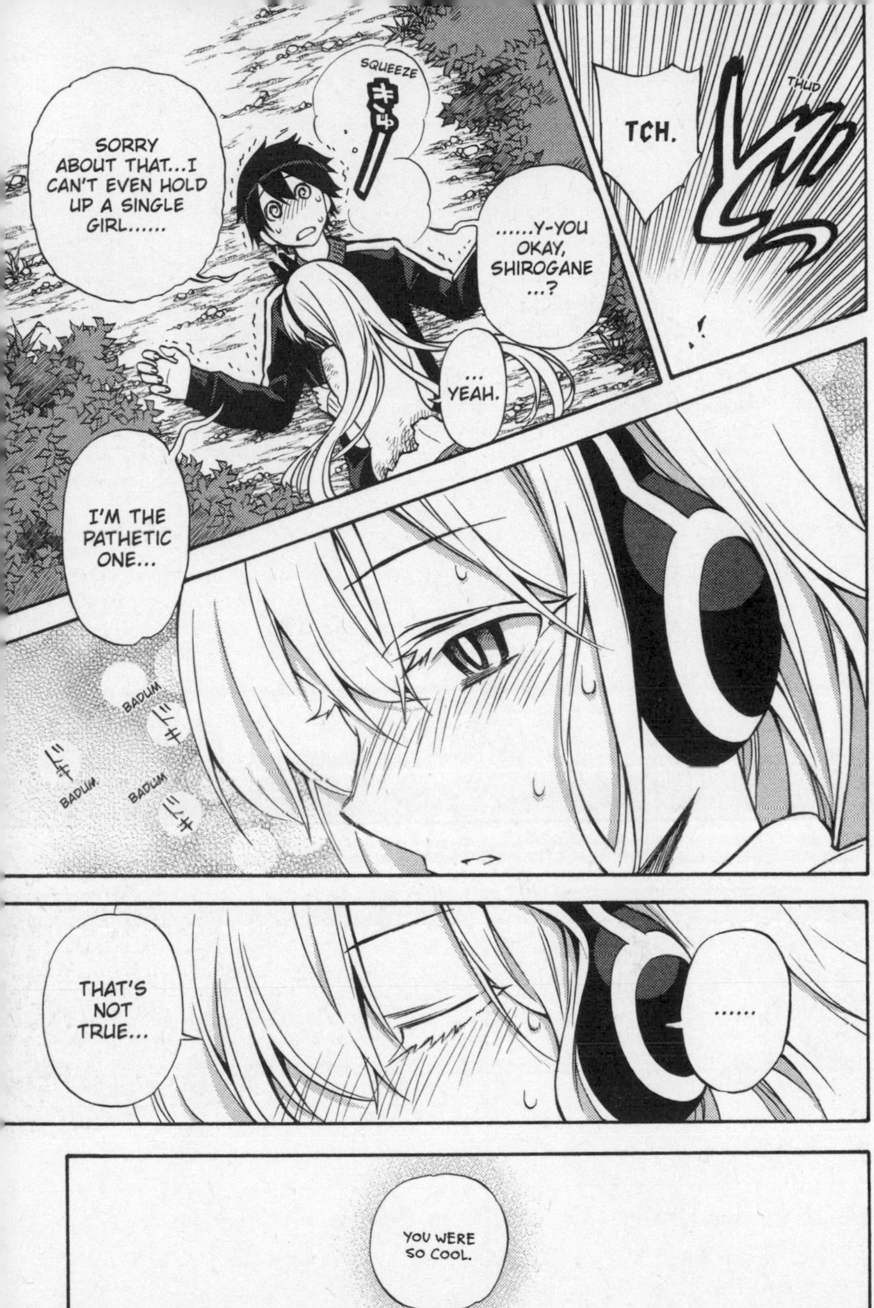
THUD
TCH.
......Y-YOU OKAY, SHIROGANE...?
... YEAH.
SQUEEZE
SORRY ABOUT THAT...I CAN'T EVEN HOLD UP A SINGLE GIRL......
I'M THE PATHETIC ONE...
BADUM
BADUM
BADUM
......
THAT'S NOT TRUE...
YOU WERE SO COOL.

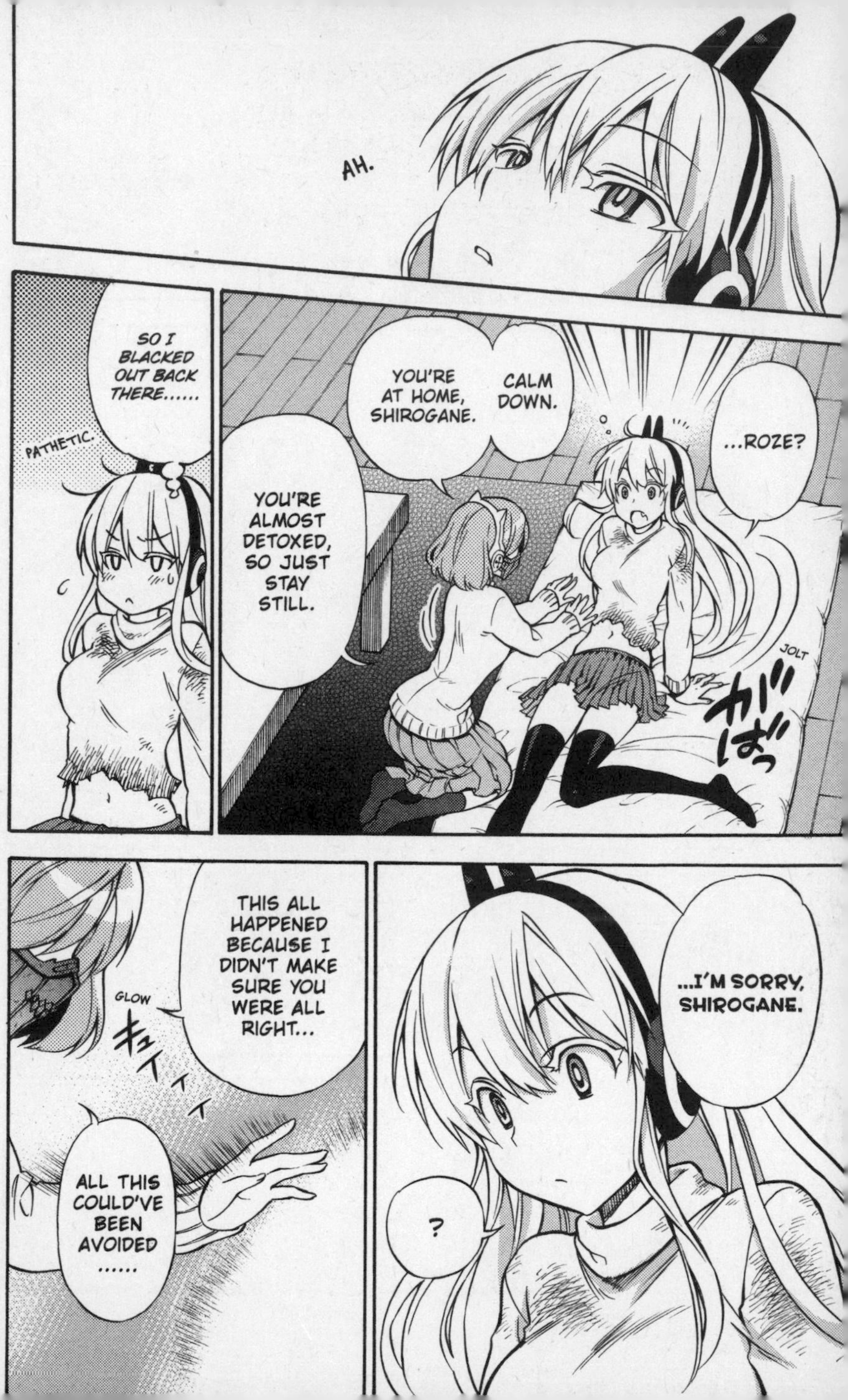
AH.
...ROZE?
JOLT
がばっ
CALM DOWN.
YOU'RE AT HOME, SHIROGANE.
YOU'RE ALMOST DETOXED, SO JUST STAY STILL.
SO I BLACKED OUT BACK THERE......
PATHETIC.
...I'M SORRY, SHIROGANE.
?
THIS ALL HAPPENED BECAUSE I DIDN'T MAKE SURE YOU WERE ALL RIGHT...
GLOW
キュイイイ
ALL THIS COULD'VE BEEN AVOIDED ......

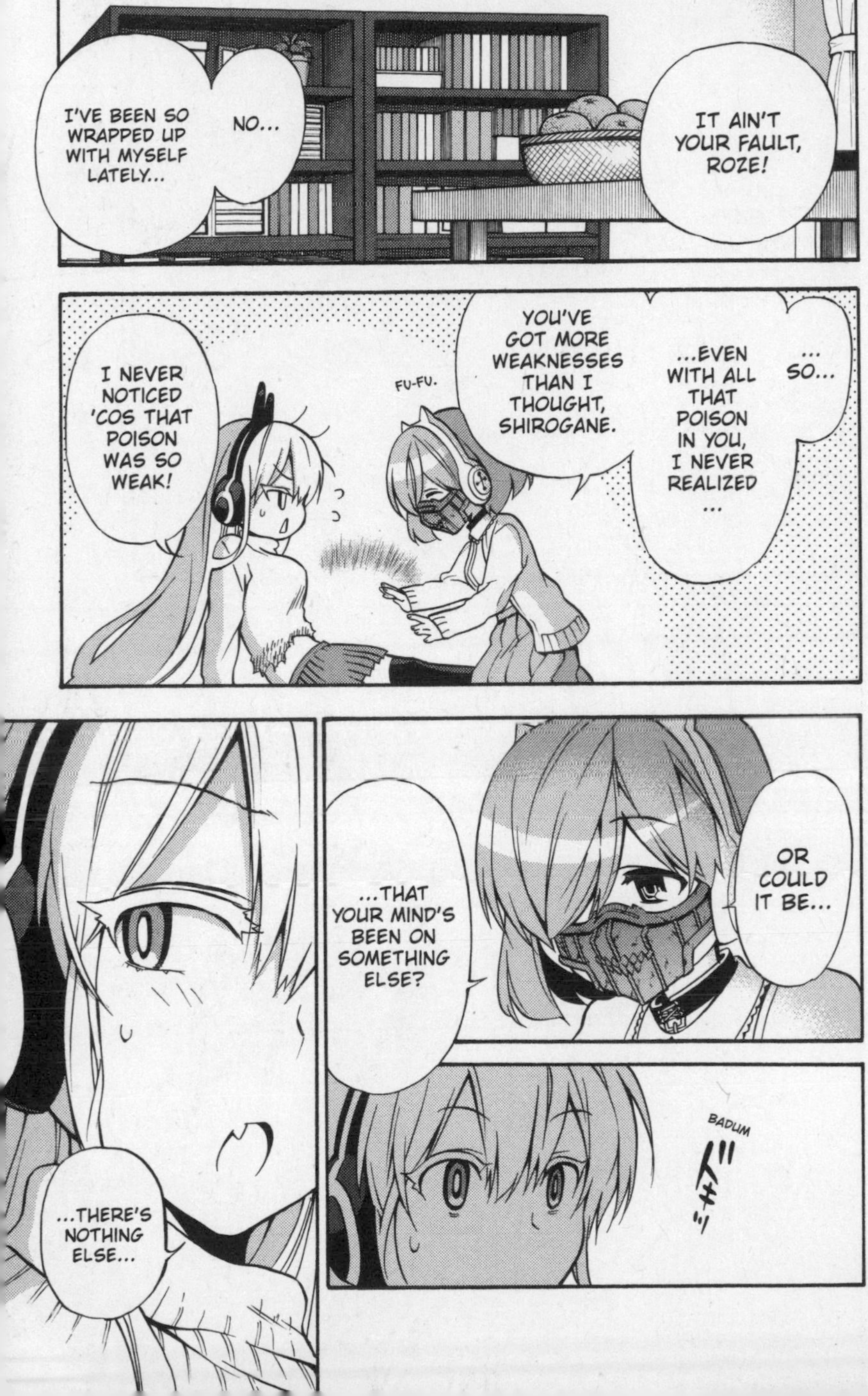
IT AIN'T YOUR FAULT, ROZE!
NO...
I'VE BEEN SO WRAPPED UP WITH MYSELF LATELY...
... SO...
...EVEN WITH ALL THAT POISON IN YOU, I NEVER REALIZED ...
YOU'VE GOT MORE WEAKNESSES THAN I THOUGHT, SHIROGANE.
FU-FU.
I NEVER NOTICED 'COS THAT POISON WAS SO WEAK!
OR COULD IT BE...
...THAT YOUR MIND'S BEEN ON SOMETHING ELSE?
BADUM
ドキッ
...THERE'S NOTHING ELSE...

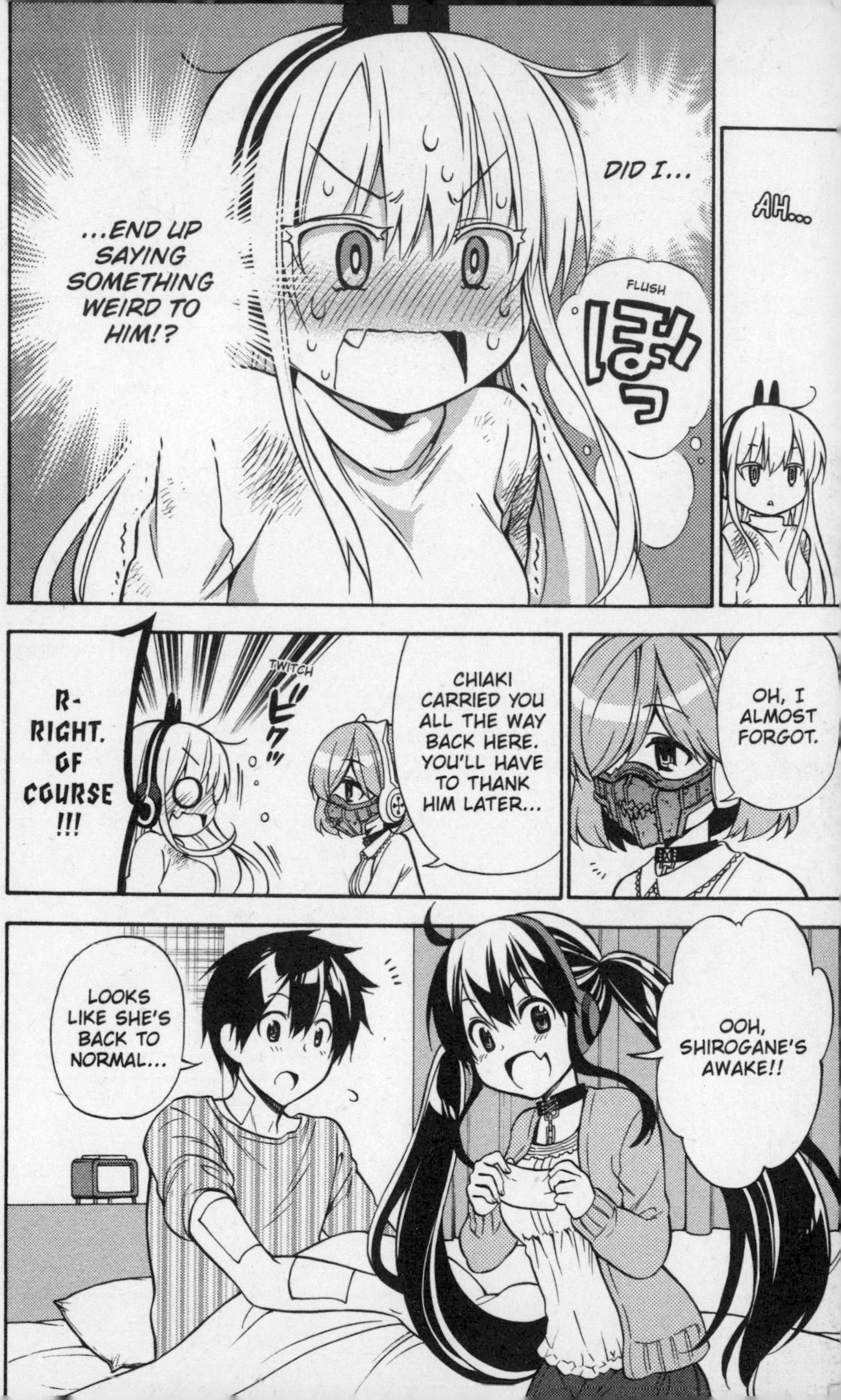
AH...
DID I...
...END UP SAYING SOMETHING WEIRD TO HIM!?
FLUSH
ぼっ
OH, I ALMOST FORGOT.
CHIAKI CARRIED YOU ALL THE WAY BACK HERE. YOU'LL HAVE TO THANK HIM LATER...
TWITCH
ビクッ
R-RIGHT. OF COURSE!!!
OOH, SHIROGANE'S AWAKE!!
LOOKS LIKE SHE'S BACK TO NORMAL...

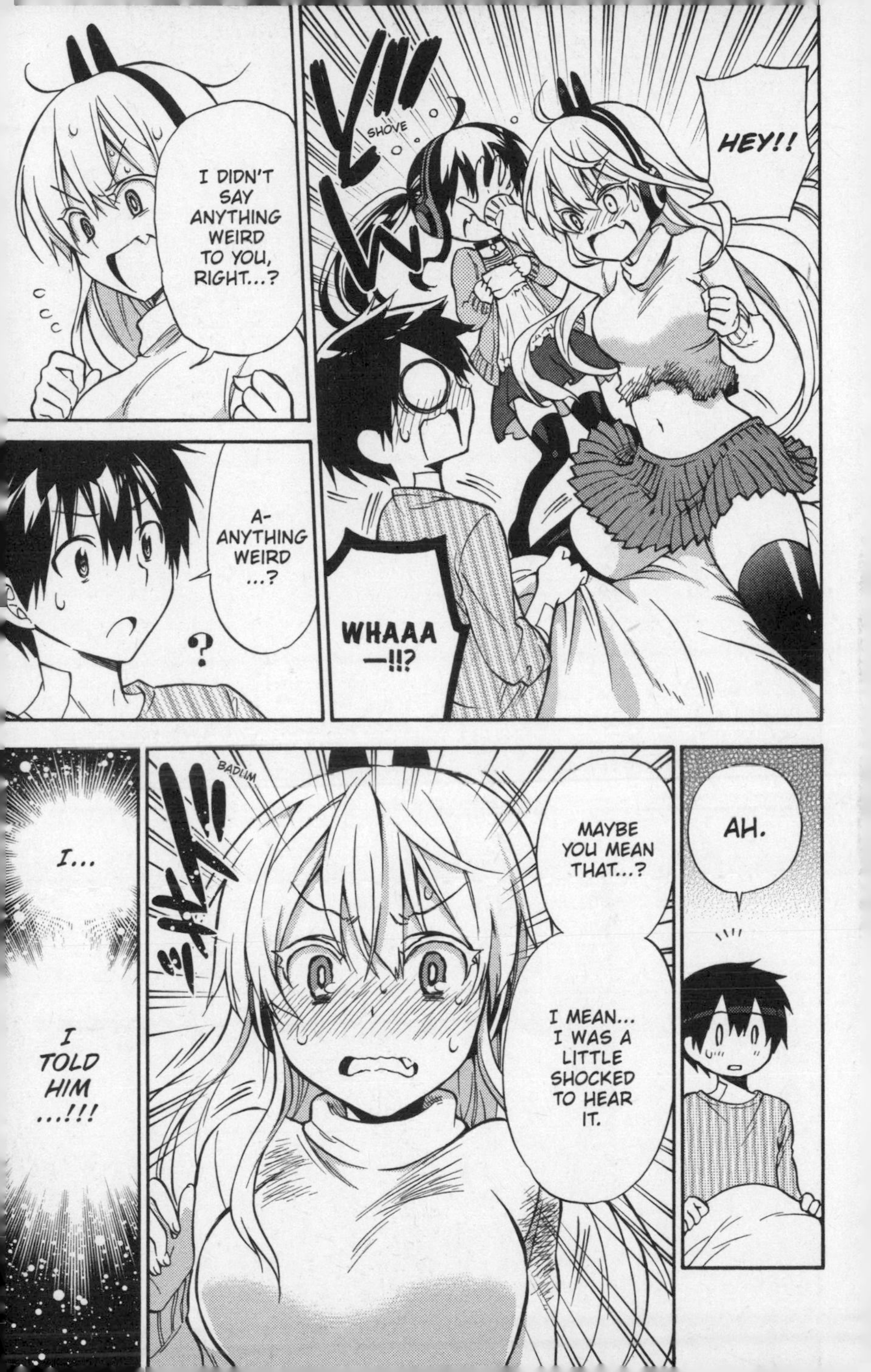
HEY!!
SHOVE
WHAAA—!!?
I DIDN'T SAY ANYTHING WEIRD TO YOU, RIGHT...?
A-ANYTHING WEIRD ...?
AH.
MAYBE YOU MEAN THAT...?
I MEAN... I WAS A LITTLE SHOCKED TO HEAR IT.
BADUM
I...
I TOLD HIM ...!!!

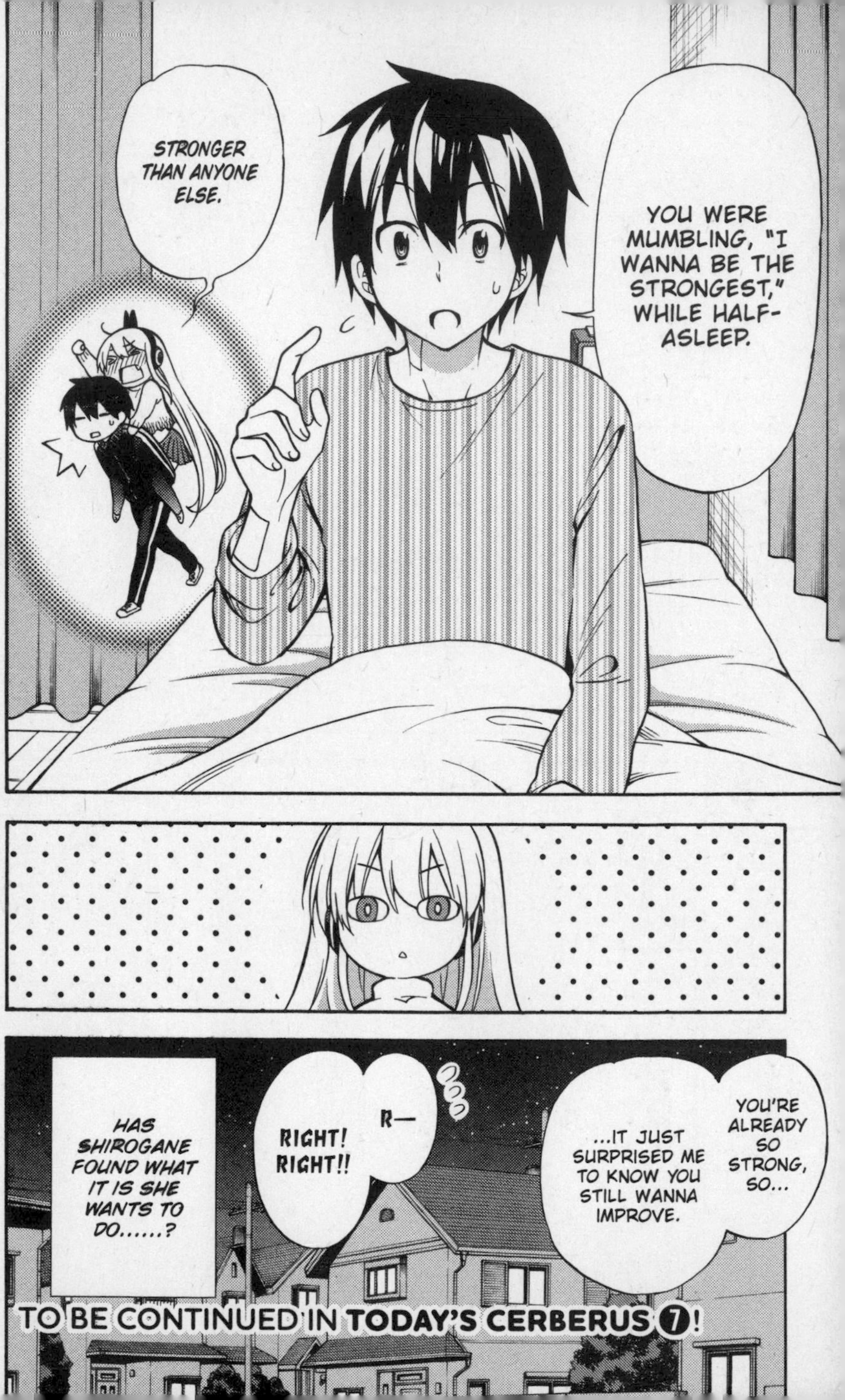
YOU WERE MUMBLING, "I WANNA BE THE STRONGEST," WHILE HALF-ASLEEP.
STRONGER THAN ANYONE ELSE.
YOU'RE ALREADY SO STRONG, SO...
...IT JUST SURPRISED ME TO KNOW YOU STILL WANNA IMPROVE.
R—
RIGHT! RIGHT!!
HAS SHIROGANE FOUND WHAT IT IS SHE WANTS TO DO......?
TO BE CONTINUED IN TODAY'S CERBERUS 7!

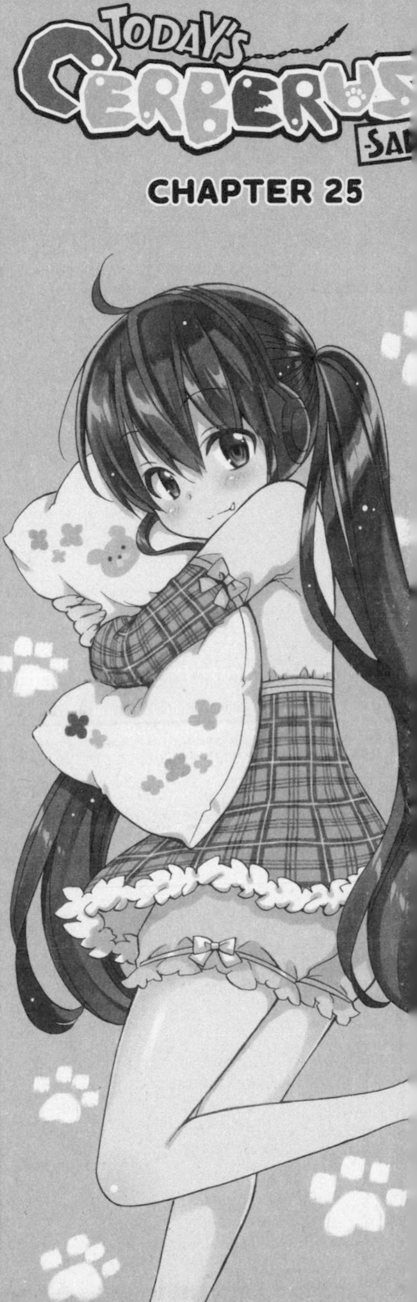
TODAY'S CERBERUS
CHAPTER 25

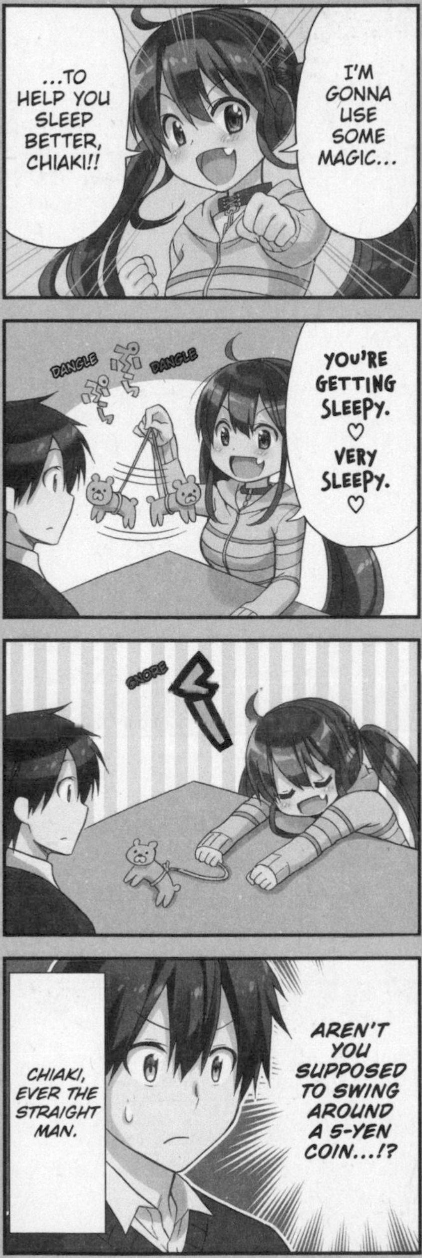
I'M GONNA USE SOME MAGIC...
...TO HELP YOU SLEEP BETTER, CHIAKI!!
YOU'RE GETTING SLEEPY. ♡ VERY SLEEPY. ♡
DANGLE
DANGLE
SNORE
AREN'T YOU SUPPOSED TO SWING AROUND A 5-YEN COIN...!?
CHIAKI, EVER THE STRAIGHT MAN.

TODAY'S CERBERUS -SAN

CHAPTER 26

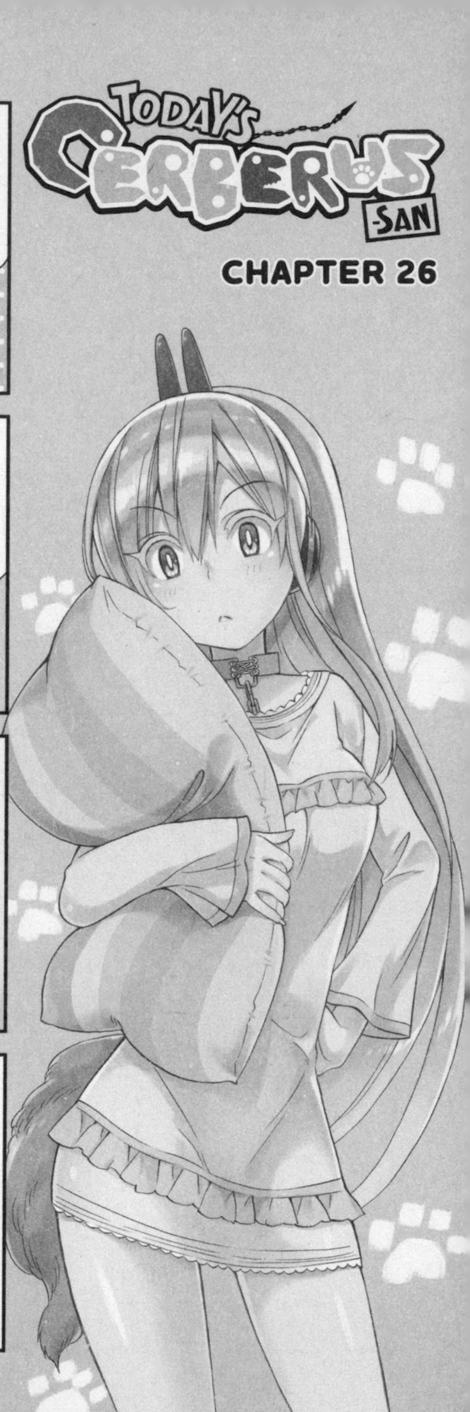

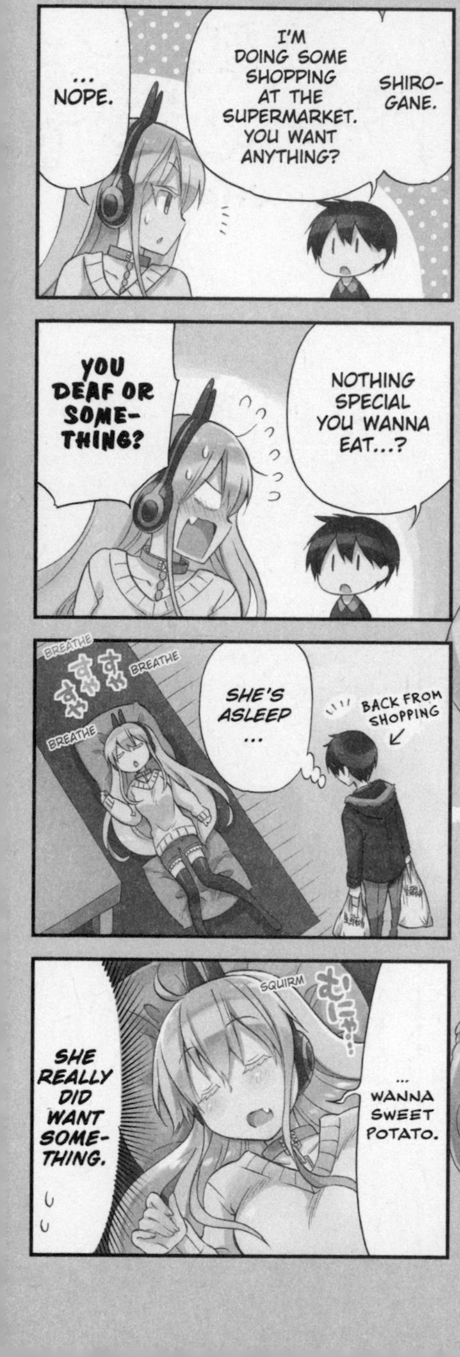
SHIRO-GANE.
I'M DOING SOME SHOPPING AT THE SUPERMARKET. YOU WANT ANYTHING?
... NOPE.
NOTHING SPECIAL YOU WANNA EAT...?
YOU DEAF OR SOME-THING?
BACK FROM SHOPPING
SHE'S ASLEEP ...
すやすや
BREATHE
BREATHE
BREATHE
... WANNA SWEET POTATO.
むにゃ…
SQUIRM
SHE REALLY DID WANT SOME-THING.

TODAY'S CERBERUS-SAN

CHAPTER 27

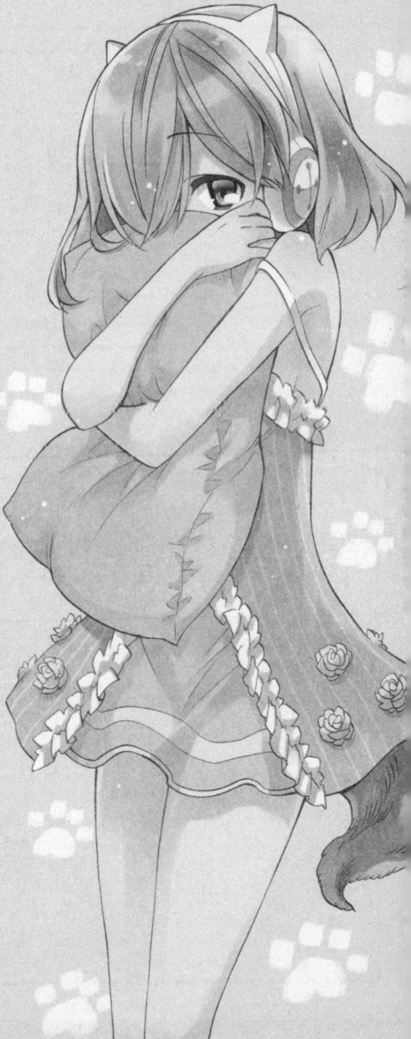

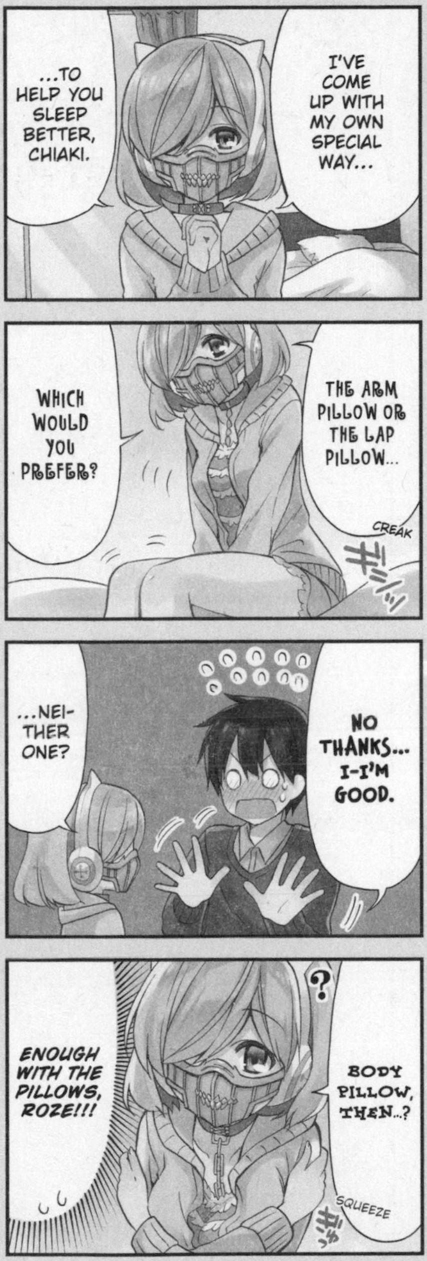
I'VE COME UP WITH MY OWN SPECIAL WAY…
…TO HELP YOU SLEEP BETTER, CHIAKI.
THE ARM PILLOW OR THE LAP PILLOW…
WHICH WOULD YOU PREFER?
CREAK
NO THANKS… I-I'M GOOD.
…NEITHER ONE?
?
BODY PILLOW, THEN…?
ENOUGH WITH THE PILLOWS, ROZE!!!
SQUEEZE

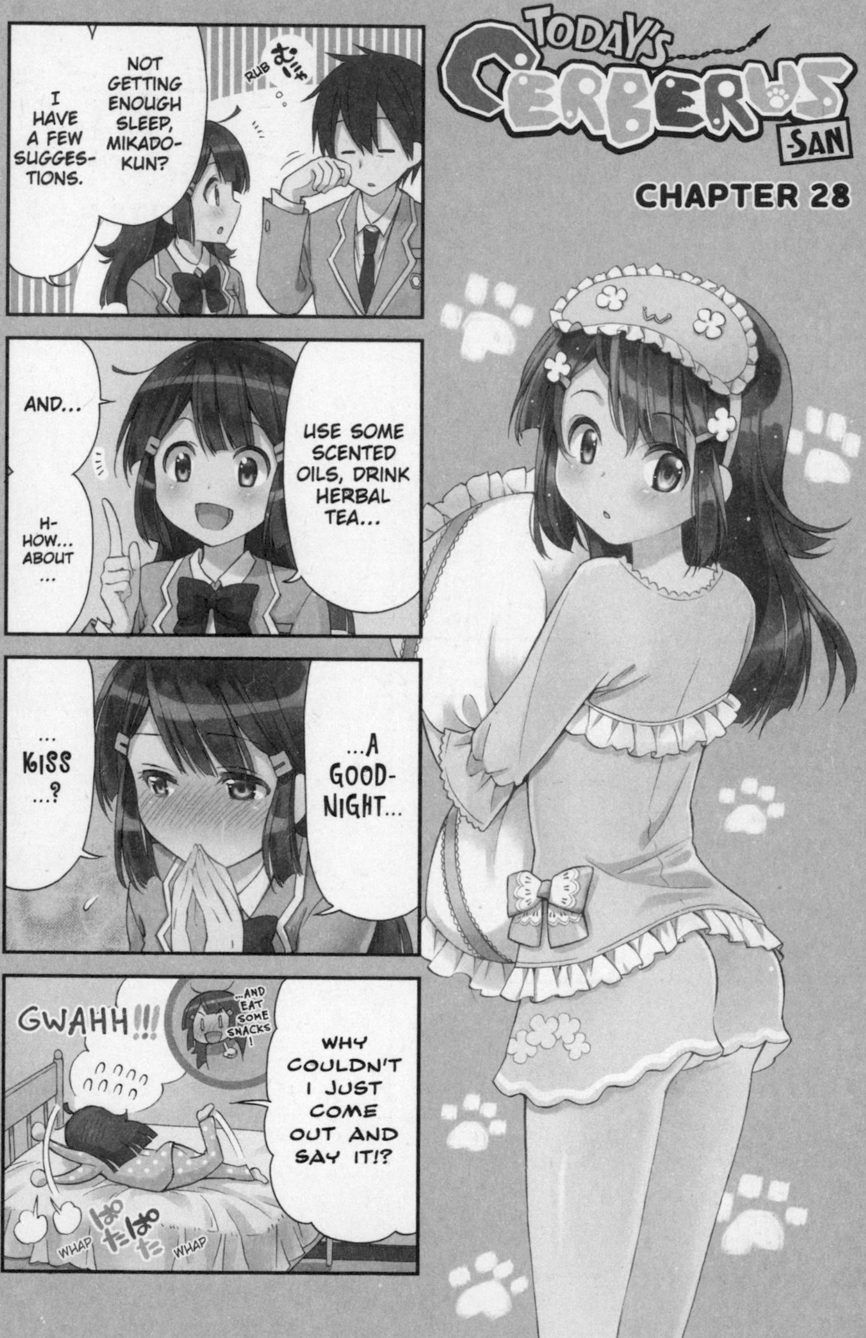
TODAY'S CERBERUS -SAN
CHAPTER 28
RUB むにゃ
NOT GETTING ENOUGH SLEEP, MIKADO-KUN?
I HAVE A FEW SUGGES-TIONS.
USE SOME SCENTED OILS, DRINK HERBAL TEA...
AND...
H- HOW... ABOUT ...
...A GOOD-NIGHT...
... KISS ...?
WHY COULDN'T I JUST COME OUT AND SAY IT!?
...AND EAT SOME SNACKS!
GWAHH!!!
WHAP ぱたぱた WHAP

TODAY'S CERBERUS-SAN

CHAPTER 29

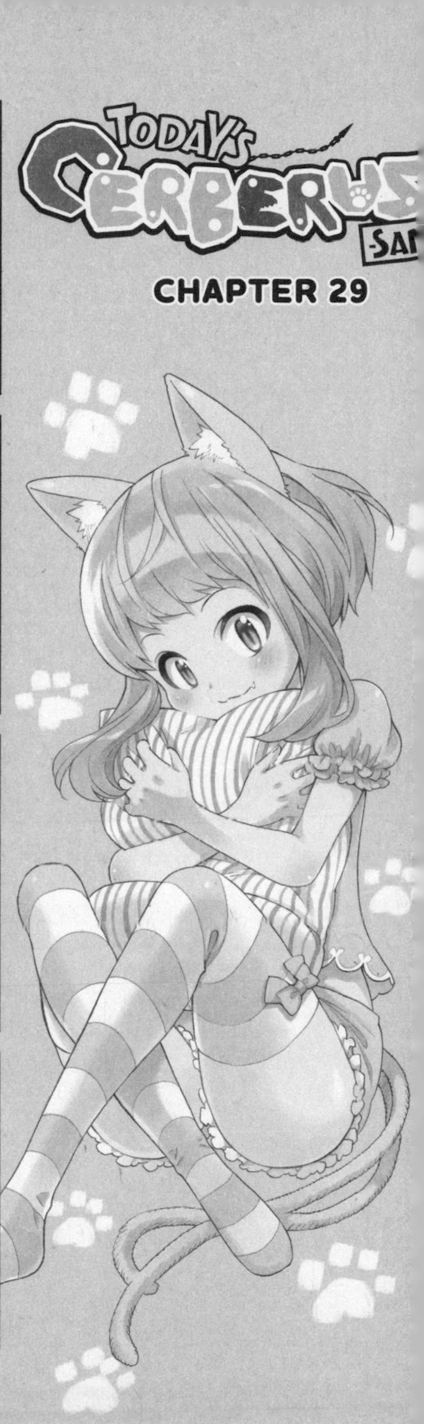

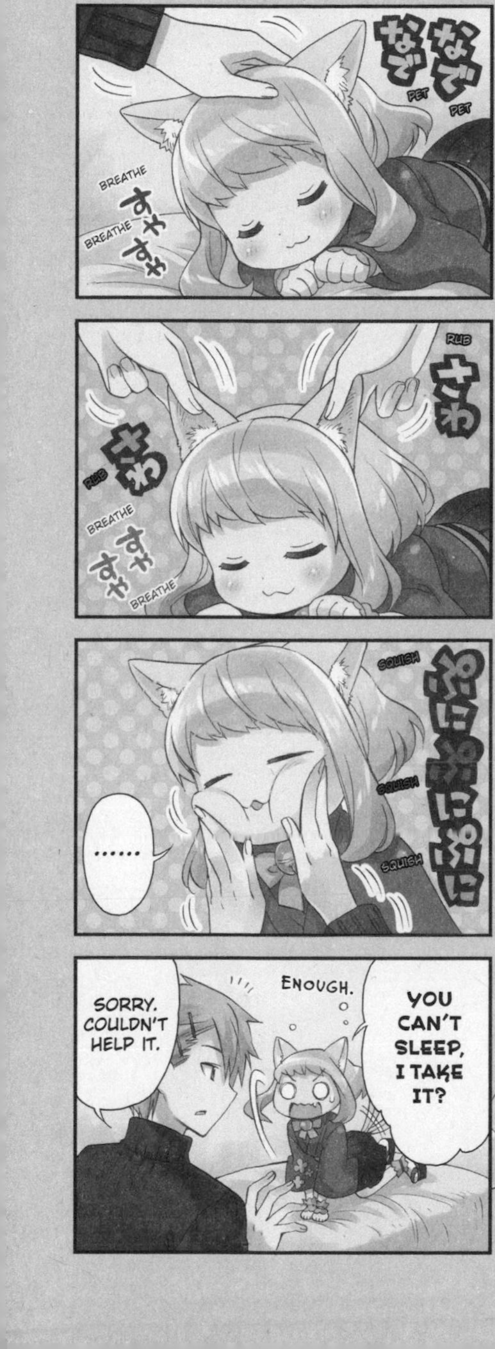
なで なで
PET PET
すやすや
BREATHE BREATHE
さわ さわ
RUB RUB
すやすや
BREATHE BREATHE
ぷにぷにぷに
SQUISH SQUISH SQUISH
......
YOU CAN'T SLEEP, I TAKE IT?
ENOUGH.
SORRY. COULDN'T HELP IT.

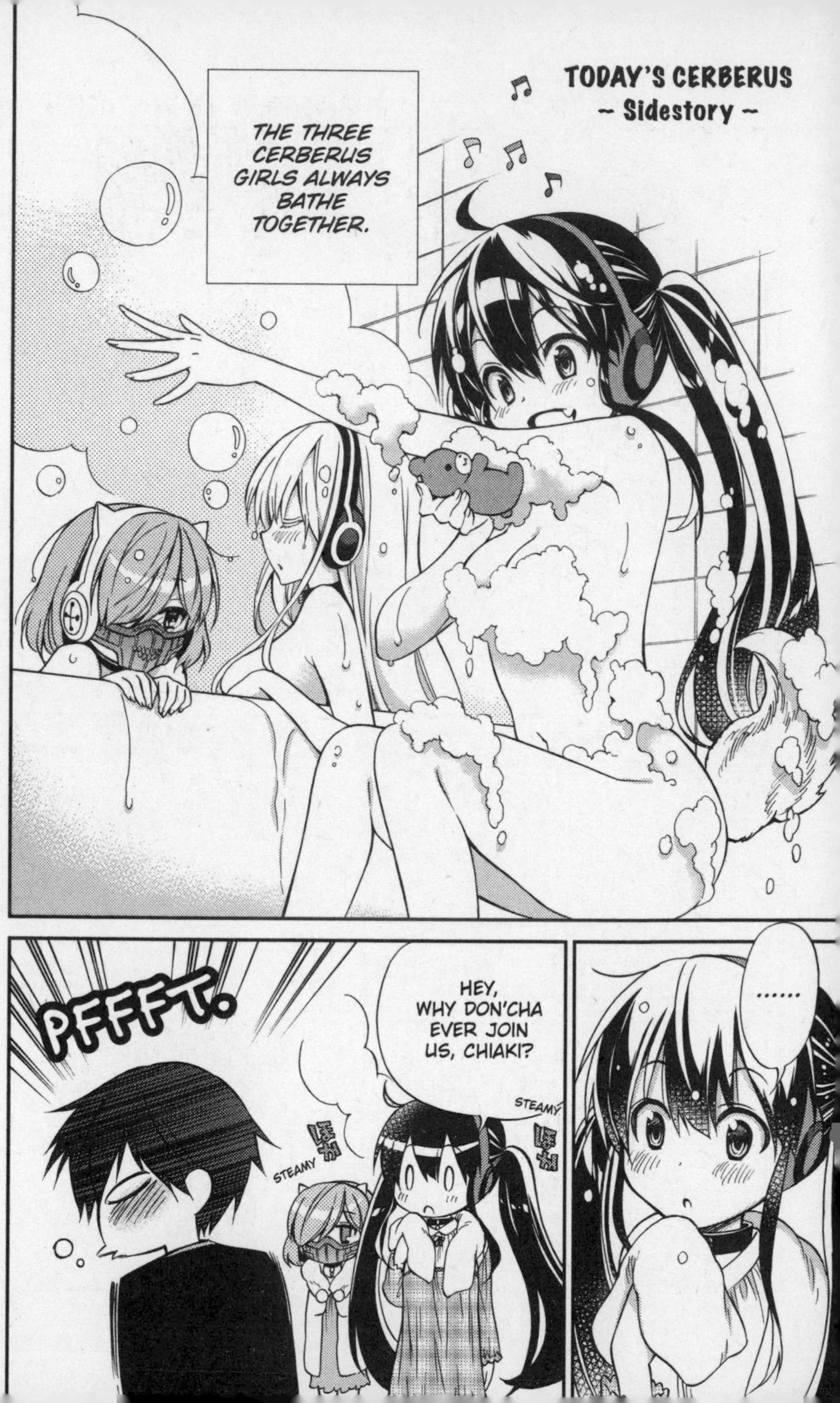
TODAY'S CERBERUS
~ Sidestory ~
THE THREE CERBERUS GIRLS ALWAYS BATHE TOGETHER.
......
HEY, WHY DON'CHA EVER JOIN US, CHIAKI?
PFFFT.
STEAMY
STEAMY

A BEAR OF AN INVITATION

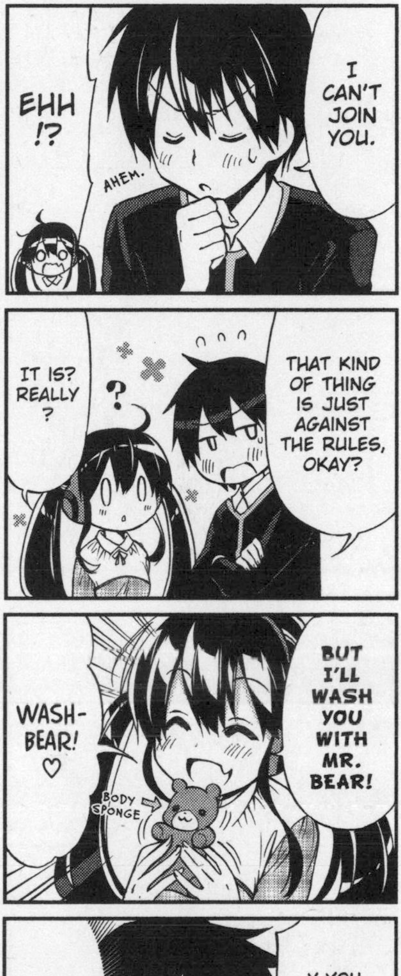
I CAN'T JOIN YOU.
AHEM.
EHH !?
THAT KIND OF THING IS JUST AGAINST THE RULES, OKAY?
IT IS? REALLY ?
BUT I'LL WASH YOU WITH MR. BEAR!
WASH-BEAR! ♡
BODY SPONGE
Y-YOU DON'T HAVE TO WASHBEAR ME!!!
WHAT AM I SAYING ...!?

WITS' END

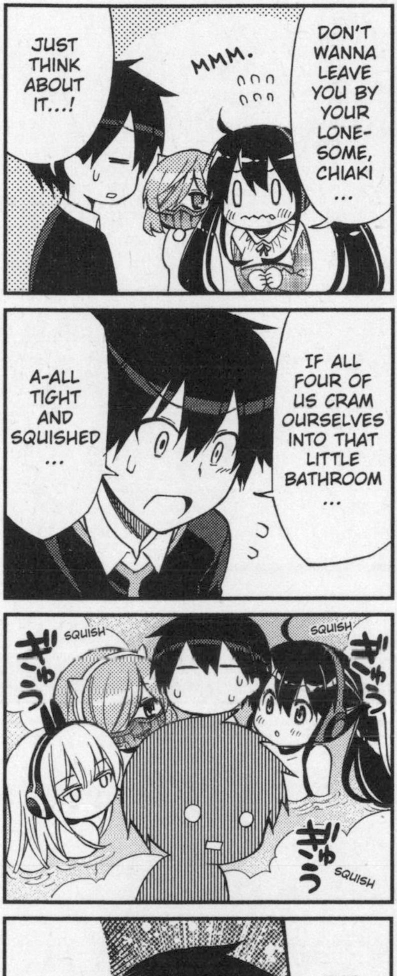
DON'T WANNA LEAVE YOU BY YOUR LONE-SOME, CHIAKI ...
MMM.
JUST THINK ABOUT IT...!
IF ALL FOUR OF US CRAM OURSELVES INTO THAT LITTLE BATHROOM ...
A-ALL TIGHT AND SQUISHED ...
SQUISH
ぎゅう
SQUISH
ぎゅう
ぎゅう
SQUISH
THE BATH WOULD JUST EXPLODE !!
WHAT AM I SAYING !!?

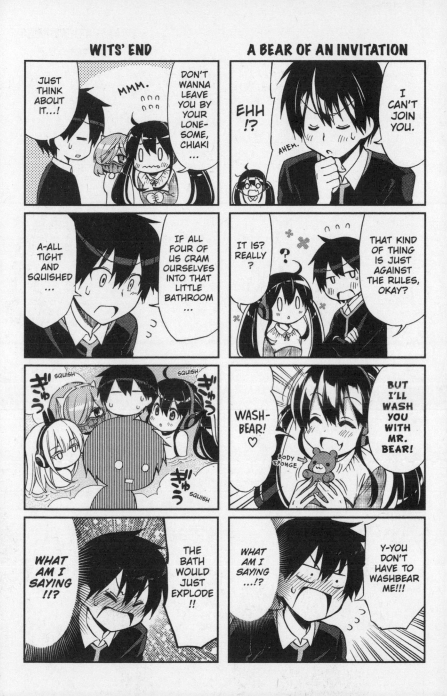

COMPETITION

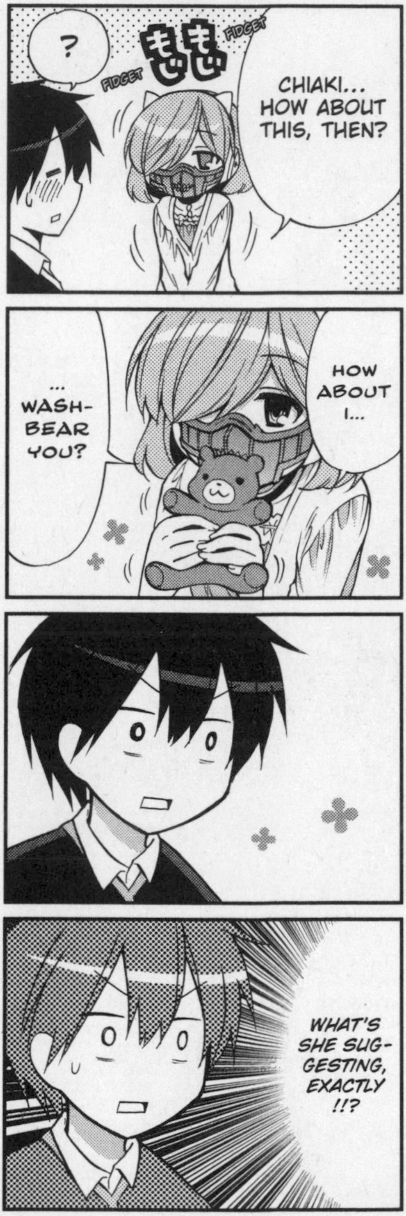
CHIAKI... HOW ABOUT THIS, THEN?
FIDGET FIDGET
?
HOW ABOUT I...
... WASH-BEAR YOU?
WHAT'S SHE SUG-GESTING, EXACTLY !!?

CARELESS

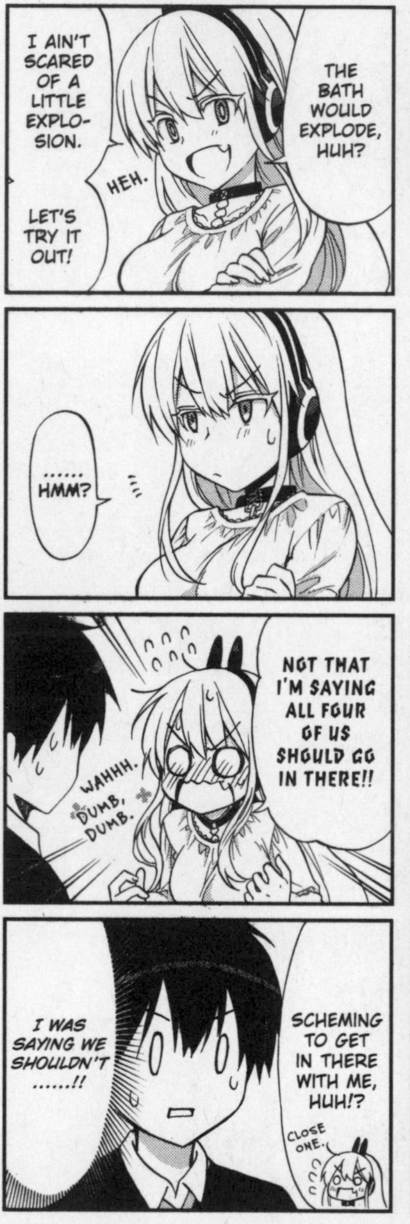
THE BATH WOULD EXPLODE, HUH?
HEH.
I AIN'T SCARED OF A LITTLE EXPLO-SION.
LET'S TRY IT OUT!
......HMM?
NOT THAT I'M SAYING ALL FOUR OF US SHOULD GO IN THERE!!
WAHHH.
DUMB, DUMB.
SCHEMING TO GET IN THERE WITH ME, HUH!?
CLOSE ONE.
I WAS SAYING WE SHOULDN'T ......!!

STRAIGHTFORWARD

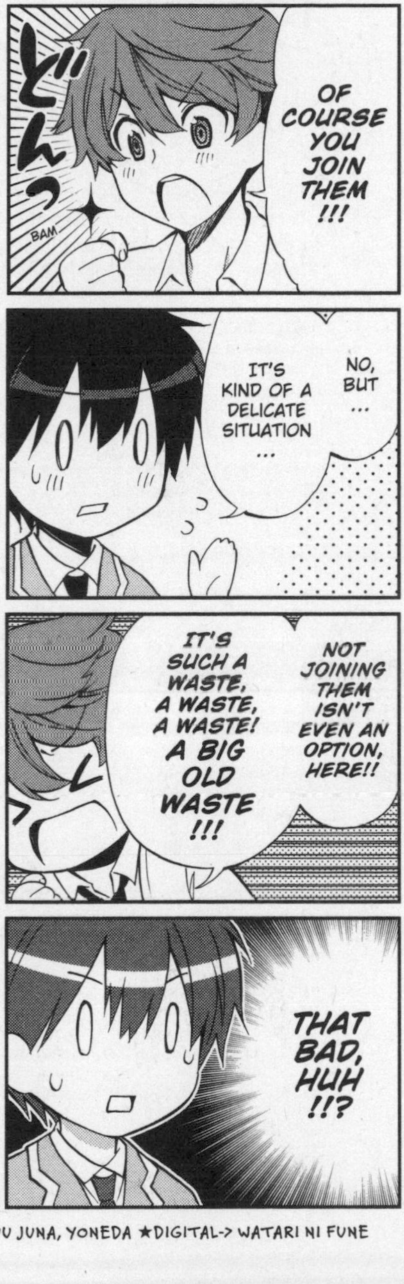
OF COURSE YOU JOIN THEM!!!
BAM
NO, BUT ...
IT'S KIND OF A DELICATE SITUATION ...
NOT JOINING THEM ISN'T EVEN AN OPTION, HERE!!
IT'S SUCH A WASTE, A WASTE, A WASTE! A BIG OLD WASTE!!!
THAT BAD, HUH!!?

UNMENTIONABLE

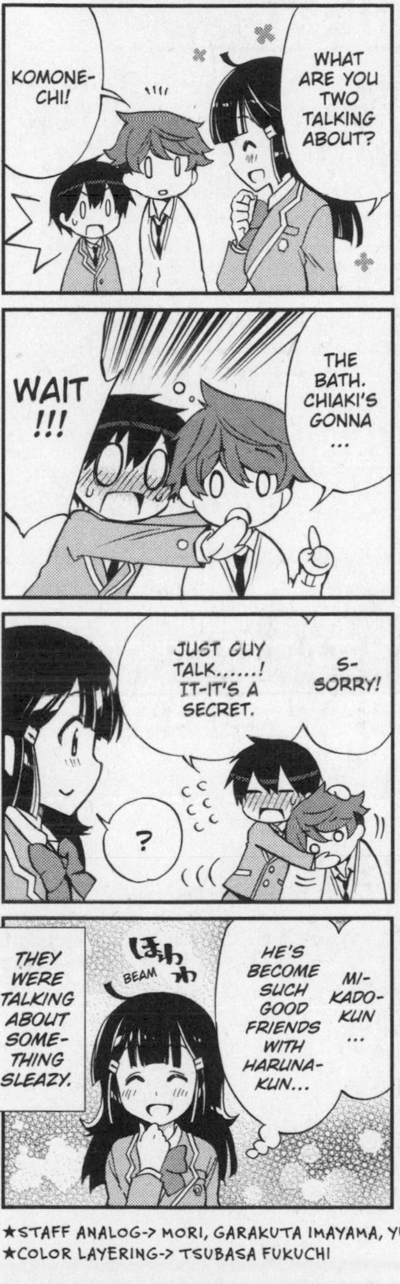
WHAT ARE YOU TWO TALKING ABOUT?
KOMONE-CHI!
THE BATH. CHIAKI'S GONNA ...
WAIT!!!
S-SORRY!
JUST GUY TALK......! IT-IT'S A SECRET.
?
MI-KADO-KUN ...
HE'S BECOME SUCH GOOD FRIENDS WITH HARUNA-KUN...
BEAM
THEY WERE TALKING ABOUT SOME-THING SLEAZY.

★STAFF ANALOG-> MORI, GARAKUTA IMAYAMA, YUU JUNA, YONEDA ★DIGITAL-> WATARI NI FUNE
★COLOR LAYERING-> TSUBASA FUKUCHI

TODAY'S CERBERUS ❻

Ato Sakurai

Translation: Caleb Cook • **Lettering: Bianca Pistillo**

TODAY'S KERBEROS Vol. 6 ©2016 Ato Sakurai/SQUARE ENIX CO., LTD. First published in Japan in 2016 by SQUARE ENIX CO., LTD. English translation rights arranged with SQUARE ENIX CO., LTD. and Yen Press, LLC through Tuttle-Mori Agency, Inc.

English translation ©2017 by SQUARE ENIX CO., LTD.

Yen Press
1290 Avenue of the Americas
New York, NY 10104

Visit us at yenpress.com
facebook.com/yenpress
twitter.com/yenpress
yenpress.tumblr.com
instagram.com/yenpress

First Yen Press Edition: November 2017

The chapters in this volume were originally published as ebooks by Yen Press.

Yen Press is an imprint of Yen Press, LLC.
The Yen Press name and logo are trademarks of Yen Press, LLC.

The publisher is not responsible for websites (or their content) that are not owned by the publisher.

Library of Congress Control Number: 2016946072

ISBNs: 978-0-316-43575-8 (paperback)
           978-0-316-41607-8 (ebook)

10 9 8 7 6 5 4 3 2

WOR

Printed in the United States of America